T0354800

KARL MARX *and* OTHER SOCIALISTS

PROBLEMS OF SOCIALISM, THE FALL OF COMMUNISM AND A PROPER SOCIALISM/ECOLOGY

LOUIS PATSOURAS

authorHOUSE®

AuthorHouse™
1663 Liberty Drive
Bloomington, IN 47403
www.authorhouse.com
Phone: 1 (800) 839-8640

Published by AuthorHouse 11/04/2015

ISBN: 978-1-5049-1569-4 (sc)
ISBN: 978-1-5049-1568-7 (e)

Library of Congress Control Number: 2015909603

Print information available on the last page.

Table of Contents

Table of Contents

This work is dedicated to my grandfather, Theofanis Stratoudakis; my parents, William and Helen; my brothers, Frank and Peter; my history professors, Dr. Henry N. Whitney, Dr. Sherman Barnes, Dr. Harvey Goldberg; my liberal and leftist friends, Jerry Hirsch, Irving Chudner, Sheldon Wolfe, Dr. Boris Blick, Dr. Morris Slavin, and Leon Ancely; to Jeffery Martin, who aided in this work's preparation.

And to my daughter, Patricia, 1956 - 2014

Introduction

No one in the 20th century has been defended or hated as much as Karl Marx, who was not only the preeminent thinker of socialism, but the inspirer of the two main social revolutions of the 20th century in Russia and China. But Marx was also one of the chief founders of democratic socialism, which, after the fall of Soviet Communism and probable fall of Chinese Communism, is the principal form of socialism in the contemporary world.

This work on Marx, which delves into his and Friedrich Engels' thought, is divided into various chapters, including "economics," "human nature" and "imperialism," each of which begins with a general introduction of Marx and Engels. The aim here is to usually present the ideas of Marx and other socialists with their opponents to provide a dialectical dynamic of conflicting ideas/social reality.

A brief essay now follows on 20th-century Communism, which saw itself as based on the ideas of Marx.

Marxism itself by its very nature is a controversial philosophy. It was, after all, the principal opponent of liberalism/capitalism in the 20th century. Thus, any study of Marx's thought is fraught with the dangers of ideology, of subjectivism, which, however, cannot be avoided in analyzing social thought. Marx himself, as an opponent of capitalism, saw that it was to be superseded by socialism through the aegis of the class struggle pitting the majority workers against the minority bourgeoisie. It is this outlook that has brought about the antagonistic relations between Marxism and Liberalism in the economic, social, political, and cultural arenas, principally between Communist/socialist parties and those defending capitalism.

It is a truism that Communist governments, born from the chaos of war, revolution and civil war, have been run by one-party dictatorships, brooking no internal opposition. Thus it is that in contradistinction to the developed nations, like the United States and those in the European Union, Communist nations had no free elections (free elections in the Soviet Union led to its demise and the fall of Communism there), and no civil liberties, as freedom of speech, press, and assembly, all rigorously controlled by Communist governments.

To be sure, Soviet Communists, for instance, nationalized industry, collectivized agriculture, industrialized rapidly, and instituted extensive social welfarism within the context of some general equality. In achieving these goals, the Soviet Communists, again as an example, committed many atrocities, such as the elimination of the richer farmers (kulaks) as a class and the murder and imprisonment of hundreds of thousands of Communists in party purges, including the formation of the infamous Gulag, the system of prison labor which devoured up to twenty million people. This Stalinist terror abated under Stalin's successors, but the other features of the Soviet regime continued.

Soviet Communism is obviously an excellent example of how historical forces have mis-shaped the ideas and ideals of great thinkers – Marx in this instance. In attempting to reform this Soviet "socialism" in the 1980s, Mikhail Gorbachev, the leader of the Soviet Communist party, unleashed class forces that resulted in the demise of the Soviet Union and the consequent rise of a bourgeois kleptocracy.

To be sure, Communist governments are not alone in perpetrating atrocities. The United States alone broke hundreds of treaties with Native Americans resulting in many massacres and resettlements. The many imperialistic crimes of the United States outside its continental boundaries (especially in the Philippines and Vietnam), Britain, France, the Netherlands, Germany, and Belgium, among others, also are numerous. Then, too, the recent terrorism of American client governments against leftist insurgencies in Central America has resulted in the deaths of hundreds of thousands. American complicity in overthrowing the democratic socialist government of Salvador Allendale Gossens in Chile, which led to the murder of thousands, was another instance, as was also the case of American involvement in aiding the rise of Suharto in Indonesia, with up to a million murdered, mostly communists.

Also of note here is the cumulative genocide of World Wars I and II, of a million Armenians by the Turks during the former, and more than six million Jews and Gypsies in the latter, plus the slaughter of many others. Finally the holocaust of the two world wars just mentioned was under the rule of the nobility/bourgeoisie engaged in rival imperialisms.

A raging controversy exists on whether Marx's thought was responsible for the authoritarianism/totalitarianism in the former Soviet Union and in contemporary Communist states like China, Cuba, and North Korea. The view of four anti-Marxists during the Cold War on this issue will now be presented, to be followed by my defense of Marx that disputes their assertions.

The four are J.L. Talmon, Hannah Arendt, Bertram Wolfe, and Karl Popper. For Talmon in his *The Origins of Totalitarian Democracy*, there was a direct lineage between "modern totalitarian democracy" and Marx, who inherited the traditions of the Enlightenment's certainty of the natural over the supernatural, Rousseau's concept of the general will and the putsch-communism of Babeuf's *Conspiracy of the Equals*. His remedy was for an open and democratic process for change based on empirical "trial and error."

Arendt in *Origins of Totalitarianism* charged that Marx's historical materialism, which paralleled Darwin's biological determinism of certainty and unceasing change, would employ the shortcut of terror to achieve socialism, instead of seeking patient democratic reform.

Wolfe, in *Marxism: One Hundred Years in the Life of a Doctrine*, faulted Marx for a dogmatism and hubris based on his belief of discovering the laws of history, leading to his advocacy of the end justifying the means.

The most balanced of these critiques was by Popper in *The Open Society and its Enemies*, which applauded Marx for his telling critique of a capitalist society replete with "injustices and inhumanity," and sympathized with Marx's passionate desire to free the working class from capitalist oppression. But he feared Marx's "religious element," involving the prophecy of an inevitably successful working-class revolution against capitalism, viewing it as the principal culprit of

Communism's deformity, preventing "cool and critical judgment" as a means to make social change. He traced this "religious" flaw to Marx's Hegelian totalitarianism ensconced in the dialectical method, whose obsession of "making heaven on hearth" was inimical to the aspirations of an open society. Popper's alternative to Marx called for democracy as the means to bring about social reform in piecemeal fashion.

These critiques of Marx postulated that his dialectic, with its supposed certainty for socialism, forced history to follow a preordained schema to achieve it. But Marx's dialectical yardstick for progress was clear and unequivocal, calling for the socialization of property to be run by "united cooperative societies," pervasive democracy – representatives held to the specific instructions of voters – full civil liberties, and an end of repressive bureaucracy, with most governmental and productive functions to be locally or regionally run in a democratic manner.

That oppressed classes, like the working class, often have a messianic and conformist social psychology is axiomatic, but to blame the Marxist dialectic for the crimes committed by Communist governments is as logical as to blame Jesus of Nazareth for the crimes of organized conservative Christianity or to blames Adam Smith for the crimes of liberalism/capitalism. To accuse Marx of being responsible for the crimes of 20th century communism is to fetishize and put into a Procrustean bed Marx's heuristic dialectic which enriches the content of historical happenings.

It is also useful to recall that in contrast to Marx's generous vision of society, a large segment of Liberalism in the 19th and 20th centuries opposed progressive social-welfare legislation (like old-age pensions, prohibition of child labor, providing the indigent with sufficient food and shelter, the eight-hour day, and national health insurance), working class initiatives in the work place (legalizing trade unions and the strike), and extending the suffrage to workers and women.

As for blaming Marx for having a future component in his social thought, for positing a socialist future, we defend this aspect of

Marx's views by asserting that social thought by its very nature is concerned not only with the past and present, but also the future, the last view being intertwined with the former two. Thus, as between the Marxist and Liberal views of posterity (the exception being radical democrats like Rousseau and Jefferson), as enunciated by conservative Liberalism and its offshoot of social Darwinism, the latter is intrinsically more authoritarian/totalitarian than the former because it forever condemns humanity to an inordinate amount of socioeconomic and attendant inequalities with their concomitant elements of alienating force and power.

It should be noted that despite Marx's erroneous predictions of 19th century socialist revolutions, the two seminal 20th-century revolutions – the Russian and the Chinese – were in Marx's name; and despite their deformations and demise of the first and probable failure of the second as of now, their social impact on the 20th century has been second to none

Furthermore, the socialist project continues throughout the world in the form of social democracy/democratic socialism. Indeed, today, with few exceptions, socialism and a rapidly expanding working class are more intimately intertwined than ever. In fact, the thesis of global capitalism of today is forming its antithesis, the international working class.

Chapter One: Overview of the Lives of Marx and Engels

Karl Marx (1818-83) was born into an upper-middle class German-Jewish family from Trier, an old city in the Rhineland, the third of nine children, five of whom died in infancy, of Heinrich and Henriette (née Pressburg) Marx. Marx's parents came from families possessing wealth and learning, of many rabbis. Although Henriette was religious, Heinrich, whose father was an Orthodox rabbi, became a disciple of the Enlightenment, an admirer of French culture, a deist and democrat, particularly influenced by Jean-Jacques Rousseau, Voltaire (Franćois Marie Arouet), John Locke, and Immanuel Kant. Furthermore, to escape religious restrictions by Prussia (it annexed the Rhineland after the fall of Napoleon) on German Jews, who, although citizens, could not practice law or attend public schools, Heinrich converted to the Prussian Evangelical (Lutheran) Church in 1817, the children following in 1824 and wife in 1825.

Marx, a brilliant student, received an excellent education: He was tutored at home to age twelve, graduated from the Trier high school in 1835, studied law at the University of Bonn in 1835-36, attended the University of Berlin from 1836-41, concentrating on history, philosophy, and jurisprudence. He was awarded the Ph.D. in 1841 at the University of Jena. His dissertation, indicating his love of Hellenic civilization and philosophy, was entitled "Differences between the Democritean and Epicurean Philosophy of Nature." He also could fluently read four foreign languages – Greek, Latin, French, and English.

Soon after the completion of his university studies, Marx married Jenny von Westphalen in June 1843, the daughter of Ludwig von Westphalen, a Prussian government official who was not only a good intellectual, but also a St.-Simonian; he befriended the young Marx who considered him his second father. The marriage at first was stormy, but became pacific with time. Marx and Jenny had six children, three of whom survived, Jenny, Laura, and Eleanor; he also had a son, Fred Demuth, with the family's live-in maid, Hélène Demuth.

After graduation, Marx embarked towards radical journalism in 1842-43, moving to Cologne, serving as an editor-in-chief of the *Rheinisch Zeitung*. In its columns, he courageously attacked the Prussian Monarchy's opposition to democracy and its stifling press censorship and delved into the poverty of the Rhineland's peasantry. The government closed the paper in late 1843 for its bold actions, Marx resigning just before, traveling to Paris with Jenny.

It was in the 1843-44 period that Marx broadened his intellectual horizon by reading the works of French utopian socialists, particularly impressed by the Comte de Claude Henri de Rouveroy Saint-Simon.

Fredrick Engels (1820-95), Marx's intimate collaborator, was born into a wealthy Rhineland German family from Barmen, of pious Calvinists, his father Caspar being a successful textile manufacturer. Engels was not as formally educated as Marx, leaving high school before graduation at age seventeen. This did not, however, detract from his intellectual brilliance. Like Marx, an omnivorous reader, he was well versed in science, history, and philosophy, with an unusual ability to master languages: English, French, Italian, Spanish, Russian, and other Slavic languages, including Arabic and Persian.

Engels, unlike Marx, never married, but was a lifelong companion of Mary Burns, an Irish worker in his Manchester textile mill; for reasons of respectability, they did not live together; when she died in 1863, her sister Lydia became his companion – Engels married her on her deathbed in 1878.

Like Marx, Engels spent most of his adult life in England, from 1842-1844 and from 1850 to his death in 1895: in Manchester, managing the family's textile mill with a partner; in London, soon after his retirement in 1869, living close to Marx, seeing him daily. Engels, an able manager/businessman was quite wealthy. By 1860, his income was a thousand English pounds per year (an average English worker in 1875 earned under forty pounds per year). In 1864, he inherited a small fortune of ten thousand pounds from his father. On retirement, he invested his money in railroads and gas and water works, receiving 4.5 percent annually. Engels was very generous to the Marx family, donating money periodically, and when retiring providing Marx a 350-pound annuity.

Engel's socialist activity began in 1842 as a communist, influenced in this decision by Moses Hess, a German-Jewish socialist and early Zionist, also important in contributing to Marx's understanding of economics and sociology. Engels, as will be observed, was instrumental in Marx's becoming a communist in 1844.

Before proceeding, an important question: Why did Marx become a communist? There is perhaps no one answer to resolve this question. In fact, it might be unanswerable. Marx did not have a severe Oedipus complex that would rail against patriarchal authority; indeed, he loved his father and disliked his mother. He had all the advantages of a wealthy family and a splendid education, a promising journalistic or academic career being a certainty, yet he gave this up for a revolutionary socialism. Ultimately, it was Marx's great empathy/sympathy for the oppressed working class that best explained his Communism.

Notes

A) The Lives of Marx and Engels

1) There are many excellent biographies on Marx: The latest by Francis Wheen, *Karl Marx: A Life* (New York: W.W. Norton, 2000), presents a lively and sympathetic portrait of his life, which includes many of his faults, like constant begging for money, quickness to take offence, cantankerousness with friends, and addiction to smoking and alcohol. The classic one is by Franz Mehring, *Karl Marx: The Story of His Life*, trans. Edward Fitzgerald (Ann Arbor: Univ. of Michigan Press, 1962); first published in 1918. Three rather recent ones sympathetic to Marx include: Maximilian Rubel and Margaret Manale, *Marx Without Myth: A Chronological Study of His Life and Work* (New York: Harper Torchbooks, 1976). Saul K. Padover, *Karl Marx: An*

Intimate Biography (New York: McGraw-Hill, 1978); and Jerrold Seigel, *Marx's Fate: The Shape of a Life* (Princeton: Princeton Univ. Press, 1978). These two are hostile to Marx, but contain valuable information: Robert Payne, *Marx* (New York: Simon and Schuster, 1968); and Fritz J. Raddatz, *Karl Marx: A Political Biography* (Boston: Little, Brown, and Co., 1978). On Engels, see W.O. Henderson, *The Life of Friedrich Engels,* 2 vols. (London: Frank Cass, 1976).

B) Works of Marx/Engels

Marx and Engels have a large corpus of writings. Among the principal works are: Karl Marx, *Capital: A Critique of Political Economy*: Vol. I, *The Process of Capitalist Production*, trans. From the German by Samuel Moore and Edward Aveling (Chicago: Charles H. Kerr, 1906); Vol. II, *The Process of Circulation of Capital*, trans. from the German by Ernest Untermann (Chicago: Charles H. Kerr, 1907); Vol. III, *The Process of Capitalist Production as a Whole*, trans. from the German by Ernest Untermann (Chicago: Charles H. Herr, 1909). Vols. II and III of this work are extensively edited by Engels from Marx's drafts and notes after his death. Hereinafter, *Capital*, I, II, and III. Karl Marx, *Theories of Surplus Value* (Selections) (New York: International Publishers, 1952). Karl Marx, *Grundrisse: Foundations of the Critique of Political Economy*, trans. from the German and Foreword by Martin Nicolaus (New York: Random House, 1973). Hereinafter, *Grundrisse.* David McLellan, editor and translator, *The Grundrisse* (New York: Harper Torchbooks, 1971), is an excellent condensation of this long work. Referred to as McLellan, *Grundrisse.* Karl Marx and Frederick Engels, *Manifesto of the Communist Party* (New York: International Publishers, 1948). Hereinafter, *Manifesto.* Karl Marx and Frederick Engels, *The German Ideology*, Parts I and III, edited with an introduction by R. Pascal (New York: International Publishers, 1947). Karl Marx, *Class Struggles in*

France, 1848-1850 (New York: International Publishers, 1964). Karl Marx, *The Eighteenth Brumaire of Louis Napoleon* (New York: International Publishers, 1926). Karl Marx, *The Civil War in France* (New York: International Publishers, 1933). Karl Marx, *A Contribution to the Critique of Political Economy* (New York: International Library Publishing Co., 1904). Frederick Engels, *Anti-Dühring or Herr Eugen Dühring's Revolution in Science* (Moscow: Progress Publishers, 1975); parts of this work are in a more popular version, *Socialism: Utopian and Scientific* (New York: International Publishers, 1935). Fredrich Engels, *The Peasant War in Germany* (New York: International Publishers, 1926). Frederick Engels, *The Condition of the Working Class in England* (Stanford, CA: Stanford Univ. Press, 1968) Frederick Engels, *The Origin of the Family, Private Property and the State*, introduction and notes by Eleanor Burke Leacock (New York: International Publishers, 1972). If other editions of these works are employed, they are duly noted with appropriate endnotes.

Almost all of the works of Marx and Engels, which have been prepared by editorial commissions in Great Britain, the United States, and Russia, have been published by 1999. In English the title is *Karl Marx and Frederick Engels, Collected Works in English*, in fifty volumes. Publication in the U.S. is by International Publishers in New York, 1975. Hereinafter, *MECW.* Other notable collections include Lloyd D. Easton and Kurt H. Guddat, editors and translators, *Writings of the Young Marx on Philosophy and Society* (New York: Doubleday and Co., 1967). Hereinafter, *Young Marx.* Lewis S. Feuer, *Marx and Engels: Basic Writings on Politics and Philosophy* (Garden City, NY: Anchor Books, 1959).

C) Works on the Ideas of Marx/Engels

Richard N. Hunt, *The Political Ideas of Marx and Engels:* Vol. I: *Marxism and Totalitarian*

Democracy, 1818 – 1850; Vol. II; *Classical Marxism, 1850-1895* (Pittsburgh: Univ. of Pittsburgh Press, 1974, 1984). Hal Draper, *Karl Marx's Theory of Revolution;* Vol. I: *State and Bureaucracy;* Vol. II: *The Politics of Social Classes;* Vol. III: *The 'Dictatorship of the Proletariat';* Vol. IV: *Critique of Other Socialism* (New York: Monthly Review Press, 1977, 1981, 1986, 1989). George Lichtheim, *Marxism: An Historical and Critical Study* (New York: Frederick A. Praeger, 1961). David McLellan, *The Thought of Karl Marx* (London: Macmillan, 1971). Istvan Meszaros, *Beyond Capital; Towards a Theory of Transition* (New York: Monthly Review Press, 1995).

Chapter Two: Roots of Marxism: The Western Radical Tradition

It is a truism that Marxism is a synthesis of German philosophy, French materialism, and English economics. But from a broader perspective, Marxism may also be seen as embodying the progressive aspects of the principal sources of the Western tradition, like the Hebrew, Greek, and Roman experiences; the socioeconomic, cultural, and political struggles of the masses against elites from antiquity on (Spartacus was Marx's favorite hero) in various revolutions, including religious, but particularly since the advent of the Industrial Revolution in 18th century England, the Enlightenment of the 17th and 18th centuries, and of the 19th century utopian socialism and radical Romanticism.

Since Marxism is a socialist movement, we begin with a brief definition of socialism and a few generalizations on human history before delving into the Western radical tradition. Socialism, as it has developed through the millennia, advocates a society of a general socioeconomic, political, gender, and cultural equality based on the principles of direct or representative democracy where technology is in the hands of cooperative and public bodies in various proportions. Although not against the private ownership of small individual/family property, socialism rejects employing the labor of others for profit. It also believes in the freedoms of speech, press, religion, and assembly, and insists on the cooperative brotherhood of all people.

Forms of socialism have been the norm of the human condition, certainly until the New Stone Age beginning ten to twelve thousand years ago – Marx's "primitive communism." But with the advent of civilization or class/oppressive societies, the first large scale attempt to effect a general equality, a form of proto-socialism occurred in the 8th and 7th centuries B.C.E., with the Hebrew Prophetic Revolution. Its principal social critics and visionaries (Amos, Micah, and Isaiah) launched a sustained criticism of a society based on a divisive socioeconomic and political inequality, viewing it as an abomination displeasing God, leading to the destruction of Israel and Judah through foreign conquest. However, a righteous remnant would be ultimately saved to live in a society of equality and abundance, of peace and joy.

This was the first recorded instance of the millenarian social psychology of the oppressed poor who employed God as a vehicle to aid them in establishing a just society. Examples: of Amos, a "herdsman and fruit picker," who characterized the rich and powerful, as those who "lie on ivory beds surrounded with luxury," and "trample on the poor and steal their smallest crumb by...taxes, fines, and usury." Of Isaiah: "How dare you grind my people in the dust like this," and "You buy property so others have no place to live. Your homes are built on great estates so you can be alone in the midst of the earth."

The great Old Testament law codes, of Deuteronomy and Leviticus, outgrowths of the Prophetic Revolution, called for progressive measures (applicable only to Hebrews), including abolishing interest on loans, canceling all debts every seven years (for instance, if one borrowed money in the fifth year it would be canceled in the seventh), freeing of debt slaves after six years, with resources to begin a new and independent life, a tithe to aid the indigent, election of officials ("Judges") by the people, and restoration of property to owners/descendants every fifty years. These laws (some might have been practiced for a generation) permitted private property of the small-type variety, ensuring a general equality. Indeed, the prophets promised a utopian future of justice and general abundance, an end to physical suffering, a cooperative nature in which "deserts bloom," and peace and tranquility for everyone as nations will "beat their swords into plowshares and their spears into pruning forks."

Greek philosophy, in which Marx and Engels were well versed, was the second great stream of Western culture/tradition. Some background: Heraclitus (c. 535-475 BCE), a pantheistic mystic and father of the dialectical method of philosophy, held that permanence is an illusion, that the only certainty within the cosmos was change, and that everything or any unity originated and ended with antithetical opposites in strife within it, ever evolving into new combinations.

Democritus (460-370 BCE), a strict materialist, denied any spiritual non-material world, including the soul. His atomic theory postulated that atoms or unseen building blocks of nature always existed which could not be created or destroyed (we now know that the primordial element of which the other elements come from is hydrogen). The observable material world, then, becomes an illusion. These atoms combined to form our and other worlds, either growing or decaying, governed by natural laws allowing for no deviance. He also had a theory of human progress based on technology, postulating that early humanity lived in a nomadic hunter-food gathering mode, but that with the taming of wild grasses or agricultural revolution, humanity settled down. Mining, metallurgy and other signposts of civilization soon developed.

Epicurus (342-270 BCE) followed the atomic theory of Democritus, but also held that a human soul existed, composed of unseen atoms dispersing at death. Gods were also real, but made up of matter! His atoms, contrary to Democritus', swerved at times allowing for some freedom and indeterminacy, including for humans. Marx preferred this view to the strict Democritean one.

The Greek Communist tradition of the Pythagoras/Socrates/ Plato/Antisthenes/Diogenes of Antiope complex is also important. It began with the 6th century BCE Greek mathematician, social reformer, and mystic Pythagoras, who wished for a virtuous elite to live pacifically and communistically (no private property) so as to avoid the contamination of exploiting others. One of his maxims insisted that there was no forgiveness for those possessing wealth while poverty existed.

The Pythagorean tradition was well ensconced in the Socrates/ Plato/Antisthenes/Diogenes of Antiope axis in the 5th to 4th centuries B.C.E. Socrates, the greatest of the Greek philosophers, like Jesus of Nazareth, never wrote anything; we know of him only through his brilliant socialist pupil, Plato. But his other devoted student, Antisthenes (the founder of the Cynics), whose student was Diogenes of Antiope, was also of importance to socialism.

Plato, although an elitist and arch anti-democrat (an admirer of Spartan aristocracy), was basically in the socialist tradition. In *The Republic*, whose central character was Socrates, he well understood that in a world of economics scarcity and labor division, class struggle, which invariably weakened the city state, was the norm, one between a grasping ruling wealthy elite (more wealth equaled less virtue) and the many average and poor citizens. To remedy this, he sought a society of justice leading to social harmony and happiness.

Its basic outlines were: Power was firmly lodged in the hands of a small communist elite or guardian class that numbered less that ten percent of the people (although economically unselfish they competed with one another for grades on examinations and honors); it comprised the philosophers or intelligentsia and the military, themselves highly educated, who not only rejected private family property, but also gender inequality (the top generalship was held by a male, however). The basis for this elite was their superior biological intelligence and exemplary lifestyle relative to that of the general population. The average people, the class of the appetites, being normally selfish in a world of scarcity, continued to have and indulge in the imperfections of private family and private property, although the guardians limited the amount of the latter element.

Plato attempted to resolved the antagonistic social relations of class society based on an insufficient economic surplus to give everyone the good life. But, in his social diagram, the guardians, who had the time to cultivate their intellectual and military "virtues," exploited the appetite class. Furthermore, it is historically impossible for the "virtuous" few – be they cleric/philosophers or Communist bureaucrats in authoritarian societies – to long remain egalitarian, as the Soviet Communist experiment has proven. They are not, after all, hermetically sealed from the inherent tensions of societies with insufficient technological development/economic surpluses and the specter of war. To be sure, Plato confirmed the truism that even in societies malformed by economic scarcity/steep labor division, the possibility of communism, although a deformed one, still existed.

Antisthenes, whom Plato characterized as "Socrates gone mad," was certainly an audacious thinker, wishing to erase distinctions between Plato's guardians and masses, all citizens to live in equality in a society devoid of private property, private marriage, and formal government. Attempting, like Plato, to solve the problem of labor division and low technological level with its accompanying scarcity, he advocated an ascetic lifestyle, living among the masses, urging them to change the status quo. Diogenes of Antiope extended these views to include a general pacifism and the end of slavery, of equality between Greeks and others.

These socialist notions continued in Stoic philosophy that pictured a primeval golden age of a bountiful nature and egalitarian societies of brotherly love being undermined by the rise of private property and its train of horrors and vices, like strife/war for material possessions and accompanying deceit and jealousy. It should also be noted that during the Hellenistic Age, with the destruction of the Greek city states and their liberties by large empires (of Alexander the Great, his successors, and Rome), a spate of utopias appeared. One was Iambulus' *Isles of the Blessed* or *Island of the Sun*, of an austere communist society in a pacific world. This escapism at once denoted intense alienation, but also a thirst for social justice.

The influence of Aristotle on Marx, whom he called the "greatest thinker of antiquity," should also be noted. Marx drank deeply from Aristotle's *Politics* on automation of machinery and in focusing on the class struggle, openly endemic in the Greek city-states. Automation, to be fully explored later, envisaged a world where workers were superfluous. As for the class struggle, he saw a normal one between the aristocrats/oligarchs, or wealthy, whose social psychology emphasized that individuals were unequal, rulership belonging to the few as they were more virtuous, and the democrats, or average citizens who favored freedom and equality. For him, the inequality of property ownership or economic inequality was the main factor causing this class struggle.

He also noted that within the ruling classes a status conflict existed between the aristocrats, whose wealth/power was based on large land holdings, and the oligarchs, who were merchants and whose wealth/power was derived from trade, the latter wishing to share power with the former. In this socioeconomic, socio-psychological, and political diagram, the slaves or human machines of the society were not considered fully human; they simply furnished the labor power to allow citizens the necessary time to cultivate themselves intellectually and to participate in political life.[1]

The next great historical force in the West to promote a general equality and brotherhood, was Christianity, a multi-layered religion most heavily influenced in its ethical and millenarian conceptions by the Hebrew Prophetic tradition, but also by Pythagoreanism, Buddhism, Zoroastrianism, and Greek mystery religion, a religion which insisted on human gods.

Christianity's rise was certainly a resultant of the class struggles among the Roman Empire's free and slave masses and equestrian and patrician elite capped by divine emperorship. Indeed, it was a serious attempt to promote a world of equality in one replete with inequality and oppression. Lest it be forgotten, Christianity was an underground millenarian religion in its early centuries, one with its own counterculture to the dominant institutions of Rome, whose man-god, Jesus of Nazareth, would soon return to destroy the world of privilege and power symbolized by the man-god Roman emperor. It was with good reason that the Roman authorities regarded the early Christians as subversives.

By the 4th century of the C.E., the overwhelming economic and other powers of the military/ landed elite transformed Christianity into a conservative religion, the Constantinian Church. But despite the many conservative strictures in the New Testament, as of slaves to obey their masters (perhaps ruses to appease the authorities), many revolutionary parts condemning wealth and power remained: The story of Jesus and the rich man, including the famous "It's easier for a camel to squeeze through a needle's eye than for a wealthy man to get into God's domain" – Mark 10:17-31, Matthew 19:16-30, and Luke 18:18-30; in Matthew 6:24 of not being able to "serve two masters, God and money"; in Timothy 6:10, "For the love of money is the root of all evils"; in Luke 6:20 ff., where the poor inherited "the kingdom of God," but not the wealthy; in the Epistle of James 5:1, where the rich were cursed with "miseries that shall come upon you. Your riches are corrupted and your garments are moth eaten. Your gold and silver is cankered; and the rust of them shall be a witness against you and will eat your flesh like fire." Furthermore, the millenarian communism of the early Jewish Christians in Jerusalem (the "Ebonite's" or the poor) as described in the Acts of the Apostles, waiting for the Messiah and quick end of the present world, is well known.

It should also be noted that Christianity has a strong tradition of a human-only revolutionary Jesus of Nazareth: The synoptic gospels, Mark, Matthew, and Luke, emphasized this Jesus who in the Gospel of John was transformed into a divine savior of the world. There was also a fifth Gospel, that of Thomas, who nowhere mentioned Jesus' divinity. For interested readers on the complexity of the Christian Gospels, see *The Search for the Authentic Words of Jesus: The Five Gospels, by the Jesus Seminar,* 1993, a collaborative work of seventy-four biblical scholars.[2]

In the Middle Ages, two noteworthy expressions of Christian socialism were noted in St. Francis of Assisi in the 13th century and the defrocked English priest John Ball, one of the leaders of the English Peasants' Revolt of 1381. St. Francis, ever solicitous of human beings and animals, dreamt of a world without the curse of property (private or collective) and urged the members of his monastic order to work with their hands. As for Ball, he uttered a profound socialist truth: "When Adam delved and Eve span, who was then the gentleman?"

Christian socialism received a great boost forward with the advent of the Protestant Revolution or Reformation in the 16th century, specifically its left wing. This was exemplified in the millenarian Anabaptist/Pietistic tradition (closely related to the 1524-1525 German Peasants' and Workers' Revolt, resulting in a spontaneous series of uprisings against the power structure) that envisioned a society along the lines of general socioeconomic equality, either through the predominance of small property or of communism.

It was during the late Renaissance and early period of Protestant Revolution and Catholic response, a time of social unease, that a spate of socialist utopias, of which Marx and Engels were well aware of, appeared. The prototypical one was Sir Thomas More's *Utopia* (from the Greek *outopos* or "no place.") It presented a detailed account of a communist society without Plato's starkly elitist diagram, featuring a general socioeconomic and gender equality linked to democracy, although a status difference existed between a minority intelligentsia, elected to the magistracy, and others. Contrary to Plato's guardians, More allowed for the nuclear family's existence, satisfied that the other institutions encircling it would prevent any undue selfishness in favoring one's progeny over those of others. This progressive utopia also abolished wage labor since work was regarded as integral to a way of life, not as a commodity or cost of production. The workday itself was six hours.

More, an acute social critic, who understood the various levers of economic and social power portrayed government as a "conspiracy of the rich, who in pretense of managing the public, only pursue their private ends." This paradigm pitted the nobility and wealthy few ("drones") against the farmers and workers, or the poor, who, laboring "as hard as a beast at labor," lived like "draft animals," invariably "worn out by age and sickness." Furthermore, echoing Jesus of Nazareth and Plato, he opined that "while money is the standard of all things, the most unworthy tend to acquire most of the wealth."

Other well-known utopias of this period were Tomas Campanella's *City of the Sun* and Valentin Andrea's *Christianapolis*. Like More, Campanella and Andrea rejected private property and wage labor and favored democracy. Andrea was the first to discuss integrated labor or the combination of manual and mental labor to transcend the curse of labor division and consequent general inequality.[3]

The English Revolution of the 1640s also enhanced human liberation through its principal progressive current, the Levellers, whose main spokesperson, John Lilburne, representing the lower-middle class, attempted to restrain power and privilege by popular democracy, widespread distribution of property, and religious tolerance. This movement began modern radical republicanism.

But socialist ideas were not forgotten during this revolution. Gerrard Winstanley of the communist Diggers, in *The New Law of Righteousness* and *Law of Freedom,* in a pantheistic and rationalist vein, propounded a democratic communist society which abolished private property and wage labor for one whose production was based on separate households sharing a common storehouse and annual parliamentary elections through universal suffrage.[4]

The classical materialist/skeptical mind was overthrown by the rise of an otherworldly Christianity based on the supernatural and redemption of the individual after death in a future life. But inexorably, it returned with the revival of trade and commerce and town life in the late Middle Ages, followed by the Renaissance, or revival of Greek and Latin learning, then by the capitalist Commercial Revolution (1400-1700), the rise of the Scientific Revolution of the 16th and 17th centuries (Galileo Galilei, René Descartes, and Sir Isaac Newton come readily to mind here) and the Age of Enlightenment of the 17th and 18th centuries.

To be sure, Marx and Engels, heavily influenced by the science and materialism of the Scientific Revolution/Age of Enlightenment, appreciated the materialist thought of the following: Baruch Spinoza, whose pantheism had nature as god, making religious doctrine irrelevant; Thomas Hobbes' and his *Leviathan*, with its realistically brutal world of strife and oppression – indeed a totalitarian one under the aegis of the state run by a sovereign; Locke's *Essay Concerning Human Understanding*, with its materialistic/sensate view of social reality; and the French materialists and/or communists, like Baron Paul Henri Thiry d'Holbach, the Abbé Gabriel de Bonnot de Mably, and the Abbé Morelly. Finally, they were well acquainted with and influenced by the works of the three principal radical thinkers of the Enlightenment: Rousseau, Diderot, and Voltaire.

Jean Jacques Rousseau, the neurotic and brilliant scion of lower-middle-class Protestants from Geneva, was the outstanding radical-liberal thinker of the period. With two seminal works justifying equality – *Discourse on the Origins of Inequality* and *The Social Contract* – he was a proto socialist and the inspirer of the great French Revolution. In the former work, he formulated that large private property came about only with the rise of civilization and the state, the latter being an instrument of the strong and wealthy. Thus, since property was not a "natural" right, but a conventional one, it could be regulated by society. In the latter work, he challenged the privilege of monarchs, nobility, and wealthy in the name of equality, liberty, and popular sovereignty, which he associated with the concepts of "social contract," and "general will," both linked to small private property. For him, individuals voluntarily made a social contract for establishing government or sovereignty whose legislation was under the aegis of the general will or the majority in the context of a general socioeconomic and political equality, in which small non-exploitative property dominated, i.e., individuals might own only what they directly worked on. Ideally, political decisions were made on the basis of direct democracy, but he also accepted a representative one. In this milieu of a general socioeconomic equality, he averred that individual interests were essentially similar to the public or common good; in class-ridden societies, the common good was subverted by the economically strong who inordinately manipulated the political process to further their interests at the expense of the many. He defended general equality also on the basis that an individual alone, without society, could not achieve much, that humans were social animals, and that a general equality furnished the optimum conditions for liberty, itself only formal with great socioeconomic inequality.

Perhaps the central figure of the Enlightenment, the son of a lower-middle-class skilled worker, Denis Diderot, was an audacious thinker who at once embraced atheism/materialism and the social ethics of Jesus of Nazareth. An archenemy of organized religion, with its intolerance and distorted view of social and physical reality, of kings and nobility, he favored an egalitarian republican society of small property owners. His view of human nature, influenced by the sensationalism of Protagoras and Locke, which modern socialism generally follows, was that: "Nature has not made us vicious; it is bad education, bad examples, and bad legislation that have corrupted us." He obviously supported the American Revolution; he died before the French Revolution. His most enduring contribution to humanity was his general editorship of the seventeen-volume *Encyclopedia* (with eleven volumes of illustrations), which assembled the knowledge of the past "to change the general way of thinking." Diderot was Marx's favorite prose writer.

Francois-Marie Arouet Voltaire was not an egalitarian. He endorsed an enlightened monarchy and detested the masses whom he called, "the cattle." But as an advocate of free speech and a determined enemy of Catholicism, which to him represented religious superstition and intolerance, he was a progressive thinker.[5]

The great social revolution of the 18th century, which intimately involved the peasantry and workers, was the French; the American Revolution also did so, but it occurred in a distant colony. It was this revolution, with its shibboleth of "Liberty, Equality, and Fraternity," well studied by Marx and Engels, that presented to them and other radical and socialist revolutionaries great hope to change society for the better; this despite the fact that the revolution failed.

The general left in the French Revolution were the Jacobins led by the indomitable Maximilien Robespierre, the principal actor of the Committee of Public Safety in the 1793-94 period, when the revolution reached its furthest left point. A disciple of Rousseau, he would abolish not only the aristocracy based on birth/wealth, but all large existing socioeconomic inequalities by progressive taxation, to be further erased at death with steep testamentary taxation. After all, property was a creature of social convention, not a natural right, allowing for its widespread use, with its corollary, the right to work. He also promoted democracy, allowing for male universal suffrage in a one-house legislature, the last being enshrined in the 1793 Constitution. He was aware that these principles were not easily arrived at, for the masses, lacking education – and being poverty stricken – were under the cultural hegemony of wealth, the normal enemy of the revolution. This was depicted in his confidential work, *Catechism*. A deist, he was an arch proponent of religious liberty. He was also against workers' unions – indeed, all corporate bodies, as is evidenced by his being for the Chapelier law. But large factories scarcely existed at this time in France.

To the left of Robespierre were the Hébertists, named after Jacques-René Hébert and the Enragés whose leaders, principally Jacques Roux and Jean-François Varlet, represented the *sans culottes* or the workers of Paris, savaged by high food prices, while wealthy speculators enriched themselves. Their aim was to extend the revolution by alleviating worker discontent through deepening the class struggle against the rich through more democracy and direct action.

As for a purely socialist current in the Revolution, there was the Society of Equals, founded in 1796 by François-Noel Babeuf and others, including Philippe Michel Buonarroti, who influenced many of France's leading 19th-century socialists, like Louis Blanc and Louis-Auguste Blanqui. This was the first major secular communist group in the modern era. Its May 1796 revolt in Paris was suppressed by Napoleon Bonaparte, Babeuf and thirty others being guillotined and twenty-four being deported, among them Buonarroti. Marx and Engels especially honored Babeuf as a leading communist revolutionary and as a principal precursor of their communism.[6]

In addition to the legacy of Babeuf, Marx and Engels were especially indebted, in the words of the latter, to "three great utopians," contemporaries or nearly so of them, who paved the way for the "science of socialism": Claude-Henri de Rouveroy de Saint-Simon, Charles Fourier, and Robert Owen.

Engels asserted that the first was not even a socialist, as his "workers" included manufacturers, merchants, and bankers, the last of great importance inasmuch as they "direct the whole social production by the regulation of credit" who were involved in battle with the "idlers," or the parasitic nobility and clerics. "Science" and "industry" would propel the planned society of abundance forward, which also guaranteed work for all. Furthermore, Engels saw that Saint-Simon was important in the history of ideas in that he was the first to state that "politics is the science of production, and foretells the complete absorption of politics by economics," or the chief aim of society was to develop the productive forces, the key in insuring the good life for all, especially poor farmers and workers, "'La classe la plus nombreuse et la plus pauvre.'" This technocratic view of society neglected the class struggle of workers against the bourgeoisie, but as yet outside of England, the working class was a minority of the population.

With respect to Fourier, Engels did not focus on his small utopian communes or phalansteries combining labor, capital, and talent/ managerial skill, but on his acute criticism of bourgeois society, like "swindling speculation" and oppression of women; "he was the first to declare that in any given society the degree of woman's emancipation is the natural measure of the general emancipation." Engels then delineated Fourier's division of historical periods comprising "savagery, barbarism, the patriarchate, civilization;" the last being that of bourgeois society since the 16th century, one in which "'poverty is born of superabundance itself,'" accentuating "'every vice practiced by barbarism in a simple fashion into a form of existence, complex, ambiguous, equivocal, hypocritical.'"

As for Robert Owen, Engels had nothing but the highest praise for this "materialist" and "communist," in which "every social movement, every real advance in England on behalf of the workers links itself on to the name of Robert Owen." In this vein, he observed Owen's struggle to better the lot of English workers, like the first labor law in 1819, "limiting the hours of labour of women and children in factories," and of being the "president of the first congress at which the trade unions of England united in a single trade association," entitled the Grand National Consolidated Trades Union of Great Britain and Ireland in 1833. Then, too, he was important in introducing "as transition measures to the complete communistic organization of society" of "cooperative societies for retail trade and production," which have "given practical proof that the merchant and manufacturer are socially quite unnecessary." But Engels did not recount Owen's social experiments, as a benevolent capitalist in

New Lanarck, Scotland, and in New Harmony, Indiana, in founding a short-lived communist colony.[7]

Engels did not neglect the great debt owed by him and Marx to these prominent German philosophers of the 18th and early 19th centuries: of Kant, whose critical views of ethics deeply influenced Johann Gottlieb Fichte, whose vitalistic atheism and socialism were duly noted, and of Georg Wilhelm Friedrich Hegel.[8]

During his university years, Marx was deeply attracted to Hegel's thought. Although a conservative in his later years, an apologist of the Prussian monarchy, Hegel had been a radical youth, an ardent advocate of the French Revolution and a religious rebel, condemning religion, including Christianity, for its "contempt of humanity." He also had an unrestrained utopian streak that proposed a society of freedom to "seek neither God nor immortality outside themselves," and the end of social oppression and the state itself. Even after becoming a political and religious conservative, he continued in *Philosophy of Right,* and *Phenomenology of the Mind* to emphasize such themes as alienation, the evils of increasing socioeconomic inequality, and the predatory individualism of the times. One of his most cogent revolutionary themes contrasted the parasitical master classes in history with the workers who, through their creative use and understanding of technology, would free themselves from them. Underlying Hegel's philosophy is the dialectical nature of social life, of ceaseless change inherent in human affairs where the idea/reality (thesis) inevitably develops within itself a counterforce (antithesis), which ultimately envelopes it to form a synthesis of the two, becoming the new thesis.[9]

Ludwig Andreas Feuerbach was also of great importance in forming Marx's thought. In his *Theses on the Hegelian Philosophy*, he formulated that history was propelled forward by the totality of the material conditions encompassing the human world, a view rejecting any supernatural intervention. And, in *The Essence of Christianity,* he postulated that theology was actually anthropology, that humanity created religion, not vice versa, a view critical of Judaism and Christianity.[10]

In the realm of economics, Marx was rapidly mastering its intricacies through careful reading, as early as the middle 1840s, of well-known British economists, including Adam Smith, David Ricardo, and James Mill, as well as leading French figures like Jean-Baptiste Say and J.C.L. Simonde de Sismondi, among others.[11]

Notes

1) On Judaism, including its strong messianism, see, for instance, Martin A. Larson, *The Religion of the Occident or the Origin and Development of the Essene-Christian Faith* (Paterson, NJ: Littlefield, Adams, and Co., 1961), pp. 195-225. Amos 5: 11, 6:4; Isaiah 4:15, 5:8. on the rich oppressing the poor. On utopianism, see Isaiah 2:4, 11:2, 28:17, 32:4-5 and 17, 35:1-10; Jermemiah 30:8, 31;12-13, for instance. On the Code of Deuteronomy (late 7th century BCE), see Deuteronomy 15: 1-6, 13-14, 23:19-20. On the Code of Leviticus (early 6th century BCE), see Leviticus, 25:8-28. On Greek philosophy, see: T.V. Smith (ed.), *Philosophers Speak for Themselves: From Thales to Plato* (Chicago: Chicago Univ. Press, 1956), pp. 5-45 on earlier Greek philosophers, as Heraclitus and Democritus. Ernest Barker, *Greek Political Theory: Plato and His Predecessors* (London: Metheun, 1960), pp. 63-98 on Sophist political thought, including its utopian element; most of the work is devoted to Plato's *The Republic* and *The Laws*. Thomas Cole, *Democritus and the Sources of Greek Anthropology* (Cleveland, OH: Western Reserve Univ., 1967), chaps. 8 and 9, for instance. Aristotle, *The Politics*, translated and introduced by T.A. Sinclair (Baltimore, MD: Penguin Books, 1966), pp 126-91, for instance. On Pythagoras and Pythagorianism, see Larson, *Religion of the Occident*, pp. 155-76. On Greek philosophy and Marx, see George E. McCarthy, *Marx and the Ancients: Classical Ethics, Social Justice, and Nineteenth-Century Political Economy* (Savage: MD: Rowman and Littlefield, 1990), pp. 19-119, for instance. On Marx's quotation on Aristotle, see *Capital*, I, 446.

2) Robert W. Funk, Roy W. Hoover, and the Jesus Seminar (translators and commentators), *The Jesus Seminar: The Search for the Authentic Worlds of Jesus* (New York: Macmillan, 1993), pp. 38ff. For more information on Christianity, see chapter on religion.

3) On utopia, there are many works, my favorite being by Marie Louise Berneri, *Journey Through Utopia* (Boston: Beacon Press, 1950). Also see Lewis Mumford, *The Story of Utopia* (Gloucester, MA: Peter Smith, 1959) and Martin Buber, *Paths in Utopia* (Boston: Beacon Press, 1960). For the persistence of utopia, see Karl Mannheim, *Ideology and Utopia: An Introduction to the Sociology of Knowledge* (New York: Harvest Book, 1963). Engels, *Anti-Dühring*, p. 27, for instance.

4) On the Levellers and Diggers, see Christopher Hill, *The Century of Revolution* (New York: W.W. Norton, 1966), pp. 129-33 ff., for instance. On Winstanley and the Diggers, see Lewis H. Berens *The Digger Movement in the Days of the Commonwealth; As Revealed in the Writings of Gerrard Winstanley, The Digger, Mystic, and Rationalist Communist and Social Reformer* (London: Holland and Merlin, 1961). Engels, *Anti-Dühring*, p. 27 refers to the "great English Revolution, the Levellers."

5) On the Enlightenment in general, see the classic by Ernst Cassirer, *The Philosophy of the Enlightenment* (Boston: Beacon Press, 1960) and Alfred Cobban, *In Search of Humanity* (New York: G. Braziller, 1960). Thomas Hobbes, *Leviathan or the Matter, Forme, and Power of a Commonwealth Ecclesiastical and Civil,* ed. and intro. by Michael Oakshott (London: Basil Blackwell, n.d.). On Locke, see, for instance, Ruth W. Grant, *John Locke's Liberalism* (Chicago: Univ. of Chicago Press, 1987). On Rousseau, see Ernst Cassirer, *The Question of Jean-Jacques Rousseau,* (New York: Columbia Univ. Press, 1954). Jean-Jacques Rousseau, *The Social Contract and Discourses*, trans. and intro. by G.D.H. Cole (New York: E.P. Dutton, 1950). On Diderot, see Carol Blum, *Diderot: The Virtue of a Philosopher* (New York: Viking Press, 1974). On Voltaire, see Ben Ray Redman (ed.), *The Portable Voltaire* (New York: Viking

Press, 1960). On French socialists in the eighteenth century, see, André *Lichtenberger, Le Socialisme au XVIII siècle: etudes sur les idées socialistes dans les ecrivains francais du XVIII siècle avant la rèvolution* (Paris: F. Alcan, 1895). Locke, Rousseau, Spínoza, Diderot, the French materialists, Babeuf, the French Revolution are mentioned, for instance, alone in Engels, *Anti-Dühring*, pp.25-33. Hobbes is mentioned, for instance, in *Capital*, I.

6) On the American Revolution, see, for instance, Grant Wood, *The Radicalism of the American Revolution* (New York: A.A. Knopf, 1992). My favorite work on the French Revolution is by the Trotskyist Daniel Guerin, *La Lutte de classes sous la Première République; bourgeois et "bras nus"* (1793-1797) (Paris: Gallimard, 1946). On Babeuf, see J.L. Talmon, *The Origins of Totalitarian Democracy* (London: Secker and Warburg, 1952), pp. 167-247 on "Babouvism."

7) Engels, *Anti-Dühring*, pp. 303-15. For more on Saint-Simon, Fourier, and Owen: Frank E. Manuel, *The New World of Henri Saint-Simon* (Cambridge, MA: Harvard Univ. Press, 1956). Nicholas V. Riasnovsky, *The Teaching of Charles Fourier* (Berkeley, CA: Univ. of California Press, 1969). G.D.H. Cole, *The Life of Robert Owen* (London: Macmillan, 1930). On the rich resistance movement of the early English working-class to socioeconomic and political oppression, see the incomparable work of E.P. Thompson, *The Making of the English Working Class*, (London: Victor Gollancz, 1964), pp. 9-212, for instance.

8) Engels, *Anti-Dühring*, pp. 33-37 and 173, for instance.

9) On Hegel, see Carl J. Friedrich, *The Philosophy of Hegel* (New York: Modern Library, 1954); and Georg Luckacs, *The Young Hegel; Studies in the Relations Between Dialectics and Economics* (Cambridge, MA: MIT Press, 1976), pp. 1-17, which includes material on Hegel's early radicalism.

10) On Ludwig Feuerbach, see his *The Essence of Christianity*, trans. George Eliot, intro. Karl Barth (New York: Harper Torchbooks, 1957), for instance, the first twelve chapters.

11) See chapter on economics.

Chapter Three: Revolutionary Communism

When Marx repudiated Hegel's idealism, he largely employed the materialist critique of Feuerbach, although retaining the Hegelian dialectic of conflict. In this vein, Marx critiqued Hegel's social construct. In *Critique of Hegel's Philosophy of the State* (1843), he rigorously criticized Hegel's pronouncements that the Prussian bureaucracy under a monarchy represented the universal interests of the people. For Marx, this was patently untrue because "bureaucracy possesses the state's essence, the spiritual essence of society, as its private property." Thus, bureaucracy presented a false consciousness because there were two intentions to everything, a "real and a bureaucratic meaning," which bifurcated "knowledge" and "will." Furthermore, bureaucracy encouraged a pervasive secretiveness and accompanying "subordination and passive obedience" to survive in its labyrinth. Indeed, for him, a repressive bureaucracy was a normal malformation of a society characterized by sharp individual and social antagonisms:

> In bureaucracy the identity of the state's interest and
> particular private purpose is established in such a way
> that the state's interest becomes a particular private
> purpose opposed to other private purposes.

Ultimately, for Marx, bureaucracy ceased to exist only when the "particular interest becomes universal."

Then, too, he rejected a constitutional monarchy on the basis that it regarded the people as subordinate to it, affirming the political ideas of the French Revolution in its most radical phase, that "Democracy is the essence" of a constitution. Specifically, he rejected Hegel's Prussian monarchy as the final step of the dialectic for a democracy in the form of universal suffrage, to lead to the idea of communism or the end of social classes and the state.[1]

In the mixture comprising civil liberties, freedom of the press is of critical importance, for without the free exchange of ideas, a *sine qua non* for informed citizenship, a flourishing democracy is impossible. In two lengthy articles, "Comments of the Latest Prussian Censorship" (1842) and "The Defense of the Moselle Correspondent: Economic Distress and Freedom of Press" (1843), Marx passionately defended freedom of the press as an elementary human right for a vibrant community life. In 1848-49, as leading editor of the *Neue Rheinische Zeitung*, he continued to plead for press freedom against Prussian censors whose response to government criticism was either censorship or suppression.[2]

Marx's next step was to find the human agency that would lead to communism. In descending from the realm of the Absolute or Spirit to the merely human, Marx's mindset, at once thoroughly sociological and philosophical, impregnated with the Prometheanism of radical Romanticism, unequivocally identified socialism with the struggles for freedom of the most oppressed group in modern society, the proletariat. In *Toward a Critique of Hegel's Philosophy of Right: Introduction* (1843), Marx discovered the proletariat as the vehicle whose emancipation would necessarily free humanity from monarchy and bureaucracy:

> In the formation of a class with radical chains, a class in civil society that is not of civil society, a class that is the dissolution of all classes, a sphere of society having a universal character because of its universal suffering and claiming no particular right because no particular wrong is perpetrated on it; a sphere...finally, that cannot emancipate itself without emancipating itself from all the other spheres of society, thereby emancipating them... This dissolution of society as a particular class is the proletariat.

Indeed, the proletariat became identified with philosophy itself: "As philosophy finds its material weapons in the proletariat, the proletariat finds its intellectual weapons in philosophy." Marx had identified the antithesis of the despotic nation state and private property in the working class that through revolution would destroy both, thus liberating itself and all of humanity. [3]

The *Introduction* was Marx's preface to becoming a Communist in the spring of 1844, in which Engels ably assisted. This conversion took place in Paris where Marx had been living since October 1843 in close contact not only with German socialists, but with such well-known French socialists as Louis Blanc and Pierre-Joseph Proudhon.[4]

In quick succession after 1844, Marx and Engels (singly and jointly) wrote a series of works which focused on the key role of their newly discovered working class to act as the basic catalyst to overturn capitalism for socialism: *The Holy Family* (1845), *The German Ideology* (1846), and *The Poverty of Philosophy* (1847).

But Marx was not merely a philosopher, but also a dedicated revolutionary. While in Paris in the mid-1840s, he often attended meetings of the League of the Just, a miniscule and clandestine communist-inclined organization of German workers. After his expulsion from Paris in the winter of 1845, Marx spent three years in Brussels, where, with Engels, he formed the communist Correspondence Committee in 1846. In February 1847, Marx and Engels joined the London-based League of the Just, which by June of that year became the Communist League, a secret Communist organization (1847-52), in which Marx was the president of the Brussels branch. Marx and Engels, as a front for the League, soon founded the Brussels German Working Men's Society. Marx contributed a substantial portion of his inheritance from his father's estate to arm members of the League for a future working-class uprising. The League itself neither swore its members to secrecy nor insisted that they be professional revolutionaries. Although it proselytized for membership secretly at first – it was forced underground as an illegal organization – it eventually recruited members legally and openly.[5]

It was as members of the Communist League that Marx and Engels participated in the 1848 Revolution. When revolution first erupted in Paris, Belgian authorities briefly arrested Marx as a dangerous radical and expelled him to France where he was warmly received. After a stay in Paris, he went to Cologne in April of 1848 to participate in the 1848-49 revolutionary events as the chief editor of the *Neue Rheinische Zeitung* (Engels was also one of its editors). His articles were revolutionary to say the least: he hailed the June 1848 workers' uprising in Paris as a milestone in the struggle of the proletariat against the bourgeoisie. In February 1849, he successfully defended himself against the government's charges of being disrespectful to the authorities and for inciting revolution.

But reactionary elements in government soon gained the upper hand, forcing the newspaper's closure in May 1849. Undeterred, Marx and Engels traveled in the Rhineland, to garner support for a Frankfurt revolution. When this project failed, Marx left for France in June and by August 1849 arrived in London where he resided until his death. After Engels participated in some fighting alongside the revolutionary Baden army, he also left for England.[6]

During this tempestuous revolutionary period, including its aftermath, Marx and Engels together penned five well-known works.

In *The Communist Manifesto* (February 1848), Marx and Engels foresaw an imminent working-class communist revolution, with cooperation from other socialists and radical middle class, stressing the need for democracy (a revolutionary concept for this period), "to wrest by degrees all capital from the bourgeoisie,"[7] and proposed reforms, including a steeply graduated income tax, free universal education, and abolition of inherited property.[8]

Later in 1848, the two wrote the *Demands of the Communist Party in Germany*, whose aim was to forge an alliance between the industrial workers (less than five percent of the population), the peasantry who formed the majority, and the rather numerous urban petty bourgeoisie. Their seventeen-point program featured such progressive proposals as universal manhood suffrage at age twenty-one, wages for representatives to allow workers' participation as legislators, the nationalization of banking and transport, right to work, free education, a steeply graduated income tax, abolition of feudal dues, and separation of church and state.[9]

In their March 1850 *Central Committee Address to the Communist League*, Marx and Engels, foreseeing imminent revolution, urged workers to arm themselves in clandestine societies. Although the revolution itself would be made by workers cooperating with sections of the middle class to establish a middle-class government, independent local councils of armed workers would also exist, permitting a proletarian revolution to overthrow the bourgeoisie. It is undeniably true that this document called for a Blanquist-like putsch by a revolutionary working-class minority, but this at most was a brief aberration; in all probability, Marx and Engels opposed this position made by a divided committee.[10]

Soon after the failure of the 1848 revolutions, Marx penned two brilliant works on French developments during and after them – *Class Struggles in France* (1848-1850) and *The Eighteenth Brumaire of Louis Napoleon*. The two covered the 1848-50 events in France in similar fashion, but the latter adds the stormy history of Louis Napoleon's coup d'état in early December 1851. Both works amply indicated Marx's mastery in delineating the discrete class forces and their shifting alliances in this turbulent period: the large landowners, the old nobility tied to the Bourbons, the "finance aristocracy," the industrial bourgeoisie aligned to the Orleanist Bourgeois Monarchy, petty bourgeoisie (shopkeepers and so forth), the peasantry, workers, and lumpenproletariat. Marx had the petty bourgeoisie fighting against the June 1848 Paris proletarian revolution (which Marx eulogized as the "first great battle" of the proletariat), only to become reconciled with the workers in February 1849 when the *haute bourgeoisie* insisted through the government that the almost-bankrupt shopkeepers pay their debts.[11]

As for Louis Napoleon's rise, Marx blamed the peasantry (two-thirds of the population), who were against higher taxes proposed by the Republic, for their overwhelming electoral support of his presidency. In the class progression, Marx especially feared the *lumpenproletariat*, the thoroughly pauperized and demoralized part of the proletariat (the drifters and criminals) who unwittingly served reaction; the young males of this group formed the *Garde Mobile*, which aided in crushing the June workers' revolution. In both works, Marx applauded the Parisian proletariat for toppling Louis Philippe in February 1848, locating the immediate cause of the revolution in the poor harvests of 1845 and 1846 and the consequent economic depression.[12]

During the 1850's, Marx and Engels again believed that a working-class revolution was imminent in Europe, beginning in England and France and perhaps spreading to Germany and elsewhere, linking it to economic depression exacerbating worker misery. Marx viewed a working-class revolution in one nation as a catalyst for others, which, however, would be met by the determined resistance of the nobility/ bourgeoisie of surrounding nations; he was aware of this being so in the French Revolution and in 1848-49. Again, with the eruption of the Paris Commune in 1871, Marx saw this uprising, which he characterized as non-socialist, as premature and destined to fail. He vigorously defended it and was hopeful concerning future socialist revolutionary outbreaks.

It is important to note that in his revolutionary scenario, Marx was not a pure technological determinist. In the capitalist era, he held that the level of technology/industrialization at any given time was simply one of many variables in gauging the possibility of revolution. Thus, for instance, although France had a smaller working class than England, because of past revolutionary experience, like the French Revolution and 1848, he regarded French workers as more revolutionary than their English counterparts. Furthermore, late in life, he even envisaged the possibility of a socialist revolution in a Czarist Russia whose overwhelming majority of the people were in the peasantry ensconced in the *mir,* a largely collectivistic village commune responsible for the payment of taxes to the government. This revolution would then spark one in the West, which, in turn, would presumably aid the drive for Russian socialism. In a letter to Vera Zasulich, a Russian revolutionary socialist, in 1881, he averred that:

> If the revolution comes at an opportune moment,
> if it concentrates all its forces to ensure the free
> development of the free commune, this community
> will soon develop into an element that regenerates
> Russian society and guarantees superiority over
> countries enslaved by the capitalist regime. [13]

Marx's revolutionary scenario, as might be readily observed, was replete with the indeterminacy of the present, of the unexpected to occur. In allowing the superstructure (former political and social struggles) to assume an important role for change, Marx did not place the working class in a Procrustean bed.

But there was also a powerful reformist position in Marx and Engels to change capitalism peacefully, especially by the 1860s. They foresaw that socialism might arrive peacefully in selected nations where democracy was in its early stages, like England, the United States, France, and Holland. Engels and Marx were among the principal fathers of the German Social Democratic Party. In his later years, Engels worked indefatigably for this party to increase its electoral strength.[14]

Marx's commitment to democracy was best illustrated by the specificity given it in *The Civil War in France* (1871). In this detailed blueprint for a future socialist society, emulating the governmental model of the 1871 Paris Commune, Marx assigned to democracy the primary role to insure orderly social progress, as well as to prevent the evils of excessive bureaucracy from deforming socialism. Democracy was the pervasive instrument in choosing representatives: Those elected at the local communes would choose delegates to the district level, who in turn would select deputies to a national assembly, still bound by the specific instructions of the voters. The power of the people also was manifested in their being able to recall before the expiration of their terms all judges and representatives.

He also applauded these undeniably egalitarian features of the Commune's government: that its council included workers and that councilors were remunerated at average workers' wages.

He then commended the Commune's proposed handling of most governmental functions in local and district communes under the watchful eyes of the people, and its desire for a "national militia" to forestall the formation of a military caste. Marx then importantly indicated his approval of linking political to economic democracy when he characterized the Commune's economic formulations as "united co-operative societies" that would "regulate production upon a common plan," and he opined: "What else, gentlemen, would it be but Communism possible Communism."[15] These formulations of Marx featuring mass democratic participation were also in his "Trade Unions – Their Past, Present, and Future", when he envisaged trade unions as:

> Centers of organization of the working class, as the
> medieval municipalities and communes did for the
> middle class. If the trade unions are required for the
> guerrilla fights between capital and labor, they are still
> more important as organized agencies for superseding
> the very system of wage labor and capital rule.[16]

To be sure, Marx's egalitarian/mass democratic views were ensconced in a framework of continuing technological development, even automation, to infinitely expand human creativity and usher in more free time, thus elevating the importance of science and education in the future communist society.[17]

Although these ideas of Marx on the economic and political organization of society had many similarities to anarchism, Marx still insisted that the state remain. Nevertheless, there was an evolution in his thought, from the rigorously centralized state of the *The Communist Manifesto* to the sharing of power between the local, district, and national levels expressed in *The Civil War in France*. [18]

In summary, the Marxist vision of the first stage of a future socialist society was profoundly egalitarian and democratic in the economic and political spheres, the essence of its "dictatorship of the proletariat."

One might object that Marx's diagram of a future socialist had many gaps. For instance, Marx did not delve into the relations between the representatives of the people and united cooperative societies, or how the representatives of the people bound by specific instructions would deal with the myriad disagreements that any complex society encounters. He was not drawing a complete picture (if he did it would have been at his own peril) presenting a general outline for a future socialist society, and expecting the socialists of the future to work out the various problems that they would encounter, leaving this legacy for socialism: that it rest upon universal suffrage, civil liberties/individual freedom, and on "united co-operative societies" in which the working class was master of its own fate, free to make mistakes as all classes and groups do, learning through experience on how to perfect the cooperative/egalitarian principle which is the seedbed of socialism.

Marx's insistence on basic wage equality and popular participation in running society was closely followed by V.I. Lenin's *State and Revolution*, written just prior to the 1917 Bolshevik Revolution, a "quasi-anarchist" work.[19] But these pervasively democratic and egalitarian precepts of Lenin were outweighed by the Soviet Communist Party's militaristic model of "democratic centralism," which ultimately reduced most party members to becoming mere ciphers.

Though the Bolsheviks promised to fulfill Marx's dreams of equality and democracy, they partially succeeded in the first element, but abysmally failed in the second. Engels himself rightly foresaw in *The Peasant War in Germany* that a socialist revolution might atrophy under certain circumstances, as when economic developments were not yet propitious for socialism, thus forcing the leadership not to represent their "party" or "class", but "the class for whose domination the movement is then ripe."[20]

Similar to Engels, Lenin and Leon Trotsky, the two principal leaders of the 1917 Communist Revolution in Russia, were fearful that if a Russian socialist revolution did not spread to the industrial West, it was predestined to fail. When Trotsky first developed his theory of permanent revolution in *Results and Prospects,* which predicted that the Russian proletariat would replace the Russian bourgeoisie as the leading class to overthrow Czarism, he also warned that socialism in Russia could not be successfully consolidated without the support of the Western working class that would not only have to prevent its governments from intervening against the Communists, but also preserve the revolution by extending it to the West.[21]

Although the Western working class was able to prevent a massive intervention to crush the Bolsheviks (limited troop deployments and other aid by the West to the Whites obviously prolonged a bitter three-year civil war), it was not able to make its own socialist revolution. For Trotsky, this was the decisive element in misshaping subsequent developments in the Soviet Union, which came to be dominated by a newly formed Communist bureaucracy that arose from the inevitable scarcity of economic backwardness.

> The basis of bureaucratic rule is the poverty of society in objects of consumption, with the resulting struggle of each against all...When the lines are very long it is necessary to appoint a policeman to keep order. Such is the starting point of the power of the Soviet bureaucracy. It knows who is to get something and who has to wait. [22]

Notes

1) On differences between Feuerbach and Marx, see David McLellan, *The Young Hegelians and Karl Marx* (New York: Frederick A. Praeger, 1969), pp. 85-116. On the *Critique of Hegel's Philosophy of the State,* see *Young Marx,* pp. 186-87.

2) *Young Marx,* pp. 67-92 for the first article; and pp. 143-48 for the second. On Marx's newspaper editorships and fight against press censorship, see Saul K. Padover, editor and translator, *On the Freedom of the Press and Censorship, Karl Marx* (New York:

McGraw-Hill, 1974), pp. 145-51 on articles concerning these matters.

3) *Young Marx*, pp. 262-63 on the long quotation; p. 263 on the other.

4) Rubel and Manale, *Marx*, pp. 31 and 38-49; Hunt, *Political Ideas of Marx and Engels*, I, chap. 3.

5) For Marx and Engels' activity just before the 1848 Revolution, see Oscar J. Hammen, *The Red 48ers; Karl Marx and Friedrich Engels* (New York: Charles Scribner's Sons, 1969), pp. 136-81.

6) On Marx and Engels in 1847-48, see Hammen, *Red 48ers*, pp. 185-403; McLellan, *Marx*, pp. 189-403; McLellan, *Marx*, pp. 189-225; Rubel and Manale, *Marx*, pp. 73-87; p. 71 – Marx predicted in London in 1847 that the working-class revolution would first erupt in England, and, then, spread to Germany, France, and Poland. Also, Hunt, *Political Ideas*, I, 147-48 ff.

7) *Manifesto*, p. 43.

8) Ibid., p. 30.

9) Marx and Engels, "Demands of the Communist Party in Germany," in Hunt, *Political Ideas*, I, 182-84.

10) *MECW*, 10, 1849-51 (1978), 227-87 is the "Address of the Central Authority to the League" (March 1850). On Marx's rejection of Blanquism, see Hunt, *Political Ideas*, I, 182-84. Draper, *Karl Marx's Theory of Revolution*, III, 14-71.

11) Karl Marx, *Class Struggles in France (1848-*1850) (New York: International Publishers, 1964), pp. 38, 56-64 ff.

12) Karl Marx, *The Eighteenth Brumaire of Louis Napoleon* (Chicago: Charles H. Kerr, 1913), p. 132.

13) On the revolutionary temperament of Marx and Engels, see McLellan, *Thought of Karl Marx*, pp. 196-211; Lichtheim, *Marxism,* pp. 122-27. *MECW*, 46, *1880-1883* (1992), letter, Marx to Zasulich, March 8, 1881, 71-72.

14) George Lichtheim, Marxism New York: Praeger, 1962, pp. 127-29.

15) On the various quotations, see Marx, *Civil War in France,* pp. 40-44. On Marx and Engels tolerating religious freedom, see Hunt, *Political Ideas*, II, 173-82. On Marx and Engels on the

temporary suspension of civil liberties following a civil war, see ibid., pp. 182-200. On "dictatorship of the proletariat," see Draper, *Dictatorship of the Proletariat*, pp. 111-44.

16) *MECW.*

17) Marx, *Grundrisse*, pp. 689-712.

18) *Manifesto*, p. 30 on rigorous state centralization. On the problem of "centralism versus decentralism" in Marx and Engels, see Hunt, *Political Ideas*, II, 147-61.

19) V.I. Lenin, *State and Revolution* (New York: International Publishers, 1932), pp. 35-44. Lichtheim, *Marxism*, p. 351.

20) Friedrich Engels, *The Peasant War in Germany* in Feuer, *Marx and Engels*, p. 435.

21) On Trotsky's theory of permanent revolution, see Isaac Deutscher, *The Prophet Armed: Trotsky: 1879-1921* (New York: Oxford University Press), pp. 145-74. Leon Trotsky, *The Permanent Revolution and Results and Prospects* (New York: Merit Publishers, 1969), pp. 104-06 on the necessity of the Western proletariat to support the revolution for its success in Russia. On Lenin's insistence on the need for assistance from the Western working class to achieve socialism in Russia, see Alfred G. Meyer, *Leninism* (New York: Frederick A. Praeger, 1962), pp. 220-21 ff.

22) Leon Trotsky, *The Revolution Betrayed* (New York: Pathfinder Press), p. 112.

Chapter Four: The Drift of History

A) Dialectical and Historical Materialism

It was only after Marx discovered the proletariat as the medium to liberate itself and humanity in *Toward the Critique of Hegel's Philosophy of Law: Introduction* that he and Engels formulated their view of history or historical materialism. Although Marx never used the terms "historical materialism" and "dialectical materialism," he employed those of "dialectical method" and the "materialistic basis" of history.[1]

This view of the world was first revealed in *Theses on Feuerbach* (1845) and other works where Marx and Engels employed variations of the Hegelian dialectic, but they rejected Hegel's idealism (primacy of spirit) for a materialism where "the idea is nothing else than the material world reflected by the human mind, and translated into forms of thought."[2] As expressed in *The German Ideology*, "life is not determined by consciousness, but consciousness by life."[3] They pictured social reality as consisting of various interdependent and contradictory elements, ever evolving in a milieu of conflict punctuated with periodic sharp breaks, especially as humanity, interacting with nature to survive, developed civilization with its train of antagonistic social relations, not only among individuals, but more significantly among classes.[4]

A more comprehensive view of the dialectic, with Greek philosophy as its bedrock, follows: For Heraclitus: "You could not step twice in the same rivers, for fresh waters are ever flowing on." "War is father of all and king of all; and some he made gods and some men, some slaves and some free." "Opposition unites. From what draws apart results the most beautiful harmony. All things take place by strife."[5] Protagoras further developed the dialectic, from the Greek word "dialego," to choose, as the process in which truth emerges from the clash of opposing views – a method extensively used by Socrates in Plato's *The Republic*.[6]

There are arguments over the elements of the dialectic. For instance, in the struggle between thesis and antithesis, is the resulting synthesis merely the antithesis, or are there elements of the thesis, which have attached themselves to the antithesis, that still survive in the synthesis? The intricacies of these disputes are of no interest here, but suffice it to say that some commentators believe that Marx was influenced not only by Hegel's dialectic, but Bakunin's conception of it, which favored the position that the antithesis so overwhelms the thesis that scarcely any vestige of it remained in the synthesis.[7]

The Marxian historical dialectic itself asserted a primary interaction between social class and technology resulting in a class struggle (in the contemporary world, primarily the working class and the bourgeoisie), including past social happenings (revolutions, for instance) and various alienations that would lead to socialism/communism. In this complexity of change, unities, like labor and capital, formed an unstable and changing nexus, leading to class conflict and social change. But this level of contradiction/conflict was linked to the technological one, of humanity's increasing mastery over nature influencing the creation of new social formations/alignments, again interacting upon the general historical tendency, which, in itself, progressed unevenly, especially in the short run. Also, we might envision the dialectic as an intellectual instrument that assigned more importance to certain elements in influencing others for change; this combined the logic of reason with selected empirical observation.[8]

Marx himself, and for that matter Hegel as well, did not employ the terms "thesis," "antithesis," and "synthesis" in their description of social reality (the terms were used by Fichte), but they do approximate their general view of it.[9]

Parenthetically, it was not Marx, but Engels in his later years, who promoted "dialectical materialism" to explain both the natural and social worlds in a philosophically rigid manner alien to Marx's flexible view, which stressed a continual openness, combining theory and praxis in determining the truth of the moment as it related to the general drift.[10]

37

We may compare Marx's dialectical and historical materialist model to the Freudian one of the human personality, determined by the dynamic interplay of a basic biological nature with that of culture in the mixture of id, ego, and superego, conscious and subconscious. In the course of everyday life, the individual is usually not aware, for instance, of the influence of the subconscious on his conscious actions, but this does not allow him to escape its various manifestations.[11] The models of Marx and Freud are dialectical, multi-layered, and heuristic, providing rich openings of insight into the human condition.[12]

Finally, is there a link between the revolutionary Judeo-Christian tradition and Marx's Hegelian dialectic to usher in the new society or utopia? Epistemologically, there is no connection, for the first uses the power of the supernatural to bring it about, while the second does so by noting past and present historical progression. But in the realm of social psychology, the two have a common thread – that the oppressed masses will achieve a just society against their present rulers whose wealth and power is inimical to general human happiness.[13]

A recent work on dialectics by Bertell Ollman, *Dialectical Investigations,* states that:

> Dialectics is not a rock-ribbed triad of thesis-antithesis-synthesis that serves as an all-purpose explanation; nor does it provide a formula that enables us to prove or predict anything; nor is it the motor force of history. The dialectic, as such, explains nothing, proves nothing, predicts nothing, and causes nothing to happen. Rather, dialectics is a way of thinking that brings into focus the full range of changes and interactions that occur in the world.

And:

> Dialectics restructures our thinking about reality by expanding our notion of anything to include, as

aspects of what it is, both the process by which it has become that and the broader interactive context in which it is found.

And:

> Dialectics restructures our thinking about reality by replacing the common sense notion of "thing," as something that *has* a history and *has* external connections with other things, with notions of "process," which *contains* its history and possible futures; and "relation," which *contains* as part of what are its ties with other relations.

This view includes "finding and tracing four kinds of relations identity/difference, interpenetration of opposites, quantity/quality, and contradiction," allowing one to transcend "focusing exclusively on appearances, on the evidence that strikes us immediately and directly," that "can be extremely misleading." [14]

These four elements may be employed by socialists to understand contemporary dialectical reality as part of a historical progression involving economics, sociology, political science, and social psychology embedded in past and present class struggles.

Marx's dialectical method was a wager that the drift of history should favor the socialist project, which has been having many difficulties in the present. In this regard, in *The Eighteenth Brumaire of Louis Napoleon*, Marx admonished socialists that:

> Men make their own history, but not just as they please. They do not choose the circumstances for themselves, but have to work upon circumstances as they find them, have to fashion the material handed down by the past. [15]

On the question of historical materialism intertwined with the dialectical method, the single fullest explanation was in Marx's *A Contribution to a Critique of Political Economy*:

1. In the social production which men carry on they enter into definite relations that are indispensable and independent of their will; these relations of production correspond to a definite stage of development of their material powers of production.

2. The sum total of these relations of production constitutes the economic structure of society – the real foundation on which rise legal and political superstructures and to which correspond definite forms of social consciousness.

3. The mode of production in material life determines the general character of the social, political, and spiritual processes of life.

4. It is not the consciousness of men that determines their existence, but, on the contrary, their social existence determines their consciousness.

5. At a certain stage of their development, the material forces of productions in society come in conflict with the existing relations of production – or what is but a legal expression for the same thing – with the property relations within which they had been at work before.

6. From forms of development of the forces of production these relations turn into their fetters.

7. Then comes the period of social revolution.

8. With the change of the economic foundation the entire immense superstructure is more or less rapidly transformed.

9. In considering such transformations the distinction should always be made between the material transformation of the economic conditions of production which can be determined with the precision of natural science, and the legal, political, religious, aesthetic, or philosophic – in

short, ideological forms in which men become conscious of this conflict and fight it out.

10. Just as our opinion of an individual is not based on what he thinks of himself, so can we not judge of such a period of transformation by its own consciousness; on the contrary, this consciousness must rather be explained from the contradictions of material life, from the existing conflict between the social forces of production and the relations of production.

11. No social order ever disappears before all the productive force, for which there is room in it, have been developed and new higher relations of production never appear before the material conditions of their existence have matured in the womb of the old society.

12. Therefore, mankind always takes up only such problems as it can solve; since, looking at the matter more closely, we will always find that the problem itself arises only when the material conditions necessary for its solution already exist or are at least in the process of formation.

13. In broad outlines we can designate the Asiatic, the ancient, the feudal, and the modern bourgeois methods of production as so many epochs in the progress of the economic formation of society.

14. The bourgeois relations of production are the last antagonistic form of the social process of production – antagonistic not in the sense of individual antagonism, but of one arising from conditions surrounding the life of individuals in society; at the same time the productive forces developing in the womb of bourgeois society create the material conditions for the solution of that antagonism.

15. This social formation constitutes, therefore, the closing chapter of the prehistoric stage of human society.

Engels in *Socialism, Utopian and Scientific* had a more succinct account:

> The materialist conception of history starts from the proposition that the production of the means to support human life and, next to production, the exchange of things produced, is the basis of all social structure; that in every society that has appeared in history, the manner in which wealth is distributed and society is divided into classes or orders is dependent upon what is produced, how it is produced, and how the products are exchanged. From this point of view, the final causes of all social changes and political revolutions are to be sought...in the economics of each particular epoch.[16]

In this model, the base comprised the "mode of production" or the "productive forces" and the "mode of distribution," of social classes, or "relations of production." The first element consisted of the economic-technological base of society whose major segments included manufacturing, transportation and the practical science involved with constructing, maintaining, and operating its complex clockwork, transforming the raw materials of nature into goods and services. The second, encompassing the social classes of society, involved not only the social relations or labor divisions to service the technological-productive sphere, but also the ownership and control of property and attendant power patterns. In a capitalist society, for example, bourgeois ownership and control of the productive forces was axiomatic, allowing for a basic command not only of the economic realm, but also of the social, political, and cultural spheres.[17]

On the relative importance between "productive forces" and "relations of production," contemporary scholars like Gerald A. Cohen, John McMurty, and William H. Shaw have the former shaping the structure of the latter, while Melvin Rader and Bertell Ollman assign a considerable role for the latter in determining the former in a dialectical interplay.[18]

Above this base, Marx, especially in *A Contribution to the Critique of Political Economy*, described a superstructure that formed "the legal, political, religious, aesthetic, or philosophic – in short, ideological forms in which men become conscious of this [class] conflict and fight it out."[19] Generally, traditional Marxists, like Engels, although allowing a dialectical interplay between the base and superstructure, allotted primary importance to the former, especially the productive forces, in determining the general historical drift.[20]

Theorists like Cohen, McMurty, and Shaw today staunchly defend this model.[21] Shaw, for instance, opines that the forces of production determine the relations of production, and that revolutionary social changes occur only when an "economic disequilibrium rocks the rest of society's relations and greatly strengthens the impulse to harness the productive forces satisfactorily."[22] He categorically rejects the notion of some Marxists that the productive forces and class structure equally influence each other. He bases this on various arguments; one principally being that for capitalism to develop, the productive forces must reach a certain high level, and that Communism or the absence of class again involves a yet higher level of production.[23] Thus, even a rigorously ecologically oriented society would have to organize the requisite high productive levels for the elevated standard of life required for socialism. The development of new technologies to cope with pollution, while also expanding the productive forces, is imperative in this progression.

Rader, a distinguished American social philosopher, has ably disputed this traditional model of Marxism, much of it formulated before such works as *The Economic and Philosophical Manuscripts*, *The Grundrisse*, and others were discovered:

> *In Marx's more organic formulations, there is no sharp dualism or clear-cut distinction between the productive forces and the productive relations, the*

> *polity and the economy, theory and practice, science*
> *and industry, culture and base. All of them not only*
> *interdependent but interpenetrate.*[24]

This view, holding that Marx's dialectical system necessarily conceives society and its development from an organic perspective, is buttressed by many quotations from *The Economic and Philosophical Manuscripts, The Grundrisse,* and other works, in which Marx employs terms like "organic" and "totality."[25] Moreover, Rader insists that the class structure and productive forces "overlap" since "both include the organization of the work process and the division of labor among the working personnel,"[26] thus disputing the fundamentalist version of productive forces having primacy over relations of production and superiority of the base over the superstructure.

Let us now wend our way through the labyrinth of the base and superstructure model in positioning some leading elements, which comprise it in light of Rader's analysis. To begin, where should science be located in the diagram? On the one hand, its critical link to the expansion of the productive forces cannot be denied, but, on the other hand, following older Marxian interpretations, the ideas of science belong to the superstructure, or should science be located in both base and superstructure? Now, in agreement with Rader, there is no reason not to definitely place science in the base, with the productive forces. Today, much of pure science, for instance, is rapidly applied to technological development.[27]

More questions arise. One is whether science and its application to technology are free of class domination or class conflict. The laws of nature have obviously nothing to do with class, but their use in technology certainly does. For instance, under capitalist socioeconomic and political relations, the technological innovations to expand productive forces at a lower cost has a tendency to cheapen and make redundant the labor of large groups of workers who are thus economically victimized. On the other hand, new decentralist technologies, like solar power, clash with established centralist ones, like the oil and electric-power industries that heavily pollute the ecostructure and whose political power prevents sufficient government aid in research and subsidies/tax breaks for these new innovations to take off. In this scenario, the contours of Rader's model are displayed in the dialectical interplay among research, technology, class struggle between labor and capital, and between small and large capitals, and their influencing state responses.

As for the problematic to the state's place in the base-superstructure diagram (traditional Marxists situated it in the superstructure), it should be, at once, in both base and superstructure because it has always played a decisive role in shaping the leading contours of the productive forces and of rising new social-class formations. Indeed, may not the state also be now seen as a productive force, as Rader suggests?[28]

All in all, Rader's organic model certainly seems reasonable. But I still support much of the fundamentalist model in the sense that some elements in the base, like the technological/productive forces and social structure, are more important in influencing the superstructure, like social thought, including religion, than vice-versa.

Marx's theory of historical development revolved around the class struggle, where technology and social structure interacted upon one another to promote change. This was a humanistic view of history, which specifically placed human action in the vortex of change to determine humanity's fate. In this model, revolutions (at times) would erupt when the various economic, social, political and other elements were too contradictory and conflict-ridden, although change might also come about peacefully via democracy.[29]

B) Historical Progression

The kernel of Marxian thought concerning historical change, involving the clash between the "forces of production" or technology and the "existing" [class] relations of production or the "property relations," encompassed six historical periods: the primitive, the Asiatic, the ancient, the feudal, and the modern...modes of production.

And the future socialist one.

Under the rubric of primitive cultures or those before civilizations, Marx and Engels allowed for two general phases, as enunciated in *The German Ideology* and in *The Origin of the Family, Private Property, and the State.* In the early historical dawn or in the savage phase, humanity, with its low-level technology, lived in small groups, which hunted and foraged for food, with such tools as small, relatively sharp stones, and later with spears and "bow, string, and arrow." It was followed by the higher barbarian one, which by its middle point, about ten or so thousand years ago, the Agricultural Revolution occurred, when women developed agriculture (men, animal husbandry, permitting extensive village life). Engels was correct when he characterized the first as "the period in which man's appropriation of products in their natural stage predominates," or food gathering, and the second as "the period in which man learns to breed domestic animals and to practice agriculture, and acquires methods of increasing the supply of natural products by human activity," or food production.

Generally speaking, Engels was again accurate in observing that early humanity living in small groups was egalitarian, from the savage stage to well into the middle stage of barbarism or to the Agricultural Revolution. Early human groups lived in bands promiscuously in the savage phases; in the early barbarian stage there was the "paring family," of a man and woman cohabiting, often serially, and then, sometime after the Agricultural Revolution, the rise of the dominant patriarchal family occurred, solidifying itself with the advent of civilization. (Minoan civilization might be an exception to this condition, with men and women most probably being equal, and in the Egyptian one, women enjoyed much, although not absolute equality with men.) Engels was aware of the many nuances here, as proportions of patrilineality and matrilineality. From today's anthropological knowledge, Engels may be incorrect in some areas here, but his general views are in the mainstream.

Civilization, or the Marxian ancient and "Asiatic" mode period, followed the higher stage of barbarism, which, with its ever higher economic surpluses, saw the early formation of class society that presupposed proliferation of labor division and accompanying status, and finally, class divisions, reflecting in varying degree the rise of private and various corporate properties. Engels' view of civilization ("the stage of development in society at which the division of labor, the exchange between individuals arising from it, and the commodity production which combines them both come to their full growth and revolutionizes the whole of previous society") is itself contemporary.

By the time that civilization first developed in the Middle East, Egypt, Crete, China, Upper India, and Greek society they were so well advanced that writing was invented, a critical means for keeping records and tracking taxes. To be sure, although these early civilizations differed among themselves in some respects (for instance, the Minoan had a high standard of life for the average citizen), they were all class societies.

We may add that Engels was incorrect when he had "slave labor as the dominant form of production" in the earlier civilizations; or when he had 365,000 slaves in Athens as opposed to 90,000 citizens because slaves were a minority of the Athenian population. There was some slavery in the early civilizations, although not much at first and only becoming prevalent in the first millennium B.C.E., the overwhelming majority of the population being in a serf-like class position in most of them.

It was also with the advent of civilization, with its writing component, that the general dichotomy between manual and mental labor began, the latter being in the superior position requiring formal education, usually common among the ruling groups and their ancillaries.

These events led to the rise of the state, of an organized society with fairly defined boundaries possessing an independent government whose essence of sovereignty allowed it to make and administer laws ultimately based on coercion. It was usually governed by small elite groups of nobles and priests, whose apex was occupied by a preeminent leader, like Pharaoh, sitting in cities controlling the countryside; they were followed in the class progression by merchants, artisans, free farmers, serfs, and slaves. Invariably, the ruling groups governed in an authoritarian/ totalitarian manner; later even democratic republics emerged, like Athens, which had extensive slave populations.

Specific instances of the process leading to the state/civilization complex, with quotations from Marx and Engels, are illustrated in *The German Ideology*, where the rise of the state was related to "the latent slavery of the family," proliferation of "labor division," and increasing "conflict between the interest of the individual and individual family and the communal interest." *The Origin of the Family* conceptualized that to keep class antagonisms in check "a power, apparently standing above society, has become necessary to moderate the conflict and keep it within the bounds of 'order'; and this power, arisen out of society but placing itself above it and increasingly alienating itself from it, is the state." But in *Socialism, Utopian and Scientific*, the "state was the official representative of society as a whole…it was this only in so far as it was the state of that class which itself represented, for the time being, society as a whole; in ancient times, the state of slave-owning citizens; in the Middle Ages, the feudal lords; in our own time, the bourgeoisie." To be sure, Marx and Engels were aware that with the rise of modern democracy, control of the state apparatus became a point of contestation between the proletariat and bourgeoisie.

In association with the state, there was the realm of law, itself closely correlated to the political hegemony of any ruling class. But in the modern period, as the working class became ever more numerous and politically active against the bourgeoisie, laws should become more favorable to its interests and aspirations. In this instance, current law is an accurate reflection of the relative strength of these two classes.[1]

The historical drama from primitive society to villages in the New Stone Age to the state/civilization complex as developed by Marxism and others is now the common wisdom of historians and social scientists. A typical example is a history textbook by Philip Lee Ralph, et al., *World Civilizations*: The authors have "hunter-gatherers in Western Asia developing agriculture and domesticating animals," allowing for "surplus production" and permanent settlements or villages, associated with a large increase in population and growing labor division. Warfare began, for "there was loot in a village." Over a period of time, as villages were combined through alliances and war, an upper class of full-time military and priestly functionaries emerged, ruling the underlying village population from cities. Unflinchingly, the authors accepted that this process was based on "subduing and exploiting others." [2]

Once the state/civilization was in place, Marx and Engels in a normal Eurocentric perspective, focused on the Greek and Roman experiences. The *Communist Manifesto*, for instance, noted the many classes in Rome, like the "patricians, knights, plebeians, and slaves." [3] Indeed, in the earlier stages of Greek and Roman society, war, trade, and widespread slavery often subverted the predominance of small property. In Rome, for instance, success in war enriched the senatorial aristocracy and their allies, the knights or bankers/merchants, while impoverishing the plebeians who were forced to compete with a large slave class working on the large latifundias and in cities. To be sure, slavery did not allow for a well-developed capitalism to develop in Rome, as agriculture always dominated.

Parallel to the ancient and feudal production was Marx's Asiatic, fashioned as much by geography as by technological development and state of class struggle. For Marx, the necessity for water to irrigate large tracts of land in India, Persia, and Egypt demanded the "centralizing power of government" to undertake this massive public-works project. These "oriental despotisms," ultimately resting on a myriad of villages and each heavily taxed collectively, were characterized by "three departments of government: finance, or the plunder of the interior; War, or the plunder of the exterior; and finally, the department of Public Works." This arrangement prevented the socioeconomic dynamism for a progressive capitalism to develop.

Although Marx abhorred British rule of India, he also saw its positive side of introducing capitalism through "English steam and free trade." Marx concentrated on the Indian variety of the Asiatic mode of production, marked by "caste" and "slavery," built upon "that peculiar combination of hand-weaving, hand-spinning and hand-tilling agriculture which gave them self-supporting power."

Marx's Asiatic mode of production shared common features with both the ancient and medieval European modes. The three were led by warrior/administrative bureaucracies, heavily taxing the rural masses, with the town/bourgeoisie sphere being clearly ancillary to that of the countryside. But in the medieval European one (we highlight Western Europe here as Central and Eastern Europe have a different development), although kingship was weak at first, it strengthened itself at the expense of the nobility by its alliance with the bourgeoisie, a development decisively aided, as Marx pointed out, by a successful imperialism overseas.

The Asian bourgeoisie could not achieve this pattern for developing capitalism. China, for instance, was not overly imperialistic with its emperorship being too strong to require the assistance of the bourgeoisie against a relatively weak landlord/gentry class, which was involved in civil wars related to dynastic changes. Furthermore, because they manned the higher positions of an examination system for choosing government officials, the gentry were largely pacified. In India, various invasions, especially the Turkic Moslem in the modern period, and the persistence of caste, weakened the capitalistic spirit.[4]

The class struggles associated with the fall of Rome and rise of Christianity, of slaves versus freemen (the latter involved with various class divisions – plebeians, knights and patricians), along with the decline of trade, led to the gradual end of slavery (a third of the people during Rome's Empire period) and consequent rise of serfdom, embedded in maorialism/feudalism, with its master class of nobility. This social construct was largely made up of serfs, but free farmers and slavery still existed. Serfs collectively were forced to work half the land of the nobility for about half the time in "workweek", this onerous tax being augmented by many other, total taxation on them being more than seventy-five percent of their time and production.

Manorialism/feudalism, with its many variants, existed in many parts of the world, including Europe (in Russia it was near slavery, lasting to the 1860s), China, Japan, and the Ottoman Empire. The primary class struggle under this system was obviously between serfs and the nobility, serf rebellions being common enough, like those of the 14th century in Europe, of the Jacquerie in France and of the English peasantry under John Ball and Watt Tyler. There were also many in Russia, including the one under Emelian Ivanovich Pugachev in the late 18th century.

In the Middle Ages, the economic scene was dominated by small private property in the towns with attendant petty industry and trade; even the manor allowed small strips of individual land ownership for serfs and free peasants. As Engels observed:

> The instruments of labour – land agricultural implements, the workshop, the tool - were the instruments of labour of single individuals... and therefore, of necessity, small, dwarfish, circumscribed... [and] belonged as a rule, to the producer himself.[5]

In this local and regulated small production/trade pattern, the realities of just price and fair profit permitted a large dosage of socioeconomic solidarity; the large and impersonal laissez- faire model would later shatter it.

The rise of capitalism for Marx and Engels was a significant event in history. *The Communist Manifesto,* for instance, observed: "From the serfs of the middle Ages sprang the charted burghers of the earliest towns. From these burgesses the first elements of the bourgeoisie were developed." Thus it was that the capitalist class, or bourgeoisie, was from the bourg, or town, whose free citizens were mostly former serfs escaping from manorial obligations. It was this "oppressed class" that became a formidable force in alliance with the monarchy against the nobility.[6]

In *Capital*, Marx saw that although "certain towns of the Mediterranean" were capitalistic rather early (like Florence and Venice), capitalism basically began in Northwestern Europe in the 16th century, aided by the general end of serfdom in the 14th century, itself much related to the Black Death. In this progression, the classic capitalistic nation for him was England, although preceded by such capitalistic ones as Venice, Genoa, and the Netherlands.

The Commercial Revolution, from about 1400 to 1700, and the almost parallel Agricultural Revolution, primarily fueled this early capitalism for Marx. He associated the former with the Western imperialism – Portuguese, Spanish, Dutch, French, and English in the "discovery of America...the East Indian and Chinese markets, the colonization of America, trade with the colonies." The latter occurred primarily in England with the development involved in "the so-called primitive accumulation," the "historical process of divorcing the producer from the means of production," or "the servitude of the labourer," to capital.

The importance of Western imperialism/colonialism and the accompanying wars among the great powers to control the commerce of the oceans cannot be underestimated in the development of modern capitalism. Wars among Britain, Spain, the Netherlands, and France strengthened royal power and its bourgeois allies against the nobility, with the exception of the middle class in Spain decimated by the expulsion of the Jews in the 1490s. Wars themselves contributed to strengthening war industries and increasing national debts, both related with the founding of great banks, like the Bank of England in 1694, which granted safe havens for investors, while raising taxes and perpetuating sharp class divisions between capital and labor. The advent of the joint-stock company, the forerunner of the modern capitalist corporation – with its many stockholders to pool their capital for business ventures and its limited liability provision – also reinforced capitalist development. Furthermore, the huge profits from the sugar and slave trade also hastened the advent of the Industrial Revolution as a large part of merchant- capital profits in these and other areas was invested in industry. Marx's succinct formula on this early capitalism was: "Colonial system, public debts, heavy taxes, protection, commercial wars, etc., these children of the true manufacturing period, increase gigantically during the infancy of Modern Industry." [7]

Within this general picture of capitalist development, Marx focused on England, the nation best exemplifying capitalism; Marx prefaced this with the correct observation that English workers and farmers before the dawn of capitalism enjoyed much higher living standards than during his lifetime: Despite the already large landholdings of the nobility, there was widespread ownership and use of land by a rather well off peasantry and a "general prosperity of the towns."

For Marx, the rise of early capitalism in England, comprised these domestic elements: (1) "The breaking up of the bands of feudal retainers"; (2) "transformation of arable land into sheep-walks" (for the production of profitable wool); (3) the "forcible driving away of the peasantry from the land, to which the latter had the same feudal right as the lord himself," through "the usurpation of the common lands"; (4) "The destruction of the old nobility by the great feudal wars" or the Wars of the Roses in the last part of the 15th century, establishing a "new nobility... for which money was the power of all powers"; (5) Henry VIII's confiscation of the lands of Catholic monasteries (the English Catholic Church owned about a third of the land), either dispensed freely to "royal favorites, or sold at a nominal price to speculating farmers and citizens, who drove out *en masse*, the hereditary sub-tenants and their holdings into one." Some of the land was also given to the newly established Anglican Church. Thus, it transpired that land tenure in England was heavily concentrated. To this mixture, he added the continual development of "usurer's capital and merchant capital," reinforcing "royal power, itself a product of bourgeois development." It should be added that even before Henry VIII and the War of the Roses, royal power in England had stripped the nobility of much of its military and other prerogatives, forcing it to the capitalist path. The brutal Norman conquest of England in 1066 was the basis of this extensive royal power that politically unified England.

Marx did not neglect the principal venue – the countryside where most people worked – for the primitive accumulation of English capitalism. Capitalist property relations were well established by the 15th century, England being the first large nation (the Netherlands preceded it) to have a unitary capitalist market in which producers were compelled to compete on the basis of market price. This cardinal fact was related to the Agricultural Revolution, or rise of "scientific agriculture," in which, as Marx exclaimed, "the irrational, old fashioned methods of agriculture are replaced by scientific ones," as "modern industry annihilates the peasant, that bulwark of the old society, and replaces him with the wage labourer."

In addition, England (compact in size with no great geographical barriers) possessed an excellent transportation system of roads and waterways close to the ocean.

In this account of the origins of modern capitalism, the latest Marxist views, those of Robert Brenner and Ellen Meiksins Wood, emphasized the importance of rural capitalist property in the genesis of modern capitalism.[8]

We delve more closely into (3) or the enclosure movement, a political/judicial crime, well described in *Capital*. Its essentials included dispossessing the peasantry of the Commons or common land, including copy holders (farmers having a "copy" of rights to land they farmed for centuries, but having no clear deed and title) by about three thousand parliamentary commissions each consisting of four to five members – gentry and bourgeoisie – of the House of Commons.[9]

Some statistics on England to show the concentration of wealth and population migration to the cities: In 1640, in percentage of land ownership, the Crown, two percent; a hundred and thirty noble families, seven percent; and under two thousand wealthy capitalists or the gentry, seventy-six percent – they leased their lands to tenants, who, in turn, hired agricultural workers. By 1700, London, the hub of capitalist England, had a population of 575,000 (the largest city in Europe) of the 5.5 million people in England. The English population almost doubled in a hundred years, being nine million in 1800; this as a result of more food produced by the Agricultural Revolution, the introduction of new crops, like the potato, and improved transportation. By the middle of the 18th century, a fourth of the English population lived in cities, and by 1830, when the first phase of the Industrial Revolution was completed, it was two-thirds, as opposed to two-fifths in France and Italy and three-tenths in Prussia.[10]

Alongside the emptying of the countryside through the Agricultural Revolution/enclosures complex, Marx recounted the savage disciplining of the English and other working classes through legislation to extract as much surplus value from them as possible to increase profits. Some leading English examples follow: Under Henry VIII, "Beggars old and unable to work receive a beggar's license. On the other hand, whipping and imprisonment for sturdy vagabonds." This was soon increased to "whipping...to be repeated and half the ear sliced off," for a second offense, while a third one resulted in "execution."

Under Edward VI, "if anyone refuses to work, he shall be condemned as a slave to the person who has denounced him as an idler," with the master himself having "the right to force him to do any work, no matter how disgusting, with whip and chains." If the worker, then, ran away for a "fortnight, he is condemned to slavery for life and is to be branded on the forehead or back with the letter 'S'," an additional infraction leading to execution. Under James I, "anyone wandering about and begging is declared a rogue and vagabond," who, after a series of unsuccessful corrections, was to be executed. In this mercantilist stage of capitalism, involved with primitive accumulation of capital, work was thus compulsory; in the later one of industrial capitalism, unemployment was favored to keep wages down and profit margins up. [11]

Before observing the modern working class, a brief description of earlier ones is in order for historical perspective. A working class certainly existed in classical Athens and Rome, but it was not numerous because of slavery and small petty production. But in Renaissance Italy, large working classes existed in towns and cities. In 14th century Florence, for instance, the *ciompi*, or woolen workers, employed in large factories comprised a third of the population. In periods of economic crises, they fought for workers' rights, seizing the government for six weeks in 1337, proposing a reform program to reduce taxes, provide for more employment, and ensure working-class representation in government. The experiment failed, with the nobility/bourgeoisie launching a successful counter-offensive to recapture the government.[12]

The medieval craft guilds, consisting of skilled workers and small proprietors, were petty- bourgeois institutions. But as the bourgeois spirit became ever more pronounced within the guilds, with masters keeping new masterships in the family, frustrated journeymen organized illegal and clandestine unions. The *compagnonnages* in 18th century France was the first modern workers' unions.[13]

It was during the Commercial Revolution in England that there emerged a widespread domestic system employing off-season farm workers to labor at home for capitalists in the clothing and other industries on a piece-rate basis; in 1750, half the people were engaged in this rural manufacturing, a halfway point between petty/individual production and the factory system.[14]

The advent of the Industrial Revolution in England in the mid-to-late 18th century represented for Marx the furthest point or synthesis of the many earlier elements discussed. In this progression, he mentioned capitalist-inventors, like Arkwright and his "throstle-spinning wheel" and Watt and his "steam-engine," replacing "the handicraft and manufacturing systems in those spheres of production that it first seized upon." This new "giant, modern industry," of "steam and machinery revolutionized industrial production."[15]

In the new configuration of capitalist production, Marx observed a factory setting allowing capital to profit from cooperative labor division so very necessary to expand labor's productive power; this in conjunction with the machine "which is the starting point of the industrial revolution," that "supersedes the workman, who handles a single tool." In great detail, he then delved into what made a machine, as opposed to a tool: "All fully developed machinery consists of three essentially different parts, the motor mechanism, the transmitting mechanism, and finally the tool or working machine." And, "from the moment that the tool proper is taken from man, and fitted into a mechanism, a machine takes the place of a mere implement."[16]

In this new system, the "labourer becomes a mere appendage to the machine," making the "product of his past labour work on a large scale gratuitously, like the forces of nature," as "machinery" makes "machinery," which "lessens its value relative to its extension and efficacy." [17]

Marx emphasized that the "productiveness of a machine is… measured by the human labour-power it replaces," thus it "raises the degree of exploitation." Of course, if human labor was less expensive than a machine, the later was not employed. The introduction of machinery, for him, also tended not to decrease, but to increase the workday, for capital wished to derive as much surplus-value value from the machine as quickly as possible; in tandem with this was the "increasing intensity of factory labour," or speed-ups.[18]

The modern factory system, for Marx, with its many horrors, normally elicited working- class responses in the forms of mass demonstrations, formation of unions, and strikes. He also noted the 1847 ten-hour-day law for women and children in Britain, a reform which accelerated economic concentration (larger enterprises could better absorb rising labor costs than smaller ones), and resulted in the "destruction of petty and domestic industries," the "last resort of the 'redundant population,'" thus the "sole remaining safety-valve of the whole social mechanism," preparing the way for a "new society" or socialism.[19] To be sure, these tendencies are continuing today.

We have already observed Marx's first three historical periods – the primitive, ancient/Asian, and medieval. The fourth, or contemporary capitalist period, was qualitatively different for Marx from periods two and three for the class struggle intensifies. This condition was because of the interplay of these principal factors: the qualitative change in technology, now of an infinitely more dynamic character than hitherto, which exacerbated the new class struggle between the working class and the bourgeoisie. This was because ever-larger aggregations of capital linked to this technology brought about these conflicts between the contending classes: as the bourgeoisie accelerated technological development to continually lower per-unit cost of production to increase profit margins, making for more unemployment of workers, recurring depressions would continue (the result of imbalances between production and consumption), destroying ever more small businesses and throwing ever-more petty bourgeoisie into the working class, itself continually becoming ever more numerous and relatively impoverished. The working class itself, ever more educated and aware of its being exploited by the bourgeoisie (the technology at the least demands an extensive general education) would increasingly become more class conscious and opt for socialism.[20]

The last, or fifth period, projected into the future, was that of "socialism," to come about either gradually or by revolution, to be followed by its higher phase, or communism. It would begin with workers acquiring "possession of the means of production in the name of society," and instituting a pervasive democracy at work and in political life, insuring a general equality in all avenues of community life.

These developments for Engels would end the reign of the state as a "repressive force" of class rule as "state interference in social relations becomes in one domain after another, superfluous, and then dies out of itself; the government of persons is replaced by the administration of things, and by the conduct of processes of production." In this progression: "The state is not 'abolished.' *It dies out.*"

Presumably the higher level of "communism would be achieved when the dichotomy between manual and mental labor was transcended by integrated labor and the enormous increase of productive forces would make for a general abundance superseding the limitations of traditional or subsistence economics based on exploitative surplus-value. This would allow for Marx's good society based on the phrase (first enunciated by Pythagoras), "from each according to his ability, to each according to his need," intertwined with the spirit of mutual aid explicit in the ethics of Marxism.[21]

Notes

A) Dialectical and Historical Materialism

1) On theories of history, see Patrick Gardiner (edited with Introductions and Commentary), *Theories of History* (New York: The Free Press, 1959), pp. 124-38 on Marx. Fromm, *Marx's Concept of Man*, p. 9.

2) *Capital*, I, 25, for instance.

3) Marx and Engels, *German Ideology*, p. 15.

4) *Capital*, I, best expresses this view in general.

5) See, for instance, T.V. Smith, ed. and trans. *Philosophers Speak for Themselves: From Thales to Plato* (Chicago: Univ. of Chicago Press, 1956), pp. 1-10 on Heraclitus. The quotations are on p. 11.

6) Ibid., pp. 60-63, on Protagoras.

7) On this argument, see Gustav A. Wetter, *Dialectical Materialism: A Historical and Systematic Survey of Philosophy in the Soviet Union* (New York: Frederick A. Praeger, 1963), pp. 7-10.

8) On the dialectic, see, for instance, Bertell Ollman, *Dialectical Investigations* (New York: Routledge, 1993), pp. 9-19 on "The Meaning of Dialectics." Also, see Robert H. Heilbroner, *Marxism: For and Against* (New York: W.W. Norton, 1981), pp. 29-58.

9) Heilboner, *Marxism*, p. 42.

10) Lichtheim, *Marxism*, pp. 255-58 and 297 ff.

11) On Freud, see Philip Rieff, *Freud: The Mind of the Moralist* (New York: Doubleday Anchor Books, 1961). Herbert Marcuse, *Eros and Civilization: A Philosophical Inquiry into Freud* (New York: Vintage Books, 1955), pp. 20-49, for instance.

12) On the dialectic as heuristic, see Melvin A. Rader, *Marx's Interpretation of History* (New York: Oxford University Press, 1979), p. xxii.

13) For a defense of Marx's utopianism, see George Sciabella's review of Isaiah Berlin's "The Crooked Timber of Humanity: Chapters in the History of Ideas" in *Dissent,* Fall, 1991, pp. 596-600. On the social psychology of oppressed groups, see Norman Cohn, *The Pursuit of the Millennium: Revolutionary Messianism in Medieval and Reformation Europe and Its Bearing on Modern Totalitarian Movements* (New York: Harper Torchbooks, 1961).

14) Ollman, *Dialectical Investigations,* pp. 10-11 on the quotations.

15) Karl Marx, *The Eighteenth Brumaire of Louis Napoleon,* trans. Daniel De Leon (Chicago: Charles H. Kerr, 1913), p. 23.

16) Karl Marx, *A Contribution to the Critique of Political Economy* (Chicago: Charles H. Kerr, 1911), pp. 11-13; I have numbered the sentences. Engels, *Socialism, Utopian and Scientific,* p. 54.

17) On elements involving productive forces, see *Capital,* I, 41-43 on commodities and use-values, 197-98 on human labor-power and raw materials, 397 on science as a productive force, 121 on labor division. On the thesis that the proletariat, as a revolutionary class, is a productive element, see Marx, *Poverty of Philosophy,* p. 159. Gerald A. Cohen, *Karl Marx's Theory of History: A Defense* (Princeton: Princeton Univ. Press, 1978), pp. 28-62. John McMurty, *The Structure of Marx's World-View* (Princeton: Princeton Univ. Press, 1978), pp. 54-99. William H. Shaw, *Marx's Theory of History* (Palo Alto, Calif.: Stanford Univ. Press, 1978), pp. 8-52.

18) Cohen, *Marx,* pp. 134-74. Shaw, *Marx,* pp. 53 ff. McMurty, *Marx,* pp. 188-239. Rader, *Marx,* pp. 3-18. Ollman, *Alienation,* pp. 240 ff., example.

19) Cohen, *Marx,* p. vii, trans. of Marx's "Preface" to *A Contribution to the Critique of Political Economy.*

20) McMurty, *Marx,* p. 158.

21) McMurty, *Marx,* pp. 188-239. Cohen, *Marx,* pp. 134-74. Shaw, *Marx,* pp. 53-82.

22) Shaw, *Marx,* p. 63.

23) *Ibid,* pp. 61 ff.

24) Rader, *Marx,* p. 10.

25) *Ibid*, pp. 58-59, for example.

26) *Ibid.*, p. 25.

27) *Ibid.*, pp. 27-33.

28) Ibid., pp. 35-41.

29) On the economic, social, and other elements of the dialectic, see Georges Gurvitch, *Dialectique et sociologie* (Paris: Flammarion, 1962), pp. 118-52.

B) Historical Progression

1) Engels, *Origin of the Family*, p. 93 on the quotations on savagery and barbarism, pp. 94-146 on the family, p. 233 on the quotation on civilization. Marx and Engels, *German Ideology* in Guddat and Easton, *Young Marx*, pp. 422-25 on labor division and so forth. Engels, *Origin of the Family*, p. 229; and Engels, *Socialism*, p. 69. On law, specifically social legislation in England, see *Capital*, I.

2) Philip Lee Ralph et al., *World Civilizations: Their History and Their Culture*, I, 8th ed. (New York: W.W. Norton and Co., 1991), pp. 14-26.

3) *Manifesto*, p. 9.

4) Marx's most extensive comments on the Asiatic mode of production is in the article, "The British Rule in India," June 10, 1853, in Karl Marx and Frederick Engels, *On Colonialism: Articles from the New York Tribune and Other Writings* (New York: International Publishers, 1972), pp. 35-41.

5) Engels, *Socialism*, p. 55.

6) *Manifesto*, pp. 9-11 on last three quotations.

7) On the various elements leading to early capitalism which leads to the Industrial Revolution, the best of Marx is in *Capital*, I, 618-848. On the first quotation, see *Manifesto*, pp. 9-10; for the second *Capital*, I, 830.

8) On the horrific exploitation of the English rural proletariat, see *Capital*, I, 739-66. Marx remarks on p. 739 that: "Nowhere does the antagonistic character of capitalistic production and accumulation assert itself more brutally than in the progress of

English agriculture." Also, see *ibid.* 788ff. on general English developments. On early capitalism, see the excellent Marxist work of Ellen Meiksins Wood, *The Origin of Capitalism* (New York: Monthly Review Press, 1999). She examines various works on the genesis of capitalism by Adam Smith, Max Weber, and leading Marxists – Maurice Dobb, Paul Sweezy, Perry Anderson, and Robert Brenner – before presenting her thesis on it. At bottom, she concludes, along with Brenner, that capitalism or the accumulation of capital has basically rural, not urban, origins.

9) Marx, *Capital*, I, 788-805.

10) An excellent work on Modern Europe, replete with statistics is by Eugene Weber, *A Modern History of Europe: Men, Cultures, and Societies from the Renaissance to the Present* (New York: W.W. Norton, 1971).

11) Ibid., pp. 806-08.

12) On the *Ciompi,* see Gene Brucker, *Renaissance Florence* (New York: John Wiley and Sons, 1969), pp. 46-48, 66-68, 79, 136, 151-52.

13) On the craft guilds, see *Capital*, I, 394; Engels, *Anti-Dühring,* pp. 320-23.

14) On domestic industry, see *Capital*, I, 509 ff.

15) *Capital*, I, 411-12 and 417. *Manifesto*, p. 10.

16) *Capital*, I, 407-08.

17) Ibid., pp. 421-26 on the quotations.

18) Ibid., pp. 427-436 and 440 ff. On the quotations and other material.

19) Ibid., p. 456 on the ten-hour day and p. 552 on the quotation.

20) These patterns are observed, for instance, in *The Communist Manifesto, Grundrisse,* and *Capital.*

21) On the two phases, see Karl Marx, *Critique of the Gotha Program* (New York: International Publishers, 1933), pp. 29-31 on the quotations. Engels, *Socialism, Utopian and Scientific*, pp. 69-70. Marx and Engels, *German Ideology*, p. 24. To arrive at a proper socialist society, traditional Marxists should go back to Marx with his strong libertarianism and reconcile with anarchists – anarcho-communists and revolutionary syndicalists. The basic

difference between Marxists and anarchists over the question of voting for parliamentary elections is now outmoded. We now know that the conquest of state power by socialists does not guarantee socialism; witness the experiences of the Soviet Union and China. I also factor in the need for an alliance between the working class and lower-middle-class which furnishes the bulk of mass mental labor; unless this is accomplished, I doubt any socialist success in the near horizon. See, for instance, Ernest Mandel, *Marxist Economic Theory* (New York: Monthly Review Press, 1975), II, 605-730. Ernest Mandel, *Late Capitalism* (London: NLB, 1975), pp. 184-222. Herbert Marcuse, *Eros and Civilization; A Philosophical Inquiry into Freud* (New York: Vintage Books, 1961), pp. Vii and 127-43. On anarchism, see Jean Grave, *La Société future* (Paris: P.V. Stock, 1895); and *L'Anarchie, son but, ses moyens* (Paris: P.V. Stock, 1899). Murray Bookchin, *Post-Scarcity Anarchism* (Berkeley, CA: Ramparts Press, 1971), pp. 94-106. On recent socialist planning models employing computers, see Fikert Adaman and Pat Devine, "On the Economic Theory of Socialism," *New Left Review*, no. 221, Jan/Feb. 1997. On computers, robots and automation, see Rifkin, *End of Work*, pp. 128-62. On computers, also see, *New York Times*, Dec. 10, 1996, p. C2. Mészáros, *Beyond Capital*, p. 710, asserts that under socialism, production is to be carried out "by a system of self-determined co-ordination of labour, from the local to the global levels."

Chapter Five: Anarchism

Marxism's great competitor during his lifetime and afterward was anarchism. A social vision with many similarities with Marxism, it had enough differences with it to produce great enmity between the two.

Anarchism, as part of socialism, is a comparatively new movement. Generally speaking, it is socialism without the formal state and other bureaucratic structures. The early strongholds of anarchism in the late 19th century were in France, Spain, Italy, Switzerland, the United States, and Russia. This vibrant philosophy has had such adherents as the novelist Leo Tolstoy, the naturalist/social critic Henry David Thoreau, the poet Percy Shelly, the playwright Henrik Ibsen, the painter Camille Pissarro, and the philosopher Jean-Paul Sartre.

Anarchism's major thinkers – William Godwin, Pierre-Joseph Proudhon, Michael Bakunin, and Peter Kropotkin (with the exception of the latter who died in 1921) – flourished in the 19th century. Godwin, with Proudhon, was the principal founder of modern anarchism. This noted English intellectual, a friend of Samuel Taylor Coleridge and father-in-law of Shelly, was influenced by two broad historical streams: the radical part of the Enlightenment, which stressed equality and virtue through reason, and the radical religious fundamentalism of England that equated government with religious persecution and favored egalitarian collectivism. In 1793, he wrote a comprehensive anarchist work entitled *An Enquiry Concerning Political Justice and Its Influence on General Virtue and Happiness,* a clear enunciation of decentralization, in which local communes would run the affairs of society. This free and equal society would be underpinned by equal distribution of property to engender a spirit of fraternity, banishing the insecurities of an acquisitive past. The present would yield to the future by the persuasion of reason through free speech.

The first anarchist movement was established among the French proletariat in the Paris of the 1860's, heavily influenced by Proudhon's ideas of mutualism (only he can be considered as the equal to Marx in breadth of social criticism and influence; he also was one of a few socialist leaders from a working-class family).

Mutualism was based on the small individual property of farmers and artisans, rejecting large- scale economic organization that would engender hierarchy and consequent subordination of the many to the few. Some economic inequality would exist as intensity and longevity of work would vary by individual. However, one could not hire (exploit) the labor of another. A rough political framework provided for local autonomous communes to federate loosely under a common constitution.

Proudhon basically envisaged a peaceful socioeconomic transformation from capitalism to socialism. He would have a central national bank invite bourgeois deposits, then make low or interest-free loans to workers to aid them in starting their self-managed industry. To expect the bourgeoisie to cooperate in this progression was naïve.

Alongside Proudhon mutualism in anarchism was the revolutionary collectivism propounded by Bakunin, a Russian nobleman who endured prison and much hardship for the cause of social revolution. He was an elitist, for the spearhead of change would come from a small cohesive group through propaganda by deed, acts of individual and collective terrorism against the power structure to inspire the workers to revolt. Indeed, he founded the International Social Democratic Alliance in 1868 expressly for this purpose. In the economic sphere, undoubtedly influenced by the increasing industrialization in Europe, which Proudhon had not sufficiently anticipated, he saw agro-industrial activity as being conducted by large collectives. But he would agree with Proudhon that decentralization must dominate politically in a federation of local communes.

Anarchism, Proudhonian and Bakuninist, played an important role in the first significant socialist-inspired revolution in history: the Paris Commune of 1871, which as legend, helped to inspire the various socialist revolutions of the 20th century. The Commune came about as a result of French reverses in the Franco-Prussian War of

1870-71 that produced animosity between radical Paris, wishing to continue the fight and the conservative and royalist cliques that would negotiate with the Prussians.

The Commune's strong anarchist factions espoused these aims: the creation of a decentralized society composed of local autonomous communes federating at the national level; the destruction of bourgeois property and end of wage labor by cooperative ownership and management of production; representatives popularly elected, receive average wages, and be subject to immediate recall; the replacement of military caste by the armed people; and the extirpation of religion by secularism.

The destruction of the Paris Commune brought about the end of anarchist activity for a decade in France, but anarchism survived in the Jura Federation of Switzerland and in some American and Spanish circles. It was during this low point of the 1870's that a new change came into anarchist thought. Elisée Reclus, a member of the Paris Commune and noted geographer, and some of his militant comrades, advocated a system of collectivism that would be coupled with free distribution of goods from centrally located warehouses. On the one hand, there was the fraternity of community; on the other, the individual's autonomy and sense of freedom were reinforced by the very cooperative and egalitarian structure itself: anarchist communism.

The leading anarchist communist was Peter Kropotkin. He was destined for a brilliant military career (indeed he was a close favorite of Tsar Alexander II) but he renounced his class privileges to join forces opposed to the autocracy. In 1872, he became a member of the First International and of a revolutionary circle in Russia whose aim was to create armed peasant bands to destroy Tsarism. He endured prison from 1874 to 1876 for revolutionary activity, but escaped. From 1877 to 1881 he was in Geneva, Switzerland, where anarchist activity was strong, and from 1881 to 1886 in France, spending most of the time in prison for alleged activity in an anarchist conspiracy against the existing order. After release from prison in 1886, he was expelled for lecturing on anarchism. From 1886 to 1917, he lived near

London, occupying himself as a naturalist and in anarchist research. He visited the United States twice: in 1897 on a speaking tour and in 1901 as a lecturer on Russian Literature at the Lowell Institute in Boston. With the advent of the March 1917 Revolution in Russia, he returned there and died in 1921.

Kropotkin is most notably known for his work entitled *Mutual Aid; A Factor in Evolution* (1905), with its optimism for human progress to end class oppression. While not denying the element of struggle for survival of animal life in nature, it was seen as occurring basically outside each species. Within the group, the dominant pattern for survival was that of mutual aid. For example, he saw that most of the work done by humans was that of a peaceful and cooperative nature, which more than counterbalanced human aggression. The categorical imperative of this message is clear and urgent, one that echoes perhaps more strongly today than during Kropotkin's generation: humans must learn to curb any need to dominate others or they will destroy themselves.

In the generation prior to World War I, when anarchist theory was refined and broadly disseminated throughout the world by book and pamphlet, the French contingent played a decisive role (it took about ten years after the destruction of the Paris Commune for French anarchism to spring back). By 1880, some viable groups were formed, the most important of which was the Social Study Group of the Fifth and Thirteenth Wards of Paris founded in 1880 by Jean Grave and some of his friends. Grave was the principal intellectual of French anarchism before World War I and chief disciple of Kropotkin. In addition to writing such outstanding polemical and theoretical works as *The Dying Society* and *Anarchy* and *Future Society*, he was an indefatigable editor of the anarchist weeklies, *The Revolt (La Révolte)* (1887-1894) and *The New Times (Lest Temps Nouveaux)* (1895-1914), the latter being the leading intellectual weekly of anarchism of the period.

Anarchists criticized bourgeois society, wishing to create a revolutionary situation to destroy and replace it with anarchism. Grave, for example, sketched this in *The Dying Society* and *Anarchy*, a notable work that received high praise from the French intellectual community:

> Anarchy is the negation of authority. Authority, however, pretends to justify its existence by its necessary defense of existing social institutions: the family, religion, property, etc. and as such has created a complex of machinery to assure its power and sanction. It has made the law, the courts, legislative power, the executive, etc. In confronting this situation anarchism should attack all social prejudice, examine in depth all human understanding, and finally demonstrate that its conceptions conform to the basic physiological nature of man that follows the laws of nature. The present society, established contrary to all logic and good sense, is unstable and rocked by revolution, which come from the accumulated hatred of those ground under by its arbitrary institutions.

For anarchists, the bourgeois order represented authority, embedded in the nexus between private property and oppressive social stratification, with its concomitants of militarism, racism, and nationalism – any condition which prevented the fulfillment of mutual aid. The chain of authority was ultimately capped by the state and private property, both intermeshing and protecting each other.

The obvious importance of the state in modern life was also duly noted. In its hands were the laws and courts that regulated all avenues of life – economic, social, and political. The means of coercion, too, were under its mantle, that of the police and military. Such authority was irrational and representative of man's antisocial side, as it was well illustrated by the anarchist view that the state's waging organized war showed its aim to conquer and exploit, which by engendering fear, stifled dissent and encouraged conformity, all in the name of defeating an enemy. This led to a patriotism that was inextricably linked with the militarism and colonialism of aggressive nationalism, forces antithetical to the anarchist ideals of pacifism and internationalism. The state leviathan's basic irrationality also reflected the intense social tensions of a class society dominated by the bourgeoisie.

Tied to an oppressive class structure and the bourgeois state was exploitative private property, which, under capitalism, resulted in an unequal socioeconomic exchange between capitalist and worker, thus intensifying socioeconomic inequality and exploitation. In this condition, the worker felt alienated, used as means for the accumulation of capital, to be corrected by a classless and egalitarian society, seen as a necessary human prerequisite for the following reasons: first, since humans were equal in essential qualities, any differences could only be minimal and unimportant; second, since the world's natural resources were the result of natural forces, they should be (as categorical moral imperative) the equal birthright of all; and third, since the present technologic-cultural level was the result of the past experience of all mankind, it should be in collective hands, not in those of any particular group.

In the world of authority, the new machine technology did not enhance the human condition; instead of widening mental and spiritual horizons, it restricted them. The monotony and humdrum routine of narrow specialization at work made workers "machines of machines," ever more dependent on capitalists. Indeed, every advance in technology could only bring more wealth to the bourgeoisie at the expense of the proletariat whose insecurity and misery would increase by more unemployment. The new arbiter of value and reality, the market, viewed labor itself as a mere commodity, a cost of production.

The institution of religion finally encircled this world of misery. In teaching respect for established authority, in calling for patience and self-sacrifice, for promising future happiness as a palliative to present suffering, and for engendering human weakness by its aura of mystery and stress on eternal punishment, religion further helped to disarm the masses by rationalizing institutionalized oppression. Ultimately, anarchism opposed religion by a secular humanism, where humans as the center of things would try to understand themselves and nature with no reference to any higher power. To be sure, this critique is very similar to that of Marxism.

Paradoxically, despite intense hope for revolution, a strong countertrend of reform already existed by about 1900 within socialism, including anarchism. As early as the 1870's, the Marxian socialist party in Germany, for example, had a revolutionary rhetoric but concentrated on vote-getting reformism. The Marxists in France also had accepted the game of electoral politics as early 1880. As between Marxists and anarchist communists, the latter remained more revolutionary. Anarchists, for example, would never participate in elections, which were seen as a bourgeois delaying tactic to forestall revolution. They saw socialist deputies as corrupted by the very bourgeois power structure which they wished to change (anarchists were anti-Parliamentarian), for the success of electoral office would demand compromise and general acceptance of the status quo. When pessimistic, however, even anarchist communists would admit that a few generations of reform might be needed to precede revolution.

Thus, reform itself would propel revolution, each reform strengthening mutual aid in an evolutionary pattern in which the masses, generally ignorant of the whole social process and still rather passive under the impress of authority, could yet understand the importance of pushing for specific changes. Anarchists were also aware of irrational forces in history, where the very oppression in the social arena made it all the more difficult for change to occur.

The revolution itself might be delayed or postponed, but ultimately not denied. In time, reform would lead to a point where the socioeconomic and cultural strength of the masses would be so overwhelming that revolution would occur. Social tensions in this pattern were seen to increase as groups approached political and cultural equality. This has been confirmed by the experience of the 20th century, in which the forces of change have made more progress than in the last few thousand years.

The revolutionary pattern for change would be aided by these elements: Technology's inner logic not only determined class structure but also created the various economic and social dislocations, which manifested themselves in social antagonism and tensions. In the agricultural Middle-Ages it was serfs versus nobility, while in the industrial 19th and 20th centuries it was the proletariat versus bourgeoisie. Although some reform was possible, inherent economic contradictions of capitalism would remain. Capitalism motivated by profits would constantly introduce labor saving machinery, which would result in unemployment and depressed wages. Capitalists would also attempt to procure new markets and new sources of raw materials through colonial expansion, but as the colonies would develop economically they would compete with the home markets, thereby putting capitalism in an even more desperate situation. (These views are similar to Marx's).

Revolution was inevitable after these contradictions emerged. The revolutionary spearhead, in France, for example, would comprise the industrial workers and small artisans – one-third of the French in the latter part of the 19th century – who would be supported by the majority of peasantry, half the population, most of whom had little or no land. Compared to the Marxists, the anarchists were more hopeful of the revolutionary potential of the peasantry. There would be no collectivization of small rural property holdings used directly because ownership of small property was not seen as counter-revolutionary. In time, the strengthening of mutual aid would lead to normal collectivization.

The revolution would be made by the people, but what about the role of a revolutionary elite? Anarchists saw its necessity, but only as secondary to the action of the masses. In the 1870's and 1880's, the Bakuninist faith in small clandestine groups committing propaganda by deed was prevalent, but by the turn of the century, anarchist activists stressed the importance of mass organization. The Marxists also underplayed the role of small elites in changing society. The view of both is sociological where history is seen as mass movement in which the individual, even the great one, only acts as a point of reference for effecting change.

The revolution was seen as transcending nationalism because the ruling groups would never allow any local anarchist success.

This emphasis on proletarian internationalism was also influenced by the events of history, where the forces of reaction cooperated to crush change, as in the 1815-1848 Metternich period, and the 1848 revolutionary wave.

The greatest difference between anarchists and Marxists was in their respective post-revolutionary vision. Basic issues were involved: the state and counter-revolution. The anarchists would immediately abolish the state along with all of its various arms: the army, the courts, the police force, and the bureaucracy; classes would be swept away; all exploitative private property would be expropriated and social hierarchy would be abolished; authority in all of its various forms would be uprooted to complete the revolution. This process would take only a few months. In its call for the immediate and total destruction of the state, anarchism was not as technologically deterministic as Marxism, which usually saw that mankind would have to wait until the future for a productive level substantial enough to eliminate the antagonism between mental and manual labor. Anarchists stressed the fact that in a socialist revolution general enthusiasm would buttress mutual aid and human solidarity to such an extent (economic equality and local participatory democracy would be prevalent) that any contradiction between manual and mental labor would not have sufficient weight to maintain the state. In fact, the anarchists were afraid that if the state were not destroyed during a socialist revolution, its continued existence would foster a new bureaucratic elite that would restore capitalism.

For Marxists, however, the state would have to continue under socialism; only in the distant future would it wither away. It was needed to organize the workers and state institutions (army and so forth) against any possible bourgeois counterrevolution, and social tension would still exist between manual and mental workers, the latter managing and coordinating affairs and thus receiving higher wages. For Marxists, this pattern was necessary, for they accepted large-scale industrial enterprise with its hierarchy. Only in the future, as the differences between manual and mental labor would end because of a very high technological/cultural level, would the social problem be eliminated in a stateless world of social harmony.

The conflicting currents of anarchism and Marxism collided in the First International (1864-1876), which was formed to promote greater working-class activity, both nationally and internationally. Although in the earlier congresses the differences between Proudhonian Mutualists, Marxists, and others did not lead to any appreciable disunity, in later ones a bitter struggle erupted between the Bakuninist-inspired anarchists and the Marxists. The former, rejecting reformism, desired immediate revolutionary action by small and clandestine groups, advocated complete group autonomy within the International, and resolutely opposed the state. The latter, however, were rapidly becoming cautious and reformist in strategy: They downplayed revolutionary action for the present, accepted bourgeois cooperation for social reform, insisted on centralization within the International, and envisaged the state to slowly wither away, even with the advent of socialism.

These basic differences led to the eventual split between anarchists and Marxists in the eventful Hague Congress of 1872. The anarchists left to found a rival Saint-Imier International that lasted to 1877, while the weakened First International expired a year earlier.[1]

Notes

1) On anarchism in general, see George Woodcock, *Anarchism: A History of Libertarian Ideas and Movements* (Cleveland, OH: Meridian Books, 1962) and James Joll, *The Anarchists* (New York: Universal Library, 1966). For the long quotation, see Jean Grave, *La Société mourante et l'anarchie*, preface by Octave Mirbeau, (Paris: Tresse et Stock, 1893), pp. 1-2. Also, see Louis Patsouras, *Jean Grave and the Anarchist Tradition in France* (Middletown, NJ: Caslon, 1995), which presents an appropriate background on anarchism in general, including Proudhon, Bakunin, Kropotkin, and revolutionary syndicalism.

Chapter Six: Economics

A) Background

This chapter is divided into four parts: 1) A brief introduction on Marx's economics; 2) a sketch of the capitalist classical economics and selected followers; 3) Marx's economics; and 4) and Thorstein Veblen, a leading American economist, the Great Depression, the New Deal, and John Maynard Keynes, the foremost capitalist economist of the 20th century.

It was Marx who principally placed economics in its broad sense at center stage in understanding history, focusing on its underlying importance in forming human institutions, like the family, state, religion, and classes; thus, he was not simply an economist, but a political economist and more, as he wove their connecting threats to general culture and to the drama of class/class struggle related to an ever-changing technology.

Marx's wide-ranging readings on economics – from Aristotle and Mercantilists, to the Physiocrats, Adam Smith and the classical British Economists (Thomas Robert Malthus, David Ricardo, and John Stuart Mill) and their epigones – was related to understanding the subject from the perspective of the working class in its struggle against the bourgeoisie.

In his economic speculations, Marx concentrated on capitalism with its contradictions, viewing it as a necessary, but transitory, step in the march of history leading to socialism. Although inimical to an economically subjected and alienated working class, capitalism expanded the productive force, while in the process creating a large working class that, in turn, would overthrow it to liberate itself and all of humanity.[1]

Marx analyzed the economic contradictions within capitalism, especially depressions and capital's tendency to become ever more concentrated, conditions resulting in ever more acute class struggles, while the productive forces were generally expanding.

B) Capitalist Economics

The principal thinkers of capitalist economics were the English classical economists, led by Smith, followed by Malthus, Ricardo, and Mill, who became a socialist. With the exception of Mill, reflecting the hegemony of the nobility/bourgeoisie, they regarded entrepreneurs as the mainspring of economics, with workers and peasantry as mere ciphers. This could not be otherwise for a deeply divided class society, when, even in 1900, 1 percent of the English people owned 75 percent of the wealth.

The shibboleths of the first three economists and their followers, with the partial exception of the first, raised the sacrosanctity of private property, the beneficence of free trade, with legislation to only aid entrepreneurs, like enforcing individual liberty to make contracts, including children with their employers, but prohibiting workers to form unions and to employ the boycott and strike against capital. Thus, their scant concern for the plight of workers, except for the first, who were seen only as vehicles to enrich the bourgeoisie, indeed to live at a precarious subsistence level doomed to everlasting poverty because of their supposed individual/collective improvidence.[1]

Smith, a professor of moral philosophy at the University of Edinburgh, wrote the masterwork, *Wealth of Nations* (1776), which is to capitalism what Marx's *Capital* is to socialism for ethical and intellectual justification. He principally observed that economic activity was distinctly related to social class – workers with labor, capitalists with profit, and landlords with rent. He himself disapproved of landlords, viewing them as parasites, having a monopoly price on food: "They love to reap where they never sowed." He also regarded the monarch, army, church, and bureaucracy as part of the unproductive sector, but glorified the industrialist/entrepreneur as the great accumulator of wealth.

To achieve maximum results for capital accumulation and economic efficiency, Smith employed the model of the self-regulating competitive market of many small producers (no oligopoly monopoly), or "invisible hand," to not only determine wages, prices of goods, and profits, but simultaneously to also promote beneficially the "society" at large.[2] More capital, itself from profit, invited more investment to produce more goods leading to higher wages and lower prices for commodities.

The state itself for Smith played a positive role: It maintained the military, the justice system and public education, subsidized some industry – that of shipping to aid national defense – and regulated the price and quality of bread because it was too important a commodity for only private markets to control. He would also impose steep taxes on luxury goods to fund welfare laws for the poor, and even advocated progressive income taxes. Furthermore, in contradistinction to many of his followers, he displayed a deep sympathy for workers, demanding that they be "tolerably well fed, clothed and lodged."

On the economic relations between labor and capital, Smith employed an antagonistic model between them, workers fighting for higher wages, capitalists, for lower, but capitalists being fewer in number and economically stronger than workers, who without employment were soon penniless, had the advantage. Furthermore, he pointed out that law favored capitalists because it deemed strikes illegal for higher wages and shorter workdays.[3] Like Marx, he saw that "civil government…is in reality instituted for the defense of the rich against the poor, or those who have some property against those who have none at all."[4]

On differences in human intelligence, with obvious implications concerning the possibility for at least a future socioeconomic equality, Smith was very generous, holding that "the difference of natural talents in different men is, in reality, much less that we are aware of," being "not so much from nature, as from habit, custom, and education." He was also aware that labor division was basically responsible for the mental degradation of workers.[5]

A free trader, Smith not only opposed tariffs and guilds (unions), but business combinations (monopoly is a tax on consumers), particularly suspicious of business: "People of the same profession or trade meet together but the conversation ends in a conspiracy against the public or in some diversion to raise prices."

Despite the misgivings that Smith evinced toward capitalists, he assigned to them the central role to accumulate capital and taking for granted an economically motivated individual with a "predisposition to barter and exchange."[6] Never economically satisfied, they pursued private ends to make more money, but also helped the general community, like employing others. In the area of technology to create wealth, Smith, although aware of machinery, did not dwell on its importance to increase output, but focused on labor division's key role in doing so.

On commodity value, Smith upheld the labor theory of value or that "labor...is the real measure of the exchangeable value of commodities," although this fact "is not altogether so natural and obvious."[7] The principal source of the modern labor theory of value was Locke's Chapter V in the second of the *Two Treaties of Government*, proposing that human labor, intermixing with nature common to all, created property, a concept elaborated on by Smith, Malthus, and especially Ricardo, whom Marx built upon to justify his socialism. But there was ambiguity in Locke's labor theory of value. On the one hand, he averred that: "One can have as much property as he can use of to any advantage of life before it spoils. Whatever is beyond this is more than his share and belongs to others." On the other hand, he claimed: "The turfs my servant has cut become my property without the consent of anybody." In the first statement, he undoubtedly referred to the state of nature, while in the second, to civilization, in which the employer owned a worker's time and labor.[8]

All in all, Smith was a progressive political economist. Although a supporter of capitalism, his favorable views on social welfare, sympathy for workers, and advocacy of progressive income taxation were magnanimous.

An influential conservative, whose views are still in vogue, was Thomas Robert Malthus, an upper-middle class Anglican parson whose *An Essay on Population* wrestled with the still perplexing problem for capitalists – the need for inexpensive labor, but fear that overpopulation might lead to social catastrophe. It began with two basic claims: that humanity required food to exist and that male/ female passion resulted in the having of children.

In this nexus, population would tend to increase more than the available food supply – food at an arithmetic rate, population at a geometric one. But the dire consequences of this were mitigated by two checks – positive, like sickness/starvation and war, and preventive, like continence and late marriage, themselves not being sufficient to prevent the horrific poverty of English workers. Ultimately, this model held that overpopulation is basically impossible in the long run because in the short run it would simply lead to higher death rates.

On to this conflict-ridden model, which supposed a struggle among individuals for food – not an unreasonable assumption considering that much of the population was on the brink of starvation at times – Malthus justified the wealth of capitalists and accompanying poverty of the workers thus: A proponent of economic progress represented by capital requiring inexpensive labor for profit, he related this condition to the especially sinful nature of British workers who, in begetting too many children, kept wages low and profits high. But if workers became more "virtuous" by having fewer children, higher wages and lower profits would follow, causing economic downturn and more unemployment. In this scenario, the working class was doomed to everlasting poverty.[9]

Malthus unalterably inimical to workers' aspirations, proposed that to insulate them from the egalitarian ideas of the French Revolution, they be taught to accept their lowly lot in life; any attempt to change the status quo being foolhardy. In this vein, Malthus attacked egalitarian notions of Paine, Godwin, and the views of Owen, as well as others favoring contraceptives to decrease the birth rate, employing his original sin argument, of naturally selfish and lazy humans who must be forced to work by fear of starvation, any leveling resulting in overpopulation and social disaster.[10]

Malthus' model of wealth and poverty pleased the wealthy who could exploit workers with the clear conscience that God himself ordained it. Being a good parson, Malthus, had religion admonishing workers to have less sin/sex, but since most of them were evil, reformation was not possible.[11] He neglected some of the obvious causes for high working-class birth rates: High infant mortality rates, the necessity for child labor to provide for basic family needs, and reliance on children to care for old or incapacitated parents during a time of no social security.

Aware of economic downturns and the social instability caused by high unemployment, Malthus opposed an overly rapid industrialization/urbanization of England, preferring the continuance of a stable gentry landowner class to employ agricultural laborers, thus rejecting Smithian free trade for tariffs on food, despite their impeding industrialization by increasing the price of labor and decreasing profit/investment.[12]

The conservatism of Malthus was also noted by his opposition to the Speenhamland System of 1795, with its basic assumption that the workers and indigent had the right to live, with the aid of government welfare to the indigent and subsidies to wage workers to attain a minimum wage, thus protecting them from the most savage effects of the labor market. The Poor Law of 1834 annulled these provisions, integrating labor fully into the self-regulated capitalist market. Relief for the indigent continued, but now only in workhouses (indoor relief), leading to the breakup of families.[13]

The Malthusian socioeconomic picture accurately portrayed the conservative mindset of a triumphant bourgeoisie during the early stages of industrialization, reflecting the relatively low level of production and accompanying sharp class division between the poor or workers and their class superiors, the bourgeoisie and nobility, proclaiming that workers were eternally doomed to the mutilations of poverty.

In the genealogy of Malthus' views, we must consider Joseph Townsend, an upper-middle class reactionary Anglican minister who espoused an embryonic Darwinian doctrine that condemned the poor, always multiplying, to poverty and early death. His *A Tract of the Poor Laws by a Well-Wisher of Mankind* opposed poor relief on the basis that in aiding the hungry it "tends to destroy the harmony and beauty, the symmetry and order, of that system which God and nature have established in the world." Indeed, workers should not be too far from hunger, for "hunger is not only peaceful, silent, unremitted pressure, but, as the most natural motive of industry and labour, it calls forth the most powerful exertions." And, he recommended that "the poor should be to a certain degree improvident...to fulfill the most servile, the most sordid, and the most ignoble offices in the community." This, in turn, would allow the nobility/bourgeoisie, "the more delicate...to procure those callings which are suited to their various dispositions."[14]

From a wealthy Sephardic Jewish family (his father, a banker), Ricardo made money by playing the stock market, became a Quaker (his wife was one) and a member of the House of Commons, and extensively corresponded with Malthus. In *On the Principles of Political Economy and Taxation*, following Smith, he divided the socioeconomic pie into three parts – wages/workers, profits/ capitalists, and rents/landowners. Wages, representing labor, would remain at a subsistence level, which, however, varied according to society's economic development. Wages themselves revolved around the natural price of labor (the Malthusian one where births and deaths were in equilibrium), contrasted to the market price fluctuating to reflect disparities in the birth-death ratio of available labor. Profits were related to wages inversely, higher wages equaled lower profits, but lower wages equaled higher profits. As for rents, they represented the prerogatives of gentry landowners, whom Ricardo pictured as parasites: Contrary to creative entrepreneurs, they simply leased land to tenants who hired agricultural laborers, and with the general increase in population and demand for more food, simply elevated rents, making food more costly and, consequently, labor more expensive, thus lowering profit margins for industrialists. The end result was the tendency toward zero profit or economic stagnation. Although aware of technology's ability to raise crop yield even with the employment of more marginal or less fertile land, he underestimated it.

In the area of how value was determined, Ricardo refined Smith: The real values of commodities vary inversely with the productivity of labor in the making of them. The trend in the natural exchange values of commodities corresponds roughly to the relative amount of labor embodied in their production.[15]

John Stuart Mill, a most important economic and social thinker, did not ultimately defend capitalism, unlike other classical economists. Although his economic conceptions were deeply indebted to Ricardo, a deep social concern for workers led him to a socialism in which workers' producer and other associations, having abolished the wage system, were collectively owned. Workers elected and removed management. An arch-opponent of capitalism, he proposed that democracy and capitalism were incompatible for the social and cultural powers of the wealthy over the working class were so pronounced that it did not have a proper enlightened self-interest. With his wife, Harriet Taylor, he authored *The Subjection of Women*, a significant work on women's liberation, and defended the Paris Commune of 1871.[16]

Malthus' chief acolyte was Herbert Spencer. To indicate the superiority of capitalism to socialism, he principally identified socialism with primitive cultures, past civilizations, and economically underdeveloped areas, calling Native American cultures north of the Rio Grande River, as well as Native American civilizations, socialist, while in the contemporary period he equated the Montenegrins as such. He disliked the collectivistic aspect of these societies, or their sense of social solidarity, which, contrary to his economically calculating bourgeois family (he favored the differences between the "ethics of family life and the ethics outside the family") did not make as great an ethical distinction between the private and public spheres. And he solemnly affirmed that the socialist principle of loving all children impartially was "biologically fatal" and "psychologically absurd."[17]

Socialism itself, for him, insured "an industrial subordination parallel to the military subordination," in which "obedience is requisite for the maintenance of order, as well as for efficiency, and must be enforced with whatever rigour is found needful." Thus, socialism would be organized hierarchically, with "multitudinous officers, grade over grade, having in their hands all authority and all means of coercion." This "bureaucracy" would run roughshod over all other social formations, including elected representatives of the populace, forming themselves into a "new ruling class" that "would wield a power far beyond that of any past aristocracy."[18]

In the economic realm, the followers of the classical economists were ensconced in the neo- classical school, which included William Stanley Jevons and Alfred Marshall, and today, one as well-known as Milton Friedman, a leading exponent of the Chicago school and the leading Republican economics guru since the 1970s. Their economics focused on the concepts of "equilibrium" and "marginal analysis:" The first referred to the economy at average levels of production and consumption at any given time, which might be affected by forces of disequilibrium (shortages, new industries, and so forth), with their influence on prices; the second involved the attaining of maximum efficiency in allocating capital for profit.[19]

An examination of Friedman's basic economic and social views follows: Friedman formulated the theoretical basis for "Supply-Side" economics or "Reganomics," which slashed the taxes for the wealthy and corporations more so than for the working and lower-middle classes to stimulate investment and consumer spending. To be sure, the capitalist world was awash with capital from the oil-producing nations. Also, under President Regan, the rise in social- security taxes more than offset savings for workers from modest tax reduction.

A believer in laissez-faire economics and the inviolability of private property, which he equated with liberty, Friedman held that big government was its mortal enemy, the *sine qua non* for the possible rise of socialism; he thus favored a spurious individual freedom and responsibility, or "rugged individualism," which masked a murderously competitive society and the authoritarian ethos of the corporation, which he conveniently ignored. He pictured himself as a traditional liberal of the 19th century variety whose constant refrain was to cut federal social-welfare programs, perpetuating individual dependence on government while fostering economic incentives of the more resourceful and successful, i.e., the wealthy.

Although Friedman liked to often quote Smith, his fear of government or collective effort to solve socioeconomics problems made him a Spencerite, although a moderate one. Friedman himself claimed that he "is not an anarchist" (there is a quasi-anarchist strain in Spencer), that the government had a proper role in protecting property and citizens from internal and external enemies, intervening to "enforce contracts," safeguard consumers against "technical monopolies," and to aid the mentally ill and children.

But he was against government subsidies to farmers and other business in the form of tariffs and collusion with business to raise prices, as the Texas Railroad Commission, which raised oil prices by reducing output. As a corollary to this, he disapproved of any close regulation of industry, as by the Interstate Commerce Commission. He also opposed public housing, minimum wage laws, social security programs as now constituted, rent controls, and other present social welfare programs for the poor and unemployed. In their stead, he proposed a system of cash subsidies supplemented with a negative income tax. As for taxes, he favored a federal flat-rate income one, steeply regressive, falling most heavily on the working and lower-middle classes, now proposed by the Republicans.

In his analysis of economics, Friedman blithely overlooked the free gifts to capital, which it received from workers and government/society: from the former, extraction of surplus-value; from the latter, public education to cheapen labor relatively, fire and police protection, tax abatements, community revenue bonds, laws and supreme court decisions protecting corporations (which are simply seen as persons, despite their immense economic power), research and development assistance, and low taxes. He was also oblivious to increasing corporate mergers and tendency to ever more oligopoly, or to the truism that American capitalists in the main favored high tariffs not too long ago to allow infant American industry to survive, or to the high costs of militarism/imperialism intimately related to the bourgeois ethic, or to government guarantees to corporations doing business abroad, or to the interference of international economic bodies in the internal affairs of poor nations, or pollution, or to the waste of scarce economic resources by the affluent in conspicuous consumption.

Ultimately, was not Friedman's "free trade" mantra simply an apology for Western and Japanese capital to rule the world?[20]

C) Marxist Economics
A. Labor Theory of Value

Before delving into Marx's labor theory of value, a brief background of it is appropriate: It was first well described by Aristotle, followed by Locke, Smith, and Ricardo. Its first socialist exponents – who argued that everything made by labor should go to it – were English "Ricardian" socialists, who, as Lichtheim asserted, "blazed the trail for him [Marx]," most notably Owen, John Gray, William Thompson, and Thomas Hodgskin.[1]

In Marx's labor theory of value, there were two primary creators of wealth – land, with its fertility of soil and natural resources, and labor-power, including the "degree of productivity of social labor."

It was the exploitative nature of economic relations between workers and capitalists that allowed for rapid capital accumulation and an ever-larger working class to develop, leading to the accumulation of wealth for the bourgeoisie, and an increase of relative misery for workers.[2]

The means by which the bourgeoisie differentiated itself from the proletariat was through surplus-value, Marx's central economic concept that explains the struggle between the proletariat and bourgeoisie: Marx held that the very labor-time of workers belonged to capital.[3] But human labor, for him, unlike other commodities, was a "universal value-creating element, and thus possesses a property by which it differs from all other commodities," so "if such a thing as the value of labour really existed, and be really paid this value no capital would exist, [the capitalists] money would not be turned to capital." Thus, when Marx discussed labor, he employed the term "labor-power," in which the "value of labour is in fact the value of labour- power, as it exists in the personality of the laborer, which is as different from its function, labor, as a machine is from the work it performs."[4]

This labor-power denoted capital's using living labor to extract from it more than exchange values, or values far exceeding the exchange variety, i.e. of surplus-value, ever-widening the socioeconomic gulf between labor and capital, clearly formulated first in the *Grundrisse* and the major theme of *Capital*. This view conceptualized human labor as not simply another commodity, but as a unique and transcendent entity, deserving the highest respect and dignity, the mainspring for material/spiritual progress.

In opposition to this view of work was the bourgeois perspective, which regarded labor as a commodity; the entrepreneur was simply being efficient to continually drive down labor costs or number of workers with redundant ones thrown into the industrial reserve army. The unemployed would be utilized as relatively inexpensive labor in the future.

Marx began his examination of surplus-value with the simple commodity, "an object outside us, a thing that by its properties satisfies human wants of some sort or another," and thus a use-value through "use or consumption." These use-values "constitute the substance of all wealth, whatever may be the social form of wealth."[5]

In the process to accumulate more use-values or capital, capital was expressed in terms of money: "Money...as capital has lost its rigidity and from a tangible thing has become a process," a "measure of value which is immanent in commodities, labour-time."[6] Or,

> Like every individual subject within circulation, the
> worker is the owner of a use value; he exchanges this
> for money, for the general form of wealth, but only in
> order to exchange this for commodities, considered
> as the objects of his immediate consumption, as the
> means of satisfying his needs.[7]

The worker's use-value itself was necessarily consumed, any savings being for old age, to prevent becoming a public burden. Thus, although the proletariat's labor-power was employed only to furnish its basic needs, for capitalists, workers' use-values were used to create more use-values or to expand existing capital.[8]

Thus, where M= money and M 1 = money after a commodity was sold, M 1 must be more than M. Marx called this increase over labor-power's "original value," "surplus-value" or the exploitation of labor-power.[9] Specifically: "This surplus-value is the difference between the value of the product and the value of the elements consumed in the formation of that product; in other words, the means of production and the labour-power."[10] Jerold Seigel's *Marx's Fate* expressed this cogently: "The value of the surplus labor that arose from the difference between the concrete labor the worker sold and the abstract labor power the capitalist bought Marx called 'surplus-value.'"[11] It might appear that capitalist profit came only when selling products, and not from the surplus labor-power and use-values of workers, but for Marx, it was directly extracted from workers in the productive process itself.[12]

In exchange value itself (if not sold it lost its original value), the value of a commodity was ultimately determined by "the labour-time socially necessary…required to produce an article under the normal conditions of production, and with the average degree of skill and intensity prevalent at the time."[13] There were also different kinds of labor: "Skilled labour" is "simple labour intensified…a given quantity of skilled being considered equal to a greater quantity of simple labour."[14] Of course, there were free goods, like air, as no labor was involved in their making, indicating that use values combined nature and labor-power.

The increase of surplus value, of S extracted from workers by capital, is the problem to be delved into, but first a preliminary examination of capital itself.

For Marx, total capital, or TC, comprised two parts: constant capital, or CC, made up over everything that labor produced in the past (plant, equipment, raw materials and so forth), and variable capital, or VC, which represented wages or labor-power advanced by capital to labor before it produced a commodity.

The inner logic of capitalism dictated that TC increase through VC. As for the rate of profit, it was divided by S, or surplus value, by TC, or total capital. Now, let us assume that an enterprise owned a TC of 500 units, 410 of CC and 90 of VC, and that the profit or surplus value was 90, added to the pre-existing capital, making in now 590. Profit here would be 18 percent or 90 over 500. As for the rate of exploiting workers (surplus value) in this instance, the S, or 90, over VC or 90, would equal 100 percent, itself divided into two equal parts: surplus labor (numerator) and necessary labor (denominator).[15]

Marx related his labor theory of value with that of labor division in the factory and elsewhere for production to formulate that modern production by its very nature was of a cooperative or social nature. Thus, he claimed that wealth should be the patrimony of everyone, not only of the wealthy and privileged.[16]

From his concept of surplus-value, Marx grafted his "relative surplus-value" one, or "the reduction of necessary labour time relative to population."[17] It was made possible by ever-increasing technological productivity/exploitation of workers requiring fewer of them to make more commodities.

Relative surplus value itself, for Marx, did not imply the automatic "shortening of the workday"; only working-class action could accomplish it.[18] But its increase permitted the wealthy to enjoy more "luxuries," the better maintenance of the "'ideological'" classes, such as government officials, priests, lawyers, soldiers, etc.," and more wealth for "those who have no occupation but to consume the labour of others in the form of rent, interest, etc." – or the upper- middle class and wealthy. Thus is was, for him, that the 1861 census of the English and Welsh population indicated a servant class in private homes of 1.2 million, while 1.1 million toiled in various cloth industries, 643,000 in mines, and 397,000 in metal works.[19]

In commenting on machinery and its multiplication of human labor, Marx also touched on automation. In the *Gundrisse* he observed:

> But once into the production process of capital,
> the means of labour passes through different
> metamorphoses, whose culmination is the *machine*,
> or rather, an *automatic system of machinery*...the
> *automatic* one...set in motion by an automaton, a
> moving power that moves itself.[20]

Automation itself opened the possibility to transcend the labor time/surplus value horizon as the science/technology level would now be so high that:

> As soon as labor, in its direct form, has ceased to be
> the main source of wealth, then, labor time ceases, and
> must cease, to be its standard of measurement, and
> thus exchange value must cease to be the measurement
> of use-value. The surplus labor of the masses has
> ceased to be a condition for the development of wealth
> in general in the same way that the non-labor of the
> few has ceased to be a condition for the development
> of the powers of the human mind in general.[21]

To be sure, this development is now much closer to reality than in Marx's time in the economically developed nations.

B. Wages and Unemployment

As already observed, Marx did not regard labor as only a cost of production like other commodities,[1] as determined by bourgeois socioeconomic relations, including the business cycle.[2] Instead, the working class itself should determine the various costs of production. But he would permit a wage system in the transitional phase leading from capitalism to socialism, like different rates of remuneration between manual and mental labor outside the capitalist market, efficient, but not at the expense of brutalizing workers or wasting their labor- power to make for class-induced luxury items.[3] In fact, since the working class would control working conditions and the amount of surplus-labor to be extracted from itself, work increasingly would become ever more "human" and creative, with machinery ever more automated; the "measure of wealth is then not any longer... labor time, but rather disposable time."[4]

This Marxian view of labor was antithetical to the bourgeois one promoted by Smith and the others. Thus, for Marx, workers, not possessing any capital under capitalism, were forced to sell the only "product" they have, their labor-power/time in the market place to capital, its average price like other commodities, determined by the necessary labor time to perpetuate it, involving varying levels of subsistence, as in "food, clothing, fuel, and housing," which "vary according to the climate and other physical conditions of his country." And:

> In contradistinction...to other commodities, there enters into the determination of the value of labor-power a historical and moral element. Nevertheless, in a given country, at a given period, the average quantity of the means of subsistence necessary for the laborer is practically known.[5]

In his analysis of wages under capitalism, Marx also distinguished between "time-wages" and "piece-wages," the latter being particularly reprehensible, the "most fruitful source of reductions of wages and capitalistic cheating," for "they furnished to the capitalist an exact measure for the intensity of labour."[6]

On the question of "national differences in wages," Marx again was exceedingly perceptive, stating that "in proportion as capitalist production is developed in a country, in the same proportion do the national intensity and productivity of labor there rise above the international level." Thus, "the relative value of money will, therefore, be less in the nation with more developed capitalistic mode of production than in the nation with less developed." From this:

It follows, then, that the nominal wages, the equivalent of labor-power expressed in money, will also be higher in the first nation than in the second; which does not at all prove that this holds for the real wages, i.e., for the means of subsistence placed at the disposal of the laborer.

To be sure, average wages under capitalism are related to the general level of productive forces and the state of the class struggle waged by the working class against the bourgeoisie; when the latter element is weakened by various conditions, the primary one being divisions within the working class itself because of a lack of class consciousness, median real wages invariably fall precipitously. Thus it is that the per capita GDP differentials between the most economically advanced nations and least developed ones were three to one in 1800 and sixty to one in 2000, although real median wages have dropped by a tenth in the United States in the last 27 years.[7]

In an arresting passage in *Capital* I, Marx intertwined the problems of wage exploitation and unemployment under capitalism thus: "Labour-power is only saleable so far as it preserves the means of production in their capacity of capital, reproduces its own value as capital, and yields in unpaid labor a source of additional capital."[8] Otherwise, it was unemployed.

Unemployment, or the "industrial reserve army" or "relative surplus population," was for Marx a general tendency of industrial capitalism, not only related to capitalist property relations and control of technology to maximize profits, but to the organic composition of capital, in which the constant part of plant and equipment inexorably increased relative to that of the variable one of wages. Thus, it was "in the absolute interest of every capitalist to press a given quantity of labor out of a smaller rather than a greater number of labourers, if the cost is about the same,"[9] or that machinery produced more goods at a lower cost than workers *per se*, being more reliable and not prone to cause social friction as workers did.

This reserve army for Marx "belongs to capital as absolutely as if the latter had bred it at its own cost." Thus, this unemployment, "independently of the limits of the actual increase of population... creates, for the changing needs of self-expansion capital, a mass of human material always ready for exploitation," or capital required a "relatively redundant population of labourers...than suffices for the average needs of the self-expansion of capital." He also saw that the unemployed or "relative surplus population" was used by capitalists as a threat to keep workers obedient, confirming the "domination of capital" over workers. Of course, unemployment tended to rise and fall in conjunction with the trade cycle.[10]

The reserve army itself comprised four groups of workers: the "floating," "latent," "stagnant" or "surplus population," and "paupers": The first, of the increasing number of unneeded workers even in good times; the second, those from the countryside serving as a reservoir for industry; the third, those employed irregularly, coming from "decaying branches of industry;" and the last, the "dead weight of the industrial reserve army," the "demoralized and ragged, and those unable to work...the sickly, the widows, etc."[11]

Ultimately, for Marx:

The greater the social wealth, the functioning capital, the extent and energy of its growth, and, therefore, also the absolute mass of the proletariat and the productiveness of its labor, the greater is the industrial reserve army...*This is the absolute general law of capitalist accumulation.* But he qualified this by stating that it was "modified in its working by many circumstances."[12]

Automation under capitalism, for Marx, would also tend to more unemployment; in fact, in a futuristic vein, he went to the past, quoting from the paean to it in Aristotle's *Politics*:

> If every tool, when summoned, or even of its own
> accord, could do the work that befits it, just as the
> creations of Daedalus moved of themselves, or the
> tripods of Hephaestos went of their own accord to
> their sacred work, if the weaver's shuttles were to
> weave of themselves, then there would be no need
> either of apprentices for the master workers, or of
> slaves for the lords.[13]

This condition would allow for a technology so very automated that direct human labor in the production process would become redundant, making the concept or surplus-value itself ever more tenuous as applied to living labor. Under this arrangement, exploitation of workers would intensify, as surplus-value would rise astronomically, obviously leading to the proliferation of the service industries so noticeable today. In this instance, capitalists also extract a secondary surplus-value from the remainder of society, furnishing them with the necessary support system to engage in this form of operation, as in education and other infrastructure.

Of course, one could take this argument on automation to the extreme. For instance, suppose that capitalists finally possessed automated systems of production in which robots not only produced other robots, but programmed to think abstractly and plan for the future, as in the quotation of Aristotle's just employed by Marx; and suppose the bourgeoisie would have total power in their hands – would normal surplus value related to human-labor time/technology then be inoperative as a concept? Yes, but before this happened, the class struggle should achieve socialism; if not, a worst-case scenario would be for a small group of capitalists running the world devoid of all other human beings as they would simply be redundant. We relate these observations to Marx's views on automation in the *Grundrisse*, already examined.

C. Economic Fluctuations

Recurring economic fluctuations, or Marx's "trade cycle," in which increased economic activity was followed by economic downturns (some more severe than others and affecting the whole range of economic activity on a national and even international levels), are recent historical phenomena, beginning in the early 19th century, intimately related to the rise of industrial capitalism and the socioeconomic division between workers and capitalists.

Economic crises, of course, existed before this time. Monarchial defaults to bankers in Spain-Austria and France in the 16th century resulted in financial crises in Lyons and Antwerp. When the Seven Years' War ended in 1763, the London stock exchange witnessed a speculative frenzy leading to a steep fall. There were also crop failures resulting in food shortages and consequent higher food prices, thus fewer purchases of other commodities in the cities, leading to higher unemployment there. Furthermore, "panics" occurred, like the Mississippi Bubble in France in 1720, engineered by the Scot John Law, economically ruining many French investors following a wild outburst of speculation for a company with limited resources and prospects. Except for food shortages, the other examples scarcely affected the fortunes of most of the people as they were engaged in agriculture.[1]

Capitalist downturns and their causes were prominently analyzed in the *Manifesto*, the three volumes of *Capital, Theories of Surplus Value,* and the *Grundrisse*. To be sure, they were intimately related to the conflicts and contradictions stemming from the labor theory of value in a capitalist society. An obvious one by Engels was: "The contradiction between socialized production and capitalistic appropriation manifested itself as the antagonism of proletariat and bourgeoisie," economic crises exacerbating the class struggle.[2] In *Capital* I, Marx himself duly enumerated the many economic crises in England until the 1860s: 1815-21, 1826, 1830-31, 1840-43, 1847-48, 1851, 1857, 1862-63.[3]

An early depression occurred from 1815-21 after the Napoleonic Wars, ending large government military orders and discharging hundreds of thousands of military personnel, while a more efficient factory system replaced workers in household industries. Crop failures, in raising the price of food in the cities, also contributed to depression, triggering the 1848 Revolution in France.

Marx was not the first commentator to discuss economic downturns, being heavily indebted to Malthus in this instance. But first some background: Smith, a late 18th century figure, understandably had no theory of a sustained depression. As for Ricardo, he assigned the post- Napoleonic war depression and rise in unemployment in Britain to the Corn Laws or high tariffs on food that made capital relatively more expensive because of higher labor costs, too simplistic.

But Malthus, noting industrialization, propounded a general theory of depression, emphasizing that effective demand was not of sufficient magnitude to purchase what industry produced, of overproduction relative to consumption. Thus, he recommended that government keep up employment in depression periods through public works to improve the infrastructure, like refurbishing railways, canals, and railroad lines. He also justified the existence of large landowners/tenants and their agricultural workers and retainers, the many government workers, and the Church of England as outlets for consumption, as stabilizing elements. To be sure, Jean Charles Leonard Simonde de Sismondi, a Swiss economist, also formulated a theory of under-consumption inherent in industrial capitalism, also influencing Marx in this area.[4]

We begin a detailed Marxist analysis on depression with this revelatory passage in the *Manifesto*:

> For many a decade the history of industry and
> commerce is but the history of the revolt of modern
> productive forces against the property relations that
> are the conditions of production, against the property

relations that are the conditions for the existence of
the bourgeoisie and of its rule.

These "periodic commercial crises" that "put the existence of
the entire bourgeoisie on trial, each time more threateningly," were
caused by an "epidemic of overproduction," involving "too much
means of subsistence, too much industry, too much commerce."
Furthermore:

> The productive...forces of society no longer tend to
> further the development of conditions of bourgeois
> property; on the contrary, they have become too
> powerful for these conditions, by which they are
> fettered...and bring disorder into the whole of
> bourgeois society, endanger bourgeois property.[5]

Or, the increasing socialization of production under capitalist
auspices collided with the limitations of capitalist accumulation of
private property from the labor of workers through surplus-value.

More specifically, Marx observed that the "life of modern
industry becomes a series of periods of moderate activity, prosperity,
over-production, crisis, and stagnation," in which "machinery" itself
contributed to "uncertainty and instability," engaged as it were
in making too many goods, with consequent unemployment, as
capitalists competed among themselves for market share.[6] These
cycles, for him, occurred approximately every ten years, "interrupted
by smaller oscillations;"[7] their length and regularity is arguable,
Marx being among the first to discuss them in great detail.[8]

Depressions, for Marx, were caused by these general factors.
Fixed capital – itself largely used to improve technology, to
produce more and to simultaneously deskill and cheapen labor, thus
improving profit – could not in the long run keep profit margins high
enough as there invariably would be this contradiction (of too many
goods produced relative to demand, the specter of overproduction).
Furthermore, successive economic crises could not but get worse, as

capital would become ever more concentrated and technologically efficient as it overwhelmed smaller enterprise. Economic bigness, i.e. economics of scale, in other words, would simply exacerbate overproduction. The credit system was involved in this depression scenario, for as profits fell, many companies could not repay their loans to banks, causing bank failure. It is true that Marx lived before the rise of a pervasive large-scale oligopoly/monopoly, but he and Engels, as in the *Manifesto*, predicted its coming. Monopoly itself was known to Marx, the one of the English East India Co. being obvious.

Furthermore, Marx was aware that stock market and other speculations were also endemic destabilizing factors, especially as economic "centralization" proceeded, allowing "money lenders" or "parasites a fabulous power not only to decimate the industrial capitalists periodically, but also to interfere in actual production in the most dangerous manner." The Russian economic collapse following the fall of Communism is a good example of this.

Now, as production stagnated and banks were either failing or making less profit on loans, other bankruptcies, unemployment and wage cuts of workers accelerated, further depressing demand. In the meantime, capitalists were forced by competition to lower prices of their commodities, further depressing profit and the value of their capital.

These manifestations for Marx were ultimately caused by a socioeconomic imbalance between surplus-value extracted from the workforce or wages and the dynamism of the machine technology, which to be used by capitalists as efficiently as possible must produce as much as possible at a profit. Competition, to be sure, inexorably would force down prices, but not enough for workers to purchase back what they produced. He was also acutely aware of the waste in luxuries by the wealthier classes and the military as outlets for consumption, but believed that they were still insufficient to prevent depression. To put it candidly, overproduction was the primary cause of depression, obviously related to the other causes. Finally, he prophesied that depressions would become ever more prolonged and severe as capital and production became ever more concentrated, leading to capitalism's collapse.

The upward cycle of the economy, for Marx, would begin when a sufficient amount of old capital was destroyed, thus lowering the proportion of constant to variable capital and consequently increasing profit, related to wages sufficiently falling to the point of making surplus-value once more profitable. To say the least, the economic devastation in the form of human misery and lost production caused by depressions are of immense proportion.[9]

D) Veblen, Great Depression, New Deal, and Keynes

Veblen, who died just before the Great Depression, essentially continued Marx's view on the normality of the trade cycles in the United States. He regarded capitalist economic downturns as normal "under the consummate regime of the machine, so long as competition is unchecked and no *deus ex machina* interposes," i.e. the state. His business cycle ran thus: In good times, prices, profits, production, and unemployment were high; in bad times, credit became negative, capital itself shrinking as stock and bond prices fell. In this pattern, he related business or the pecuniary to the industrial arena, "industrial depression is primarily a depression in business." More explicitly:

> Industrial depression means that the businessmen engaged do not see their way to derive a satisfactory profit from letting the industrial process go forward on the lines and in the volume for which the material equipment of industry is designed.

As such, Veblen defined "overproduction" as a "state of affairs that prevails when business cannot make a good profit from the goods sold at particular price," there being "too many competitive producers and too much industrial apparatus to supply the market at reasonable prices."

The return on investment was primary for Veblen in explaining economic downturn: "New investments are made on the basis of current rates of interest and with a view to securing the differential gain promised by the excess of prospective profits over interest rates." But in a depression, industry itself could not perform at its maximum rate to make a "reasonable" profit. The new and dynamic machine technology exacerbated this: "Machine process, ever increasing in efficiency, turns out the mechanical appliances and materials with which the processes are carried on, at an ever decreasing cost." This, in a normally competitive market, resulted in lower prices, but only the newer plants, those with the latest technology, could reap cost advantages allowing them to under-price their less technologically advanced competitors, forced out of business with consequent unemployment of labor.

Another cause for depression, according to Veblen, involved periodic battles between competing business groups to acquire particular companies through "(money) coercion," inflicting "pecuniary damage" and "a set-back to the industrial plants concerned and a derangement, more or less extensive, of the industrial system of large."

Was it possible, then, for Veblen, for capitalism to prevent depression by not overproducing, through wasteful private leisure-class expenditure ("conspicuous consumption") and increased government spending in "armaments, public edifices?" At first, he claimed that the only way out for capitalism was to have business combinations become near monopolies or preferably "trusts," monopolies to regulate output, thus prices and profit, in addition to effecting "considerable economies in the cost of production," to further increase profit. Or:

> But when the coalition comes effectually to cover its
> special field of operation, it is able not only to fix the
> prices which it will accept (on the basis of what the
> traffic will bear), but also in a considerable measure to
> fix the prices or rates which it will pay for materials,

labor, and other services (such as transportation) on a similar basis – unless it should necessarily have to deal with another coalition that is in similar position of monopoly.

This formation of monopoly to obviate depression by Veblen was theorized as a means of overcoming the rages of deflation which intense competition contributed to: In 1866, the U.S. wholesale price index stood at 174; in 1880 at 100, and in 1890 at 82. The depressions of 1873-76 and 1893-97 were partly caused by larger firms successfully driving smaller ones into bankruptcy or simply annexing them.

Monopoly itself was legalized by the Trust, first used by Samuel Dodd, a Standard Oil Company lawyer, in the 1880s. This legal arrangement had competing companies assign their stock to a group of trustees, who, in turn, issued new stock certificates, enabling them to exercise control over the various companies, including the regulating of prices and production.

The Sherman Anti-Trust Act of 1890, specifically enacted to destroy Trusts, was employed in the first two decades of the 20th century to do so in celebrated cases as that of the Standard Oil Company in 1907, settled in 1911, and the National Packing Company in 1907, settled in 1921. But even with these successes, bigness in business continued in the form of oligopoly, in which several producers with interlocking directorates would agree to restrain output and price competition. (The interplay of capital and technology obviously promoted this bigness.) As early as the turn of the century, 1 percent of the industrial firms produced about one-third of the manufactured goods in America.

For Veblen, another way out of depression was for business to engage in the conspicuous consumption of military goods or war preparedness, under the guise of "patriotism." This state of affairs, for him, also inculcated a sense of servility among the general population, reflecting the rise of the military, in the process stifling an overt class struggle against the bourgeoisie by unemployed and impoverished workers. (This happened in Nazi Germany, for instance, in the 1930s under Nazism, which embarked on a war economy in preparation for conquest.) But Veblen warned business that patriotic fervor may undermine the economic prerogatives of business or "sacrifice the profits of the businessman to the exigencies of the higher politics," or to government control under the aegis of a military-industrial complex.[1]

In his later works, especially, *Absentee Ownership and Business Enterprise in Recent Times: The Case of America* (1923), Veblen stated that even business mergers/concentration could not prevent depression because it resulted in a "prudent measure of unemployment," causing an imbalance between production and consumption deleterious to the economic process. Or:

> Unemployment, in other words 'sabotage,' to use a word of later date, was becoming an everyday care of the business management in the mechanical industries, and was already on the way to become, what it is today, the most engrossing care that habitually engages the vigilance of the business executive.[2]

All in all, from an over-arching perspective, Marx and Veblen believed capitalism could not overcome the contradictions imposed by private property or the capitalist economic/social structure and dynamic technology.

We now observe the specific causes of the Great Depression in the United States, itself part of a worldwide condition in the capitalist world: In the 1919-29 period, while real wages increased 26 percent, productivity rose 40 percent. This was reflected in huge average annual corporate profits, 730 million dollars in the 1916-25 period, as opposed to 1.4 billion dollars in 1926-29; and corporate cash surpluses in billions of dollars mounted from 3.5 in 1921 to 9 in 1929. There were large amounts of money in the hands of speculative capitalists who only put down 5 percent of a stock's value to purchase it, rapidly driving up the stock market; in 1922 the Dow Jones Stock Average was 50; by 1929, just before the crash, it was 200. Banks themselves employed depositors' monies for market speculation, this in an economy dominated by big business; the largest 200 corporations controlled half the non-banking corporate wealth. Oligopoly reigned – in terms of respective market percentages – three auto companies held 82; four meat packers, 70; Aluminum Company of America, 100; nine steel companies, 80. The free market was a myth here, as "administered prices" of the large corporations were designed to hold prices of commodities up, disregarding fluctuations of demand. Thus, in the early 1930s, although iron and steel production dropped 80 percent, the price fell only 6 percent (inelastic pricing). But where there was intense competition among many producers, as in agriculture, the price declined precipitously, although not production, a bushel of wheat, $1.05 in 1929 and 39 cents in 1931 (elastic pricing). Also, since the Germans could not pay the Allies for World War I reparations, the Allies could not honor American loans to them, signifying the collapse of the international credit market. Then, too, the richest 2 to 5 percent owned between 60 and 75 percent of the wealth.

In October 1929, British investors left the U.S. market in droves when British interest rates were raised to 6.5 percent. The market plummeted 30 percent. Although from November 1929 to April 1930 the market went up 50 percent, it inexorably decreased to its nadir in 1932, losing 89 percent of its highest value in 1929. To be sure, in the 1930-33 period, about 5,000 banks failed, with depositors losing all of their savings, the price index dropping by a fourth and private investment fell in billions of dollars from 15 to less than 1. Interest rates decreased slowly from 5 percent to 3.8 percent, their low in 1936 at 1.7 percent), and unemployment sharply increased from 3 percent in 1929 to 25 percent, its peak during the depression.

The federal government itself would act, although neither too promptly nor efficaciously, to prevent the horrendous socioeconomic misery of unemployment. President Herbert Hoover in the 1930-32 period engaged in some government pump priming, averaging 2.5 billion dollars a year. But with the advent of the New Deal under

President Franklin Delano Roosevelt in 1933, pump priming was rapidly increased, reaching $15 billion by 1936, itself aiding private investment, at $10 billion by 1936.

Furthermore, the New Deal enacted legislation to prevent mass starvation, initiated relief programs and restarted the economy by providing jobs through measurers like the Federal Emergency Relief Administration, Public Works Administration, the National Industrial Recovery Act (its section 7a gave labor the right to organize effectively, preventing employer coercion to form unions, which once having the majority of workers in a plant could bargain collectively), Civilian Conservation Corps, and National Youth Administration. It also aided business through the Reconstruction Finance Corporation (begun by Hoover in 1932), lending money usually to big business, totaling $15 billion from 1932 to 1941, with most being repaid; in fact, this agency realized a half-billion dollar profit.

Then, the federal government intervened in other areas – protecting savings accounts by the Federal Deposit Insurance Corporation (FDIC), divorcing speculative from commercial banking by the Glass-Steagall Act, providing pensions for the elderly and assisting families by the Social Security Act, and promoting regional economic development by the Tennessee Valley Authority.

But these and other acts did not end high unemployment, which dipped to 14 percent by 1937, rose to 19 percent in 1938, fell to 17 percent in 1939, and was still 10 percent in 1940. Only the advent of World War II solved the unemployment problem. Indeed, without massive government assistance, and/or war, capitalism is neither viable economically, nor can it end large-scale working-class misery.[3]

In his *General Theory of Employment, Interest and Money* (1936), Keynes was most troubled by inherent capitalist instability, to be corrected by state action and even some socialism. Primarily, his analysis denied the validity of Say's Law, that production or supply automatically created its own demand, because under capitalism, money demand ultimately mattered; without it, the unemployed/underemployed simply could not purchase available goods.

His remedy was massive government intervention to restart the economy through lower interest rates, monetary expansion or inflation, and public investment in public works, to be partly financed by higher taxes on the wealthy. This scenario candidly admitted that capitalism could not survive without extensive government assistance, thus promoting large-scale government spending, inviting in the back door an increasing group of government bondholders as key economic players.[4]

But this was not all, for with continuing economic stagnation, Keynes in "Democracy and Efficiency," in 1939, proposed a system to ensure prosperity which he termed "Liberal Socialism."

> A system where we can act as an organized community
> for economic purpose and to promote social and
> economic justice, while respecting and protecting the
> individual – his freedom of choice, his faith, his mind
> and its expression, his enterprise and his property.

To ensure these wishes, Keynes favored an amalgam of capitalism and some state socialism in the form of many quasi-public corporations run by a managerial elite, the chief architects of his new society, preserving the power of a now chastened and public-spirited bourgeoisie, a pious, but unrealistic view of them.[5]

This mixed-economy model was partly adhered to in Western Europe after World War II, with extensive nationalizations of industry and finance and rising social welfarism, but the hegemony of the bourgeoisie returned in the "free market" economics of the International Monetary Fund (IMF), World Bank (WB), World Trade Organization (WTO), and various free trade blocs, as the European Union (EU), and extensive privatization.

Louis Patsouras

Notes

A) Background

1) On Marxist Economics: Marx's key works on this are the *Grundrisse*, and *Capital*, I, II, and III; they not only present his economic doctrines, but his familiarity with various Western economists and profound understanding of economic and related developments especially in Western Europe, particularly Britain. On favorable interpretations of Marx's economics, see, for instance, Leo Rogin, *The Meaning and Validity of Economic Theory: A Historical Approach* (New York: Harper and Brothers, 1956), pp. 332-410). Paul M. Sweezy, *The Theory of Capitalist Development: Principals of Marxian Political Economy* (New York: Monthly Review Press, 1956). Ernest Mandel, *Marxist Economic Theory*, 2 vols. Trans. by Brian Pearce (New York: Monthly Review Press, 1968), I, ch. 3 on "Money, Capital, Surplus-Value," for instance.

B) Capitalist Economics

1) Rogin, *Meaning and Validity*, pp. 14-331 on the Physiocrats, Adam Smith, David Ricardo, Thomas Robert Malthus, and so forth.
2) Bruce Mazlish, ed. *An Inquiry into the Nature and Causes of The Wealth of Nations, Representative Selections* (Indianapolis, IN: Bobbs-Merrill, 1961), pp. 162 ff.
3) ibid., pp. 65-66.
4) ibid., p. 257.
5) Ibid., pp. xvii and 16-17.
6) Ibid., p. 17.
7) Ibid., pp. 31 and 33.
8) E.A. Burtt, ed., *The English Philosophers, From Bacon to Mill* (New York: Modern Library, 1967), ch. 5 of Locke's "Concerning Civil Government," pp. 413-23. On Smith, see Robert L. Heilbroner, *The Worldly Philosophers: The Lives, Times, and*

Ideas of the Great Economic Thinkers (New York: Simon and Schuster, 1953), pp. 33-66.

9) Thomas Robert Malthus, *An Essay on the Principle of Population*, intro. By T.M. Hollingsworth (London: Dent, 1892), pp. 5-11 on subsistence tending to increase arithmetically, while population increases geometrically. This work was first published in 1798; its fifth edition (1817) opposed birth-control measures, Books I and II, entitled "The Checks on Population."

10) Ibid., Book, III, pp. 1-29 and Book, IV, pp. 200-15.

11) Ibid., Book, III, p. 25.

12) Ibid., Book III, pp. 97-125.

13) Ibid., Book IV, pp. 200 ff.

14) K.R. Popper, *The Open Society and Its Enemies*, Vol. I: *The Spell of Plato*; Vol. II, *The High Tide of Prophecy: Hegel, Marx, and the Aftermath* (New York: Harper Torchbooks, 1963), II, 710.

15) On Ricardo, see Heilbroner, *Worldly Philosophers*, pp. 67-95; Rogin, *Meaning and Validity*, pp. 110-56; the quotation is on p. 118. David Ricardo, *On the Principles of Political Economy and Taxation*, intro. By F.W. Kolthammer (New York: E.P. Dutton, 1937), pp. vii-xiii on his life; pp. 5-32 on value; on p. 11, "of labor, as being the foundation of all value, and the relative quantity of labor as almost exclusively determining the relative value of commodities"; pp. 52-63, on wages; on p. 61, that the poor, with the aid of the legislature, "regulate the increase of their numbers, and to render less frequent among them early and improvident marriage"; pp. 64-76 on profits; on p. 71, their "natural tendency... is to fall" as more food for more people necessitates "more and more labor," which is offset by "improvements of machinery," and so forth.

16) On Mill's socialism, see Rogin, *Meaning and Validity,* pp. 280-88. John Stuart Mill, *Principles of Political Economy; With Some of Their Applications to Social Philosophy* (New York: Augustus M. Kelley, 1965), pp. 199-237 on property and socialism. This work is first published in 1848; by the third edition in 1852,

Mill is a socialist. William Stafford, *John Stuart Mill* (London: Macmillan Press, 1998), pp. 122-30.

17) J.D.Y. Peel, ed. and intro., *Herbert Spencer on Social Evolution: Selected Writings* (Chicago: Univ. of Chicago Press, 1972), pp. 244 ff.

18) Ibid., pp. 246-49 for the quotations.

19) On the neo-classical economists, see, Rogin, *Meaning and Validity*, pp. 454-80 on Jevons, pp. 554-616 on Marshall. On Friedman and "Supply-side economics, see Charles K. Wilber and Kenneth P. Jameson, *Beyond Reaganomics: A Further Inquiry into the Poverty of Economics* (Notre Dame: IN: Univ. of Notre Dame Press, 1990), pp. 64-67, 92-121.

20) On Milton Friedman, see his (with the assistance of Rose D. Friedman), *Capitalism and Freedom* (Chicago: Univ. of Chicago Press, 1962), pp. 22-55, 177-89, for instance. Milton and Rose Friedman, *Free to Choose: A Personal Statement* (New York: Harcourt, Brace, Jovanovich, 980), pp. 38-149, for instance. Milton and Rose Friedman, *Tyranny of the Status Quo* (San Diego, CA: Harcourt, Brace, Jovanovich, 1984), pp. 1-67, 105-31, for instance.

C)

a) Labor Theory Value

1) Lichtheim, *Socialism*, p. 139 on the quotation, and pp. 124-41.

2) *Capital*, I, 673; on "primitive accumulation," see 784-848. Ibid., pp. 586-88.

3) Ibid., pp. 592-93 for the three quotations.

4) Ibid., pp. 41-42 for the three quotations.

5) On money, see *Capital*, I, for the first quotation and *Grundrisse*, p. 283 for the second.

6) *Grundrisse*, p. 283.

7) Ibid., p. 265.

8) *Capital*, I, 168.

9) Ibid., p. 232.

10) Seigel, *Marx's Fate*, p. 308.
11) *Capital*, I, 221 ff.
12) Ibid., p. 46.
13) Ibid., p. 51.
14) Ibid., pp. 235 ff.
15) Ibid., pp. 357-58.
16) *Grundrisse*, p. 769.
17) *Capital*, I, 352.
18) Ibid., pp. 486-88.
19) *Grundrisse*, p. 692.
20) McLellan, *Grundrisse*, p. 142.

b) Wages and Unemployment

1) See previous section of this chapter.
2) See previous section of this chapter.
3) Karl Marx, *Critique of the Gotha Program: With Appendices by Marx, Engels, and Lenin.* ed. by C.P. Dutt (New York: International Publishers. 1938), pp. 8-9 ff.
4) *Grundrisse*, p. 708. István Mészáros, *Beyond Capital: Towards a Theory of Transition* (New York: Monthly Review Press, 1995), pp. 745 ff.
5) *Capital*, I, 189-90.
6) Ibid., p. 605.
7) Ibid., pp. 611-13 on the last three quotations. Wage ratios between workers of advanced nations as against poor ones are common knowledge. On real median wages falling in the U.S., see, for instance, Lawrence Mishel, Jared Bernstein, and John Schmitt, *The State of Working America* (Washington, DC: Economic Policy Institute, 1996), pp. 129-237, on wages; but from 1997 to 2000 they have increased about five percent.
8) *Capital*, p. 678.
9) *Capital.*, p. 697.
10) *Capital.*, pp. 693-701 on the quotations.
11) Ibid., pp. 703-07.

12) Ibid., p. 707.

13) Ibid., pp. 445-46.

c) Economic Fluctuations/Depressions/Capital Concentration

1) For general accounts on trade or business fluctuations, see Wesley Clair Mitchell, *Business Cycles and their Causes* (Berkeley: Univ. of California Press, 1971), pp. 149-71 for a succinct account. A.W. Mullineux, *Business Cycles and Financial Crises* (Ann Arbor: Univ. of Michigan Press, 1990), for a "neutral" business approach; see chap. 4, for instance. For a Marxist interpretation, see Ernest Mandel, *Late Capitalism* (London: Verso, 1978), pp. 562-89.

2) Frederick Engels, *Socialism*, p. 59.

3) *Capital*, I, 497.

4) Rogin, *The Meaning and Validity of Economic Theory*, pp. 185-92.

5) *Manifesto*, pp. 14-15 on the quotation.

6) *Capital*, I, 495.

7) Ibid., 694.

8) Ibid., 690-94.

9) Marx/Engels on tendency to increasing economic crises under capitalism, including long-run factors, see, for instance, *Capital*, I, 681-711, 836-37; *Capital*, III, 247-81, 292-305, and 568; Marx, *Theories of Surplus Value*, pp. 376 ff.; *Grundrisse*, p. 692 on the "automatic system of machinery," and pp. 745-58, on general tendency of profit to fall. Also, see commentaries on the subject by Rogin, *Meaning and Validity of Economic Theory*, pp. 358-410; and Sweezy, *Capitalist Development*, pp. 147-55. On Marx's most timely remarks on financial machinations in the mixture for depression, see his *Capital*, III, 678-79 of the David Gernbach translation, intro. Ernest Mandel (London: Penguin Books, 1991).

d) Veblen, Great Depression, New Deal, and Keynes

1) Thorstein Veblen, *The Theory of Business Enterprise* (New York: Scribner's, 1904), pp. 213-91 for most of the quotations. The long quotations are on pp. 213 and 261. On background material, see, for instance, Jonathan Hughes, *American Economic History* 3rd ed. (Glenview, IL: Scott, Foresman and Co., 1990).

2) Thorstein Veblen, *Absentee Ownership and Business Enterprise; The Case of America* (New York: Augustus M. Kelley, 1964), p. 112 on the long quotation. (First published in 1923).

3) On the factors leading to the Great Depression, see, for instance, John Kenneth Galbraith, *The Great Crash, 1929* (Boston: Houghton Mifflin, 1961), pp. 1-199. On the New Deal, see, for instance, William E. Leuchtenburg, *Franklin D. Roosevelt and the New Deal* (New York: Harper Torchbooks, 1963), pp. 41-275.

4) John Maynard Keynes, *General Theory of Employment, Interest, and Money* (New York: Harcourt, Brace, 1936), pp. 33 ff., 219 ff., and 275 ff.

5) John Maynard Keynes, "Democracy and Efficiency," *New Statesman and Nation*, Jan. 28, for the quotation.

Chapter Seven: The Working Class and Class Chain

A) Marx's and Engels' 19th Century Working Class

Although the industrial revolution in the mid-18th century England marked the beginning of the modern working class, workers would not become the majority of the population until the early decades of the 19th century. But inexorably, the working class would increase numerically and spread to other nations.

In the U.S. in 1860, during the early stage of industrialization, workers already comprised 4.3 million of a 31.5 million population, and 12 million of 75 million by 1900. In France, outside of Paris and Lyon and some areas in the north, a proletariat scarcely existed before the 1850s, but by 1866 there were 4.5 million workers in a population of 30 million, and by 1906, 7.23 million workers of 39 million. In Germany in the 1840s, only 4 percent of the male population worked in factories, but by 1914 it was 12 percent. Still, in the early part of the 20th century, more than two-fifths of the French and at least one-third of the American workforces were still in agriculture. Indeed, American society was characterized by a pervasive petty-bourgeois spirit based on the family farm and small urban business; but by 1950, only 18 percent, and by 1970 only 9 percent of the active working population were self-employed or employed others, the same in 2000.[1]

We first comment on two key works on working-class life: Engels' trail-blazing *The Condition of the English Working Class in England in 1844* (1845) and Marx's *Capital*, I (1867).

Engels, with much first-hand observation, painted a credible picture of the poverty and subsequent ills besetting English workers and hated Irish immigrants making up the bottom of the working class. He minutely described working-class life: housing, poor and rapidly built, with neither heat nor water, usually entire families living in a room, an eighth living in cellars, human and other waste thrown into the streets; diet, for the better-off workers included meat and vegetables each day, while the poorer workers ate less meat, with the Irish eating only potatoes; high unemployment, especially during the bottom of a business cycle, with consequent begging and higher death rates for lack of food, starvation common; long hours of daily work, up to 18; considerable pollution of air and water, industrial and human wastes causing it; the British working class, reacting to its poverty and degradation organized the Chartist movement under Robert Owen and others.[2]

Capital I was not only a critique of capitalist economics but a minutely detailed history of the horrors of working-class life, especially in 19th century Britain. Marx followed Engels' work (he often quoted from it) and many others, including a plethora of government reports depicting the various facets of working-class life dominated by the slum, long hours of work in hellish working conditions for men, women and children; high unemployment, especially during economic downturns; high death rates, begging, petty criminality to stay alive, starvation; and laws, like the Poor Law of 1834, which literally made poverty a crime, with its workhouse provision breaking up families. In the chapter on history, some of the horrid details of the rise of capitalism have already been amply indicated, but more will be presented to emphasize the salient fact that Marx's empiricism in describing the intense social misery of working-class life is second to none.

Marx's specificity of working-class misery, itself closely related to the class struggle, was well delineated: In chapter 10, "The Working Day," which comprised a tenth of the volume, Marx indicated the gravity of the problem, with extensive background from the middle of the 14th century. He, then, observed the long work days of up to 15 hours and even more (like 20 hours for Scottish railway workers), including women and boys working 12-hour shifts – even at night. Furthermore, he recounted the frenzied attempts of the factory owners to keep the working day as long as possible, bitterly opposed to shortening it (Factory Acts of 1833, 1844, 1847, and 1850) and their attempts to circumvent it.[3]

Chapter 15, "Machinery and Modern Industry," comprising a sixth of the work, again intertwined the development of machinery to capitalist exploitation of workers and their alienating degradation. Again, Marx presented many concrete and detailed examples in various industries of the effects of machinery associated with capitalism.

In the "hardware industry of Birmingham" and nearby, "30,000 children and young persons, beside 10,000 women" were engaged in "very heavy work"; and "young people are worked to death at turning the looms in silk weaving when it is not carried on by machinery." He described work of children in the "tile and brick-making" industry (it was compared to similar conditions in coal mines) where "boys and girls" as young as age 4 labored 15 hours or more a day under abhorrent working conditions, including lifting up to 10 times their weight daily from clay pits. Death rates climbed and lives were demoralized, "making them in after life lawless, abandoned, (and) dissolute." Then, too, he was aware of the high accident rates in the mills, an example being in a scotching mill near Cork, Ireland.[4]

Other areas which Marx covered included pauperism, "or that part of the working-class which has forfeited its condition of existence (the sale of labor-power, and vegetates upon public alms"). In 1865, out of a population of 24 million in the United Kingdom, more than 1 million were thus officially designated. Many simply died of starvation.[5]

In the realm of housing, Marx described the slums in London and other cities as a "housing inferno," full of "ragged Irishmen or decayed English agricultural labourers." He quoted Dr. Embleton that the "spread of the typhus has been the overcrowding of human beings, and the uncleanliness of their dwellings.'" Slum housing itself, for this physician, was devoid of "space, light, air, and cleanliness.'"[6]

The very poverty of working-class parents would also force them at times to auction weekly their children, 9 years or older, in "public markets."[7]

In the leading non-agricultural industry, cloths ("cotton, woolen, worsted" and the like), Marx (who maintained that the cotton segment promoted slavery in the United States) saw that most of its labor was provided by boys and girls; in 1861, out of 643,000 operatives, only

18,000 were "males above 13 years of age." He then exclaimed that the 1850 Factory Act still allowed children from age 11 to 13 to work 12 hours a day (an hour-and-a-half of which was for lunch and rest) from Monday to Friday and 7 ½ hours on Saturday.[8]

Marx also explored the deteriorating and negative effects of work and health and life longevity of workers in the pottery industry, drawing from reports of factory inspectors on their being ravaged by pulmonary and other diseases, themselves associated with the progressive physical deterioration of children, men, and women.[9]

On wages in England and Ireland, Marx's lengthy investigations from Blue Books of Parliament accurately indicated their diminution in the 1797-1815 period as a certainty, although noticing that in the 1849-59 period they rose in England, but not significantly. As for education of working-class children, Marx decried its very paucity before the Factory Act of 1864, which required that children have elementary education before being employed; in fact, he pointed out that they attended school for half the day and worked the other half. It would soon lead to universal primary school education in 1870.[10]

Other notable commentaries on working-class life in novels and social histories/surveys include Charles Dickens' *Oliver Twist* (1828), *Nicholas Nickleby* (1839), and *Hard Times* (1845); Benjamin Disraeli's *Sybil* (1845), Victor Hugo's *Les Miserables* (1862), Emile Zola's *L'Assamoir* (1877) and *Germinal* (1855), as well as Charles Booth's 17 volume (1891-1903) massive survey, *Life and Labour of the People in London.*

It is a truism that socioeconomic conditions for workers in the West improved during the course of the 19th century. This amelioration, not of great proportion when measured against the increasing wealth of the bourgeoisie, was largely because of continual working-class initiatives, ably assisted by progressive liberals, against entrenched conservative liberals.

Let's begin with the number of hours a day/week of work. Certainly, this problem has much to do with the quality of life. (May Day, the most celebrated working-class holiday and institutionalized by the Second Socialist International in 1889, had as its principal aim the 8 hour day). In France, for instance, during the 1815-48 period, a 15-hour a day, 6-days-per-week was standard; in the 1852-70 period a 12-hour, 6-day week was common; by 1900, a 10-hour, 60- hour week was general in the industrialized nations.[11]

What about working conditions? There is ample evidence, from government sources, novels, and memoirs that the 19th century factory was a veritable hellhole, easily qualifying for Dante's "Inferno." The mixture of an unsafe and unsanitary work environment, with many hours of work, destroyed the health of workers rapidly.[12] Graphic accounts of this were depicted in Upton Sinclair's *The Jungle* (1906),[13] and in Marx's careful reading of English government commission reports in *Capital*.[14]

We now observe real wages of workers in France, England, and the United States during the 19th century: In the first, they doubled in the 1814-1914 period. In the second, wages doubled between 1800 and 1860 and from 1860 to 1905. Regardless, the average English worker only earned about a third more than his French counterpart. In the third, real wages from 1860 to 1890 increased only slightly. Despite the rise in real wages, the standard of life was so low to begin with that the increases were not important enough to justify optimism. Real wages were especially low in the first half of the century.

To indicate the intense poverty of the proletariat in the 19th and early 20th centuries, representative working-class budgets will be presented: for a Parisian in the1860s – 1,100 francs for food, 300 for rent, 100 for laundry, 75 for heat and light, and 300 for other expenses (food along being about 60 percent of the budget); for the 1880s in England, about 60 percent went for food and drink; for an American in 1900 (American workers already enjoyed the world's highest living standards, followed by their British counterparts at about two-thirds their level), food still took 45 percent, followed by rent at 25 percent.[15]

In the realm of housing, most of the working-class families in Paris and London inhabited one room apartments, with sewage thrown into the streets to be collected. Not until the end of the century were running water and central heating available to most urban inhabitants of Western Europe and the United States. Paris, for instance, did not have safe water and proper sewage systems before its rebuilding in the 1860s.

Not surprisingly, these conditions contributed to much higher mortality rates in working-class areas than in those of the middle class: In Paris, for instance, cholera and smallpox epidemics in the first half of the century ravaged the former areas while sparing the latter. (Cholera is induced by the contamination of food and water by bacteria from feces.)[16] The infant mortality rate in Paris in the first half of the 19th century was twice as high for the proletariat as for the bourgeoisie.[17]

Scant and poor food, horrid housing and sanitation, and child labor led to the physical deterioration of the working-class youth. For instance, in 1830-48 France, nine-tenths of young workers reporting for military duty did not pass their physical examinations.[18]

Unemployment itself was always a constant nightmare for workers. In *Capital*, Marx alluded to the permanence of an "industrial reserve army," or unemployment under capitalist arrangements, that ravaged workers but benefited capital, for it created a reserve army "for the changing needs of the self-expansion of capital, a mass of human material always ready for exploitation,"[19] and it regulated "the general movements of wages" tied to the trade cycle, i.e., unemployment tending to depress wages.[20] At times, unemployment was astronomically high: In Manchester, for instance, from 1841 to 1842, from 50 to 75 percent, a figure sometimes replicated in other European industrial areas. Even in a frontier America, two depressions in the last of the 19th century, 1873-80 and 1893-97, were especially severe, unemployment averaging about 12 percent in both.[21]

Pauperism itself, due mainly to unemployment, linked to illness and older years was often very high: In Paris, from 1847 to 1851, as much as one-third of the working class; in 1845 England, as much as one-sixth; and for Marx in *Capital* in 1860 Belgium as much as a half. With low wages and pauperism, the possibility of mass starvation existed: Langer estimated that whereas in 16th century Europe about one-fifth of the people were "on the brink of starvation," this rose to one-third by the 19th century.[22]

In this milieu of grinding poverty, a stable family life for the working class was difficult to achieve, especially for the poorer segments. In mid-19th century Paris, grim statistics revealed that one-third of the children were illegitimate, with infanticide being common. Not surprisingly, Parisian workers were replaced by immigrants from the provinces.[23] With economic survival so meager, the labor of women and children was prevalent before and after mid-century, although more common before than after. It was not unusual in England, for instance, to have four-, five-, or six-year old children working in factories. Six-year-old girls pushed coal carts in the coal mines in the 1840s. Langer had the majority of the labor force in mills before 1850 in England, France, and Germany made up of women and children under the age of sixteen, the former earning a half; the latter, a fourth, of the adult male average.[24]

Working-class misery often resulted in criminality, i.e., stealing simply to survive, mostly of the petty variety, although organized gangs existed. About 10 percent of the populations in the large cities were "criminals." Streets in working-class neighborhoods were especially unsafe at night and much of society's conversation was preoccupied with robberies and murders.[25]

As for working-class women, earning half less than men in the context of an ongoing patriarchy, they were clearly subordinate to their males. Bourgeois relations were replicated in the working-class family, with the males representing the bourgeoisie, the females, and the workers. Often, women, to avoid starvation, became part-time prostitutes before marrying; many, however, could not escape from the degradation. One estimate, for about 1850, had 80,000 prostitutes in London and 50,000 in Paris.[26] Patriarchy allowed men, more so than women, to momentarily escape their living hell in alcohol, tobacco, and gambling. In England, between a fourth to a third of a working-class family's income went for these pastimes in pubs that were male preserves.[27]

What about education and literacy for the proletariat in this period? In France, illiteracy among workers was high before midcentury. It was only in 1868 that a law provided for free universal public education to age 12. In England, it was not until the Forster Education Act in 1870 that universal primary education was instituted. In the United States, where a policy for education did not exist outside of land grants, public education was rudimentary; by 1900, manual workers had about four years of education, while white-collar workers had 8.[28]

The paucity of social legislation in the first half of the century and even afterward was well illustrated in France and England. In France, only two laws, which were often flagrantly broken, protected workers. The law of March 22, 1841, regulated child labor in manufacturing establishments of more than 20 workers (only an extremely small percentage of factories): A child had to be at least 8 years old to work; from the age of 8 to 12 only 8 hours a day was permitted; from the age of 12 to 16, no more than 12 hours. For night work, one had to be 13 years old, two hours of which being the equivalent of three in the day. The law of 22 February 1851 on apprentices stipulated a few hours of release time to attend school and no more than a 10 hour day to age 14. In England, over the bitter opposition of the Liberals, who were for "the liberty of the subject," the Tories passed Factory Acts by the first half of the century. The first, of 1833, forbade children under the age of 9 to perform factory work, while those from age 9 to 13 could labor for 48 hours a week, and those from 14 to 18, 68 hours a week. The second law, of 1842, prohibited all females and males under the age of 10 from working in the mines. The third, of 1847, decreed a 10-hour day for women and children under age 14. Again, these laws were difficult to enforce in many instances.[29]

In the United States, economic misery among workers should not be underestimated, despite their being better off than workers of other nations. Robert H. Bremner, a respected American social historian in *From the Depths: The Discovery of Poverty in the United States* (it examined the problem of poverty from the 1850s to the 1920s) had Jacob Riis (*How the Other Half Lives*) estimating that between "twenty to thirty percent of New York's population lived in penury" in the early 1890s; and Father John A. Ryan, a Catholic economist, saw that in the early 1900s, 60 percent of the male workers did not earn a sufficient wage to support their families properly, thus necessitating the labor of women and children.[30]

In addition to facing the obscenity of poverty, workers were often legally treated like children by employers. The *livret* (notebook), which indicated a worker's performance and behavior at work (carried by French workers from the middle of the 18th century to 1890, except for brief periods) was correctly seen by workers as equivalent to a prostitute's permit.[31] In England, at least until the 1860s, there was a double-standard regarding breach of contract involving worker and employer – the worker could be imprisoned, but an employer only required to pay monetary compensation after a successful civil suit against him. These are some leading examples of what R.H. Tawney in *Equality* called the "moral humiliation" of being a worker.[32]

Proletarian socioeconomic misery may be contrasted to the waste of the wealthy. Marx, for instance, remarked that in 1862 England, female servants, 15 percent of the work force numbered a million, while workers and managers in factories totaled only three-quarters of a million, and he favorably compared the opulent lifestyle of the bourgeoisie with that of the nobility.[33] Veblen, in *The Theory of Leisure Class* (1899), noted that the bourgeoisie were merely the last in line of a succession of parasitic ruling classes.[34] To buttress this argument, in 1891 England, a quarter million males, comprising the idle rich, had neither trade nor profession. And, in 1900 England, while most of the workers labored under the poverty line of 50 pounds per year, the peerage, with an annual income of 50,000 pounds per year, enjoyed the luxury of 300 to 400 room castles on 50,000 acre estates, while their poorer cousins, the gentry, were force to subsist on a 3,000 pound annual income, and live in only 30 to 50 room manors on 3,000-acre estates.[35]

As for concentration of wealth, which Marx had predicted as one of the outcomes of capitalism, the top 1 percent of the population owned 68 percent of the private wealth in Great Britain in the early

1900s. During the same time, 47 percent of private wealth in the United States was owned by the top 1 percent.[36]

Unions are key organizations to protect the working class in modern society; in fact, their legal status and restrictions imposed on striking and picketing is an index of working-class power. Their fortunes in selected nations were: France's Le Chapelier law of 1791 expressly forbade all workers' and employers' combinations – it was primarily directed against the former. Article 216 of the Civil Code (instituted by Napoleon Bonaparte) prohibited combinations from raising wages, while article 1781 gave the employer's word in a dispute more weight than the workers. In the French penal code, articles 291-94 prohibited an association of 20 or more persons, while articles 414-16 declared strikes and picketing illegal. Under Louis Napoleon workers could strike (1864) but could not belong to unions until 1868. With the Paris Commune's destruction in 1871 these rights were abrogated. It was only in 1884 that the Third Republic allowed unions to exist and to strike (this did not include government workers).

In England, the Combination Laws of 1799-1800 declared unions illegal, but they were relaxed in 1824 and in 1825 allowed workers to organize them, but not to strike. Only by the Union Laws of 1871 and 1875, which repealed the 1825 act, were unions and strikes made fully legal and collective bargaining and peaceful picketing permitted. In Germany, unions became fully legal in 1890, in Russia in 1906.[37]

In the political arena, workers were excluded from voting for much of the century. In France, under the Bourbon restoration and Orleanais rule (1814-48), male suffrage was highly restrictive, only the nobility and *haute bourgeoisie* could vote.[38] Universal male suffrage was the product of the 1848 revolution. In Britain male suffrage in the 1832 reform bill increased to 15 percent; in 1867 it reached 30 percent (skilled workers were now included); in 1884 it rose to 60 percent; and by the early 20th century there was universal male suffrage. The nobility, however, in the House of Lords, had the power of indefinite veto, which was modified in 1911 to just over two years. In Germany, before the 1848 revolution, democracy was nonexistent. A parliament (*land tag*) based on two house, a house of lords or upper house of the nobility and a house of representatives, or lower house of the people dominated by the bourgeoisie, was established in Prussia in 1850; the king, however, had veto power over all legislation passed by this parliament. With the advent of the German Empire in 1871, there was universal male suffrage for the *Reichstag* (the lower house) that could not initiate legislation, only veto that from the upper house, or *Bundesrat*, an organ under the control of the Kaiser and the other princes – the chancellor himself was responsible to the Kaiser, not parliament.

Under Bismarck, the *Reichstag* in 1878 passed the Exceptional Laws that attempted to destroy the German socialist party (it drove the socialists underground) by rigorously harassing its newspapers and meetings, although socialist candidates were permitted to run for office. The socialists thrived under persecution and the government made an about-face in 1890. In Russia, the autocracy was somewhat modified by the 1905 Revolution that established a parliamentary system (four *Dumas (parliaments)* met to 1918). The second *Dumas* (1907), elected by universal male suffrage, was soon prorogued and a system of class voting was inaugurated which favored the nobility and bourgeoisie at the expense of the peasantry and workers. In the United States, democracy was tarnished because until the 17th amendment to the Constitution (1913), state legislatures elected the Senate. Furthermore, the Supreme Court could declare any law unconstitutional. Also, many African-Americans were denied elementary civil/human rights, especially in the Deep South until the mid-1960s. American women themselves did not universally vote until the 19th amendment to the Constitution was passed in 1920. From a broad perspective, women, or the lower half of the working class, did not vote in most democratic nations until after World War I, and only after World War II in France and Italy.[39]

The last arena concerns the view of the workers by the bourgeoisie, almost uniformly unfavorable. The chasm in living standards between the two classes would make this frame of mind almost axiomatic. Invariably, in the novels of Honore´ de Balzac, Eugene Sue, and others, the middle class characters would portray workers as beastly or as ugly creatures.[40]

How could it be otherwise?

B) Marx and Class

Marx, of course, was not the first to discover the concepts of class and class struggle. Thinkers, as varied as Plato, Aristotle, James Harrington, Thomas Jefferson, Rousseau, Alexander Hamilton, James Madison, Owen, and Saint-Simon, likened social class to unequal property division and social conflict. Indeed, Marx was not even the first to call for a working- class revolution; the disciples of Saint-Simon did.[1]

But Marx was the first to see class and class struggle as central categories in the unfolding of history leading to socialism, insisting on this in a well-known letter to Joseph Wide-eyed in March 1852:

> As far as I'm concerned, the credit for having discovered the existence and the conflict of classes in modern society does not belong to me. Bourgeois historians presented the historical development of this class struggle and economists showed its economic anatomy long before I did. What I did that was new was to prove 1) that the existence of classes is linked to predetermined historical phases of the development of production; (2) that the class struggle necessarily leads to the dictatorship of the proletariat; and (3) that this dictatorship itself is only the transition leading to the abolition of all classes and the establishment of a classless society.[2]

In a systematic manner, Marx in *Capital III* left less than two pages on what constituted a class, stating that there were three general classes in the modern world, workers tied to wages, capitalists to profit, and landlords to rent; but, then, he added many discrete status groups within them, complicating the class picture. He, then, abruptly terminated the discussion.[3]

But Marx's works were replete with past and current class struggles, between proletariat and bourgeoisie. From a broad theoretical perspective this comprised Marx's historical materialism: It theorized that the base or substructure, comprising the productive forces (labor-power, science and technology) and the relations of production or "economic class structure," determined by labor division and property relations, "at a certain stage of their development conflict with one another," led to "social revolution." Thus, classes and accompanying class struggle, the motor force of history, formed in the base, in turn, interacted dialectically with the superstructure or the domain of ideology or "the legal, political, religious, aesthetic or philosophic" arenas, "in which men become conscious of the [class conflict] and fight it out."[4]

To be sure, for Marx, the class struggle in the main favored the master classes over the subaltern ones, the former being socioeconomically, politically, and culturally dominant over the latter; this was ultimately reflected by their basic control of the state or means of violence and by the fact that the subjected classes were either divided by status groups or too preoccupied by the daily struggle to simply stay alive, a key precondition being obedience to the status quo. But on a personal level, class differences were deeply felt, the starting point for the class struggle.

Indeed, class conflict, even if the master classes thoroughly dominated the subaltern ones, as in the Roman Empire, of senators and equestrians over plebeians and slaves, could lead to the destruction of the state by outside forces. There were not many slave rebellions in the Roman Empire, but large-scale slavery certainly led to the dire consequence of not having a large citizen army to adequately protect it from small populations of Germans in many tribes. In the end, this resulted in ending large-scale slavery and rise of Feudalism/manorialism.

The best known instance of class struggle was in the *Communist Manifesto*, which began thus:

> The history of all hitherto existing society is the
> history of class struggles. Freeman and slave,
> patrician and plebian, lord and serf, guild master and
> journeyman – in word, oppressor and oppressed –
> stood in constant opposition to one another, carried
> on an uninterrupted, now hidden, now open flight,
> a fight that each time ended, either in revolutionary
> reconstruction of society at large, or in the common
> ruin of the contending classes.

In the present capitalist era, the primary class struggle for Marx was between workers and the bourgeoisie because increasing increments of capital resulted in more wage workers, suffering under the onus of relative or increasing economic deprivation and powerlessness, exacerbated by the ever-recurring economic crises with their train of massive unemployment. In this process, the petty bourgeoisie (small capitalists, office workers, and so forth) would be absorbed either by larger capital formations or thrown into the working class by changing technologies and universal education, reducing the relative advantage of mental over manual labor.[5] But despite the hope for an immediate working-class revolution, working-class unity was difficult to achieve because workers, at first, even more so than the bourgeoisie, were divided by an increasingly complex labor division and concomitant status gradations, lacked a general working-class consciousness (many were and are recent arrivals from countryside with its intense parochialism),[6] and were usually demoralized by the cruel economic whip of low wages, brutal working conditions, long workday, poor housing and deficient diet.[7]

Both Marx and Engels analyzed the cultural hegemony of the bourgeoisie over the proletariat, as in *The German Ideology*, in which the "ideas of the ruling class," i.e. the bourgeoisie, were "the ruling ideas," making for a false consciousness among workers, distorting their view of social reality and hampering unity. For both, this was reinforced by the fact that the bourgeois intelligentsia basically defended their class interests at the expense of the proletariat.

For Marx, these divisions within the working class were also exacerbated by ethnic and religious differences. In a letter of 9 April 1870 to S. Meyer and A. Vogt, he remarked that because of the "constantly increasing concentration of tenant farming, Ireland supplies its own surplus to the English labor market, and thus forces down wages and lowers the moral and material condition of the English working class." Thus, there emerged in England "a working class *divided* into two *hostile* camps, English proletarians and Irish proletarians," in which the "ordinary English worker hates the Irish worker as a competitor who lowers his standard of life. Indeed:

> In relation to the Irish worker he [the English worker] feels himself a member of the ruling nation and so turns himself into a tool of the aristocrats and capitalists of his country *against Ireland*, thus strengthening their domination *over himself*. He cherishes religious, social, and national prejudices against the Irish worker.

The Irish worker, in turn, regarded the "English worker at once the accomplice and stupid tool of the *English rule in Ireland*." Marx, then noted that this intraworking-class division was "artificially kept alive and intensified by the press, the pulpit, the comic papers, in short by all the means at the disposal of the ruling classes." Its resolution, for him, was for the British workers to support Irish national emancipation, in the process of which they and Irish workers would unite against common the enemy, the bourgeoisie.[8]

Ethnic and religious divisions within the working class are common. The United States is a good example of this. In the last 50 years, more than 150 million immigrants worldwide have left poorer nations for wealthier ones. Today, for instance, 9 percent of German workers are foreigners. The influx of these immigrants, many being refugees and "illegals", comprised almost half the population increase in the First World.

By the year 2000, almost half the world's people live in urban areas, most being workers, a process which is accelerating rapidly, so rapidly that by the next half century, the overwhelming majority should be living in urban areas as workers, barring some catastrophe, perhaps an ecological breakdown or large-scale war. It is within the large urban complexes of today and future that working-class unity should be achieved through the interaction of technology and class struggle.

For Marx, the underlying antagonism between the workers and capitalists was based in the exploitation of the former by the latter. Specifically, workers directly engaged in the processes of production, as in fabricating and transporting commodities, were directly exploited, while commercial, office, and service workers indirectly so as they did not directly make surplus-value.[9]

From a broad perspective, we shall contrast the changing class character of Western Europe and the United States between the mid-19th century and the late 20th century to indicate not only the large numerical increase of the working class, but also its partial rise to power to where it is now at center stage in political developments. In the earlier period, Marx, for example, noted many social classes and class fractions in early industrial France and in an industrially well- developed England and Wales.[10] In the later period, Marxists still observed class and status complexity within a general pattern of increasing social polarity between the proletariat and bourgeoisie. But there were crucial differences between the two periods. In the earlier one, an urban proletariat forming a significant part of the work force, if not its majority, did not exist outside of England and Wales where workers comprised two-thirds of their work force.[11] Outside of the United States, where slavery existed alongside a robust economy, most of the people were either farm laborers and tenant farmers or small "independent" farmers mired in a largely marginal economic position, invariably in a highly dependent relationship to the nobility or bourgeoisie. As for the petty bourgeoisie, it was not large. But in the contemporary class structures of these advanced areas, farmers were a relatively insignificant part of the work force of mostly blue- and white-collar workers. The white-collar group, for example, at the time of Marx'' death was less than 5 percent of the work force, but a fourth of it in the 1940s and more than a third in the 1980s.[12]

It is these white-collar workers, among Marx's "nonproductive" workers, who caused the most controversy concerning their class position. For example, Marx did not disagree with S. Laing's assigning to the middle class such occupations as "officials, men of letters, artists, and school-masters," but strenuously objected when he included better-paid factory workers.[13] But he then presented an example where occupation was not eternally fixed to one particular class, indicating that classes evolved. The case in point was with commercial workers, now in the petty bourgeoisie, as "the better paid class of wage workers...whose labor is classed as skilled and stands above average labor," who performed such mental labor as language translation, thus alluding to the dichotomy between manual and mental labor as related to class differences. But he foresaw that in the future, many of these commercial workers would become members of the working class because of increased "division of labor in the office" that would result in "a one-sided development of [their] capacity," and decreasing skills that would be "more rapidly, easily, universally, and cheaply reproduced with the progress of science and public education."[14]

But even before the rise of the white-collar workers, Marx observed the increasing number of "unproductive" members of the "working class," in the service sector. For instance, in 1861 England and Wales, there were about 1.2 million "servants," as against 1.6 million workers in mining, steel, and various textile enterprises,[15] relating this phenomenon to intensified capitalist exploitation of productive workers through a long workday and increasing technological sophistication. He also formulated that as technology under capitalism became more complex, it required, on one hand, a better-educated work force (thus alluding to the increasing number of technical schools necessitated by modern technology), but that, on the other hand, it simplified industrial processes to cheapen relatively the work of labor.[16] This dynamic technological element allowed for more status complexity within the working class and for generally decreasing class differences between them and the petty bourgeoisie. Today, much more so than in Marx's time, because more education is needed to potentially or actually serve a more complex technology, many workers, including petty-bourgeois brain workers, come closer to Marx's ideal worker under socialism:

> Modern industry, indeed, compels society, under penalty of death, to replace the detail worker of today, crippled by lifelong repetition of one and the same trivial operation…by the fully developed individual, fit for a variety of labors, ready to face any change of production, and to whom the different social functions he performs, are but so many modes of giving free scope to his own natural and acquired powers.[17]

Today, in following the socioeconomic methodology of Marx, who can dispute that part of mental labor, especially in the mass occupations like teachers, nurses, and engineers, can as easily be assigned to the upper half of the working class (many earn less than unionized blue-collars) as to the lower-middle class, and, of course, former lower-middle class clerks are now indisputably proletarians. This problem is further explored later in the chapter.

C) Socialist Debates on Class

Debates over class boundaries among socialists have been of long duration. Even before the outbreak of the first World War, in the world's largest and most disciplined socialist party, the German Social Democratic Party, the orthodox Marxist Karl Kautsky envisaged a sharper class struggle between proletariat and bourgeoisie on the basis of the increasing proletarianization of large segments of the petty bourgeoisie, while the revisionist Marxist Eduard Bernstein held that an attenuated class struggle would occur between them through the *embourgeoisement* of large sections of higher-paid workers.[1]

To test the validity of these theses, we examine in chronological order the following key works of the last fifty or so years in the U.S. and Europe, specifically the French for the latter, commenting on the size of the two numerically largest classes adjacent to each other in the class hierarchy of economically advanced nations, the working and the lower middle: *White Collar* (1951) written by the leading American sociologist, C. Wright Mills, who, although a socialist, was closer to Karl Mannheim than Marx; *Class and Class Conflict in Industrial Society* (1959) by Ralf Daherndorf, a Weberian German sociologist favoring open/evolutionary social democracy, whose views challenged the following works of these outstanding Marxist scholars: *Classes in Contemporary Capitalism* (1974) by Nicos Poulantzas, a former member of the Greek Communist Party and Trotskyist who became a leading commentator of Marxist thought in France; *Labor and Monopoly Capital* (1974) by Harry Braverman, an American skilled worker; and *Class, Crisis and the State* (1978) by Erik Olin Wright, an American sociologist.

In *White Collar*, Mills envisaged the rise of a new American working class, comprising not only blue-collar workers, but also an increasing number of white collars. He saw that because of inexpensive land and high wages, the U.S. had a traditionally large middle class; the majority of free Americans were independent farmers in the early 19th century.[2] His general class alignments in 1870 were 33 percent for the old middle class (most were independent farms and businessmen), 6 percent for the new middle class (salaried professionals and managers), and 61 percent for wage workers; in 1940 the respective figures for the three classes were 20 percent, 25 percent, and 55 percent.[3] The sharp decline of the old middle class was largely due to a diminishing farm population and rapid rise of the new middle class, mostly officer workers, salespersons, and school teachers.[3] Mills' proletariat in 1940 of skilled, semiskilled, and unskilled workers was mostly of the last two categories, 41 percent alone being semiskilled.[4]

The progressive dissolution of differences between the new middle class and workers in the last half-century, for Mills, was striking. In 1890-1900, the average white-collar worker earned twice the income and enjoyed twice the education of the blue-collar, eight years to four; by the 1940s, white-collar income advantage had slipped to a 4:3.3 ratio and the educational gap had narrowed to twelve years/eight years.[5]

These tendencies led Mills to predict a new working class in the next generation, formed by the lower white-collar and traditional blue-collar workers, principally on the basis of similar income and the near universality of a high school education. This reflected the technological reality of "increased rationalization," linked to the lowering of skill among white-collar workers that has resulted in their more "factory-like" work.[6]

Dahrendorf constructed a basically Weberian model of social class in *Class and Class Conflict in Industrial Society,* focusing primarily on the importance of "authority," with bureaucracy and status differences taking precedence over property relations and class strife. But, he admitted that for 19th century capitalism, Marx was essentially correct in assigning ownership of the productive forces as the basis for "authority" or social power.[7] Specifically, for Dahrendorf, "authority" was the decisive element, even more important than property, in determining class and status,[8] influenced here by the centrality of the Kaiser principle in German history.

Two examples presented by Dahrendorf in which "authority" overrode Marx's "class" were: (1) Contemporary Western capitalism or "post-capitalism" was characterized by a split between stockholders and managers of corporation; (2) In Communist nations, although the bureaucracy did not own the means of production, it was the overarching authority, and as such enjoyed its perquisites.[9] But the first point is disputable inasmuch as Kolko, in *Wealth and Power in America*, argued that the managerial sector has a high degree of stock ownership. Of those earning a hundred thousand dollars yearly in 1950 (they owned between 65 to 70 percent of corporate stock), 47.7 percent was in the hands of managers. This view, followed by Domhoff in *Who Rules America?*, sees corporate management as an integral part of the capitalist elite, much of which is made up of upwardly mobile middle-class persons, intimately sharing its mindset, a not unreasonable assumption.[10]

As for the second, in which authority was seemingly devoid of property ownership, control of the means of production was itself a form of ownership. Neither Marx[11] nor Lenin foresaw this condition under socialism; the latter's *The State and Revolution* (1917), following Marx's egalitarian and democratic propensities,[12] called for worker control of industry and general economic equality, leading such an astute commentator as George Lichtheim to characterize this position as "quasi-anarchist."[13] Furthermore, Darendorf did not answer why Communist nations, despite their large wage differentials, were still more economically and socially egalitarian than capitalist ones. Should I dare say that because the means of production had been nationalized, the form of ownership of Communist elites did not give them as much economic power and privilege as their capitalist counterparts in the West and Japan?[14] But he was correct in that part of an authoritarian/bureaucratic Communist elite and rising capitalists of the 1980s used their "authority" to overthrow the Soviet system and seize power in the 1990s, acquiring much of Russia's wealth and bringing a train of socioeconomic inequality even greater than in the U.S. But this "authority" from a Marxian perspective might be explained by status/class terms.

Dahrendorf's view of society emphasized stability over conflict, but recognized the latter's importance: "society is...a relatively integrated system of conflicting structural forces, even more a permanently changing structure of integrative and disruptive factors."[15] For short- run analysis, I doubt that a Marxist could fault this: Marx's *The Eighteenth Brumaire of Louis Bonaparte* amply delineated this. This focus on the near-term allowed Dahrendorf to assert that most changes in history did not involve revolution.[16] But seminal developments are intimately linked to the revolutions of the last three centuries, beginning with the English.

The end of contemporary revolution, for Dahrendorf, was predicated on the rise of the white-collar workers, but "there is no word in any modern language to describe this group that is no group, class that is no class, and stratum that is no stratum."[17] He assigned two-thirds of them to the bourgeoisie (those with a bureaucratic position and, thus, authority in a state and private sectors, even post-office clerks) and one-third, like office and service workers, skilled workers, and foremen (even if salaried) to the proletariat.[18]

It would seem that the very polarity of Dahrendorf's two-class model exacerbated social tensions, but he dampened them because classes became all the more "complex and heterogeneous."[19] An example of Dahrendorfian status-group conflict taking precedence over class struggle involved skilled and unskilled workers fighting over wage demands, one's gain resulting in the other's loss.[20]

Furthermore, he saw the further weakening of class consciousness in advanced industrial society in intergenerational social mobility and multiplicity of skill gradations,[21] but did not state the obvious: that most of it, manual worker fathers to non- manual worker sons, was largely lateral movement, reflecting the changing nature of the means of production.[22] As for the proliferation of occupations, they could hinder the class struggle, but in periods of crisis, this compartmentalization could be overcome.

Despite the weakening of traditional class alignments, Dahrendorf still employed the term "class" to indicate "conflict groups that are generated by the differentiated distribution of authority in imperatively coordinated associations."[23] Indeed, for him, class conflict continued,[24] even "ubiquitous,"[25] but in an attenuated form, "institutionalized" and "far removed from the ruthless and absolute class struggle visualized by Marx,"[26] basically applicable only to "industrial conflict," now largely isolated from "general social and political problems." One of his proofs for this was the demise of traditional working-class parties.[27]

It is axiomatic that early worker resistance to bourgeois hegemony through industrial strikes and mass demonstrations for higher wages, union representation, and the vote was often met by brutal repression, thus evincing a "ruthless" class struggle. But, once workers won unions and the vote, the class struggle obviously became more "institutionalized" and less "ruthless." Also, as Lichtheim noted, generally after 1860, Marx and Engels became the fathers of democratic socialism, ardently supporting reform through the formation of trade unions and political parties to engage in a basically pacific class struggle in industry and politics. In this vein, both held the possibility that socialism could be peacefully realized in such emerging democratic nations as the United States, France, Britain, and Holland. Thus, although they saw the class struggle as the central instrument to explain social progression, it was not necessarily violent.[28]

Indeed, a "ruthless" Marxian class struggle, which Dahrendorf equated with strikes and confrontation, might indicate the general weakness of the working class; one denied access to permanent mechanisms allowing for meaningful change. Generally, with obvious exceptions, a largely tranquil class struggle waged in the political arena by political parties is more efficacious for change than narrow industrial strife. Although traditional working-class parties are now more amorphous because of the changing composition of the work force, that does not necessarily vitiate the ongoing class struggle. Today, the working class is more politicized and stronger than a hundred years ago; every European nation has a powerful and often governing socialist party. Thus, despite the fact that many socialist parties are less "Marxist" than previously, the expanding working class is now poised more so than ever to assume hegemony.

Another view of Dahrendorf had class differences diminishing because the worker now leads two lives: one at the factory, where as a worker he retains a proletarian consciousness, another, as consumer, where he loses his worker identity, consumerist fetishism wins over all![29] If that were true, Darhrendorf's post office clerk may be faced with a reverse problem: "Authority" (what great authority?) at work does not give him a higher standard of life than that enjoyed by many workers. Or, what leads to Dahrendorfian social stability with respect to workers, may in turn lead to instability for his various petty-bourgeoisie fractions that are now economically proletarianized. Poulantzas, whom I concur with in *Classes in Contemporary Capitalism*, characterized Darhrendorf's views as Weberian, "the traditional objection to the Marxist theory of classes,"[30] and asserted that Dahrendorfian class amorphousness was antithetical to Marxian concentration. [31]

For a historically brief period, one in which the traditional petty bourgeoisie was being eradicated, a new group of higher-paid workers emerged. But capitalist demands to ever reduce labor power and relatively cheapen it through new technologies routinizing labor and greater need for more education to find employment have also significantly conspired to reduce the differences between blue- and white-collar workers – thus, the emergence of the new working class. As for proletarian parties of earlier models no longer existing, the new versions simply reflect the changing nature of the working class.

Much of the working class today is reformist and under capitalist hegemony in its many forms, and divisions exist between it and the lower-middle class. But in Western Europe after World War II, the two cooperated to bring about massive social reform and much nationalization of industry. Furthermore, from a broad historical perspective, it is only when living standards rise that the working class is able to wage a more efficacious class struggle than when it was in its early formation, not far from starvation.[32]

In the last chapter of Dahrendorf's work, there was a section entitled "How People See Society": The "dominant groups," satisfied, viewed it "as ordered and reasonable," the middle groups as a "bureaucratic hierarchy in which everybody has his defined place both above and below other," while the "subjected" ones "emphasize the cleavages that in their opinion account for deprivations they feel."[33] From the perspective of wealth and power, Dahrendorf, however, minimized the reality that the two lower groups, the vast majority of the work force, have much more in common with one another than they do with elites. Only history, of course, will decide as to whether the Weberian Dahrendorf or Marx is more correct.

A rather recent and stimulating Marxist work on class in France, closely dissecting differences between its proletariat and petty bourgeoisie, is Poulantzas' *Classes in Contemporary Capitalism*. In employing orthodox Marxian methodology, Poulantzas defined classes as "principally but not exclusively by their place in the production process, i.e., in the economic sphere," and "place in the social division of labor as a whole," including the "superstructure," since "the political and the ideological" are also important,[34] and "classes exist only in the class struggle," although at times part of the proletariat favored the bourgeoisie, an example being the "labor aristocracy."[35]

Poulantzas' three classes in France were: (1) the proletariat (42 percent of the working population), of manual workers directly involved in the production and transportation of commodities, directly making surplus-value and thus directly exploited by capital.[36] Poulantzas did not enumerate the various occupations of these manual workers (as he would with the petty bourgeoisie), but following Wright, who closely analyzed Poulantzas' work, they would include "craftsmen, operatives, and labourers"[37] in such blue-collar preserves as manufacturing, construction, and transportation; (2) the petty bourgeoisie, comprising the old petty bourgeoisie (independent farmers, craftsmen, and shopkeepers) and the new petty bourgeoisie (office workers, teachers, salespersons, technicians, engineers, doctors, lawyers, and service workers like hairdressers). This class included mental labor not in the upper bourgeoisie and non-productive labor not directly exploited in the making of commodities. Thus, office workers, although exploited by their employers, were done so from funds coming from the surplus value extracted from manual workers. Even, for example, if a profession of this group was involved in "the reproduction of labor-power," like teachers, they were still in the nonproductive category. The combined petty bourgeoisie, following Poulantzas' criteria, is probably in the mid-50 percent range;[38] (3) the bourgeoisie, presumably no more than 5 percent, of large owners and those with "possession" or "the capacity to put the means of production into operation," thus including higher business management, in addition to the state and other elites.[39] (Poulantzas did not present any overall class percentages outside the proletariat).

Let us further trace Poulantzas' position on the differences demarcating the proletariat from the petty bourgeoisie. He quoted from Marx's *Capital*, III, that merchant capital did not produce any surplus-value, thus its workers did not directly create surplus-value.[40] To be sure, for Marx, commercial workers were still exploited as workers by commercial capital: "Just as the labourer's unpaid labor directly creates surplus-value for productive capital, so the unpaid labor of the commercial workers secures a share of this surplus-value for commercial capital."[41] And: "His wage [commercial worker's] is not necessarily proportionate to the mass of profit which he helps the capitalist to realize." And: "He creates no direct surplus-value, but adds to the capitalist's income by helping him to reduce the cost of realizing surplus-value, inasmuch as he performs partly unpaid labour."[42]

I do not completely disagree with Poulantzas' Marxist distinction between productive and nonproductive capital/work, but do so with his placing commercial and presumably service workers for all time with the petty bourgeoisie.[43] In fairness to Poulantzas, Marx, at times, placed along with commercial workers such nonproductive service workers as maids and grooms, in the petty bourgeoisie,[44] commercial workers being "the better paid class of wage-workers... whose labor is classed as skilled and stands above average labour."[45] But Marx foresaw that many commercial workers would become members of the working class as more labor division in the office and expansion of public education resulted in their lower relative wages, largely erasing class distinctions between productive and nonproductive labor. Especially did he emphasize the importance of wage differentials in determining class position.

The second demarcation line between proletariat and new petty bourgeoisie, for Poulantzas, involved individuals in such occupations as technicians and engineers who might also be supervisors, tying technology to supervision. As part of the process of production, this group was directly exploited by capital, as productive labor involved in the technical division of labor.[46] But, in the social division of labor, in the process of production as supervisors and/ or brainworkers, in which capacity capital used them to extricate surplus value from manual workers, they were members of the petty bourgeoisie; this command of labor would fall under Poulantzas' rubric of the political domination of labor by capital.[47] This position followed *The Communist Manifesto*, which saw workers as "privates" in the factory "under the command of a perfect hierarchy of officers and sergeants...enslaved by the machine, by the overlooker, and above all, by the individual bourgeois manufacturer himself."[48] In this instance, "sergeants" and "officers" were not members of the proletariat, although as workers still exploited by capital.[49]

Poulantzas combined both the technical and social divisions of labor into the larger complex of the dichotomy between manual and mental labor, viewed largely from educational differences, i.e., to "capitalist ideological realtions,"[50] undoubtedly influenced by the Gramscian concept of bourgeois ideological dominance over the proletariat.[51] He maintained that modes of work not associated with manual labor were invariably related with not being a worker. Thus, "the traditional esteem given to paperwork...to a certain use of speech," which workers lacked, and to the dichotomy "between general culture...and technical skills."[52] Education, for him, was the critical factor here in differentiating the petty bourgeoisie from the workers, noting that in the early 1970s, a French working-class child had a one-in-seven chance of having a "secondary higher" education, while one from the bourgeoisie, including petty bourgeoisie, had a better than a one-in-two.[53] More education, for him, was related to both higher income and class position; in the France of 1969, engineers earned three times as much as workers.[54]

Marx, however, did not always solely place mental labor within the bourgeois spectrum. One example in *Capital*, I:

> A schoolmaster is a productive labourer, when in addition to belaboring the heads of his scholars; he works like a horse to enrich the school proprietor.

That the latter had laid out his capital in a teaching
factory, instead of in a sausage factory, does not alter
the relation.[55]

Another was in his *Theories of Surplus-Value*:

A writer is a productive labourer not in so far as
he produces ideas, but in so far as he enriches the
publisher who publishes his works, or if he is a wage-
labourer for a capitalist.[56]

From a broad perspective, although Marx was certainly aware of
the antagonistic relationship between manual and mental labor, he
ultimately envisaged that this and other differences between workers
would ultimately be erased because "everyone is only a worker."

But in defense of Poulantzas, until quite recently, this labor
dichotomy situated mental labor within the bourgeoisie. Furthermore,
his recognizing the importance of the superstructure, or the political
and ideological, is invaluable in understanding the persistence of
bourgeois cultural hegemony over broad sections of the proletariat.[57]
More importantly, Poulantzas largely erased the class distinctions
between workers and large sectors of the petty bourgeoisie, there
being many gradations in the structure of mental labor:

The mental labor aspect does not affect the new petty
bourgeoisie in an undifferentiated manner. Certain
sections of it are affected directly; others, subjected to
the reproduction of the mental/manual labor division
within mental labor itself, are only affected indirectly,
and while these sections are still affected by the
effects of the basic division, they also experience a
hierarchy within mental labor itself.[58]

For him this did not only have economic consequences, but also
affected "ideological and political relations," primarily leading to the

"fragmentation and polarization of the new petty bourgeoisie" whose lower sectors are brought "close to the barrier that separates them from manual labor and from the working class."[59] But he insisted that even these lower petty- bourgeois "fractions" could never be fully integrated into the working class, leading him to reject, at least for the foreseeable future, a numerical increase of the working class to the degree where it would outnumber the petty bourgeoisie and bourgeoisie. In this regard, he claimed that between 1954 and 1968, in France, the "productive" workers or proletariat increased 5 percent, while the nonproductive workers, most in the petty bourgeoisie, rose 10 percent. But he then saw that the increase in the working class represented a greater increase than among the "nonproductive" workers.[60]

Despite this trend, Poulantzas boldly forecasted a proletarian-led alliance with fractions of the new petty bourgeoisie to achieve socialism in France because of the intervention of three recent developments: (1) the traditional petty bourgeoisie continued to decline because of the increase of capital so that by 1969 only 3 percent of the work force were independent craftsmen and 5 percent were small shopkeepers; (2) the continuing growth in education had dramatically increased the number of those receiving a baccalaureate degree, resulting in their higher unemployment and erosion of occupational mobility; (3) the income gap between blue- and white-collar workers by 1970 had narrowed to where the former, on average, were only 10 percent lower than the latter,[61] the last two elements closely related to his concept of the increasing proletarianization of those who performed lower mental labor.

Most significantly, for Poulantzas, the narrowing income gap allowed for various "fractions" of the petty bourgeoisie to come ever closer to the proletariat and their influence, like most "lower-level office workers, many of whom are women, technical personnel and lower engineers."[62] Ultimately, for him, this would result in a "polarization of the new petty bourgeoisie towards proletarian class positions" because this group "has no autonomous long- run class position, and as history has shown, it cannot in general have its own political organizations," analogous to that of a popular front between the proletariat and large sections of the petty bourgeoisie, in which proletarian hegemony prevailed.[63]

Braverman's *Labor and Monopoly Capital* importantly examined the growing contradictions, now of crisis proportion between the "scientific-technological revolution,"[64] requiring "greater worker skill through more training and education, the concomitant subdivision and routinization of work, increasing job displacement, and changes in job classification..."[65] These conditions, under a capitalism extracting ever larger amounts of surplus-value from workers, demanded "faster and more efficient methods and machinery," to further reduce "the worker to the level of an instrument in the production process,"[66] making labor more abstract, analogous to Marx's structure of labor in contradistinction to capital.[67] To be sure, for him, greater worker skill accompanied general technological advances, but even so, the requisite technical knowledge for running society was in the expertise of technicians and engineers, about 3 percent of the active work force.[68] In fact, following Marx, as technology became more complex, he envisaged more relatively poorly paid workers, as is evident today in the manufacturing, clerical, services, and retail sales areas.[69]

As for Marx's distinction between productive and nonproductive labor, Braverman, like Poulantzas and Wright, took cognizance of it, noting that commercial workers, for example, did not produce surplus-value, but in agreement with Wright generally and unlike Poulantzas, he did not place them in the petty bourgeoisie, asserting that Marx himself referred to them as wage workers.[70] Indeed, he viewed these commercial workers as part of "the vast and complicated structure of occupations characteristic of unproductive labor in modern capitalism" and duly noted that they indeed had "lost many of the last characteristics [higher wages and more skill I presume] which separated them from production workers."[71]

Braverman posited an American working class (his social framework, along with Mills' and Wright's, was the most generous in extending the class boundaries of the proletariat) of between two-thirds and three-quarters of the active work force;[72] it was divided into four main categories (he also presented the weekly median salary of each for 1971): 9.5 million skilled workers or craftsmen" at $167; 18.1 million operatives and laborers at $117-120; 14.3 million clerical workers at $115; and 13.4 million service and sales workers at $96.[73]

Braverman made a sharp distinction between the contemporary new middle class and the white-collar clerical workers. Some background of his: in the United States of 1870, less than 1 percent of the active workers were clerks; by 1900, they increased to 3 percent (4 percent in Great Britain) and by 1970, to 18 percent. Clerks for Braverman were bookkeepers, secretaries, stenographers, bank tellers, file clerks. Like Mills, he observed that in 1900 this group earned twice as much as manual workers but, as already noted, by 1971 earned somewhat less; this trend occurred also in Great Britain. About two-thirds of clerks were now women, obviously touching upon the problem of gender and work.[74]

Through rationalization, basically mechanization, the jobs of clerks, for Braverman, were now standardized and routinized, basically removing mental labor content from their work, making office and factory work essentially similar. He thus envisioned clerks as the female equivalent to male factory workers.[75] Essentially, Mills' prediction of the rise of a new social class composed of manual and lower white-collar workers, the new proletariat, had been confirmed by Braverman.

Nevertheless, there persisted, for Braverman, a new petty bourgeoisie, between 15 to 20 percent of the work force in such professionals as technicians, nurses, accountants, engineers, teachers, and scientists, forming the bulk of lower and middle management, that still identified itself with capital.[76] Along with Poulantzas and Wright, he was aware of the political and ideological domination that this group, acting for the bourgeoisie, exercised over workers. But, for him, many sections of this new middle class, again due to the inexorably rationalization of the new technologies, were already in the throes of falling into the working class, thus becoming more discontented.[77] If this scenario is correct, in the advanced capitalist nations, the new middle class will further shrink, for the working class will be joined by increasing numbers of mental workers to confront an ever-diminishing petty bourgeoisie.

Braverman's "scientific-technological revolution" has not only led to a more educated proletariat whose work is increasingly routinized.[78] but may contribute to a near-future crisis of capitalism from massive unemployment through automation. A 1988 United Auto Worker study on automation estimated the loss of more than 20 million manual labor jobs in the U.S. by the year 2000.[79] Automation and the need for more education to procure employment should inevitably intensify class tensions between the working class and bourgeoisie.

A noteworthy and recent work of Marxist scholarship on class and related problems is Wright's *Class, Crisis and the State*, whose methodology importantly employed the relatively novel concept of "contradictory class locations." Although fundamental classes were formed by "social relations of production," this did not preclude class ambiguity based on not only economic criteria, but also ideological and political ones.[80]

To be sure, Wright, along with the other commentators examined, presented a social diagram of three basic classes, the proletariat, the petty bourgeoisie, and the bourgeoisie. (1) The proletariat, from 41 to 55 percent of the work force, was made up of the usual blue-collar workers and most of the lower white-collar group, especially in the clerical and secretarial areas, in addition to workers in "political and ideological apparatuses" associated with it. Invariably, the proletariat was linked with wage labor in the "social relations of production."[81] (2) The petty bourgeoisie, of 4.5 percent, consisted of self-employed entrepreneurs and professionals.[82] (3) The bourgeoisie, at the apex of the social structure, from 1 to 2 percent, encompassed wealthy capitalists and upper management of business, government, education, and religion.[83] As may be readily seen, Wright's definite class structure was from 46.5 to 60.5 percent. The remainder was in "contradictory class locations" and in "contradictory class relations," as they related to differences among both of the bourgeois classes and the proletariat, representing the following specific conditions:

"a contradictory location within the social relations of production" related to "control over money capital, physical capital, and labor power" and a "contradictory location within the political and ideological apparatuses" that "execute but do not create state policy or...control the production of bourgeois ideology."[84]

These "contradictory class locations" were situated in two broad sets, each comprising two groups on either side of the three-class flow. The first set was situated between the proletariat and the bourgeoisie. Its first group, just above the proletariat, of "bottom managers, foremen, and line supervisors," was between 18 and 23 percent of the work force. Its second group, above the first and immediately below the bourgeoisie, was made up of "top managers, middle managers, and technocrats," numbering 12 percent. The second set was comprised thus: its first group, between the bourgeoisie and petty bourgeoisie, of "small employers" of up to 50 workers, numbered 6 to 7 percent; its second group between the proletariat and the petty bourgeoisie, of "semi-autonomous employees," including professionals like college teachers and researchers working for others, was from 5 to 11 percent.[85]

Because of his "contradictory class locations" concept, Wright's social structure had many similarities to that of the Weberian Dahrendorf, with its focus on class indeterminacy and on status groups, and to Poulantzas' class "fractions."

But Wright and Poulantzas had somewhat different interpretations of Marx, three principal elements being in question here, Wright generally following Braverman and disputing Poulantzas: (1) In the productive versus nonproductive labor controversy, Wright opposed any distinction between the two on the basis that Poulantzas himself admitted that both of these formers of labor were exploited by capital, thus making it immaterial in which form it was exploited.[86] Furthermore, he quoted against Poulantzas, Marx's well-known statement of "a schoolmaster is a productive worker," although engaged "outside the sphere of material production,"[87] thus placing even elite university professors in a "contradictory class location" because as employees, a form of surplus-value was extracted from their labor. (2) In the manual/mental labor dichotomy, for Poulantzas, all mental labor, including the lowly work of clerks and secretaries, was assigned to at least a petty-bourgeoisie location. Wright criticized this reasoning on the grounds that one could just as well use "racism, nationalism, and other ideologies of domination" to denote class differences.[88] Perhaps Wright was more correct than Poulantzas in this dispute for the present and future, but traditionally these two forms of labor had been important in determining class. (3) There was disagreement with the political criterion involving capital's command over labor, Poulantzas unequivocally locating foremen and lower management with the petty bourgeoisie, while Wright, although acknowledging some validity for this, also positioned them as workers, thus their "contradictory class location."[89]

If pressed, Wright would admit that the semi- or quasi-classes, with the exception of the entrepreneurs just above the petty bourgeoisie and the top managers, might be seen as a new middle class, occupying an "intermediate position between labor and capital," that could not but also bear the stamp of the proletariat insofar as it also labored for capital. His dynamic semi-classes have fractions or groups within them with propensities to identify themselves more so with either capital or labor in the social polarity. For instance, he claimed that engineers were not too closely attached to the bourgeoisie and middle managers.[90] In the event of an economic crisis, engineers would be more prone to embrace a proletarian class position than middle managers.

A major fault in Wright's class methodology is insistence that merely working for capital, even as a middle or higher manager, somehow makes one into a semi-proletarian. Although one cannot dispute that these groups work for capital, the economic disparities, let alone the ideological and political criteria, between them and workers are so pronounced that their "contradictory class relation" is almost meaningless in the context of contemporary social arrangements. I agree, however, with Braverman and Wright that Poulantzas' distinctions between manual and mental labor and productive and nonproductive labor are now almost without foundation in trying to distinguish a large part of the traditional petty bourgeoisie from the proletariat.

Wright was especially critical of Poulantzas' class model for being too restrictive of proletarian membership. In applying the criteria that Poulantzas employed to determine a French proletariat of 42 percent in 1970, Wright observed that this permitted an American proletariat of about 20 percent for the same period. But the class structures of the two nations were not so dissimilar as to allow for such a large disparity. Perhaps Wright misinterpreted Poulantzas' methodology on types of labor.[91]

Specifically Wright envisaged an expanding proletariat of as much as 70 percent of the work force with the addition of the two nearest "contradictory class locations." But certain methodological problems remained. For instance, one might easily conceive of "line supervisors" and "foremen" becoming proletarians, but not elite university professors.

Wright's work on class was also of value in indicating the continuing resilience of a capitalist social structure, clearly indicating that even in the late 20th century, in a highly advanced capitalist nation like the United States, half the work force was still outside the proletariat. Not tangentially, Wright also cogently explained why socialism was so weak in the United States, reflecting the unresolved conflicts engendered by fundamental division plaguing the American working class, of skill gradation, ethnicity, and gender, linking these divisions to the capitalist marketplace, embodying the pitiless economic whip.[92]

Paradoxically, the two Europeans, Dahrendorf and Poulantzas, both from nations with vigorous socialist traditions for more than a century, were much more restrictive in delineating the parameters of the working class than their American counterparts, Mills, Braverman, and Wright, from a nation with a rather anemic one.

D) Marcuse and Sartre

Two other well-known thinkers after World War II should be considered in understanding the working class and socialism – the neo-Marxist Herbert Marcuse and near-Marxist Jean-Paul Sartre: The former, a German Jew and a political philosopher, came to America as a refugee from Nazi Germany, becoming a guru of the American New Left in the 1960s and 70s. The latter, an outstanding French philosopher of Existentialism, merged it with anarchism and Marxism, especially in his magnificent *Critique of Dialectical Reason*.

For Marcuse, it is now possible in the technologically advanced capitalist nations, like the United States, to have the necessary level of productive forces to ensure a full-scale socialist society. He would end an exploitative-, hierarchical- (one of almost endless labor division), polluting-, imperialistic- (Vietnam being a prime example), totalitarian/democratic capitalist society whose façade of freedom masked an inherent authoritarianism at whose apex is a parasitic capitalist elite.[1]

But in a pessimistic vein, he did not believe that socialism was on the near horizon, especially in the United States, because its proletariat, in a dependent position, basically accepted the status quo. For him, the new technology protected the existing social arrangements by producing a sufficiently high material abundance for most workers, cloaking exploitation through the acceleration of automation, making it more difficult for workers to understand its intensity. To this, he added an administrative network, largely denying a specific focal point for anger to be directed against.[2]

There were, however, sparks of opposition to the capitalistic/technological structure among sections of the intelligentsia and middle-class youth (both with sufficient affluence and understanding to comprehend its essentially authoritarian nature), and among ethnic minorities, who daily experienced the worst features of its exploitation/repression, scarcely sharing in the cornucopia of the new consumerism.[3]

For Marcuse, the capitalistic social structure itself had an inherent contradiction pit the capitalist elite against the working class, which might either lead to Communism or some form of fascism.[4] If the workers assumed power, a greater possibility in Europe with its long socialist tradition than in the United States where it was weak, they had the proper economic conditions to succeed, i.e., an advanced technological structure.

For Marcuse, the new socialist society (basically classless and stateless in which the productive forces were in the hands of the workers) would proclaim the "self-determination of men and women" asserting "their freedom and humanity in the satisfaction of their vital material needs."[5] He also insisted on having direct democracy, where in any organization, be it economic or political, there would be effective control from below. Finally, he would eliminate the present "fragmentation of work," the extensive labor division that condemned most workers to repetitive and mindless labor, with automation and cybernetics, making work creative and supervisory.[6] These new conditions/patterns, for him, would end an alienating competition producing meaningless products for the sake of profit, "servitude in the guise of technology," and pollution.

The ultimate focus of the new socialist world, for Marcuse, was to ensure the required material abundance, for humanity's basic "moral and aesthetic needs."[7] Some conflict within it might still exist, but he believed that it could be handled "without oppression and cruelty."[8] The chances for this were likely, for him, because this socialism would contain an authentic "political freedom," transcending traditional class politics.[9]

With *Critique de la raison dialectique* in 1960, Sartre fitted his humanistic existentialist philosophy within the broader parameters of Marxism, which he recognized as the dominant contemporary philosophy describing the complexity of social reality.[10] This work, injecting Marxism with the specificity of existentialism, followed in the broad footsteps of Marx in that it envisaged history as moving toward a future state of freedom. The Sartrean vision, faithful to the Marxist and anarchist traditions in which the interaction between individual and society through various groups was at center stage, utilized the full range of their rich and complex socio-historical experiences, while exploring the individual's interior-exterior existence through existentialism.

For Sartre, scarcity underlay the historical progression, forcing individuals into performing various tasks requiring labor division and coordination, leading to domination and hierarchy as principal characteristics of the social construct. From scarcity, violence also sprang "interiorized scarcity" which "makes people see each other as the Other and as the principle of Evil." Furthermore, an economy of scarcity produced "a climate of fear and mutual distrust."[11] It was in this maelstrom that humanity made history dialectically; the dialectic itself being "the totalisation of concrete totalisation effected by a multiplicity of totalizing individualities."[12] In this historical analysis he not only delineated the larger contours of history, progressing dialectically through economic, social, political, and cultural changes, but also viewed the individual in his alienated human relationships stemming from antagonistic social relations.

Attention will be given to the Sartrean analysis of such topics as tensions within status groups, bureaucracy, the state, class struggle, revolution and critique of communist societies in order to indicate that Sartre's views followed in the footsteps of Marx.

Sartre saw alienation/subjection, tied to the individual's interaction with others, as an inherent condition of history. At first, human association was in "fused groups" (ad hoc groups devoid of structure, living in equality and fraternity), which evolved into "pledged groups" (individuals organized by a pledge of mutual obligations and rights), which in time became transformed into institutions (the state, military, and so forth), in which sovereignty or authority based on coercion was paramount. Once these last structures were in place, spontaneity and democratic forms would atrophy; indeed, bureaucracy became "the opposite of freedom." Sartre, like Orwell in *1984*, was fearful that the rise of new bureaucratic state, through its control of the communications media, could condition the masses to act against their interests, as the Nazis were able to do in their frenzied anti-Semitism, thus hindering the attainment of socialism. This attempt by the bureaucracy to influence and control events was called "other-direction."[13]

Sartre was definitely in the anarchist tradition in focusing great attention on the primary or more intimate human associations operating within the larger collectives of state and class. It was what happened in these small groups and their surrounding networks, where individuals intimately involved themselves in love and work, that he regarded as most important in determining the intensity of the class struggle in any particular period. Indeed, the very complexity and diversity in the myriad of small groups and their alienation from one another made it very difficult to achieve the unity of the proletariat.[14]

As for the state, Sartre followed the Marxist/anarchist traditions: "In this sense, for example, the nineteenth-century bourgeois state reflected the unity of bourgeois society." "The state is a determination of the dominant class, and this determination is conditioned by class struggle." "The state therefore *exists* for the sake of the dominant class, but as a practical suppression of class conflicts within the national totalisation." "In class conflicts it [the state] intervenes to tilt the balance in favor of the exploiting classes."[15]

The class struggle for Sartre, patterned basically on Marxist and anarchist precedents, was the chief propellant of history. In the present historical epoch, the ascending proletariat (the exploited) was locked in a deadly conflict with the descending bourgeoisie (the exploiters), the former as the chosen class ("the damned of the earth") to destroy the bonds of all class oppression.

His deep sympathy for the proletariat was indicated thus:

> His [the worker's] free activity in its freedom, will
> take upon itself everything which crushes him –
> exhausting work, exploitation, oppression, and rising
> prices. This means that his liberty is the means
> chosen by the Thing and by the other to crush him
> and to transform him into a worked Thing. Hence the

moment of the free contract by which in the nineteenth century, the isolated worker, a prey to hunger and poverty, sold his labor to a powerful employer who imposed his own rates, is both the most shameless mystification and reality.

Sartre also saw divisions within the two general classes: the bourgeoisie, from the petite bourgeoisie to the very wealthy, competed among themselves for profits. The proletariat, in turn, from unskilled to skilled, also competed for jobs and wages, but had a more difficult time to unite for it must overcome the alienations and divisions imposed by past generations: "The previous generation already defines their [workers'] institutional future" through various "obligations – military, civic, professional, etc." Despite these impediments, the overriding historical tendency was for the class struggle between the workers and bourgeoisie to intensify as the workers became more unified.[16]

Indeed, Sartre employed a technological perspective to postulate the progressively increasing class solidarity of the proletariat. "The machine organizes men," defining to a large degree the relations of the workers to themselves as well as to the capitalist owners. Thus, when revolutionary syndicalism was in its heyday in the early 20th century, the few skilled workers who formed the labor aristocracy could simply paralyze a factory by going out on strike. Since the labor aristocrats were not interested in the unskilled workers, mass unionism did not develop; divisions in the working class were too wide to impose unity. Today, however, with the "interchangeability of skilled workers" mass action was possible.[17] He also observed that the recent technological explosion related to the educational one, a condition allowing for a highly educated work force, largely erased former status differences, thus furthering the probability for revolution.

The "apocalypse," or the revolution, would come from individuals coalescing together in the fused groups that at a certain historical juncture would simply act in the spirit of equality and fraternity

– a view of the young Marx, who also saw imminent revolution, of Bakunin, and the Lenin of 1917 who urged the Bolsheviks to follow the masses.[18]

Sartre critiqued socialist societies in economically backward nations most perceptively. Although basically sympathetic to them, he indicated such negative features in the early stages of their development as rise of bureaucracy and its terror that culminated in the "cult of personality." These deformities, however, should be progressively resolved by "de-bureaucratization, decentralization, and democratization: and the last term should be taken to mean that the sovereign must gradually abandon it *monopoly of the group* (the question arises at the level of workers' committees)." Sartre did not go as far as anarchists to describe the new socialist bureaucrats as constituting a new capitalist class because the revolution expropriated capitalist property.[19] Sartre obviously was incorrect here, for an unrestrained bureaucracy invariably engendered capitalism.

E) Major Bourgeois Thinkers and Class

Marxism and socialism in general have had many well-known conservative opponents in the last two centuries: the American sociologist William Graham Sumner, the Italian economist and sociologist Vilfredo Pareto, and the German sociologist Max Weber. They are referred to as "The Three."

The "three" believed, like Marx, that society was divided into various social classes. But for Sumner and Pareto, class demarcations were more important in understanding social reality than for Weber, who was more concerned with differences among status groups. For Sumner, a social Darwinist, there were three basic classes: the wealthy few (the most fit), the "masses" or average people ("mediocrities"), and the working class at the bottom, composed of the unfit, a sizable minority. For Pareto, he, too, was aware of social complexity, and that the elite was generally contrasted to the masses. For Weber, the ruling elite, of Kaiser, army, and state bureaucracy (the wealthy bourgeoisie was not included) governed, although he positioned various layers of the bourgeoisie between rulers and masses.

The "three," again agreeing with Marx, saw that there were antagonistic social relations among classes. Sumner, for instance, envisioned a future America in the grips of a rising socioeconomic misery leading to increasing social conflict between the middle and working classes. For Pareto, the class struggle between rulers and ruled, being interminable, proceeded with a succession of elites using the dissatisfied, but incompetent, masses as pawns. For Weber, the basic social dynamic pitted intra-class status groups against one another, although the class struggle between the workers and middle-class was still operative.

The "three" posited a gloomy prognosis for socialism: that should it assume power, an elite would still run society and deny universal equality. Weber, for instance, emphasized that large- scale industry and proliferating labor division bureaucratized social organization (even under socialism), thus effectively negating the principle of equality. Ultimately, the "three" based class/ status inequality on a biological basis (either a strict or a modified one) and the normally acquired advantages from inherited wealth/privilege. Basically, for them, there was only contempt for the incompetent and chaotic masses and admiration for their rulers.[1]

Robert Michels, a protégé of Weber and former socialist who became an ardent admirer of Mussolini's fascism, continued emphasis on inequality. In *Political Parties* (1911), he described the oligarchic tendencies inherent in a German Social Democratic Party (the chief Marxist party of the Second International) dominated by officeholders who invariably came from bourgeois social formations. Moreover, he noted that its officeholders had a slow rate of turnover.[2]

F) Contemporary Class Structure in the United States

Contemporary class alignments in the United States in 2000 confirm that Marx's view of class, of ever-greater class polarity between the bourgeoisie and proletariat is essentially correct. The richest 1 percent ($1.1 million annually is their average income, versus $50,000 for a median family) owns 40 percent of all private net wealth (32 percent in the 1960s), including half the stock, 62 percent of bonds, 53 percent of non-home real estate. Its family minimum net wealth in 2000 is more than $4 million, quadrupling from 1979. Occupationally, 41 percent is in management, 22 percent in medicine, 12 percent in law, 19 percent in sales, and 6 percent in other areas. They are followed by the upper-middle class, the next 9 percent, with 30 percent of net wealth, many of whom are millionaires. The top 10 percent have 86 percent of net financial assets. The principal basis for this wealth, from half to three-fourths, especially for the top 1 percent, is from inheritance and income generated from it. (According the *Economist,* in 1998 the nation had 4.5 million millionaires, including 250,000 deca-millionairs, and 170 billionaires.) The next 10 percent of households have 15 percent of net wealth, and the bottom 80 percent has 15 percent of it (its lower half, 0.4 percent).

Only the richest 1 percent and, to some extent, the next tenth, have been the principal recipients in the last two decades of rising income and wealth; the top 1 percent alone received 80 percent of it, the next 10 percent most of the remainder. In 1999, the average CEO compensation in large corporations (salary, bonuses, stock options, and other perquisites) is $12.4 million, earning more than five hundred times the workers' median of $24,000 (in 1974, thirty-four to one), as opposed to a twenty to one ratio in German and sixteen to one in Japan.

With much higher salaries and the spectacular increases in stock prices in the 1990s, the top 5 percent of households (they have a lower propensity to consume with a correspondingly higher one to save) have increased their wealth/income considerably; in 1981 they have 15.6 percent of national income; in 1996, 21.4 percent, as the income differential between them and the poorest fifth increased from eleven to one in 1975 to nineteen to one in 1996. The estimated wealth of the Forbes 400 (the 400 richest households in America, 170 being billionaires) rose from $477 billion in 1996 to a trillion dollars in 1999.

The economic and social power of the top half of the wealthiest top 1 percent is a wonder to behold. G. William Domhoff in *Who Rules America Now?* examined this privileged elite, well aware of its wealth, power and social prestige through social indicators, like Registers or Blue Books, the most prestigious being the Social Register, exclusive boarding schools and social/country clubs, especially in the larger cities and elite universities. It was from this upper-class and social layers just beneath it that its top ranks were mostly recruited from. About half of the upper-class intermarried with others, obviously of lower status, but usually not much. Not surprisingly, the typical occupations of this business elite were heavily skewed to business, finance, and corporate law.

The apex of this elite was composed of the wealthiest fortunes, CEOs, and other prominent figures of the leading corporations in banking, insurance, manufacturing, media/entertainment, and those of the political, healthcare, educational, military, and religious complexes. According to the capitalist bible, *Forbes* magazine, the wealthiest 400 individuals alone were grouped into 82 families; in the early 1980s, they owned about $166 billion in corporate assets. To have basic control of a large corporation, any single person/group having only 5 percent of the stock is in good position to do so. But the 400 alone possessed stock of at least 15 percent of corporate capital worth $2.2 trillion. The stock of the 400 and their ancillaries was tied to interlocking ownership/directorship of large banks and insurance companies that administer about half the stocks and bond. The leading 21 of them (BankAmerica, Bankers Trust, Chase Manhattan, Citicorp, Morgan Guaranty, Prudential, Metropolitan, and Equitable Life, among others) had substantial shares with each other, but also with the other largest 122 corporations and their 2,259 subsidiaries. But let us broaden this list to include the Fortune 500 or the top 500 corporations. The several thousand or so leaders of these corporations – CEOs and members of the boards of directors, many sitting on two or more corporate board, of prominent people in business, former military, political, and other figures, linking business elites to others – controlled the basic economic decision-making power of the nation, indicating the preeminence of business among the interlocking pyramids of power.

In this panoply of power, successful stars in one area transferred their charisma to others. For instance, the actor Reagan, with the aid of General Electric and other corporations, became governor of California before becoming President. The billionaire Ross Perot was a perennial Presidential aspirant, as was Steve Forbes, the heir to *Forbes* magazine, and Pat Buchanan, the television personality/ commentator.

Underneath the richer classes is the lower-middle class from a fifth to a fourth of the people, primarily in the mass professions (teachers, nurses, engineers, computer specialists, lower management) and small business.

The top two classes are almost exclusively composed of mental labor, as is half of the lower- middle class. (A fourth of adults over age 24 in 2000 are college graduates who are divided into two broad groups of mental labor or Rifkin's "knowledge class," a fifth in the higher category including scientific researchers, graduate-school graduates, physicians, lawyers, and so forth), four-fifths in the lower one of the mass professions. The remainder of the class chain is composed of the working class, about two-third of the total, many of whom call themselves "middle-class," reflecting the social dynamics of a conservative society. It principally includes skilled, semiskilled and unskilled workers, many formerly unemployed workers now self-employed and usually economically marginal, the unemployed in general, welfare recipients, and most prison inmates. An increasing part of this class is now composed of clerical, retail/wholesale, service, and transportation workers.

The deepening wealth polarity may also be expressed in the following median net worth of families in dollars adjusted for inflation in 1989 and 1998 respectively: under age thirty-five, 9,900 and 9,000, down 9 percent; age thirty-five to forty-four, 71,800 and 63,400, down 12 percent; age forty-five to fifty-four, 125,700 and 105,500, down 16 percent. In ethnic terms in 1995 for median family wealth in dollars: 61,000 for whites, 7,400 for blacks, and 5,000 for Hispanics.

Two sets of percentage in income are now presented for population quintiles from lowest to highest for 1967 and 1996, respectively – 5, 10, 17, 24, 44; 4, 9, 15, 24, 49. Changes in after-tax family income from lowest to highest population quintiles from 1977 to 1999 are: minus 9, plus 1, plus 8, plus 14, and plus 43. The slight gains noted for the third and fourth quintiles are a result of a longer workweek and of more women entering the work force, as real median wages have declined 10 percent from 1973 to 2000. In comparison with other nations in after-tax income inequality between the lowest and highest population quintiles, the United States has double that of France and Germany and triple that of Japan.

In viewing this class model, the upper working class, skilled and union workers, is losing ground to mental labor lodged in the mass professions. Indeed, universal primary and secondary education and now mass college education, related to rapid technological change and desire for upward social mobility, (formal education makes up a large percentage of an individual's life in the First World) are major factors in reducing the socioeconomic distance among various forms of labor, many combining manual and mental labor, making labor ever more interchangeable. In the U.S., for instance, four-fifths of adults finish high school, a sixth have some college, a fourteenth have a two-year college degree, and a fourth are college graduates.

Thus it is that many workers are now overeducated with respect to their jobs and can rather easily learn others. As the gap between the general education level and work performed widens, itself related to capitalism's tendency to at once demand more skilled workers, but to also lessen skills and cheapen them through new technologies, there is more dissatisfaction among the more educated working and lower middle classes with the status quo.

A recent examination of relative lower salaries recently, related to the developments just discussed, follows. It is now estimated that 11 college million graduates work below their levels of skills and thus loss of salary. In colleges/universities, for instance, two-fifths of the faculty are part-timers, while in two-year colleges, about two-thirds are. Furthermore, there is an excess of graduates in science, more than a fifth, again diminishing their earnings. Yet another example involves physicians whose professional independence and loss in salary has resulted from the rise of HMOs, prompting the American Medical Association in 1999 to approve unionization.

These developments should be related to the cardinal fact that in economically advanced nations (all capitalist), the wage/salary segment of the workforce is now very high; for instance, nine-tenths in the United States, four-fifths in Great Britain and Germany, and three-quarters in France. This condition is related to the decline of small independent farmers, shopkeepers, and artisans brought by the new technologies/economics-of-scale combination and reduction of the traditionally large and concentrated industrial workforce in the economically advanced nations, now less than a fourth in the U.S., although still three-eighths in Germany; but it is rising in the newly industrializing nations like China and India. This has obviously meant the rise of the service sector, compromising three-fourths of the work force in the United States and two-thirds in Western Europe.

These occurrences in the short run have negatively impacted on organized labor in the economically advanced nations. Thus it is that today the unionized labor force is only two-fifths of the Italian, a third of the British, three-tenths of the German, a seventh of the American, and a tenth of the French. Indeed, in the U.S., lack of unionization among workers has widened the income gap between college and high school graduates from 30 percent in the 1970s to 80 percent in 2000. This happens despite the fact that large sectors of college-educated workers, like teachers, registered nurses, and males between the age of 45 and 54, have seen their earnings drop for the first two by 3.1 percent and the third by 10 percent from 1987 to 1991. In the meantime, hundreds of thousands of skilled foreign workers have been hired for limited periods by high-tech firms to cheapen the labor of native workers. Retraining of older workers and others would be an alternative to this practice, but would diminish profits.

As for the need of more skilled workers, only 5 percent of American corporations claim it.[1]

From an overall perspective, why is the American working class still in a conservative mode? After all, the two major American political parties, the Republicans and Democrats, are basically conservative, espousing the glories of an individualistic/bourgeois ethic? To explain this, the insights of Marx and others observed in this chapter offer valid explanations. But in following Marx, the class struggle in an advanced technological setting is intensifying, this despite racism and continuance of large-scale immigration which continually divide the working class. The left half of the Democratic Party may be seen as partially social democratic, while the Greens are certainly so.

Notes

A) Marx's and Engels' 19th-Century Working Class

1) On industrialization, see Tom Kemp, *Historical Patterns of Industrialization* (New York: Longman, 1978); W.W. Rostow, *The Stages of Economic Growth: A Non-Communist Manifesto* (Cambridge: At The Univ. Press, 1960). *Capital*, I, 368-556. C. Wright Mills, *White Collar: The American Middle Class* (New York: Oxford University Press, *1956)*, p. 16 has "three-quarters of the American work force engaged in agriculture in 1820," by 1880 one-half. In 1990 about two percent of the work force is in agriculture. Michael Maccoby, *The Gamesman: The New Corporate Leaders* (New York: Simon and Schuster, 1976), p. 88 for the 1950 and 1970 figures.

2) Engels, *Condition of the Working Class*, pp. 30-87 has much on slum life and poor housing; p. 85 on diet, p. 144 on prostitution, p. 145 on disintegration of working-class family life because of poverty and many hours of work; pp. 104 ff. on the super-exploited Irish; pp. 111 ff. on poor food and general environment,

including pollution of air and water, resulting in much illness and death among the working class; pp. 240-73 on Chartism.

3) *Capital*, I, 255-330.

4) Ibid., pp. 506-08 and 527.

5) Ibid., pp. 706 and 718-21.

6) Ibid., pp. 723-28.

7) Ibid., pp. 432-34.

8) Ibid., pp. 488 and 320.

9) Ibid., pp. 270-71 and 322.

10) Ibid., pp. 608 and 700 on wages; pp. 513 and 528-29 on education.

11) On the horrid life conditions (work, food, housing, high death rates, and so forth) of the various working classes in the 19th century – we have already examined Engels' and Marx's contributions on this – see: Thompson, *Making of the English Working Class*, pp. 189-349. Georges Duveau, *La Vie ouvrière en France sous le Second Empire* (Paris: Gallimard, 1946), pp. 323 ff. On wages and a 12-hour working day. Louis Chevalier, *Laboring Classes and Dangerous Classes: In Paris During the First Half of the Nineteenth Century* (New York: Howard Fertig, 1973), p. 97 and 278 ff. on *la misère*. On Europe in general, see especially William L. Langer, *Political and Social Upheaval, 1832-1852.* (New York: Harper and Row, 1969), pp. 181-213, "The Social Question." In general, for the first half of the 19th century, most workers toil at least 12-hours per day, although 15-hour days are not uncommon; Sunday at times is a day of rest. For the U.S., see Robert Bremner, *The Discovery of Poverty in the United States* (New Brunswick, NJ: Transaction Publishers, 1992). On hours of work: Gordon Wright, *France in Modern Times: 1760 to the Present* (Chicago: Rand McNally, 1960), p. 217. Duveau, *La Vie ouvrière*, pp. 233-35.

12) W.O. Henderson, *The Industrialization of Europe, 1790-1914* (New York: Harcourt, Brace, and World, 1969), pp. 123-24.

13) Upton Sinclair, *The Jungle* (New York: Doubleday, Page and Co., 1906), pp. 152-56 on horrific factory conditions.

14) *Capital,* I, 270-01.

15) Real Wages: On Great Britain, see G.D.H. Cole, *A Short History of the British Working- Class Movement, 1789-1947* (London: George Allen and Unwin, 1948), pp. 269 ff.; from 1845 to 1870 wages scarcely rose, p. 18. France: Wright, *France*, p. 217. Duveau, *La Vie ouvrière*, pp. 323 ff. On the U.S., see Puth, *American Economic History*, p. 296. Stearns, *European Society*, p. 170 states that real wages rose by a third in Britain between 1850 and 1875, and by thirty percent in France and Germany between 1870 and 1900. Langer, *Political and Social Upheaval*, p. 183. Georges Weill, *Histoire du Movement Social en France*, 1852-1902 (Paris: Felix Alcan, 1904), pp. 116-17. For England, Langer, *Political and Social Upheaval*, p. 188, states that a worker in the early 19th century could purchase much less food for his wages than he could in the year 1500. In 1500 the per capita meat consumption in Germany was about 200 pounds per year; in the early 19th century in Germany and England, it was thirty-five to forty pounds; *Capital*, I, 845-47, was aware that the American standard of life was above European levels, free land was the reason. Furthermore, Marx stated that only in North America (U.S. and Canada) and a few other colonies which have free land do wages exceed "bare subsistence."

16) On the appalling housing conditions in the 1860s in Britain, see *Capital*, I, 723-27; Frederick Engels, *The Conditions of the Working-Class in England in 1844* (London: George Allen and Unwin, 1952), pp. 23-74. On pp. 25-74. On pp. 25-28 he describes the horrid housing facilities of London workers – most lived in one-room apartments. On the lack of sanitary facilities in proletarian areas, see ibid., p. 97, where Engels describes the stench pervading the large cities. In Paris, poor housing and lack of sanitary facilities are detailed by Chevalier, *Laboring Classes*, pp. 195 ff for the first; pp. 203 ff for the second. Langer, *Political and Social Upheaval*, pp. 190-91, has workers living in one-room apartments; often several families would live in a single room.

17) Chevalier, *Laboring Classes*, pp. 332 ff. on Paris' unsafe water and disproportionately higher infant mortality rate in proletarian areas.

18) Wright, *France in Modern Times*; p. 217 on the poor physiques of working-class youth.

19) *Capital*, I, 693.

20) Ibid., p. 699.

21) Puth, *American Economic History*, 297; Hobson, *Problems of Poverty*, p. 5 has twelve percent of the British workers unemployed in 1887. Langer *Political and Social Upheaval*, p. 187, states that despite inadequate statistics on unemployment in the first half of the 19th century, "it was extensive."

22) On pauperism, see *Capital*, I, 717; Langer, *Political and Social Upheaval*, p. 187; on the "brink of starvation" statistics, see. P. 182.

23) On illegitimate children and infanticide, see Chevalier, *Laboring Classes*, Langer, *Political and Social Upheaval*, p. 196.

24) On child and woman labor, *Capital*, I, 506 ff. Langer, *Political and Social Upheaval*, pp. 185-86.

25) On poverty leading to crime, see Langer, *Political and Social Upheaval*, p. 194, pp. 275 ff; Chevalier, *Laboring Classes*, pp. 275 ff., for example; *Capital*, I, 530-31, on unemployed children becoming criminals.

26) On prostitution, see Langer, *Political and Social Upheaval*, p. 195. Philip Lee Ralph et al., *World Civilizations*, 8th ed. (New York: W.W. Norton, 1991), II, 262. Marx and Engels are certainly aware of the lowly position of working-class women; Karl Marx and Frederick Engels, *Manifesto of the Communist Party* (New York: International Publishers, 1948), pp. 26-28. Frederick Engels, *The Origin of the Family, Private Property and the State* (Chicago: Charles H. Kerr, 1902), pp. 89-90 and p. 196. On p. 89: "The modern monogamous family is founded on the open or disguised domestic slavery of women..." A recent work which intersects feminism with socialism is by Ann Ferguson. *Sexual Democracy, Women, Oppression, and Revolution* (Boulder,

Colorado: Westview Press, 1991), pp. 162-204 being especially important.

27) On working-class male domination over their women, including statistics on alcohol and tobacco, see Nicky Hart, "Gender and the Rise of Class Politics," *New Left Review*, No. 175, May/June, 1987, pp. 21-47.

28) On education and workers in the 19th century, see, for instance, Duveau, *La Vie ouvrière,* pp. 449 ff; Mills, *White Collar,* pp. 72 ff. 265 ff. Wright, *France*, pp. 218-19. J. Salwyn Schapiro, *Modern and Contemporary European History (1815-1952)* (Cambridge: Riverside Press, 1953), pp. 133-34.

29) Robert H. Bremner, *From the Depths: The Discovery of Poverty in the United States* (New York: New York University Press, 1956), p. 83 and p. 153.

30) Duveau, *La Vie ouvrière*, pp. 231-35 on the *livret.*

31) *Capital*, I, 464. R.H. Tawney, *Equality* (London: George Allen and Unwin, 1931), p. 37.

32) Karl Marx, *Theories of Surplus Value*, Part I, Vol. IV of *Capital* (Moscow: Foreign Languages Publishing House, n.d.), p. 195. *Capital*, I, 488, on fifteen percent of the workers being servants.

33) Thorstein Veblen, *The Theory of the Leisure Class: An Economic Study of Institutions,* intro. C. Wright Mills (New York: Mentor Books, 1957), see. pp. 80-87, "The Pecuniary Standard of Living."

34) Barbara Tuchman, *The Proud Tower: A Portrait of the World Before the War: 1880-1914* (New York: Macmillan Co., 1966), pp. 26 ff.

35) T.B. Bottomore, *Classes in Modern Society* (New York: Pantheon Books, 1966), p. 38. Arthur S. Link: *A History of the United States since the 1890's* (New York: Alfred A. Knopf, 1958), p. 23.

36) On labor unions, see David Caute, *The Left in Europe since 1789* (New York: World University Library, 1966), pp. 136-52.

37) Wright, *France*, p. 144, after the 1830 Revolution the male voters increased from 90,000 to 170,000.

38) This survey can be easily followed by reading standard works in European and American history. I recommend an old

favorite – Schapiro, *Modern and Contemporary European History (1815-1952)*. A recent favorite is by Eugene Weber, *A Modern History of European: Men, Cultures and Societies from the Renaissance to the Present* (New York: W. W. Norton, 1971). On American History, I particularly favor Burner, Genovese, McDonald, *The American People*.

39) Chevalier, *Laboring Classes*, pp. 373-93, for instance.

B) Marx's Views of Class

1) Lichtheim, *Origins of Socialism*, pp. 35-39.
2) On Marx's discovery of the universality of the class struggle in historical progression as noted in the letter, see Saul K. Padover, ed., *On Revolution: Karl Marx*, trans. by editor (New York: McGraw-Hill, 1971), pp. 133-35.
3) *Capital*, III, 1031-32.
4) On class and class alignments, indicating the inordinate power of the French bourgeoisie and nobility vis-à-vis the peasantry and proletariat, in which the social outlook of the peasantry (one of small property, poverty and isolation) allowed Louis Napoleon to gain power, see Karl Marx, *The Eighteenth Brumaire of Louis Bonaparte* trans. from German by Eden and Cedar Paul (New York: International Publishers, 1926), pp. 54-60, pp. 72-84, pp. 128 ff. Karl Marx, *The Class Struggles in France (1848-1850)*, intro by Frederick Engels (New York: International Publishers, 1964), pp. 36ff. on various groups and classes – he mentions nine. Henri Lefebvre, *The Sociology of Marx* (New York: Pantheon Books, 1968); Bober, *Marx*, 112; Shlomo Avineri, *The Social and Political Thought of Karl Marx* (Cambridge: At the University Press, 1971), pp. 17-64; Allen W. Wood, *Karl Marx* (London: Routledge and Kegan Paul, 1981), pp. 82-100. *Manifesto*, pp. 16-20; David McClellan, *The Thought of Karl Marx: An Introduction* (London: MacMillan, 1971), pp. 152-66 entitled "Class."
5) On class struggle between proletariat and bourgeoisie, the single best example in a general way is Marx and Engels' *Manifesto*, p.

19. Also, *Capital,* I, 363. More capital results in more workers; *Manifesto,* p. 15; *Capital,* I, 673. On increasing and relative misery of the proletariat, see ibid., pp. 707-17; Karl Marx, *Wage-Labour and Capital,* intro. by Frederick Engels (New York: International Publishers, 1933), p. 39 and p. 47. On Marx and alienation, see Bertell Ollman, *Alienation: Marx's Conception of Man in Capitalist Society* (Cambridge: Cambridge University Press, 1976), pp. 131-233; Erich Fromm, Marx's *Concept of Man* with a trans. of Marx's *Economic and Philosophical Manuscripts* by T.B. Bottomore (New York: Fredrick Ungar, 1966); and, Istvan Meszaros, *Marx's Theory of Alienation* (London: Merlin Press, 1970), pp. 123-89, for example. On the contradictions within capitalism that precipitate economic crises, see *Grundrisse,* pp. 745-50; *Capital,* I, 495ff., and 681ff.; *Capital,* III, 211-66 that is titled "The Law of the Tendency of the Rate of Profit to Fall"; and Paul M. Sweezy, *The Theory of Capitalist Development: Principals of Marxian Political Economy* (New York: Monthly Review Press, 1956), pp. 190-236.

6) *Manifesto,* p. 17; *Capital,* I, 685-89. On the difficulty of forging working-class unity, see Karl Marx and Frederick Engels, *The German Ideology,* Parts I and III (New York: International Publishers, 1947), p. 58, for example, in which at times workers are more hostile to one another than the bourgeoisie are to one another; Marx and Engels, *Manifesto,* p. 18 and p. 21.

7) On working-class misery, see *Capital,* I, 688-733; and Frederick Engels, *The Condition of the Working Class in England in 1844* (Oxford: B. Blackwell, 1968) – this is a pioneer work. *Capital,* I, 463 on workers being at the bottom of the labor-division hierarchy.

8) On capitalist cultural hegemony, see Marx and Engels, *German Ideology,* pp. 39-40; also see Ollman, *Alienation,* pp. 227-33 entitled "Marx's Critique of Bourgeois Ideology," in which the concepts of ideology and alienation are interwoven. On Marx's letter, see Karl Marx and Frederick Engels, *On Colonialism: Articles from the "New York Tribune" and Other Writings* (New York: International Publishers, 1972), pp. 336-38.

9) *Capital*, I, 41-221, 643ff.; *Grundrisse*, pp. 239-240ff. George Lichtheim, *Marxism: An Historical and Critical Study* (New York: Frederick A. Praeger, 1962), pp. 162-84. Jerrold Seigel, *Marx's Fate: The Shape of a Life* (Princeton, N.J.: Princeton University Press, 1978), pp. 293-336. *Grundrisse*, pp. 239ff. *Capital*, I, 41-221, 634ff. On p. 641, ibid.: The capitalist extracts "a surplus-value over and above the value of the advanced capital. This surplus-value has cost the labourer his/her labor but the capitalist nothing." *Capital*, III, 353, for example, on productive and non-productive labor.

10) Marx, *Class Struggles in France*, in which he mentions nine social groups which form five classes; the nobility that he divides into the Bourbons and Orleanists; the bourgeoisie that he divides into the financial, industrial, mercantile, and petty bourgeoisie; the peasantry; the workers, and the lumpenproletariat, workers who have become criminals. P. Noyes, *Organization and Revolution* (Princeton, NJ: Princeton Univ. Press, 1966), pp. 15ff. on the fact that only four percent of the German males in the eighteen-forties worked in factories. Carol Owen, *Social Stratification* (London: Routledge and Kegan, Paul, 1968), p. 87 has seventy-seven percent of the 1867 English work force in the proletariat.

11) *Capital*, I, 221.

12) On the rise of the new salaried petty bourgeoisie, see Ralf Dahrendorf, *Class and Class Conflict in Industrial Society* (Palo Alto Calif.; Stanford Univ. Press, 1959), pp. 52ff. Harry Braveman, *Labor and Monopoly Capital: The Degradation of Work in the Twentieth Century* (New York: Monthly Review Press, 1974), pp. 293ff. asserts that clerks in the middle of the last century were part of management, and that as late as 1900 were less than five percent of the American and British work force.

13) *Capital*, I, 221.

14) *Capital*, III, 353-55.

15) *Capital*, I, 487-88. Marx, *Grundrise*, pp. 689-712 on the importance of science to expand technology, where machines replace workers.

16) *Capital*, I, 530-35.
17) Ibid., p. 534.

C) Socialist Debates on Class

1) On debates within socialism on class boundaries/class struggle before World War I, see Peter Gay, *The Dilemma of Democratic Socialism: Edward Bernstein's Challenge to Marx* (New York: Collier Books, 1962), pp. 204-19. Also, see Marx, *Eighteenth Brumaire of Louis Bonaparte,* p. 33.
2) C. Wright Mills, *White Collar: The American Middle Classes* (New York: Oxford Univ. Press, 1951: Galaxy Book Edition, 1962), pp. 1-12. Tom Bottomore, *Marxist Sociology* (New York: Holmes and Meir, 1975), p. 12 takes note of Marx's influence on Mills regarding "classes and elite."
3) Mills, *White Collar*, pp. 63-64.
4) Ibid., p. 67.
5) Ibid., pp. 73-74.
6) Ibid., p. 297.
7) Dahrendorf, *Class and Conflict*, pp. 140-141.
8) Ibid., pp. 156-57ff.
9) Ibid., pp. 77-92 and 141ff. On (1) and (2) respectively.
10) Gabriel Kolko, *Wealth and Power in America: An Analysis of Social Class and Income Distribution* (New York: Frederic A. Praeger, 1962), pp. 67-68. William Domhoff, *Who Rules America? Power and Politics in the Year 2000*, 3rd ed. (Mountain View, CA: Mayfield, 1998), pp. 105-15.
11) Karl Marx, *The Civil War in France*, intro. Frederick Engels (New York: International Publishers, 1933), pp. 40-42.
12) V.I. Lenin, *State and Revolution* (New York: International Publishers, 1932), pp. 33-34.
13) George Lichtheim, *Europe in the Twentieth Century* (New York: Praeger, 1972), p. 142.
14) Donald C. Hodges, *The Bureaucratization of Socialism* (Amherst, Mass: University of Mass. Press, 1981), pp. 101ff. Although Soviet

income differentials have been narrowing since 1956, they are still significant – see Murray Yanowitch, "The Soviet Income Revolution," in Celia S. Heller (ed.), *Structured Social Inequality* (New York: Macmillan, 1969).

15) Dahrendorf, *Class and Class Conflict*, p. 113.

16) Ibid., pp. 129-36.

17) Ibid., p. 52.

18) Ibid., pp. 55-57.

19) Ibid., p. 56.

20) Ibid., pp. 50-51.

21) Ibid., pp. 57-59.

22) See Seymour Martin Lipset and Reinhard Bendix, *Social Mobility in Industrial Society* (Berkeley; Univ. of California Press, 1959), pp. 11-75 on "Social Mobility in Industrial Societies." In the US, for example, thirty-three percent of sons with a manual worker father moved to a non-manual occupation, while of those whose father was a non-manual worker twenty- six percent moved downward to the manual worker category. If one subtracts the downward mobility from the upward one, the latter's increase is slight, T.B. Bottomore, *Classes in Modern Society* (New York: Pantheon Books, 1966), pp. 43-44 saw economic development leading to less manual labor. Also, he noted that "most social mobility takes place between social levels which are close together." Concerning intergenerational social mobility, Lipset and Bendix, *Social Mobility*, p. 165 stressed its insignificance.

23) Dahrendorf, *Class and Class Conflict*, p. 204.

24) Ibid., p. 66.

25) Ibid., p. 210.

26) Ibid., p. 66.

27) Ibid., pp. 271-74.

28) Ibid., p. 275.

29) Ibid., pp. 272-73.

30) Nicos Poulantzas, *Classes in Contemporary Capitalism*, trans. David Fernbach (London: NLB, 1979), p. 14 on the various quotations.

31) Ibid., pp. 195-96.

32) Saul K. Padover, *Karl Marx: An Intimate Biography* (New York: McGraw-Hill, 1978), p. 260 contains the "Demands of the Communist Party in Germany" (March 1848) whose appeal was to the workers, peasants and petty-bourgeoisie.

33) Dahrendorf, *Class and Class Conflict*, p. 284 for the quotations.

34) Poulantzas, *Classes,* p. 14 for the various quotations.

35) Ibid., p. 15.

36) Ibid., p. 210ff., and p. 301; the long quotations is on p. 216.

37) Erik Olin Wright, *Class, Crisis, and the State* (London: NLB, 1978), pp. 53-61.

38) Poulantzas, *Classes,* pp. 193-94ff. and p. 301.

39) Ibid., p. 18, pp. 175-89, and p. 229.

40) Ibid., pp. 175-89, and p. 229.

41) Marx, *Capital*, III, 207-80 and 282.

42) Ibid., p. 294.

43) Ibid., p. 300. For footnotes 7 through 9, see Poulantzas, *Classes*, pp. 210-15.

44) Karl Marx, *Theories of Surplus-Value* (Vol. IV of *Capital*), Part I (Moscow: Foreign Languages Publishing House, 1963), pp. 195-96.

45) Marx, *Capital*, III, 300-01 for quotations.

46) Poulantzas, *Classes*, pp. 226-27.

47) Ibid., p. 228ff.

48) Marx and Engels, *Communist Manifesto*, p. 16. For a very similar passage, see Marx, *Capital*, I, 364.

49) Poulantzas, *Classes*, p. 226, for example.

50) Ibid., pp. 233-41.

51) Ibid., p. 237 and pp. 252-54 on Gramsci.

52) Ibid., p. 258 on the three quotations.

53) Ibid., pp. 261-62.

54) Ibid., p. 246 on earnings.

55) Marx, *Capital*, I, 558.

56) Marx, *Theories of Surplus-Value*, Part I, pp. 153-54.

57) Padover, *On Revolution*, in which Marx's *Critique of the Gotha Program* is on pp. 488-509. The material alluded to is on pp. 495-96.

58) Poulantzas, *Classes*, p. 256.

59) Ibid., p. 257.

60) Ibid., p. 301.

61) Ibid., p 309ff. on the three factors.

62) Ibid., pp. 316-26.

63) Ibid., pp. 334-35.

64) Braverman, *Labor and Monopoly Capitalism*, pp. 3ff.

65) Ibid.

66) Ibid., pp. 172. *Major Themes of the Work.*

67) Ibid., pp. 85ff. And 173ff.

68) Ibid., p. 242.

69) Ibid., p. 379.

70) Ibid., pp. 44-49.

71) Ibid., p. 423 and pp. 315ff.

72) Ibid., p. 379. Marx and Engels, *Communist Manifesto*, pp. 17-18 state that "machinery obliterates all distinctions of labor and nearly reduces wages to the same low level."

73) Braverman, *Labor and Monopoly Capitalism*, pp. 296-97 and pp. 368-69.

74) Ibid., pp. 295-97.

75) Ibid., pp. 298ff. and pp. 349ff.

76) Ibid., pp. 403-09.

77) Ibid., p. 408.

78) Bowen, *Academe*, Feb. 1980, pp. 8-18.

79) Howard Hawkins, The Potential of the Green Movement," *New Politics*, Summer 1988, p. 89.

80) Erik Olin Wright, *Class, Crisis and the State* (London: NLB, 1979), p.74ff.

81) Ibid., p. 54 and pp. 96-97; also see the class chart on p. 84.

82) Ibid., pp. 79-80.

83) Ibid., pp. 84-85 and p. 95.

84) Ibid., p. 97.

85) Ibid., pp. 74-87.

86) Ibid., p. 49.

87) Ibid., pp. 46-47, Marx, *Capital*, I, 558.

88) Wright, *Classes*, p. 53.

89) Ibid., pp. 51-52ff.

90) Ibid., p. 74ff.

91) Ibid., p. 55. For the percentage of blue-collar workers in the U.S., see Bruce Bartlett, "False Images and Political Bias," *The New York Times*, June 12, 1983, F2, who states that of the U.S. gross national product, the share of manufacturing in 1960 was 45.6 percent, in 1981 it was 45.8 percent, while salary and wage workers in this area as percentage of the new active work force fell correspondingly during this time from 31 percent to 21 percent.

92) Wright, *Classes*, pp. 91.

D) Marcuse and Sartre

1) For a sympathetic study on Marcuse, see Robert W. Marks, *The Meaning of Marcuse* (New York: Ballantine Books, 1970). Herbert Marcuse, *Soviet Marxism: A Critical Analysis* (New York: Vintage Books, 1961) is a brilliant critique of Soviet society which hopes for the continued progress of Soviet society; see pp. 146-75, for instance. Herbert Marcuse, *Counterrevolution and Revolt* (Boston: Beacon Press, 1972), pp. 1-16. Herbert Marcuse, *Eros and Civilization: A Philosophical Inquiry into Freud* (New York: Vintage Books, 1955), pp. 138-43 on the fact that higher living standards do not necessarily make for a better society.

2) Herbert Marcuse, *One-Dimensional Man: Studies in the Ideology of Advanced Industrial Society* (Boston: Beacon Press, 1964), pp. 1-48.

3) Marcuse, *Counterrevolution*, pp. 32 ff.

4) Ibid., pp. 15 and 24 ff.

5) Ibid., p. 18.

6) Marcuse, *Eros and Civilization*, p. vii envisions automation to allow for "working time becoming marginal and free

time becoming full time." Herbert Marcuse, *Five Lectures, Psychoanalysis, Politics, and Utopia* (Boston: Beacon Press, 1970), p. 67 on cybernetics and computers. Herbert Marcuse, *An Essay on Liberation* (Boston: Beacon Press, 1969), p. 69 envisages "direct democracy," in which representatives may be immediately recalled, underpinned by "equal and universal education for autonomy."

7) Marcuse, *Counterrevolution*, p. 17.

8) Marcuse, *Five Lectures*, p. 79.

9) Marcuse, *One-Dimensional Man*, p. 4.

10) On Sartre, see, for instance, Hazel E. Barnes, *Sartre* (Philadelphia: J.B. Lippincott, 1973). Pietro Chiodi, *Sartre and Marxism* (Hassocks, Sussex: Harvester Press, 1976). Mark Poster, *Existential Marxism in Postwar France: From Sartre to Althusser* (Princeton: Princeton Univ. Press, 1975). Jean-Paul Sartre, *Raison de la raison dialectique* (Paris: Gallimard, 1960). For the English translation which I am using, see *Critique of Dialectical Reason*, trans. Alan Sheridan-Smith (London: NLB, 1976), p. 882.

11) Ibid., pp. 123, 131, and 148-49.

12) Ibid., p. 37.

13) Ibid., pp. 260-504 on various human ensembles/associations and their evolvement; pp. 576-633 on institutions; p. 608 on a "pledged group" evolving into an institution; p. 658, on "opposite of freedom"; pp. 642 ff. On the bureaucratic state and Nazi anti-Semitism; p. 650 on "other direction."

14) A key argument of ibid.

15) Ibid., pp. 638-40. Italics not mine in the quotation.

16) Ibid., pp. 699 and 781-94; p. 241 for "damned of the earth"; p. 235 on the long quotation; pp. 606 ff. On institutional inertia and "obligations."

17) Ibid., pp. 240 ff.

18) Ibid., pp. 351-404 and 687 ff.

19) Ibid., pp. 661-62.

E) Principal Bourgeois Thinkers and Class

1) On Sumner, see M.R. Davis, *William Graham Sumner: An Essay of Commentary and Selections* (New York: Crowell, 1963). On Pareto and Weber, see H. Stuart Hughes, *Consciousness and Society: The Reorientation of European Social Thought, 1890-1930* (New York: Alfred A. Knopf, 1961), chap. vii. On Pareto, see James H. Meisel, *Pareto and Mosca* (Englewood Cliffs, N.J.: Prentice Hall, 1965). On Weber, see W.J. Mommsen, *The Age of Bureaucracy: Perspectives on the Political Sociology of Max Weber* (New York: Harper and Row, 1974). On the ruling elite (combinations of nobility, capitalists, and religious leaders), see William Graham Sumner, *Folkways* (Boston: Ginn and Co., 1906), p. 64. Vilfredo Pareto, *Mind and Society,* ed. Arthur Livingstone: four vols. (New York: Harcourt, Brace, and Co., 1935, III, 1423-31. Max Weber, *Economy and Society: An Outline of Interpretive Sociology,* eds. Guenther Roth and Claus Wittich, three vols. (New York: Bedminster Press, 1968), II, 941-1003. For Pareto and Weber, bureaucrats have an ancillary role to governing elites. On class structure: Sumner, *Folkways*, p. 47. Pareto, *Mind and Society*, III, 1427. Weber, *Economy and Society*, I, 302-07 on "status groups and classes. On the class struggle: William Graham Sumner, *Earth-Hunger and Other Essays* (New Haven: Yale Univ. Press, 1913), p. 289. Pareto, *Mind and Society*, III, 1431 ff. Vilfredo Pareto, *Les Systèmes socialists* (2nd. ed.; two vols.; Paris: M. Giard, 1926), I, 16 ff., accepts the class struggle, tying it to the rise of revolutionary outsiders leading the masses. On the biological superiority of the wealthy elite, see Sumner, *Earth-Hunger,* pp. 351-52.

2) Robert Michaels, *Political Parties: A Sociological Study of the Oligarchical Tendencies of Modern Democracy* (New York: Collier Books, 1962), pp. 72, 117 ff., and 348-53.

F)

1) On statistics for class in the United States – many have already been presented – see Democratic Staff of the Joint Economic Committee, *The Concentration of Wealth in the United States* (Washington, DC: Joint Economic Committee, United States Congress, 1986), pp. 24-48. Lawrence Mishel, Jared Bernstein, John Schmitt, *The State of Working America* (Washington, DC: Economic Policy Institute), pp. 273-92. Keith Bradsher, "Gap in Wealth in U.S. Called Widest in West," *The New York Times*, April, 17, 1995, pp. A1 and C4; and Nicholas D. Kristoff, "Japan Is Torn Between Efficiency and Egalitarian Values," ibid., Oct. 26, 1998, pp. A1 and A10. On inheritance and wealth, see Doug Henwood, *Wall Street* (London: Verso, 1998), pp. 68-69. On the number of millionaires and so forth, see *The Economist*, May 30, 1998. On class, I favor the views of Mills, Braverman and Wright over those of Dahrendorf and Poulantzas. On Rifkin's "knowledge class," see Jeremy Rifkin, *The End of Work: The Decline of the Global Labor Force and the Dawn of the Post-Market Era* (New York: G.P. Putnam's Sons, 1995), pp. 174-77. On the myth that many more skilled workers are needed to service the new technologies, see Kim Moody, *New Left Review*, no. 216, March/April, 1996, pp. 110-12. On new technologies lowering the income of higher professionals, see Walter Russell Mead, "At Your Service: The New Global Economy Takes Your Order," *Mother Jones*, March/April, 1998, pp. 32 ff. And Robert Reich, "Working Class Dogged," ibid., p. 40. On recent statistics on wealth, also see articles by Holly Sklar, *Z Magazine*, July/August, 1999, pp. 63-66; March, 2000, pp. 37-41. On education, see Harry Brill, "More Graduates, Fewer Jobs," *Against the Current*, Sept./Oct., 1999, pp. 34-37. On rising income inequality between college and high school graduates, see *The New York Times*, Oct. 17, 2000, p. A23. G. William Domhoff, *Who Rules America Now: A View for the 80s* (New York: Touchstone Book, 1983), on the top half of one percent, see pp. 20 ff, 41-44 ff.

Chapter Eight: The Riddle of Human Nature

That Marx had a theory of a basic human nature, related to his theory of class struggle in which the proletariat battled the bourgeoisie to attain the good society, is indisputably true. Questions concerning human nature inevitably involved Marx's views on alienation or the individual's estrangement from himself/herself and others – but with consequences.

Human nature is related to human needs. In the course of human evolution, beginning with the Old Stone Age which stretched more than a million years, near-humans and humans forged a cooperative way of life to meet their basic needs (food, water, shelter, clothing, and sex). It was characterized by the rubric of "primitive communism," one of a general socioeconomic, cultural, and political equality in the form of participatory democracy, involving intense mutual aid for survival, including altruistic food sharing, and utterly devoid of war, itself a form of suicide as the margin for economic survival was small. That this way of life is related to a basic human nature and a primitive technology is axiomatic. The basic technology of most of the Old Stone Age was that of the hand ax necessitating that humans live in small bands, usually under a hundred people, to forage and hunt.

With the advent of the Neolithic Age and its Agricultural Revolution and subsequent development of early civilization, the egalitarian way of life of the preceding hundreds of thousands of years was shattered by class-oppressive societies ruled by small elites running administrative, military, and religious hierarchies, capped by a maximum leader like Pharaoh in Egypt with combined secular and religious powers.[1]

The intention now is to cover the nature of human nature arguments – such as individuals basically being good (cooperative and non-aggressive, favoring equality) or evil (uncooperative and aggressive, promoting inequality) – and note Marx's and others' views in this respect from the mid-19th century to the present.

The beginning point in this progression are the ideas of Charles Darwin (A.R. Wallace had similar contemporary views) who revolutionized the subject of evolution and its corollary of human nature in two seminal works, the *Origin of Species* (1859) and *The Descent of Man* (1871).

In theorizing about how human nature developed, Darwin's main postulate, largely inspired by Malthus' *An Essay on Population*, held that:

> Many more individuals of each species are born that can possibly survive…there is a frequently recurring struggle for existence…[which] follows that any being, if it vary slightly in any matter profitable to itself, under the complex and sometimes varying conditions of life, will have a better chance of surviving and thus be *naturally* selected. From the strong principle of inheritance, any selected variety will tend to propagate its new and modified form.[2]

Thus it was that this upper-middle class Englishman reaffirmed the bourgeois shibboleth that individual competition manifested in the economic arena was sanctioned by nature itself, replacing a theistic god as final arbiter.

In *The Descent of Man*, Darwin extolled the importance of "struggle for existence" for bringing humanity to its present high level of development, allowing "the more gifted men… [to] be more successful in the battle for life than the less gifted." In "open competition…the most able [men] should not be prevented by laws or customs from succeeding best and rearing the largest number of offspring." But, then, Darwin qualified this line of thought:

> Important as the struggle for existence has been and even still is, yet as far as the highest part of man's nature is concerned there are other agencies more

important. For the moral qualities are advanced either
directly or indirectly, much more through the effects
of habit, the reasoning powers, instruction, religion,
and the like, than through natural selection; though
to the latter agency may be safely attributed the social
instincts which afforded the basis for the development
of the moral sense.[3]

This "moral sense" or "conscience," for him, was an integral part
of humanity's "well- marked social instincts," like "parental and filial
affections," which included being "in the society of [one's] fellows,"
and having "a certain amount of sympathy with them, and to perform
various services for them." This "sociability" was not only evident
among humans, but also among animals. Indeed, sociability and
accompanying sympathy were "increased through natural selection"
and "those communities which included the greatest number of the
most sympathetic members, would flourish best and rear the greatest
number of offspring."[4]

There is a deep ambivalence in Darwin on competition as against
cooperation among humans, which reflects the socioeconomic
contours of bourgeois society. The bourgeois model is one of intense
mutual aid in the family and among other intimates as opposed
to a lesser one for the general community. Thus, Darwin rejected
legislation to aid indigents and to permit birth control on the grounds
that they subverted natural selection. Furthermore, he was a typical
19th century racist in affirming that the "biologically inferior races"
would soon be eliminated.[5]

Darwin's biological/social/political perspective was continued
by two of his principal disciples, Spencer in Britain and Sumner in
the United States. One of the founders of sociology, the conservative
Spencer followed a view of human nature similar to Darwin's. It
maintained that, yes, humans possessed such good qualities as
curiosity, taking care of the young, and liking work, but that in
the present, they were basically proper only to buttress competing
families, not pity the economically unsuccessful, i.e. the working

class, the unfit and deficient in Darwinian natural selection. Thus, there is the paradox of "good" human qualities co-existing alongside selfish ones, like economic competitiveness to weed out the unfit, a prerequisite for human progress.[6]

Spencer reinforced this outlook by also being a disciple of Jean-Baptise de Lamrack, a French naturalist preceding Darwin, whose theory of "acquired characteristics" affirmed that offspring inherit the good and bad qualities of parents. In this model, biological fitness, including intelligence, became the decisive factor for success/goodness in a bourgeois-dominated competitive society, in which the poor/unfit were progressively eliminated, the wealthier groups becoming the majority. Thus, through the aegis of biological/economic forces, altruism, in the end, prevailed in some form of socialism, which magically overcame the Marxian law that capitalism, left to its own devices, inexorably led to ever increasing concentration of capital and ever deeper class polarity. This is the end-justifying-the-means Spenserian model.[7]

The Darwinian-based laissez-faire economics of Spencer decreed an end to all trade unions and any social legislation to aid the working class, fearing, for instance, that working-class combination contravened natural law in asking for higher wages and allowing union leaders to abrogate individual rights of workers. (But business trusts were permitted on the basis of survival of the fittest.)[8] He also precluded any state assistance/action to set minimum-age requirements for employment, inspect and regulate working conditions in factories, provide workers with unemployment insurance, initiate compulsory vaccination programs and establish compulsory and publicly-financed primary education and accompanying academic standards, but conceded private charity to aid the poor.[9] He even would deny public regulation of city "drainage systems" on the grounds that government normally bungled any economic undertaking.[10] In fact, for him, any state legislation was an attack on "voluntary cooperating." [11] Not surprisingly, he hoped that the Tory-dominated Liberty and Defense League whose shibboleth was "Individualism versus Socialism" would reverse increasing state interference in the socioeconomic realm.[12]

Although a fierce economic individualist who believed in the necessity of individual antagonistic relations, Spencer would also readily admit to the social categories of class and class struggle. For instance, "barbarous and civilized communities alike are characterized by separation into classes, as well as by separation of each class into more and less important units." And he unflinchingly accepted the resultant class struggle emanating from class differences: "So long as men are constituted to act on one another, either by physical force or by force of character, the struggles for supremacy must finally be decided in favor of some class or someone."[13] In this class progression, he considered the bourgeoisie as more genetically fit than the workers and those employed more so than the unemployed.[14] To be sure, the views of Darwin and Spencer on the genetic superiority of the bourgeoisie over workers were the prevailing ones among the bourgeoisie in the 19th century.[15]

That conservative American bourgeois academics in the second half of the 19th century and later would reflect the mindset of the Darwin/Spencer team is axiomatic, their leader Sumner, the brilliant son of an immigrant English worker. After Sumner graduated from Yale to become an Episcopalian minister, Spencer's unknowable God replaced his theism, prompting his leaving the ministry and returning to Yale as a professor of economics and sociology to expound the Spenserian creed.[16]

To be sure, Sumner was not a consistent conservative: He went awry when he opposed American imperialism in the Spanish-American War on the grounds that it was inimical to democracy and defended labor unions and their right to strike and boycott goods to test the market, a collectivistic aberration. But, apart from these follies, he followed the Spenserian track.[17]

Like Spencer, in the name of the iron law of Lamarckian/Darwinian genetics, Sumner pictured a mercilessly competitive world of self-interest and vanity outside the individual's immediate circle. Government here was not to be involved as an arbiter among different socioeconomic classes or in developing social programs to aid the poor, any attempt to do so being useless, and simply wasting monies on them.   The class progression in Sumner's social diagram, based on different levels of intelligence and competence, was of a tripartite nature: at the apex were the wealthy few, with the "genius and talent" to attain this lofty position, followed by the "masses" or "middle class," the majority of the populace, described as "mediocrities," and finally, the dregs/defectives of society, the unskilled workers and illiterates, usually in a state of criminality and dependency; there were no deserving poor. But it is comforting to note that the bottom group was now only made up of a minority of the people.[18]

The social Darwinism of Sumner also readily perceived the reality of classes and class conflict, both ultimately related to individual conflict. Thus, for him, since democracy permitted the "many and the poor" (their cupidity wished to despoil the rich of their property) to organize and contest the rulership of the rich, the end of the American frontier, with its largesse of inexpensive land and corollary of high wages, would intensify the class struggle between them. But Sumner's "natural" competitive-evolutionary struggle, curiously, would not extend to the realm of natural human rights as he neglected Locke for Edmund Burke's historical/institutional conservatism.[19]

In contradistinction to the conservative social Darwinism of Spencer and Sumner, there was the reform-minded one of Thomas Henry Huxley in England, a physician, biologist, and naturalist, instrumental in popularizing Darwin. Although he agreed with Darwin that evolution involved a struggle for existence, in which the strongest and/or those with the most cunning survived, or the existence of "animal man," he also believed that with the advent of human progress/civilization, it was possible to control this struggle through the intervention of a community-based ethics resting on the lofty concepts of loving others, the rule of law, and of impartial justice. Thus, he held that it was feasible for "ethical man" to effect social reform to help the poor, but adamantly opposed any socialist solution on the basis that natural selection not be fully impeded, the assumption being that biological inequality was linked to the socioeconomic sphere.[20]

The views of Darwin and his disciples or the conservative bourgeois position on human nature will now be contrasted to those of the left in which Marx played a prominent role. To begin, the radical liberal bourgeoisie, exponents of a general equality during the Enlightenment and later, had a view of the individual as being basically good, some leading individuals here being Rousseau, Diderot, Thomas Paine, Thomas Jefferson, and Benjamin Franklin. To be sure, conservatives, like Hobbes, Malthus, and Alexander Hamilton, opposed them. Two examples: Jefferson described average farmers in his America as "the chosen people of God, if ever he had a chosen people," basically associated them with "virtue."[21] On the other hand, Hamilton's view of the economically average was related to his Hobbesianism. "The people – the people is a great beast."[22]

That Marx had a theory of human nature is amply reflected in works like *The Holy Family, Economic and Philosophical Manuscripts, Theses on Feuerbach, The German Ideology*, and *Capital*. In the sixth thesis in *Theses on Feuerbach*, for instance, he insisted "the essence of man is no abstraction inherent in each single individual. In its reality it is the ensemble of the social relations," whose "essence, therefore, can be regarded as many individuals in a *natural way*."[23] In the *Economic and Philosophical Manuscripts* he stated:

> Man is directly a *natural being*. As a natural being, and as a living natural being, he is, on the one hand, endowed with *natural powers and faculties*, which exist in him as tendencies and abilities, as *drives*. On the other hand, as a natural, embodied, sentient, objective being he is a *suffering*, conditioned and limited being, like animals and plants. The *objects* of his drives exist outside himself as objects independent of him, yet they are *objects* and his *needs*, essential

objects which are indispensable to the exercise and confirmation of his faculties.[24]

These "drives" and "needs," for Marx, were related to a basic human nature in *The Holy Family*, composed of two parts – the "constant" and the "relative," both involved in the making of humanity in history. The former encompassed needs required to simply exist, thus "hunger was a natural need," as was sex. The latter comprised those that were socially challenged, linked to discrete socioeconomic structures, like capitalism and its power relations, or what individuals normally economically and socially desired under its hegemony, thus changeable.[25] In this instance, Marx, in *Capital I*, in criticizing Jeremy Bentham's utilitarianism, invariably associated with tying pleasure and pain to bourgeois capital accumulation, perceptively pointed out that Bentham's frame of reference for understanding human nature was the "modern shopkeeper, especially the English shopkeeper, as the normal man" for "past, present, and future." In this bourgeois world, for him, "money" is the *"object par excellence,"* bestowing power to those possessing large amounts: "My own power is as great as the power of money." This bourgeois mindset, for Marx, would apply only to periods where capitalist relations were widespread, as in his contemporary period, for "human nature" is "modified in each historical epoch," as "man is not merely a natural being; he is a *human* natural being" who was "consciously self-transcending," i.e., humanity made its own historical progression, of course consonant with the states of technology and class struggle.[26] Thus it was for István Mészáros in *Marx's Theory of Alienation* that Marx's conception of human nature comprised three dialectically linked elements, of "man," "nature," and "industry."[27]

Indeed, for Marx, with the advent of socialism, it would be possible to resurrect at a higher human level the earlier egalitarianism of primitive cultures. In this vein, he described the ideal communist in *Capital I*, of the "fully developed individual" who was "fit for a variety of labours, ready to face any change of production, and to whom the different social functions he performs, are but so many modes of giving free scope to his own natural and acquired powers."[28] In *The German Ideology*, he and Engels called for an individual who could "do one thing today and another tomorrow.[29] In *The Economic and Philosophical Manuscripts*, he postulated that under "communism" it was possible to conceive of "the return of man himself as a social, i.e., real human being, a complete and conscious return which assimilates all the wealth of previous development."[30]

In this vein, Marx conceived of free and un-alienated labor as central to the human condition, as human beings actualized themselves in life, but work itself was not an "amusement, as Fourier naively expressed it in shop-girl terms." Indeed, for him, "really free labor, the composing of music, for example, is at the same time damned serious and demands the greatest effort." Furthermore, for him, "the labor concerned with this material production" should be "of a social nature" and "have a scientific character and at the same time" be "general work," that it "ceases to be achieved by human effort as a definite, trained natural force." This work under an advanced socialism, with its advanced technology of automation, would transcend the curse of Adam and Eve, of alienating and brutal work for most individuals in a world of great scarcity and strife.[31]

In 1902, the most influential work of socialist quasi-Darwinism appeared, *Mutual Aid: A Factor in Evolution* by Kropotkin, which significantly viewed mutual aid as even more basic than "love, sympathy, and self-sacrifice," which "play an immense part in the progressive development of our moral feelings." Broadly:

> It is the conscience – be it only at the stage of instinct –
> of human solidarity. It is the unconscious recognition
> of the force that is borrowed by each man from the
> practice of mutual aid; of the close dependence of
> every one's happiness upon the happiness of all;
> and of the sense of justice, or equity, which brings
> the individual to consider the rights of every other
> individual as equal to his own. Upon this broad and

necessary foundation, the still higher moral feelings are developed.

Kropotkin was well aware that his thesis of mutual aid was antithetical to Spencer's and Huxley's social Darwinism, which he portrayed as Hobbesian. Specifically, he disagreed with their position that primitive humans, outside of their immediate group, were engaged in a "Hobbesian war of each against all."[32] He did not deny that there was a struggle for existence among "individuals of the same species for the means of subsistence," but he insisted that it was of a "limited extent," not of the same magnitude as the spirit of cooperation or mutual aid which was paramount.[33]

This close kinship between mutual aid and ethics was further amplified in Kropotkin's last work, *Ethics: Origin and Modern Development*, which employed Darwin's positive assertions on human sociability/sympathy in *The Descent of Man* as a starting point for an outline of ethics among various religious/moral philosophers. In his synthesis of what formed ethics, Kropotkin combined the biological with the sociological and psychological to present a grand design for human survival, whose basic thesis was "that the prosperity and happiness of no nation or class could ever be based, even temporarily, upon the degradation of other classes, nations, or races."[34] In this picture, modern science played its proper role to free humanity "from superstition, religious dogmatism, and metaphysical mythology,"[35] as the "I", was replaced by the "We."[36]

But Kropotkin did not have a Pollyannaish view of humanity's fate, acknowledging that oppressive societies since the rise of classes, with their antagonistic socioeconomic relations glorifying force/power and wealth, and the accompanying institutions which uphold them ("parasitic growths"), might further misshape human nature to the extent that humanity would destroy itself.[37]

Two American Progressives of the late 19th and early 20th centuries will now be examined concerning human nature: Lester Frank Ward, one of the founding fathers of sociology in America, and Veblen, already identified.

Born into a frontier family in Illinois in 1841 of a worker/farmer father and a clergyman's daughter, Ward labored on farms and in factories to further his studies to become a secondary school teacher. After being severely wounded in the Northern Army in the Civil War, he was employed as a clerk in the Treasury Dept. in Washington D.C. and attended night college, earning degrees in law, medicine, and the liberal arts by 1872, becoming a paleontologist for the government. Only toward the end of this life did Ward become an academic, a sociology professor at Brown University, authoring many works, the best remembered being *Dynamic Sociology* and *Pure Sociology.*

A radical liberal not from socialism (an intellectual ally and friend of Veblen) and an acerbic critic of conservatism, Ward castigated Malthus, Ricardo, and Spencer for being watchdogs of a brutal capitalism exploiting rural and urban labor. Along these lines, although accepting Darwinian natural selection/evolution, he conceptualized that it represented the "genetic" phase of the past, paralleled by a competitive and unsavory "animal economics," to be replaced by the new phase of human development, the "psychic" one, representing an emerging and purposeful human intelligence to consciously order human progress with planned economics to largely replace the wasteful competitive one.

A believer in the importance of a proper social environment to change human destiny, Ward favored a universal public school education in conjunction with high income and death taxes, which would mitigate the advantages of privilege based on inherited wealth. Thus, although some socioeconomic inequality continued, opportunity for individual socioeconomic mobility was enhanced, bringing about a form of meritocracy. This social model obviously included numerous governmental social services for the citizenry.[38]

In *Pure Sociology*, Ward observed that collectivism, equated with public ownership of the means of production and exchange, was further advanced on the Continent than in England and, in an opening to a possible future socialism, stated in a 1906 American Sociological Society conference that: "Every step in the direction of a true collectivism has been and must be a step in the direction of true individualism."[39]

Veblen had views similar to Ward's. He pictured historical change as itself related to a basic human nature formed by natural selection over hundreds of thousands of years when humanity in its "savage" state compelled the individual to closely cooperate with the group. This was because in comparison to many other animals, humans were weak and not swift, formidable only by virtue of their intelligence, social organization, and technology.

In this schema, group solidarity overrode individual "self-interest," itself at peace with others. Veblen contended that "savage groups" lived in an economy in which "differentiation of employments is still less elaborate and the invidious distinction between classes and employments is less consistent and rigorous" than that of barbarian or later New Stone Age groups. Thus, contrary to the barbarians, savages did not possess a "leisure class," with its train of deleterious habits and attitudes. Indeed, he emphatically remarked that savage cultures (his examples being the Andamans, Todas, and Eskimos, among others) had no "hierarchy of economic classes," living in a general equality without a "defined system of individual ownership," and were "peaceable," having "a certain amiable inefficiency when confronted with force or fraud."[40]

For Veblen, it was in the seed or "savage" period that humanity developed, in its struggle to survive, three basic "instincts" (he employed the terms "propensity" and "instinct," the second indicating a stronger and more elementary force than the former): (1) The "parental bent," which did not merely signify care for the young, but concern for or sympathy with other humans in varying degree, of humanity in general. (2) "Workmanship," the complex of elements related to human manipulation and alteration of the environment through technology, also involving the qualities inherent in doing this, like skill and perseverance. (3) "Idle curiosity," or the desire to know as much as possible of the cosmos, irrespective of material gain, or what may be termed as abstract thought in all of its ramifications.

These "instincts," for Veblen, were not to be considered in the ordinary sense of the term, like the hand-grasp of infants when presented with an object, or as "drives," like that of the sexual one or the avoidance of thirst or hunger, but as deep sociobiological qualities or attributes of the human condition, which its expanding brain developed over hundreds of thousands of years of social life. (Anthropologists, like Montagu, now assert that natural selection over the course of time conspires to replace instinctual behavior in humans, the threefold increase of the brain in the first three years of life reflecting this.)[41]

But these human "instincts," for Veblen, were partly malleable. With the advent of civilization and its corollaries of war and socioeconomic oppression, these primary attributes had been deformed by class-based authoritarian societies. But these primary "instincts," which Veblen related to socialism, would hopefully overwhelm leisure-class predatory traits.[42]

Veblen, like Marx, perceived human activity as purposeful and more than the sum of its parts in which change was inherent in human existence:

> Man's great advantage of other species in the struggle
> for survival has been his superior facility in turning
> the forces of the environment to account. It is to this
> proclivity for turning the material means of life to
> account that he owes his position as lord of creation.
> It is not a proclivity to effort, but to achievement –
> to the compassing of an end. His primacy is in the
> last resort an industrial or economic primacy. In his
> economic life man is an agent, not an absorbent; he is
> an agent seeking in every act the accomplishment of
> some concrete, objective, impersonal end.[43]

And, to sum up:

> He [man] is not simply a bundle of desires that are to
> be saturated by being placed in the path of the forces
> of the environment, but rather a coherent structure of
> propensities and habits which seek realization in an
> unfolding activity.[44]

In the last half of the 20th century, the past arguments on human nature have continued, with the addition of intelligence now in the picture assuming an important role, especially the one between ethnicity/race and class. The conservative side included the ethnologist Konrad Lorenz; Robert Ardrey, one of his popularizers; the zoologist Edward O. Wilson; the psychologist Richard J. Herrnstein; and the political scientist/sociologist Charles Murray. The left liberal and socialist camps included the anthropologist Ashley Montagu; the geologist, biologist, and science historian Stephen J. Gould; the evolutionary geneticist Richard Lewontin; the neurobiologist Steven Rose; the psychologist Leon J. Kamin; and the biologist Richard Lewis, among others.[45]

Konrad Lorenz was an eminent scientist, one the founders of ethnology, a Nobel Prize laureate in 1973 for his work in the field. In *On Aggression*, he argued that early hominids employed pebble tools to not only kill game, but also one another. Thus, since human beings came from warlike ancestors, essentially competitive and selfish, it was only normal that when humanity established large-scale institutions, like the state, war and economic exploitation became the norm.[46]

Ardrey, a popularizer of Lorenz, in *Territorial Imperative*, again alleged that man, being a descendant of a "killer-ape," was innately aggressive with a well-developed instinct of territoriality, these precedents inevitably leading to the rise of private property and consequent social inequality/hierarchy, and war. A society of equality, therefore, was simply utter nonsense.[47]

A distinguished present-day zoologist at Harvard University, Edward O. Wilson, is widely known for his *Sociobiology: The New Synthesis*, whose general outlook is Spenserian. Sociobiology itself, for him, is "the systematic study of the biological basis of all social behavior." In his study of it, he concentrates on "animal societies," but also examines "early man" and the "more primitive contemporary societies," and by extension contemporary civilized humanity.[48]

With many qualifications, Wilson postulates that human destiny lies with its genes; he is a biological determinist. Although he admits that human beings "sometimes cooperate closely," as insects do, they often "compete for the limited resources allocated to their role-sector." Winners "gain a disproportionate share of the rewards, while the least successful are displaced to other less desirable positions." Those with the better genes will move up the socioeconomic ladder, while those not as well-endowed do not. Competition also involves "competition between classes," which "in great moments of history… has proved to be a determinant of societal change."[49]

Wilson's biological determinism is of "polygenetic" nature. "Hereditary factors in intelligence," thus not only include the IQ, but also qualities of "creativity, entrepreneurship, drive, and mental stamina," which genetically may be "uncorrelated or even negatively correlated."[50] Nevertheless, these genetic qualities or traits as a whole account for why some individuals succeed, while others do not. Social and economic advantages that some individuals have over others are not delved into, although they are recognized as playing a role.

Again, with many qualifications, Wilson employs his sociobiology to explain such various social phenomena as (1) tribalism (now nationalism) and fear of the stranger, associated with territoriality; (2) why men, presumably physically stronger than women, are socioeconomically superior to them; and (3) why the higher-ranking males have more children through polygyny than the lower-ranking ones.[51] But he neglects to point out that the upper bourgeoisie of today have fewer children per capita than workers. Are the wealthy cunningly committing class suicide for their own benefit?

The biological determinism of Wilson is so ubiquitous that it even explains why human "ethical standards are innately pluralistic": Because "the genetic foundation of which any such normative system is built can be expected to shift continuously." He is also fearful that the increased "gene flow around the world" can lead to "an eventual lessening of altruistic behavior through the maladaptation and loss of group-selected genes." But to indicate the complexity of the genetic nightmare, he then asserts that "we do not know how the most valued qualities are linked genetically to more obsolete destructive ones." Thus, for instance, "cooperativeness toward group-mates might be coupled to (aggressiveness) toward strangers, creativeness with a desire to dominate," and so forth.[52]

To be sure, Wilson is afraid of a future and perfect communist society run by the acolytes of B.F. Skinner, a leading educational psychologist and novelist/social philosopher, whose *Walden II* socially plans all aspects of human life. But, of course, Wilson believes that neurobiology will have to be employed to alter the genetic makeup to make this possible. ("Only when the machinery can be torn down on paper at the level of the cell and put together again will the properties of emotion and ethical judgment come out clear.")[53] Regrettably, this form of society, for him, may have to come in order "to fit the requirements of the ecological steady state." But he consoles himself by projecting this communist society at least a hundred years into the future.[54] But he does have a way out of his nightmare, to follow Aldous Huxley's *Brave New World*, in which biological and social engineering are consciously employed to maintain social inequality.

A leading contemporary anthropologist, Montagu, acknowledges a deep debt to Kropotkin's views on evolution and the nature of man. In numerous works – *Man: His First Million Years, On Being Human, The Nature of Human Aggression, Darwin: Competition and Cooperation* – he theorizes like Kropotkin, Ward, and Veblen that Darwin overemphasizes competition and undervalues cooperation in the make-up of human nature. He believes that the primary factors insuring early human survival are "cooperation and mutual aid." Thus, *Australopithecines*, for him, are "amiable and sociable," and humanity probably inherits these predispositions, related to the maintenance of individual/group survival, so very necessary to hunter/gatherer societies.

For Montagu, the close cooperation needed for human survival is undergirded by the very act of reproduction itself and the consequent necessity to nurture progeny, central to human activity and purpose. Along with the increasing size of the human brain, associated with a more complex technological/cultural level, the necessity for learning and communicating become central for survival, speech increasingly interrelated with learning: "Speech is by nature a cooperative venture; it is designed to put one into touch with others; without someone to talk to, talking is meaningless. Without someone to answer, talking is profitless." Speech itself makes people "increasingly interdependent; they needed each other more." Indeed, without some form of love, speech and human intelligence are unimaginable; a child to survive and flourish simply needs a proper support system. Thus, not surprisingly, for him, "cooperation" and "amiability" encompass the arc of most of the human condition, being imperative elements for human survival. Biologically, then, a human is born with the capacity to love and cooperate, but if the environment denies them, in varying degree, corresponding aggressive behavior develops.

Montague presents many examples of contemporary hunter-gatherer (like the Eskimo and! Kung) behavior to bolster his generalizations about primitive societies, of their exhibiting only a minimal aggression within and outside their groups and of their intensely cooperative bent, and asks if this is not because "any undue aggressiveness might fatally upset the delicate balance" for group survival. Thus, it is likely "that in the course of human evolution as a hunter-gatherer, the highest premium is placed by natural selection on cooperative behavior, and a negative premium on aggressive traits," and that there is simply no evidence of "hostility between neighboring prehistoric populations," and if any, they are infrequent.[55] Along with Veblen, Montagu posits "that during almost the whole of man's evolutionary history he lived in peace and cooperation with his fellow man,"[56] and that the primary human drives are basically of a cooperative and pacific nature.

To be sure, along with Marx, Veblen, and Kropotkin, Montagu is aware that the evils of war and class society are of recent vintage in human development, coming about from technological and class factors, and that the partly selfish and competitive individual who has emerged since then is socially, not biologically, conditioned to act so.[57] This learned behavior can be unlearned by altering present institutions, presumably along radical republican or socialist lines. In conjunction with this, he categorically affirms that humans do not have instincts to dominate others.[58]

In the nature-of-human-nature arguments, the problem of differences in intelligence invariably crops up. It, too, occurs along divisions between conservatives opposing radical liberals and socialists. But first some background is in order.

In societies with extensive labor divisions, like those of the bourgeois-dominated and communist varieties, formal education increasingly is universally used to train and steer students into various occupations, which, of course, have different incomes and social-power related to status and class. Thus, in contemporary America, a physician and lawyer command more power/respect than a nurse, engineer, and teacher, who, in turn, are higher in the pecking order than blue-collar workers.

Not surprisingly, conservative social Darwinists, like Spencer and Sumner, were among the first to assign a higher intelligence to the bourgeoisie than to workers. Indeed, Spencer and Sir Frances Galton, a cousin of Darwin, were the first to examine closely intelligence as part of a eugenics movement to improve the English stock, basically eliminating those of low intelligence, the very poor. Galton, for instance, in many scientifically flawed studies, insisted that intelligence was inherited from parents, although conceding that environment played a secondary or minor role. He even convinced Darwin that inherited intelligence, indeed, was the key to intellectual/ material success.

The principal father of "intelligence tests was the Frenchman Alfred Binet, who in the 1905-11 period devised tests to determine how successfully school children could adapt to the demands of formal education. But he did not believe as Galton and others that he was literally measuring some definite or known quantity as "intelligence."

In the U.S., the conservative psychologists H.H. Goddard and Lewis Terman readily accepted the views of Spencer and Galton, but were influenced by Binet to devise tests to prove it. (In the American educational system, the Stanford-Binet IQ test is used to direct students into "appropriate" occupations).[59]

A recent conservative work on intelligence and ethnicity and class will serve as a prime example of continuing conservative insistence on stressing the importance of heredity over environment: *The Bell Curve* (1994), by two Harvard professors, Herrnstein and Murray. With a plethora of studies in IQ as proof, they claim that from 40 to 70 percent of intelligence is hereditary. The two, then, picture an American society formed by three distinct classes: two diametrically opposed, a college-educated "cognitive elite" and slow learners (disproportionately black) mired in the world of poverty/welfare, of out-of-wedlock children, and criminality, between them being the average workers. Thus, the resurrection of Spencer and Sumner![60]

Intelligence tests in the 20th century have yielded these results: in the United States Army Alpha Test during World War I, Eastern and Southern Europe immigrants, including Jews, scored lower than the older immigrants from Northern and Western Europe. Also, Northern blacks outperformed Southern whites. In standardized IQ tests in America after World War II, whites in general have about the same average scores, with Jewish-Americans being somewhat higher. IQ tests have also revealed that in Northern Ireland, Protestants (the dominant socioeconomic group) average ten points higher than Catholics (both are Celts); the average student in Japan has an IQ of 110 as opposed to about 100 in the United States; that American blacks with an average IQ of 85, are fifteen points lower on average than whites; that the children of American professionals, like lawyers, physicians, and engineers, score fifteen points higher than those of manual workers; and that in Japan, the Buraku-min, an ethnically Japanese group of about two million, traditionally living in ghettos because of their ancestors' lowly occupations, perform fifteen points lower than average among Japanese, but do just as well as other Japanese-Americans who achieve higher scores than the white average.[61]

Broadly, left responses to the right on intelligence conceptualize that it is formed by a complex interaction between genetic and environmental factors; that there is not only one form of intelligence, but many, and that intelligence testing itself has many flaws.

We begin with Montagu, for whom the genetic component of intelligence testing cannot be measured in any great degree, for it is inevitably intertwined with the social environment. Thus, it is incumbent for society to enrich the lives of all children.[62]

Gould, a Harvard professor and Marxist, offers a detailed critique of 19th-century craniometry and 20th-century intelligence tests in *The Mismeasure of Man*. He observed that in such tests, whose methods and data he meticulously examined, American IQ testers like the psychologists Goddard and Terman, and the British psychologist Sir Cyril Burt (they stressed the importance of heredity and scarcely noticed the role of culture/environment in the making of academic intelligence) are guilty of reifying intelligence, of trying to make concrete a complex phenomenon composed of many qualities.

Gould himself, like Montagu, rejected a biological determinism for general intelligence among humans:

> Our large brain is the biological foundation of intelligence; intelligence is the ground of culture; and cultural transmission builds a new mode of evolution more effective that Darwinian processes in its limited realm – the "inheritance" and modification of learned behavior.[63]

In *Not in Our Genes*, Lewontin, Rose, and Kamin continue in the footsteps of Montagu and Gould to attack the biological determinists whose ardent champion, Burt, is exposed as producing fraudulent studies favoring heredity over environment in forming intelligence. (Burt influences American scientists, like Arthur Jensen, who views whites and the middleclass as being innately more intelligent than blacks and workers). Indeed, the three purport that in careful but limited studies there is good evidence to support the thesis that a proper environment is decisive in improving performance on intelligence testing and decreasing failure in academic work. For instance, in a French study of working-class infants adopted by bourgeois parents, the children in question average 16 points higher than their siblings who had been raised in a working-class environment. In similar studies in the United States of adopted infant children, including African-Americans adopted by white parents, which compare the adopted to the biological children, the general consensus is that the "children reared by the same mother resemble her in IQ to the same degree, whether or not they share her genes."[64] This being the case, the authors claim that IQ can be increased "as much as social organization will allow,"[65] and that "our biology" allows us the flexibility of "recreating our own psychic and material environments"; that ultimately "our biology makes us free."[66] Gardner, a Harvard psychologist, also, disagrees with the view that there is only one kind of intelligence, that which is assigned by IQ. In addition to "linguistic" and "logical-mathematical" intelligence stressed by IQ tests, he observes others, like the "musical," "bodily-kinesthetic," "spatial," and various "personal."[67]

Surprisingly, IQ scores are rising throughout the world: "Twenty-seven points in Britain since 1942 and 24 points in the United States since 1918...with comparable gains throughout Western Europe, Canada, Japan, Israel, urban Brazil, China, Australia, and New Zealand." This indicates the importance of the various environmental factors (including test preparation) in determining "intelligence," stressed by the left, as against a supposedly and relatively fixed hereditary one, which environment cannot change much in short periods of time (the genetic pool changes only slowly), favored by conservatives.[68]

Recent studies support the views of Monagu, Lewontin, Rose, Kamin, and others on the decisive importance of environment interacting with heredity or biology in affecting intelligence and personality. In fact, a special edition of *Newsweek* in 1997 entitled *Your Child* has a series of articles based on recent studies by psychiatrists, psychologists, pediatricians, neurobiologists, and others, which indicate that early environmental factors are critical in determining intelligence and personality, as well as the plasticity of the human brain that are formed by experiences after birth; a gene needs a favorable environment to reach its fullest potential. Thus it is that children who are raised in intellectually enriched and more psychologically secure environments do better on intelligence testing and are more stable emotionally than those without these advantages. Abused and traumatized children who are subjected to great stress from fears/anxieties, however, have elevated stress hormones, like cortisone, and invariably suffer from learning and emotional problems, their hippocampus and frontal lobes (the first involves memory, while the second controls emotions), either smaller or having less neural activity than those of normal children. Positron-emission tomography (PET) scans, for instance, indicate less neural activity in the temporal lobes of children subject to extreme deprivation than for those of normal ones. (There are gradations in all of these processes and results). This, in turn, impinges on learning ability for "some percentage of capacity is lost. A piece of the child is lost forever," according to Dr. Bruce Perry of the Baylor College of Medicine. There is now even some evidence that severe trauma experienced by parents has some genetic transference influencing children's mental health, again engaging the interplay of genetics and the environment.[69]

Socioeconomic status and mental illness and their relationship to rearing children, on average, have a bearing on the good life, including intelligence. Furthermore, the multiple stresses of poverty and recent reductions of social welfare for the general population, especially the poor, do not bode well for their children. Indeed, to recapitulate the section on intelligence and class, is not life, given what we now know, more tragic than ever for the working class and especially for its poorer part than for the bourgeoisie?

From the perspective of human intelligence, there is no reason to suppose that the "average" individual is incapable of fully participating as a general equal in an egalitarian and democratic socialist society. In Japan, the average IQ of 110 allows, even by the standards of traditional intelligence testers, for the successful completion of a university education.

Some closing comments on intelligence and "race."

Recent studies employing mitochondrial DNA passed on from mother to daughter indicate that Africans have a greater genetic diversity than other population, strongly suggesting an African ancestry for modern humanity, coming from a gene pool of 20,000 or so people approximately 100,000 years ago. The recently completed genome project also attests to the fact that all human beings are 99.9 alike genetically, again indicating humanity's newness, while chimpanzees, the closest animal to *homo sapiens*, have much larger genetic differences among themselves, indicating a direct remote ancestry stretching back millions of years.[70]

Recent advances in genetics, coupled with the rise of socioeconomic inequality under present capitalistic arrangements, pose a danger to the radical republican/socialist view of society being composed of more or less equal individuals in general ability when a proper environment is given to children. Indeed, Wilson may be comforted by the scenario drawn by Lee M. Silver, a molecular biologist at Princeton University, who, in *Remaking Eden*, warns that an upper-bourgeoisie of about 10 percent of the population, through free choice and economic superiority, will be able to enrich their children through new gene-addition methods that can be passed on to succeeding generations, eventually dividing the population into two castes, the "GenRich," or synthetically "gene enriched" individuals, and the "Naturals," or average people conceived under normal natural selection. Although admitting to the key role of environment in determining personality and general achievement, Silver underscores the obvious genetic advantages of the "GenRich" over the "Naturals," further exacerbating existing socioeconomic inequalities between them. But this is not all, for he predicts that in about three centuries, any mating between the "GenRich" and "Naturals" will not usually produce offspring, and in about a thousand years the two will have "no ability to cross-breed," forming two distinct species. "Human nature" in this future society will reflect this division.[71]

Silver's views on genetic enrichment, much of it through genetically engineered "gene-packs" influencing particular skills as proficiency in music or athletic ability and even general intelligence, are not necessarily antithetical to those of Gould and others, in the sense that they may provide the necessary means to create a group of super humans. To be sure, if need be, a socialist society can genetically enrich all children, the resources for this easily coming from savings eliminating waste and war. Advanced technology itself will make it possible to transcend present labor divisions and fulfill Marx's dream of the "fully developed" individual who can perform a variety of tasks.

Final remarks on the nature of humanity: For socialists and radical liberals, the basic problem is not whether human beings are cooperative or intelligent enough to participate as equals in society, as most are. Even in the most class-ridden societies, forced cooperation is *de rigueur* in everyday life or in conducting war. That humanity is basically sociable and cooperative has been verified by history.

Rather, the problem is whether humanity can construct societies in which the cooperative and sociable spirit is established along with egalitarian and non-exploitative arrangements. The critical issue dividing the left and conservatives, which, if not resolved, may lead to humanity's either destroying itself through atomic/biological warfare or pollution, or simply divide itself into two different species.

Notes

Chapter Eight: The Riddle of Human Nature

1) On basic human needs, see, for instance Abraham H. Maslow (an ethnologist and psychologist), *Motivation and Personality*, 2nd ed. (New York: Harper and Row, 1970), ch. 1. Barrington Moore Jr. (a

sociologist), *Injustice: The Social Bases of Obedience and Revolt* (White Plains, NY: M.E. Sharpe, 1978), pp. 6-7. On primitive society, the Neolithic Age, and early civilizations, see Marvin Harris, *Culture, People, Nature: An Introduction to General Anthropology*, 5th ed. (New York: Harper and Row, 1988), pp. 162-206.

2) Charles Darwin, *Origin of Species*, 6th ed. (London: John Murray, 1859), pp. 4-5.

3) Charles Darwin, *The Descent of Man and Selection in Relation to Sex* (New York: D. Appleton, 1897), p. 97.

4) Ibid., pp. 97ff.

5) On Darwin's conservative social policies and his justification of imperialism on the basis of racial superiority, see Ashley Monagu, *Darwin: Competition and Cooperation* (New York: Henry Schuman, 1952), pp. 89-95.

6) For an excellent overview of Spencer's influence and views, see Robert L. Carneiro, ed. and intro. *The Evolution of Society: Selections from Herbert Spencer's Principles of Sociology* (Chicago: Univ. of Chicago Press, 1967); Hofstadter, *Social Darwinism in American Thought* (New York: Harper Torchbooks, 1955), pp. 31-50.

7) See Hofstadter, *Social Darwinism*; Commager, *American Mind*; and Carneiro, *Evolution of Society*, pp. ix-lvii.

8) Herbert Spencer, *The Man Versus the State* (Calwell, ID: Caxton Printers, 1969), pp. 74-75 ff.

9) Ibid., pp. 10-16.

10) Ibid., pp. 96-97.

11) Ibid., p. 59.

12) Ibid., p. 21.

13) Herbert Spencer, *First Principles* (New York: D. Appleton and Co., 1903), p. 391 for the two quotations.

14) Herbert Spencer, *Social Studies* (New York: D. Appleton and Co., 1896), pp. 149 ff. on an economic survival of the fittest that is biologically determined – the unemployed/unfit would not be aided by the state.

15) See chapter on class for details.

16) On Sumner, see the excellent biography by Harris E. Starr, *William Graham Sumner* (New York: Henry Holt and Co., 1925); Robert Green McCloskey, *American Conservatism in the Age of Enterprise: A Study of William Graham Sumner, Stephen J. Field and Andrew Carnegie* (New York: Harper Torchbooks, 1964).

17) On labor unions, see Hofstadter, *Social Darwinism*, pp. 62-63; on stand against imperialism, see Starr, *Sumner*, pp. 262 ff.

18) On Sumner's views in this paragraph (economic man, class, and so forth, see William Graham Sumner, *Folkways: A Study of the Sociological Importance of Usages, Manners, Customs, Mores, and Morals* (Boston: Ginn and Co., 1906), pp. 40 ff., and Starr, *Sumner*, p. 400 and pp. 463-76.

19) Starr, *Sumner*, pp. 432-36 and 448-59; Hofstadter, *Social Darwinism*, p. 60.

20) Thomas Henry Huxley, *Evolution and Ethics and Other Essays* (New York: D. Appleton and Co., 1896); Thomas Henry Huxley, "The Struggle for Existence," *The Nineteenth Century* (London), Vol. 23, February, 1888, pp. 161-80; on p. 165: From a moral perspective, "the animal world is on about the same level as a gladiator's show."

21) John Dewey, *The Living Thoughts of Thomas Jefferson* (Philadelphia: D. McKay, 1940), p. 76.

22) Vernon Louis Parrington, *Main Currents in American Thought*, I, *The Colonial Mind* (New York: Harvest Book, 1954), p. 305.

23) See Norman Geras, *Marx and Human Nature: Refutation of a Legend* (London: Verso Editions and NLB, 1983), p. 29 on the quotations of Marx's 6th thesis.

24) Erich Fromm, *Marx's Concept of Man*, with a translation from Marx's *Economic and Philosophical Manuscripts* by T.B. Bottomore (New York: Frederick Ungar, 1966), p. 181.

25) Marx, *Holy Family*, 128 ff, Marx, *Economic and Philosophical Manuscripts* in Fromm, *Marx's Concept of Man*, p. 182.

26) Marx, *Capital*, I, 668; Marx, *Economic and Philosophical Manuscripts* in Fromm, *Marx's Concept of Man*, pp. 163-65 and 183.

27) István Mészáros, *Marx's Theory of Alienation* (London: Merlin Press, 1970), pp. 25-26.

28) Marx, *Capital*, I, 534.

29) Marx and Engels, *German Ideology*, p. 22.

30) Marx, *Economic and Philosophical Manuscripts* in Fromm, *Marx's Concept of Man*, p. 127. See, also, Adam Schaff, *Marxism and the Human Individual* (New York: McGraw-Hill, 1970), pp. 49-102; and John Plamenatz, *Karl Marx's Philosophy of Man* (Oxford: Claredon Press, 1975), pp. 36-85.

31) McLellan, *Grundrisse*, p. 124 on the quotations.

32) On Kropotkin, see Martin A. Miller, *Kropotkin* (Chicago: Univ. of Chicago Press, 1976). Peter Kropotkin, *Mutual Aid: A Factor in Evolution* (New York: Alfred A. Knopf, 1919), pp. 5-7 on the quotations.

33) Ibid., p. 2.

34) Peter Kropotkin, *Ethics: Origin and Development* (New York: The Dial Press, 1924), p. 4.

35) Ibid., p. 5.

36) Ibid., p. 64.

37) Kropotkin, *Mutual Aid*, p. 9.

38) On Ward, see the splendid study of his life and thought by Samuel Chugerman, *Lester F. Ward: The American Aristotle*, pp. 67-84, Chapter Four, is entitled "Lester Ward: Critic"; Commager, *American Mind*, pp. 199-226, Chapter Ten, is entitled "Lester Ward and the Science of Society." I have incorporated many of their insights.

39) Ward, *Pure Sociology*, p. 561. The quotation is from Commager, *American Mind*, p. 208.

40) Veblen, *Leisure Class*, pp. 22 ff.

41) Thorstein Veblen, *The Instinct of Workmanship and the State of the Industrial Arts* (New York: Augustus M. Kelley, 1964), pp.

25-26 ff. Ashley Montagu, *The Nature of Human Aggression* (New York: Oxford Univ. Press, 1976), pp. 65-65 and 78 ff.

42) Veblen, *Leisure Class*, pp. 41-46.

43) Thorstein Veblen, "the Instinct of Workmanship," in *Essays in our Changing Order*, ed. Leon Ardzrooni (New York: Augustus M. Kelley, 1964), pp. 80-81. Veblen, *Leisure Class*, p. 259 – "the leisure class canon demands strict and comprehensive futility; the instinct of workmanship demands purposeful action."

44) Thorstein Veblen, "Why Is Economics Not an Evolutionary Science?" in *The Place of Science in Modern Civilization and Other Essays* (New York: B.W. Heubsch, 1919), p. 74.

45) The personages mentioned are usually at the top of their fields of study.

46) Konrad Lorenz, *On Aggression* (New York: Harcourt, Brace, and World, 1966), p. 231, for instance, on the hominid Australopithecus – not a direct ancestor of modern man – as a killer.

47) Robert Ardrey, *The Territorial Imperative* (New York: Athenaeum, 1966), pp. 269-319.

48) Edward O. Wilson, *Sociobiology: The New Synthesis* (Cambridge, MA: Harvard Univ. Press, 1975), p. 4.

49) Ibid., p. 554 for the quotations in this paragraph.

50) Ibid., pp. 554-55.

51) Ibid., pp. 286-87.

52) Ibid., p. 575.

53) Ibid.

54) Ibid.

55) Montagu, *Human Aggression*, pp. 135-85 on the last four paragraphs of the text.

56) Ibid., p. 301.

57) Ashley Montagu, *Man: His First Million Years* (New York: Mentor Books, 1957), pp. 105-06. Montagu, *Human Aggression*, pp. 301-02.

58) Montagu, *Human Aggression*, pp. 233 ff.

59) On salaries, see *U.S. News and World Report*, Oct. 31, 1994, pp. 110 ff., on salaries of professionals, per year in 1993/1994: for midlevel engineers, about $60,000; for lawyers, between $70,000 to $80,000 in law firms; for physicians, median incomes for those in group practice with 8 to 17 years; for internists: $142,000; for psychiatrists, $153,000; obstetricians/gynecologists, $218,000; while median earnings per year for drill press operators is $14,700; lathe operators, $27,700 and machine repairers, $30,300.

60) Herrnstein and Murray, *Bell Curve*, pp. 535-52.
On IQ testing, heredity versus environment, and so forth, the radical republican/socialist view is upheld in these representative works: Ashley Montagu, *Statement on Race*, 3rd ed. (New York: Oxford Univ. Press, 1972), pp. 115-16. Ashley Montague, *Man's Most Dangerous Myth: The Fallacy of Race*, 5th ed. (New York: Oxford Univ. Press, 1974), pp. 241 ff. Stephen J. Gould, *The Mismeasure of Man* (New York: W.W. Norton, 1983), pp. 192-223. R.C. Lewontin, Steven Rose, and Leon J. Kamin, *Not in Our Genes* (New York: Pantheon Books, pp. 83-129. Richard

61) Levins and Richard Lewontin, *The Dialectical Biologist* (Cambridge, MA: Harvard Univ. Press, 1985), pp. 120-27 ff. and 159. Jeffrey M. Blum, *Pseudoscience and Mental Ability* (New York: Monthly Review Press, 1978), pp. 25-112 and 145-95. For the conservative position, reminiscent of Spencer and Sumner, see Richard Herrnstein and Charles Murray, *The Bell Curve: Intelligence and Class Structure in American Life* (New York: Free Press, 1994), pp. 269-340, for instance, on ethnic differences in IQ. For an excellent critique of this work, see Adolph Reed Jr., "Looking Backward," *The Nation*, Nov. 28, 1994, pp. 654-62.

62) Montagu, *Man's Most Dangerous Myth*, pp. 241 ff.

63) Gould, *Mismeasure of Man*, pp. 15 ff; the lengthy quotation is on p. 325.

64) Lewontin et al., *Not in Our Genes*, pp. 127-29.

65) Ibid., p. 129.

66) Ibid., p. 290.

67) Howard Gardner, *Frames of Mind: The Theory of Multiple Intelligences* (New York: Basic Books, 1993), pp. 3-70 and 331 ff. Steven Fraser, ed., *The Bell Curve Wars: Race, Intelligence, and the Future of America* (New York: Basic Books, 1995), particularly articles by Stephen Jay Gould, Howard Gardner, Richard Nisbett, Jacqueline Jones, Andrew Hackner, and Orlando Patterson.

68) On the recent upsurge of IQ scores (the Flynn effect, after James R. Flynn, professor of political philosophy, Univ. of Otego in New Zealand), see Sharon Begley, "The IQ Puzzle," *Newsweek*, May 6, 1996, pp. 70-72.

69) See articles in *Newsweek* (Special Edition), *Your Child*, Spring/Summer, 1997: Sharon Begley, "How to Build a Baby's Brain," pp. 28-32 and p. 32 on the quotation by Dr. Perry, Marc Peyser and Anne Underwood, "Shyness, Sadness, Curiosity, Joy. Is It Nature or Nurture?" pp. 60-63; Debra Rosenberg, "Raising a Moral Child," pp. 92-93.

70) On the African connection of modern Homo sapiens, see Brian M. Fagan, *World Prehistory: A Brief Introduction* (New York: HarperCollins, 1996), pp. 81-85. Luigi Luca Cavalli-Sforza and Francesco Cavalli-Sforza, *The Great Diasporas* (Reading MA: Addison-Wesley, 1996), pp. 66-125. William A. Turnbaugh, et al., *Understanding Physical Anthropology and Archeology*, 6th ed., (Minneapolis/St. Paul: West Publishing Co., 1996), pp. 112-17. John H. Relethford, *The Human Species: An Introduction to Biological Anthropology* (Mountain View, CA: Mayfield Publishing Co. 1996), pp. 334-47. Emma Ross, "Study Links Europeans' Origins to few from Africa," *Akron Beacon Journal*, April 21, 2001, p. A2.

71) Lee M. Silver, *Remaking Eden: Cloning and Beyond in a Brave New World* (New York Avon Books, 1997), pp. 1-11, 91-125, 240-50. Also, see Jeremy Rifkin, *The Biotech Century: Harnessing the Gene and Remaking the World* (New York: Jeremy P. Parcher/Putnam, 1998), pp. 2-4, 10-31, 117-74, 222-23.

Chapter Nine: Alienation in Class Society and its Costs

The philosophical concept of alienation is important in socialist theory because of its centrality in its Marxist stream to explain the consequences of social misery/oppression; its lineage will be briefly discussed before examining the views of Marx and others, usually socialists/near socialists, on its devastating social effects under capitalism.

Alienation holds that although human beings are social animals, individuality divides them in varying degree. For instance, while others may empathize with one, only he/she experiences first hand joy and sorrow, futility and rage, life and death. In a general sense, then, alienation is concerned with the estrangement of human beings from one another, of individual dread and despair, of inner loneliness.

Alienation, however, is largely magnified in class-exploitative societies, with their inordinate competitive features, pitting, in varying degree, individuals, status groups, classes, nations, and religions against one another: since the dawn of civilization the individual has been psychologically and ethically deformed by these antagonistic/ exploitative socioeconomic and other relations. To be sure, although there was less alienation in primitive cultures than in civilization because of intense mutual aid and equality, its potential to increase based on economic scarcity and labor division was omnipresent.[1]

Allusions to alienation are of old vintage, as in the Old Testament describing early humanity's living in the innocence of equality, peace, and relative abundance in the Garden of Eden, which were destroyed when Eve, deceived by Satan who personified evil, tempted Adam to eat the apple of knowledge. Anthropologically, this myth described the consequences resulting from the Agricultural Revolution and civilization, of woman's subordination to man, of the lot of most of humanity to be brutally exploited by governing elites while the arts and sciences flourished. The not knowing right from wrong would refer to the absence of private property, which allowed for broad sexual intimacy within early communities, of group solidarity, as against its more restrictive forms with the rise of the nuclear family and its relative exclusivity from others.[2]

In the modern period, alienation was well explored by Marx; it was greatly influenced by thinkers like Rousseau, but especially Hegel, who employed the term to describe the troubled individual under civilization. In *Discourse on the Origins of Inequality*, Rousseau contrasted the tormented, yet civilized, individual at war with others, with the happy and noble savage. In *The Phenomenology of the Spirit*, Hegel observed that normally, despite alienation, human beings desired not only to fulfill themselves, but also to aid and respect others (the mutual-aid aspect). But since human existence was confronted by the perennial problem of economic scarcity, there not being enough to fully satisfy material and social human needs, conflict arose, in the course of which the winners because the masters while the losers became slaves, part of whose labor was appropriated by the former, the two fearing and hating one another. Furthermore, the masters were not creative, but parasitical, while the slaves, the productive and creative classes through their understanding of the technology, would ultimately win independence.

The importance of the concept of alienation in modern thought may also be measured by Existentialism, basically a bourgeois philosophy whose leitmotif was concerned with the essentially alienated or lonely individual engulfed in anguish and dread, whose life was essentially absurd and meaningless, without hope. Its founder is the conservative religious Danish philosopher Soren A. Kierkegaard who flourished in the first half of the 19th century. To be sure, Sartre incorporated existentialism within a Marxist framework, an exception to the rule.[3]

Marx and Engels saw instances of at least some alienation in which individuals were separated from one another in primitive cultures, marked by the first inescapable labor division or the "sexual act," with others following "naturally by virtue of natural disposition (e.g., physical strength), needs, accidents." In the early family itself, there was a form of "latent slavery," in which "wife and children are the slaves of the husband." Then, "labor division and private property are moreover identical expressions: in the one the same thing is affirmed with reference to activity as affirmed in the other with reference to the product of the activity." It is this early division of labor, for them, which "implies the contradiction between the interest of the separate individual or the individual family and the communal interest of all individuals who have intercourse with one another." And, they contended, once a society reached a sufficiently high level of technological development with accompanying labor division, "each man has a particular sphere of activity which is forced upon him and from which he cannot escape." Thus:

> A cleavage exists between the particular and the
> common interest – as long, therefore, as activity is
> not voluntarily but naturally divided, man's own
> deed becomes an alien power opposed to him, which
> enslaves him instead of being controlled by him.

This condition itself was related to the dichotomy between manual and mental labor.

Marx suggested that alienated labor, along with technological advances and greater economic surplus, led to the emergence of private property, and ultimately to class society and the state, both of which become involved in an intricate clockwork of socioeconomic, political, and cultural inequalities with their concomitant elements of conflict.

To be sure, this alienation at times was of unbearable proportion, especially when some individuals were bereft of property, while others had an overabundance of it, like under capitalism, thus "my means of life belong to someone else that my desires are the unattainable possession of someone else...that an inhuman power [capital] rules over everything."[4]

For Marx, workers were the most unfree and thus the most alienated group in capitalist society because they must sell their labor-power to capital, thus becoming commodities in which exchange value, as opposed to use value, affected almost all human activities and institutions in the competition for wealth and power among individuals, status groups, and classes. In this progression, workers had the choice either to accede to becoming commodities to make other commodities, or starve.

To be sure, as observed in *The Holy Family*, capitalists were also alienated to some degree by the capitalist market place/property, but less so than workers:

> The propertied class and the class of the proletariat present the same human self-alienation. But the former class finds in this self-alienation its confirmation and its good, its own power: it has in it a semblance of human existence; the class of the proletariat falls annihilated in its self-alienation; it sees in it its own powerlessness and the reality of an inhuman existence. In the words of Hegel the class of the proletariat is in abasement…and indignation to which it is necessarily driven by the contradiction between its human nature and its condition of life which is the outright decisive and comprehensive negation of that nature.[5]

For instance, bourgeois occupations, like physician and lawyer, were rather creative and satisfying, but the worker, being a mere commodity for the capitalist, was "exposed to all the vicissitudes of competition, to all the fluctuations of the market."

In his *Economic and Philosophical Manuscripts*, Marx stated:

> First, that the work is external to the worker that it is not part of his nature; and that consequently he does not fulfill himself in his work but denies himself, has a feeling of misery rather than well-being, does not develop freely his mental and physical energies but is physically exhausted and mentally debased.

Thus, the worker felt fully human only when performing animal functions or at home. How could it be otherwise as "the worker sinks to the level of a commodity?" For Marx, this alienation was part and parcel of a long historical process that began with the advent of "private property acquisitiveness, the separation of labor, capital and land, exchange and competition, value and the devaluation of man, monopoly and competition – and the system of *money*."[6]

In *Capital*, capitalism, with its almost infinite labor divisions, inexorably made "the laborer into a crippled monstrosity, by forcing his detail dexterity at the expense of a world of productive capabilities and instincts." And as the labor power of labor produces more capital, the greater the domination of labor by capital:

> All means for the development of production transform themselves into means of domination over, and exploitation of the producers: they mutilate the laborer into a fragment of a man, degrade him to the level of an appendage of a machine, destroy every remnant of charm in his work and turn it into a hated toil; they estrange from him the intellectual potentialities of the labor-process in the same proportion as science is incorporated in it as independent power; they distort the conditions under which he works, subject him during the labor process to a despotism the more hateful for its meanness; they transform his lifetime into working time, and drag his wife and child beneath the wheels of the Juggernaut of capital.[7]

And:

The special skill of each individual factory operative vanishes as an infinitesimal quantity before the science, the gigantic physical forces, and the mass of labor that are embodied in the factory mechanism and, together with that mechanism, constitute the power of the "master." Not surprisingly, for Marx, workers could not but be the "slaves of the bourgeois class," as they were "enslaved by the machine, by the over-looker, and above all by the individual bourgeois manufacturer himself," and once paid "set upon by the other portions of the bourgeoisie, the landlord, the shopkeeper, the pawnbroker, etc."[8]

Marx also employed three specific terms in examining alienation – "commodity fetishism," "objectification," and "reification."

The first posited: "There...is a definite social relation between men, that assumes, in their eyes, the fantastic relation between things." In a capitalist society, the fetishism of money, itself related to exchange value commoditization, representing universal capital, "conceals, instead of disclosing the social character of private labor, and the social relations between individual producers," thus leading to mystifying socioeconomic relations, denigrating labor by making it simply one of a myriad of commodities.

The second term (Marx borrowed it from Hegel) postulated that human activity expressed itself in products made, not only everyday-common ones, but also art itself. This was related to the truism that individuals invariably wished to realize themselves positively, but because of a capitalist world of exploitation/oppression: "The performance of work appears in the sphere of political economy as a vitiation of the worker, objectification as a loss and as servitude to the object, and appropriation as alienation." Thus: "So much does objectification appear as loss of the object that the worker is deprived of the most essential things not only of life but also of work."

This manifestation included the difficulty of workers procuring jobs and "that the more objects the worker produces the fewer he can possess and the more he falls under the domination of his product, of capital."

The third, intertwined with the other two, insisted that labor division under capitalism again distorted social relations, viewing individuals from the perspective of work performed, making them into things, obviously diminishing their humanity. (Althusser, a French Marxist philosopher, in *For Marx*, disagreed that reification was a Marxist concept; for him, in *Capital*, "the only social relation that is presented in the form of a thing...is *money.*" Ollman, in *Alienation*, believed otherwise.) [9]

Do the antagonistic-alienating socioeconomic relations of capitalism encourage technological innovation? Yes. But this is only part of the truth of invention/discovery: first, curiosity itself in any technological construct promotes it; second, it is the result of cooperative effort, built upon the experiences of past and present generations, increasingly more so today than before as scientific complexity constantly increases, undermining any supposed unique genius. Furthermore, socialism itself has just as much or even a greater desire to foster technological breakthroughs to raise living standards than capitalism because with the lessening of scarcity, admittedly a problem posing some relativity, human-socialist solidarity should increase. Furthermore, socialism uses inventions as much as possible to lessen routine-deadening labor while disdaining useless-alienating consumerist junk; but capitalism is unconcerned with alienation and is condemned by an archaic profit motive to promote conspicuous waste.

Non-alienating work itself is situated in a society marked by a high level of technology, especially of automation, of integrated labor, in which use value overwhelms market relations of exchange value for exploitation/profit and where participatory democracy at work/society among general equals prevails.

That the work place should make workers into simple automatons was central in the writings of Frederick W. Taylor, the father of scientific management, and practices of Henry Ford, the auto magnate who initiated the moving assembly line of the meatpacking industry, calling for a continuous synchronization between the mobile human body and the material handled, reducing work to a few bodily movements. Taylor, the principal father of work-time studies, had no less an object in mind than to reduce manual labor to a series of mindless motions, specifically removing any mental element on the factory floor, the end being a de-skilled and inexpensive blue-collar work force. Before Taylorism became widespread in the early 1900s, skilled blue-collar workers had much autonomy in the work place.

Taylorism itself was symptomatic of the fact that the power of capital led to a technology and organization which in the end reduced blue-collar workers to a generalized mass of poor and dependent retainers in an increasing labor division, itself spawning more bureaucracy, signifying the growing socioeconomic distance between capital and labor.[10] Smith himself in *Wealth of Nations* praised the increase of labor division in the Lombe Brothers factory employing children, but admitted that labor division in the main makes workers "as stupid and ignorant as it is possible for a human creature to become." [11]

Taylorism was further refined after World War II in Japan by "Toyotism," named after the labor organization pioneered by the Toyota automobile company, instituted after the crushing of Japanese unions in the Red Scare prompted by the Cold War in the late 1940s and early 50s. Its basic element was the utilization of the team approach in an assembly line, each member being able to perform the work of others, all interdependent on one another. The skills involved here were not complex, the work itself being utterly repetitive, although the simple rotation of tasks somewhat relieved the monotony. In this setting, workers occupied the bottom rung of a hierarchical structure, their immediate superior being the team leader, with no input as to how rapidly they worked or other matters, but expected to discuss among themselves as to how they should better work or exploit themselves and monitor one another. But there was more, for workers were herded to hear inspirational sermons about the glories of their company and to sing its praises.[12] This team concept was tied to lean production with its just-in-team arrival/delivery of goods and flexibility for efficient production, made possible by the electronics revolution in computers and increasing automation, including greater use of robotics.

We should also add that lifetime-employment (to age 55) policies in Japan applied only to the larger companies, employing about a fifth of the workforce. The workers of the smaller independent companies doing contract work for the leading ones, like supplying them with parts for final products (these companies in turn have smaller contractors working for them – there are up to four tiers involved here), were not promised lifetime employment and received lower wages. Even within the companies themselves, janitorial and other work was again done by outside firms. This model of capital/ labor organization resulted in further fracturing and dividing the Japanese working class.[13]

Up to now, there is only one major instance of the assembly line ever being discarded in the automobile industry. In the Volvo plant in Uddevalla, Sweden, in 1985, teams of workers, usually from 10 to 12 each, would assemble a car in its entirety. This model, which proved to be efficient enough, was inaugurated because of an acute labor shortage, but terminated with the rise of unemployment.

The moral of the story is that no one voluntarily likes to do boring/repetitive work.[14]

The delineation between work and alienation/oppression continues in many recent studies. A key one by the Marxist Braverman, *Labor and Monopoly Capital*, held that the wondrous technological advances since the 1950s only intensified worker dissatisfaction in the work place. This condition was because the technology was designed to magnify workers' powerlessness, condemning most workers to doing work requiring little or no intellectual challenge, as well as chaining them to a "round of servile duties." Indeed, as the technology advanced most workers became ever more inconsequential because they did not "own the machine and the labor power." [15] Another by the Marxist Bertall Ollman, *Alienation: Marx's Concept of Man in Capitalist Society*, saw that Marx's theory of alienation represented "the devastating effect of capitalist production on human beings, on their physical and mental states and on the social processes of which they are a part." [16]

These views were similar to those of two socialist academics who labored in factories as workers: Simone Weil, the noted French anarchist (*La Condition ouvière*), in 1930s Paris; and Richard M. Pfeffer, a Harvard Ph.D. in government and member of the John Hopkins faculty (*Working for Capitalism*), in the 1970s in greater Baltimore. Both unsparingly accused the capitalist factory system of viewing workers as things or objects to be used, caging them in a social milieu of strict bureaucracy and inhumanity, with almost endless job gradations, rules, and regulations whose aim was to exploit, divide and disempower them as much as possible. But workers might also at any moment be subject to dismissal, either singly or in groups, thrown into the whirlwind of more helplessness and despair. Furthermore, foremen treated workers like children, using harsh language and other devices to discipline them, further eroding their human dignity. The work itself was abominable with long workdays and low wages, repetitive and utterly boring, at maximum speed in hellish working environments, making a mockery of their human existence, further confirming their belonging to the inferior and humiliated class. This was not surprising since workers themselves neither owned the work place nor were consulted in the organization of work, and with their limited education, the mechanical and other principles of science remained a mystery to them, further increasing their alienation.[17]

That work basically defines a person's life, associated with status and class divisions and all they entail, was poignantly described by Studs Terkel (an icon in Left journalism) in *Working*, a magnificent tome of oral history in which more than a hundred Americans recounted how work affected their lives in general. In the continuum of work/class, this study affirmed the obvious of more losers than winners in the race for success; for most workers, jobs were usually physically exhausting and psychologically stressful, as they were caught in a hierarchic cage of humdrum work routines. But for the fortunate ones, the happy few, work was creative and often accompanied with great financial rewards. To be sure, there were a few socialists questioning the status quo. [18]

Terkel's observations were confirmed by Barbara Garson, a well-known social activist, in two works: in *All the Livelong Day*, a brilliant reportage of the work lives of blue- and white-collar workers who were stripped of all dignity and autonomy as labor division increasingly multiplied, ever more fragmenting work and accelerating its pace. In *The Electronic Sweatshop*, she indicted the new and spreading computer technology for subjecting white-collar workers to a new work slavery, the aim being to de-skill them, "restrict their autonomy," and "to make people cheap and disposable." She also observed the deleterious effects of electronic surveillance at work, recording/evaluating every second in the office assembly line, white collars being effectively proletarianized, with "Big Brother" watching them. In this critique, she followed Braverman's objections to Taylorism. [19]

Another major study on capitalist work relations in America, *The Hidden Injuries of Class*, was by two well-known Left writers, Richard Sennett and Jonathan Cobb. In addition to recounting the wasteland of work for most workers, they described the underlying social psychology of a ferociously competitive society dividing people between the successful and failures, the latter usually blaming themselves for their shortcomings.[20]

Yet another well-regarded study on the workplace is by Chris Argyris, Beach Professor of Administrative Sciences, Yale University. *Personality and Organization* relied on a number of detailed studies on work to demonstrate that workers at the lower end of the work/class progression experienced infinitely more feelings of powerlessness and frustration than those performing mental labor. Thus, assembly-line workers faced with the rapid pace and repetitive nature of their work, along with long work hours, more often succumbed to psychosomatic and related illnesses, like high blood pressure and heart disease, and were more prone to accidents than others.[21]

The problems caused by unremittingly boring/repetitive work at high speed, now often electronically monitored, have been recently examined by three studies: A report on the United States by the International Labor Organization, "Job Stress: The 20th Century Disease" (1993); Mitchell Marks' *From Turmoil to Triumph* (1994); and Jeremy Rifkin's *The End of Work* (1995). The first insisted that the annual economic costs of alienation at work on the American economy in the form of illness, absenteeism, lower productivity, and job turnover was in the $200 billion range, while in Britain, as much as 10 percent of its GDP. It also found that as many as 40 percent of Japanese workers feared death by overwork, or "karoshi."[22] The second, by a psychologist on organization and consultant to business, lamented the damage done to workers' morale and disenchantment with management in the wake of recent mergers and downsizing, increasing unemployment and work time (the latter resulting in "burnout"), and decreasing real median wages. The third, by a labor economist, reiterated in great detail the problems posed by the first and second and recommended a 30-hour work week.[23]

Before proceeding to present in some detail the annual human and material costs of an alienating class society in the U.S., usually for the 1990s, these approximate annual statistics on it are in order. There are about 2.25 million deaths from all causes, a 100 million work full-time, and the GDP is as much as $9 trillion.

The American workplace itself has been traditionally driven by violence, reflecting the classist, sexist, and racist (including ethnic and religious divisions) nature of American society. For instance, a 1996 report by the National Institute for Occupational Safety and Health revealed about 1 million crimes annually in the workplace (11 percent of the total), including 1,100 murders (4 percent of the total), and 8 million robberies. A survey conducted by the Northwestern National Life Insurance Co. of 600 workers in 1993 obtained similar results to those of the Justice Department, a sixth claiming to be physically attacked and a fifth threatened by physical harm. The "workplace avenger" who kills fellow workers and supervisors in a fit of rage is not unknown. Then, there is the specter of "covert," "passive" or "hidden aggression," directed against workplace competitors, including malicious gossip, dirty looks, rudeness, and hostile criticism, impinging on efficiency/profits, whose high costs are difficult to quantify. In a recent study of 452 anonymous employees surveyed in six states in a period of a month or less, three university professors – Robert A. Baron, Joel H. Neuman, and Deanna Geddes – more than a quarter reported experiencing such aggressions, while a sixth saw themselves at times as recipients of discourtesies, as not being informed of meetings.

Workplace aggression is undoubtedly related to the earlier bullying of children by parents, which in turn manifests itself in children bullying one another on the street and in school, including for ethnic and religious differences, especially virulent in a racist and multi-ethnic and religious U.S. where "strong (usually the majority or the stronger) prey on the "weak" or minority by speech (teasing and name calling), shunning or physical attack. At times, those picked on may resort to indiscriminate murder as in the Columbine High School case in Colorado in 2001. A recent study of bullying in school, for instance, reveals that a third of children from the sixth to tenth grades indicate verbal or physical bullying concerning race/ethnicity, religion, and disabilities, like speech.

There are also high human costs related to an unhealthy and hazardous workplace environment, including toxic air, dangerous machinery, unsafe work procedures, and speedups. According to the National Safety Council, 250,000 workers died on the job from 1970 to 1995, many from employer negligence; in this time, only four people, according to the Occupational Safety and Health Administration (OSHA) – a federal agency monitoring the workplace – served a prison sentence for subjecting workers to an unsafe work environment. But the average number of annual deaths by accidents in the 1990s has dropped by 40 percent, or to 6,000. Nevertheless, there are still from 50,000 to 70,000 annual deaths from occupationally related illnesses, like lung cancer, and 6 million are injured, of whom 1.4 million leave the workplace for varying periods of time, 50,000 permanently. OSHA itself in 1987 had less than 800 inspectors to cover 6 million work sites; in 1998, the number is 2,000.

These workplace disasters are related to an increasingly helpless work force, with ever less union protection and job security, which is constantly driven to perform ever more in less time. A 2001 report issued by the Families and Work Institute, "Overworked: When Work Becomes Too Much," claims that almost a third of the American work force believes that it is chronically overworked (the "karoshi" syndrome), up to half at times. Not surprisingly, the study concludes that this alienation results in "physical and emotional health problems," like "loss of sleep" and resentment towards bosses.

Now, to high worker mortality rates: In Indiana, for instance, construction workers, most of whom are males, live 10 years less than the national average for men, and in a study of two Lordstown automobile plants near Youngstown, Ohio, the respective mortality rates from cancer are 40 to 50 percent higher than the average. From an overarching perspective on life longevity, a *New York Times* article, "For Good Health, It Pays to be Rich and Important," reports that wealthy white men live 6.6 longer than their poorer counterparts, while whites live longer than blacks, at age 65, 7.4 years for men, and 3.7 years for women.

Tensions and conflicts at work are now exacerbated by downsizing as permanent lifetime jobs are becoming ever scarcer. Since most workers identify themselves closely with their work, intimately related as it is with socioeconomic self-worth, unemployment often results in feelings of shame and worthlessness. When debts cannot be repaid and family possessions dwindle, the psychological health of all family members is imperiled. Not surprisingly, the long-term unemployed have a 30 percent higher rate of divorce than average and abuse their children and spouses more often and more severely than others. From a general perspective, a 1 percent increase in unemployment in America results in a rise of 4 percent for suicide, almost 6 percent for murder, and 4 percent for men and 2 percent for women in admittance to state psychiatric hospitals.[24]

Middle and upper management also cannot completely escape alienation at work, especially its competitive part. Although workers in unionized corporations have some job protection from arbitrary dismissal, this is less so for middle and upper management. Furthermore, the rewards of money and power are so great for managers that they spend not only much of their lives working, but equally spend their social lives networking and politicking for promotion. In this labyrinth, uncertainty reigns. Middle management is now also being savaged by recent trends in corporate downsizing and introduction of new technologies, leading not only to mass layoffs and corresponding lower salaries, but also to increased workloads, inexorably to greater job stress and burnout. This group is also losing its favored status in the workforce because mass higher education has increased its numbers.

In the contemporary Darwinian jungle of middle and upper management, the supposed rationality and efficiency of merit in the business world is largely mythical. For instance, in promotions, more than half of middle managers readily admit that they are made on a "largely subjective evaluation or arbitrary decision."

Even top executives have been concerned with recent downsizings and increased workloads accompanying them. In a 1991 survey of senior executives in the largest thousand American companies, 54 percent feared losing their jobs and 26 percent experienced "burnout," the two leading anxieties. (Of course, senior executives usually have clauses in their contracts protecting them for a number of years in case of dismissal, but workers do not.)

Along with the irrationalities in promotion, there is the specter of inherent economic waste in the American corporation because of its conflict/alienating model in the workplace, which David Gordon, an economist, in *Fat and Mean*, contrasted with the more cooperative German and Japanese ones, necessitating that American corporations have three times as many managers and supervisors as their Japanese and German counterparts, despite recent downsizings also involving management. Whereas Germany and Japan had 4 percent of their work force as managers and supervisors, the U.S. had 13 percent in the early 90s.[25] The task is now to relate the alienation of capitalist work/technology and socioeconomic inequality to the socialization of the individual within the alienated family. It is within the family that most children first become socialized in the primary human patterns, trust and love, fear and hate. In Erik Erickson's eight stages of human psychological development, five critical ones (three to age five, like "trust versus mistrust," "autonomy versus shame and doubt," and "initiative versus guilt" – and two from ages six to eighteen) transpired when the individual was closely associated with the immediate family.

Thus it is that for the neo-Marxists Eric Fromm, as in *Escape from Freedom* and *The Sane Society*, and Theodore W. Adorno and others in *The Authoritarian Personality*, children socialized in an "exploitative child-parent relationship," itself reflecting a society deeply driven by inequality and conflict, as adults became sadomasochistic and obsessive compulsive, attempting to mitigate their insecurities through incessant work and submission to the prevailing religious, socioeconomic, and political authorities, basically intolerant of different ethnic and religious groups and those lower on the socioeconomic scale, more prone to follow Nazism and other authoritarianisms.[26]

Manifestations of the consequences of alienation/oppression in the American family include the following: Shepard, in *Sociology*, presented a series of surveys in the 1970s with these results:

> Almost seven of ten parents had used some form of violence on their children....Nearly 8 percent admitted to kicking, biting, or punching their children; 4 percent had beaten up their children; and 3 percent had threatened their children with weapons.

But there is more; statistics here encompass the 1980s and 90s: perhaps as many as a fifth of men and a third of women have been sexually abused in childhood, usually by either father, or mother, or near relative who has an essentially compulsive personality, addicted in varying degrees/combinations to work, religion, power, and sex, according to the American Psychological Association and others. The pattern of the Adornian male abuser may also be applied to females.

Is it any wonder that one of ten teenagers attempts suicide, as research from the Centers for Disease Control and Prevention states in a survey conducted in 1997. This child abuse is related to violence between spouses in a third of marriages. To be sure, there is also sibling rivalry/violence, and abuse of the elderly, especially the "weak, disabled or female." It is estimated that from half million to 2.5 million elderly parents are annually battered by their children.

The consequences of alienation also extend to the bedroom. The harried, insecure, competitive existence of modern life obviously contributes to sexual dysfunction. A recent and extensive study, conducted by Sociology Professor Edward O. Laumann and Dr. Raymond C. Rosen of the Center for Sexual and Marital Health at the Robert Wood Johnson Medical School in New Jersey, found that, of 1,750 women and 1,410 men studied (the most thorough study since the discredited Kinsey Report of the 1940s), a fourth of women fail to achieve orgasm and a third between age eighteen and 39 lack any interest in sex; for men, 30 percent have problems with premature ejaculation, and 15 percent lack sexual interest. Not surprisingly, the study concludes that poverty, various family stresses, and early and later traumatic sexual experiences like molestation and/or rape lead to the greater possibility of sexual dysfunction. Economic problems also play an important role here as women, whose incomes declined by more than 20 percent in the last three years, have a 60 percent greater likelihood of lower sexual desire than those whose incomes increased. Furthermore, more education and wealth translate into a healthier sexual life, the truism being that the bourgeoisie are less alienated than the working class.

In conjunction with these statistics, there are high divorce rates in the U.S. and in the rest of the world. In the first alone, half of first marriages, three-fourths of second, and nine-tenths of third end in divorce. To be sure, these numbers indicate a weaker nuclear family as an all-encompassing economic unit, although it is still of decisive importance in status/class relations, including social mobility.

Early emotional and physical abuses (the two are related), in addition to various socioeconomic stresses like poverty and insecurity, lead to later neurotic/psychotic behavior. According to Dr. Judith Lewis Herman in *Trauma and Recovery*, from 50 to 60 percent of psychiatric patients requiring hospitalization and from 40 to 60 percent of outpatient ones, were physically and mentally abused in childhood. To be sure, genetic predisposition may be present in mental illness, especially in psychosis, but it is certainly exacerbated by environmental factors. More than a fifth of the population today suffers annually from diagnostically recognizable neurotic symptoms like excessive anxiety and depression, pronounced phobias, obsessive- compulsive disorders, manic depression, and a little more than 1 percent are psychotic or paranoid schizophrenic. Indeed, over a lifetime, perhaps as many as 70 percent of the people have some form of mental illness.[27]

The elite of alienated societies are also composed of deeply alienated individuals, hungering for wealth and power in varying combinations, who routinely lie to defraud, and use others. These are the able sociopaths or psychopaths, the "aggressive egocentrics" and those exhibiting "paranoid, hysterical and obsessional patterns," obviously well-endowed to survive in the Machiavellian labyrinths of the higher economic and political complexes. In this respect, Hitler and Stalin come readily to mind, both psychopaths able to function and succeed in their political ambitions, undoubtedly terrifying those about them to further consolidate and maintain their power. Furthermore, as Dr. Alex Comfort, a neo-anarchist critic of culture, points out in *Authority and Delinquency in the Modern State*, paranoiacs in difficult times have a powerful hold over people as they are able through projection to identify their common hatreds, thus able to find scapegoats, like ethnic/religious minorities. Harold Greenwald, a well-known psychologist, reinforces his views:

> The reasons why we generally do not discuss the
> successful psychopath is because we would then have
> to discuss many of the rulers of the world....Many of
> the symptoms...as lack of morals and apparent lack
> of guilt, exist widely among people of power and
> influence.

Of course, through the services of the sensationalist tabloids, the general public now knows the "sins" of their "betters" or "rulers." An earlier commentary on elite psychopathology was the well-regarded work by the political scientist Harold D. Laswell in *Psychopathology and Politics* (1930), presenting detailed descriptions of personages caught in the web of neurosis and power.[28]

In observing alienation under capitalism, in which the focus is generally on the United States, there is also the awareness of the intense alienation in former socialist societies like the former Soviet Union, whose top layers rejected civil liberties and workers' control of the work place and participation in economic planning, decisive elements indicating intensely antagonistic socioeconomic and political relations. In fact, it was within this deformed socialism (it did have some socialist tendencies, like a rather high degree of socioeconomic equality and extensive social welfarism) that private capitalism developed, existing socialist tendencies obviously overwhelmed by non-socialist ones.

There are many other consequences of alienation/oppression, which in its more extreme forms manifests itself in illness, including anorexia nervosa, obesity, compulsive gambling and buying, extensive use of both legal and illegal injurious drugs, and in criminal activity. The psychic costs of these manifestations are incalculable, but the annual ones (human and economic in the 90s) are largely measurable: the first two phenomena, involving eating disorders, cause the deaths of 300,000 and economic costs in illness, work missed, and early death is certainly more than $200 billion. The third, or compulsive gambling, heavily engages 5 percent of the population, who bet much of the more than $500 billion legally wagered, and many tens of billions illegally, profits being $50 billion. Although legal gambling (most gamblers are men) pays taxes, the social costs of gambling (robbery to pay debts, child and spousal abuse, divorce, and job loss) are $90 billion in 1988. Its twin, compulsive buying (90 percent are women) wastes tens of billions of dollars.

In the realm of psychoactive drugs, legal or illegal, human and material losses are indeed very high. The two most harmful legal drugs are smoking tobacco and alcoholic drinks. Now annually, tobacco, with 50 to 60 million users, has an economic cost of $150 billion and results in more than 440,000 deaths; alcohol, with 100 million habitual users, results in the deaths of 65,000 and costs $185 billion, including treatment of 14 million alcoholics and 30 percent of 37,000 automobile deaths from accidents involving alcohol. In the area of illegal drugs, like marijuana, cocaine, and heroin, they inflict 16,000 annual deaths among 12 to 15 million addicts, 3 million being hard-core, with $200 billion in costs for purchasing the drugs, treatment, property stolen, and incarceration.[29]

Crime itself in its various manifestations denotes the lack of human solidarity in a society stricken by deep individual and social antagonisms, in which economic insecurity and competition drive individuals to be endlessly acquisitive. Crime may be divided into three parts – within the family (already examined), street, and business. The second, or street crime, of burglary and robbery (motor vehicles, jewelry, currency, and household goods) annually consumes $16 billion.

A detailed Justice Department report released in 1996, "Victim Cost and Consequences: A New Look," asserts that the total annual cost for family and street crimes – including rape, injury and murder, factoring in physical injury and psychological trauma and attendant hospitalization, time lost from work, and police and legal costs – is $450 billion. This cost neither includes the $40 billion expended for prisons and related parole and probation systems, nor does it include the $210 billion spent for business and individual security, including anti-theft devices and 1.5 million private security guards.

The third, or business crime, is all pervasive, its annual burden to the public now at $300 billion, with corporations employing kickbacks, bribery, fraud, extortion, violating federal regulations, and tax evasion, while employee embezzlement is merely in the 20 to 40 billion range. In any given decade, about a fifth of the largest 500 corporations are fined by the federal government. Among the more costly frauds/wastes annually in billions of dollars in the last decade include the Savings and Loan debacle (20), in healthcare (100).

Some of the more egregious examples of this in fines and restitution in dollars for the 1999-2000 period are Marc Rich's corporations (Rich is an international trader living in Switzerland who often shaves legality, pardoned in 2001 by President Clinton before leaving office), which paid $200 million. Prudential agreed to pay $1.7 billion to policyholders because of deceptive practices. SmithKline Beecham paid $325 million in fines for false billings to Medicare. Archer Daniels Midland, paid a $100 million fine for price fixing. Michael Milken, the "junk-bond king," paid a $1.1 billion (he will still be worth $125 million) for financial fraud. One of his cohorts, Ivan Boesky, was only fined 100 million. Martin A. Frankel, another financial wizard who fled the country to Germany, will return in 2001 to face financial fraud charges of $208 million. Blue Cross and Blue Shield of Illinois paid $144 million in civil and criminal fines. Columbia/HCFA Healthcare and Quorum Health Group paid a $1.1 billion fine for fraudulent expense claims. In 2001, Walter A. Forbes, former chairperson of Cedant is charged for causing its investors a loss of $19 billion by declaring "phony profits." Cedant itself has compensated shareholders at $2.8 billion. Furthermore, employers illegally withhold from workers $20 billion annually, according to an employer-sponsored think-tank. Lawyers and their ancillaries, of course, cannot be done away with under these circumstances; their cost, $125 billion annually.

To be sure, under the rubric of crime, these elements of it should not be neglected. Half the repairmen overcharge their clients. Furthermore, according to the Internal Revenue Service (IRS), underreporting of income is 20 percent for professionals, 30 percent for farmers, and 50 percent for small business. In any given year many of the S&P 500 corporations and individuals in the Forbes 400 do not pay any income taxes, and in cases involving more than $10 million owed between them and the IRS, its recovery rate is 17 percent, as it is faced by a multitude of lawyers, all part of a pattern (it includes $3 trillion in illegal offshore tax-free bank accounts and various domestic phony trusts) that siphons $300 billion annually from the IRS. The IRS itself has lost 19,000 employees (a third of its staff) to "streamline" the government, allowing rich tax cheaters to further flourish.

A recent United States Judiciary Committee report bewails that America is the "most violent and destructive nation on earth," with the highest homicide and robbery per capita rate among the economically advanced nations. This is reflected in statistics for 2000: prisoners number two million (a third in city and county jails, two thirds in state and federal prisons, a fifth incarcerated for drug-related offenses) of whom 46 percent are black, 34 percent white, 17 percent Hispanic, and 3 percent other, four-fifths having illegal drug and alcohol problems suggesting high stress levels and mental illness. Black males especially are in involved in this social catastrophe: almost a third of them will know prison under present incarceration rates (7 percent of them are in prison at any given time, many as repeat offenders), and of 17,000 murders per year, over half are committed by blacks. Illegal drugs, especially crack cocaine, contribute to this. These numbers should be viewed from this economic alienation: half of black men, from ages 25 to 34-years of age, are either unemployed or earn wages below the poverty line for a family of four.

It should be added that white-collar criminals involved in financial crime face less imprisonment than blue-collar crimes involving a gun. For instance, in cases of fraud, insider trading, and tax evasion of a $1 million or more, there is a maximum of three years imprisonment (often not any), though these sentences may be increased to a 5.25 year maximum sentence in 2001.[30] For comparative purposes, one selling two ounces of cocaine in New York as a first-time offender can receive fifteen years to life.

Is anyone surprised that alienation/oppression, with its train of drugs and crime, takes such a heavy toll in lives and economic resources, especially savaging minority youth in the nation's inner cities? When Louis Chevalier, a French social scientist, observed that 10 percent of Parisians in the 1850s were criminals, poverty being the basic cause, is it unreasonable to claim that this also applies for street crime in American cities today?[31]

A substantial part of the damages related to pollution, including human illness and attempts to mitigate it, are also the resultant of a class-alienated society, with its particular technological structures and consumerist demands with their inherent waste. Certainly a cooperative world like socialism is more likely to solve these problems than the present order. The following statistics are generally annual ones for the early 1990s in the U.S.: Cancer rates climbed rapidly from 1950 to 1986, as reported in a 1989 study by the National Cancer Institute. The figures depict an increase of 21.5 percent for children under age 14 and a 22.6 percent increase for adults. It may be argued that the rising adult cancer rate may be partly explained by an aging population, but this does not hold true for children. The work place itself, according to the National Safety Council, accounts for 23 to 38 percent of cancer deaths, or 150,000, which alone consumes $275 billion. As for other annual pollution costs in billions of dollars: air pollution from industry and transportation ($226 billion), on residential and industrial structures ($30 billion), the cost of polluted water on health ($1 billion), and $11 billion on recreational activity – they do not include the loss of irreplaceable natural resources in the many tens of billions of dollars. Finally, there is the toll of toxic microbes in food, which kills 9,000 people annually and causes illness in 80 million people, costing $7 billion in medical bills and work absences.[32]

According to Murry Weidenbaum, chairperson of President Reagan's Council of Economic Advisors, other wasteful annual expenditures in the 90s include $138 billion for advertising, $136 billion for deficient vehicle safety, as well as $300 billion for the military ($400 billion in 2003) and related areas.[33]

That the very wastes enumerated created jobs and great profits – not to mention special interest groups, which in an alienated class society are fearful of change lest they lost their jobs/profits – is obvious. But if class alienation can be overcome by socialism, the resultant should, within the context of contemporary technology, allow for a six-hour work day without the loss of jobs and present living standards in the U.S. and other developed nations within the near future.

In *The Culture of Narcissism*, history professor Christoph Lasch traced the American character from the 17th century Puritan centered on work as a "calling", to the 18th century "Yankee", personified by Franklin as more materialistic and individualistic but still related to some virtue and community; to the 19th-century one of unbridled individualistic success and self-improvement, to the late 20th century-one depicting the narcissistic "Happy Hooker," materialistic and acquisitive, living for the moment, consumerism equaling nirvana, but forced to conform, however, within the bureaucratic cage of monopoly capitalism, devoid of any sense of self-entitlement and power. His way out of this alienating impasse had a Marxian ring to it:

> The struggle against bureaucracy therefore requires a struggle against capitalism itself. Ordinary citizens cannot resist professional dominance without also asserting control over production and over the technical knowledge on which modern production rests...They [citizens] will have to create their own "communities of competence." Only then will the productive capacities of modern capitalism, together with the scientific knowledge that it now serves it, come to serve the interests of humanity instead.[34]

Lasch's consumerist nirvana is, of course, related to the alienation or essential meaninglessness of work for most of the work force, whose basic compensation now is to frequent the new temples/pleasures of capitalism – the retail outlets, in frequent vacations, prompted by the new priests, advertisers and salespersons, who dispense the meaning of life.

Although Marx delved extensively into the various aspects of working-class alienation at work and outside of it, he did not do so for education. To be sure, the *Manifesto* favored "free education of all children in public schools," along with "abolition of child labor in factories," and the "combination of education with industrial production, etc." But, for most 19th-century thinkers, including Marx and Engels, it was assumed that education would not be of long duration for the masses at least for the immediate future – this in a society of yet primitive technology and great scarcity from our vantage point. In Western Europe, general literacy by the mid-19th century was widespread in France and Germany. The same could be said of Britain at a later period, with most workers and farmers having, at most, a primary education.

But Marxists and other progressives in the 20th century have delved into the problems of an alienating education in bourgeois society. In the economically advanced capitalist nations, education is, along with the family, the primary transmission belt to acculturate youth to society's norms. It is only vitally involved in determining the individual's life chances or socioeconomic success.

Not surprisingly, education, as part of an individualistic/competitive society, is of a ferocious nature. Cooperation here is pictured as being friendly to one's peers and obedient to school authorities. But underneath this façade, there is the constant anxiety of being graded at every turn in relationship to the group or to long-established so-called objective criteria, a condition adversely affecting proper learning. Rewarding winners with good grades and accolades invariably humiliates average and poor students, while engendering pride among the former and resentment among the latter. This learning milieu, intrinsic to a bourgeois-dominated society, alienates in varying degree most of its students, as it is necessarily replete with boredom and futility associated with memorization and rote learning, restricting intellectual curiosity by emphasizing test grades.

With the importance of local taxation in funding education from kindergarten to grade twelve, there are also wide variations spent on children, obviously involved in the socioeconomic differences among various school districts. Socioeconomic alienation is less intense for the students of wealthier neighborhoods, allowing most of them to either attend college or to be accepted by the more prestigious colleges and universities. As observed at all levels, there is competition for grades, although in the higher socioeconomic groups it is muted with many good grades for most students as their academic intelligence, as indicated in tests, is uniformly high. In the working-class, especially its poorer half comprising a large proportion of blacks and Hispanics, great socioeconomic alienation impinges on a good education, with students buffeted by the usual problems associated with poverty, like poor academic performance and accompanying high dropout rates, in a milieu at school characterized by crumbling buildings, antiquated books, and lack of supplies – not to mention a home life encircled by economic insecurity and accompanying general chaos.[35]

Notes

1) On Marx and alienation, see Erich Fromm, *Marx's Concept of Man,* with a translation from Marx's *Economic and Philosophical Manuscripts* by T.B. Bottomore (New York: Frederick Ungar, 1969), pp. 43-58. Erich Fromm, *The Sane Society* (New York: Holt, Rinehart, 1955), pp. 120-52. Bertell Ollman, *Alienation: Marx's Concept of Man in Capitalist Society* (2nd ed.; London: Cambridge Univ. Press, 1976), pp. 131-35, for instance.

2) Genesis 2 and 3.

3) On Rousseau, see Ernest Cassirer, *The Question of Jean-Jacques Rousseau* (New York: Columbia Univ. Press, 1954). Jean-Jacques Rousseau, *The Social Contract and Discourses*, trans. and intro. By G.D.H. Cole (New York: E.P. Dutton, 1950), pp. 234-72. On Hegel, see *The Philosophy of Hegel*, ed. and intro. Carl J. Friedrich (New York: Modern Library, 1954), pp. 399-445.

4) Marx and Engels, *German Ideology*, pp. 22 ff. Fromm, *Marx's Concept of Man*, pp. 24, 93-109, and 151, the last citation is the lengthy quotation.

5) K. Marx and F. Engels, *The Holy Family or Critique of Critical Critique* (Moscow: Foreign Language Publishing House, 1956), p. 51.

6) Marx and Engels, *Communist Manifesto*, pp. 15-16; Fromm, *Marx's Concept of Man*, pp. 93-98; the long quotation is on p. 98.

7) *Capital*, I, 396 for the long quotation.

8) On the long quotation, see *Capital*, I, 462-63. On the brief quotations, *Manifesto,* p. 16 and Marx and Engels, *German Ideology*, p. 69.

9) On "commodity fetishism," see Marx, *Capital*, I, 81-87; on "objectification" see Marx, *Economic and Philosophical Manuscripts* in Fromm, *Concept of Man*, pp. 95-97; on "reification," see Ollman, *Alienation*, pp. 196 ff. and 205 ff. Louis Althusser, *For Marx*, trans. Ben Brewster (New York: Pantheon Books, 1969), p. 230.

10) On Taylorism, labor division, and so forth, see Sudhir Kakar, *Frederick Taylor: A Study in Personality and Innovation* (Cambridge, MA: MIT Press, 1970); Dan Clawson, *Bureaucracy and the Labor Process: The Transformation of U.S. Industry, 1860-1920* (New York: Monthly Review Press, 1980), pp. 38 ff., 71 ff., 126 ff., and 202-67.

11) On Smith, see *The Wealth of Nations: Representative Selections* (Indianapolis, IN: Bobbs-Merrill, 1961), pp. xvii, 3-5.

12) Daniel Singer, *Whose Millennium? Theirs or Ours?* (New York: Monthly Review Press, 1999), p. 163.

13) Ibid., pp. 163-64.

14) On the Swedish innovations to end the conventional assembly line, see Christian Breggren, *Alternative to Lean Production* (Ithaca, NY: ILR Cornell Univ. Press, 1992).

15) Braverman, *Labor and Monopoly Capital*, pp. 95, 194, and 241.

16) Ollman, Alienation. p. 131.

17) Simone Weil, *La Condition Ouvrière* (Paris: Gallimard, 1951), pp. 15 ff. Richard M. Pfeffer, *Working for Capitalism* (New York: Columbia Univ. Press, 1979), pp. 47-102, for instance.

18) Studs Terkel, *Working: People Talk About What They Do All Day and How They Feel About Their Work* (New York: Pantheon Books, 1974), cf., for instance, Mike Lefevre, factory worker, pp. xxxi-xxxviii, with David Bender, factory owner, pp. 393-97.

19) Barbara Garson, *All the Livelong Day: The Meaning and Demeaning of Routine Work* (Garden City, NY: Doubleday, 1975), pp. 38 ff., 58 ff., and 90 ff., for instance. Barbara Garson, *The Electronic Sweatshop: How Computers Are Transforming the Office of the Future into the Factory of the Past* (New York: Simon and Schuster, 1988), pp. 40-114, 166-71, 175-263.

20) Richard Sennett and Jonathan Cobb, *The Hidden Injuries of Class* (New York: Alfred A. Knopf, 1972), pp. 30 ff., 55 ff., 72 ff., 92 ff., 121 ff., 147 ff., 162 ff.

21) Chris Argyris, *Personality and Organization: The Conflict Between System and the Individual* (New York: Harper Torchbooks, 1970), pp. 76-122.

22) On the ILO report, see David Briscoe, "Labor force reluctant lot, report says," *Akron Beacon Journal*, March 23, 1993, p. D6; and Frank Swoboda, "Employers Recognizing What Stress Costs Them, U.N. Report Suggests," *Washington Post*, March 23, 1993, p. H2.

23) On recent downsizing and mergers of corporations, with resulting widespread layoffs of workers, coupled to overwork and higher stress of those working, and decreasing real wages, see Mitchell Lee Marks, *From Turmoil to Triumph: New Life after Mergers, Acquisitions, and Downsizing* (New York: Maxwell Macmillan International, 1994), pp. 3-28. Jeremy Rifkin, *The End of Work: The Decline of the Global Work Force and the Dawn of the Post-Market Era* (New York: G.P. Putnam's, 1995), pp. 182-90.
On increasing alienation in the family and work place, manifested by more stress and higher levels of violence, unsafe working conditions, more job insecurity, higher medical costs related to the preceding, and lower life longevity for workers relative to the rich, see Rifkin, *End of Work*, pp. 194-97. Blair Justice and Rita Justice, *The Abusing Family* (New York: Plenum Press, 1990), pp. 191-93. William Greider, *Who Will Tell the People: The Betrayal of American Democracy* (New York: Simon and Schuster, 1992), pp. 111-22. Ralph Estes, *Tyranny of the Bottom Line: Why Corporations Make Good People Do Bad Things* (San Francisco, CA: Berrett-Koehler, 1996), pp. 180-82. *In These Times*, Nov. 14-20, 1990, p. 16. The daily press is a good source for the consequences of alienation at work and elsewhere. For instance, at work, see *Akron Beacon Journal*, Aug. 13, 1990, p. A4; Jan. 28, 1996, pp. 14, A1 and A4; July 9, 1996, p. A3. On sabotage at work, see Mary

Curtius, *(Los Angeles Times)*, "Employee vandalism gouging companies," *Akron Beacon Journal,* Nov. 8,

24) 1998, pp. G1 and G8. On "passive aggression," see Michael Lopez *(Albany Times Union)*, "Aggression on the job: Gossip, dirty looks," *Akron Beacon Journal*, Jan. 25, 1999, p. D4. Lisa Cornwell, "Workplace violence on the rise," *Akron Beacon Journal*, Sept. 4, 1995, pp. D1 and D4. On workers competing with one another at work and its deleterious effects, see Sherwood Ross, "Competition on job is internal strife," *Akron Beacon Journal*, March 11, 1996, p. D3. On bullying at school, see Lindsey Tanner, "Bullying affects one in three, study says," *Akron Beacon Journal*, April, 25, 2001, pp. A1 and A2. On longevity of life, see "For Good Health, it Helps to Be Rich and Important," *New York Times*, June 1, 1999, pp. D1 and D9. On overworked Americans, see Diane Stafford, "Workers complain they are swamped," *Akron Beacon Journal*, May 20, 2001, p. F3.

25) On job stress and higher unemployment rates for managers, about 8 percent of the work force, see Marks, *From Turmoil to Triumph*, pp. 6-14; Michael C. Jensen, "Frustrated Middle Managers," *New York Times*, July 18, 1971, Sec. 3, p. 1. Dennis Weintraub, "Office Politics: A Deadly Game for Losers," *Akron Beacon Journal*, March 22, 1974. Earl Shorris, *The Oppressed Middle: Politics of Middle Management* (Garden City, NY: Anchor Press/ Doubleday, 1981), chaps. 6 and 7. Carl Hecksher, *White-Collar Blues: Management Loyalties in an Age of Restructuring* (New York: Basic Books, 1995), pp. 3-94. On corporate waste, see David M. Gordon, *Fat and Mean: The Corporate Squeeze of Working Americans and the Myth of Managerial Downsizing."* (New York: Free Press, 1996), pp. 33-60.

26) Erik H. Erikson, *Identity: Youth and Crisis* (New York: W.W. Norton, 1968), pp. 91-141. Erich Fromm, *Escape from Freedom* (New York: Farrar and Rinehart, 1941), pp. 141-206. Erich Fromm, *The Sane Society* (New York: Holt and Rinehart, 1955), pp. 12-52. T. W. Adorno et al., *The Authoritarian Personality* (New York: Harper and Brothers, 1950), pp. 759 ff.

27) On the family (and its discontents), see John M. Shepard, *Sociology,* 5th ed. (Minneapolis/St. Paul, MN: West Publishing Co., 1993), p. 344. John Bradshaw, *The Family: A Revolutionary Way of Self-Discovery* (Deerfield, FL: Health Communications, 1988), pp. 116, 126 ff. Dennis Coon, *Introduction to Psychology: Exploration and Application* (St. Paul, MN: West Publishing Co., 1980), pp. 420-84. Judith Lewis Herman, *Trauma and Recovery* (New York: Basic Books, 1992), pp. 103, 96-114, 122, and 135. Anne Sappington and Mike Paquette, "Family Violence," *Akron Beacon Journal*, Aug. 24, 1996, p. A8 on sexually abused children. On attempted suicide by teenagers, see *Akron Beacon Journal*, Aug. 14, 1998, p. A4. "Body-bag" journalism as daily reported on television and press presents the continuing drama/alienation of especially the economically lowest third of the people.

28) Alex Comfort, *Authority and Delinquency in the Modern State* (London: Routledge and Kegan Paul, 1950), pp. 31-65. Harold Greenwald, "Treatment of the Psychopath," p. 364, in Harold Greenwald, ed., *Active Psychotherapy* (New York: Atherton Press, 1967). Harold D. Lassell, *Psychopathology and Politics* (New York: Viking Press, 1960), pp. 1-77. This work was first published in 1930.

29) On drugs, see Steven B. Duke and Albert C. Gross, *America's Longest War: Rethinking Our Tragic Crusade Against Drugs* (New York: Jeremy P. Tarcher/Putnam Book, 1993), pp. 23-32 on tobacco, 33-42 on alcohol, pp. 54 ff. on heroin, etc. On gambling, see Marc Cooper, "America's House of Cards," *The Nation*, Feb. 19, 1996, pp. 11-19.

30) On the Senate Judiciary Report, see *Akron Beacon Journal*, March 13, 1991, p. A6. On murder and suicide, see *Mother Jones*, Jan.-Feb., 1994, p. 40. On "Victims Costs and Consequences" report, see *Akron Beacon Journal*, April 22, 1996, p. A4. On black males and incarceration, see *U.S. News and World Report*, Oct. 16, 1995, pp. 53-54. Also, see on this and related topics, David Remnick, "Dr. Wilson's Neighborhood," *The New Yorker*, April, 29/May 6, 1996. On the number of street murders and cost of

street, white-collar, and corporate crimes, see Russell Mokhiber, "Underworld U.S.A.," *In These Times*, April 1-13, 1996, pp. 14-16; Ralph Estes, "The Public Cost of Private Corporations," *Advances in Public Interest Accounting*, VI, 1995, 339-45; and Robert Sherrill, "A Year in Corporate Crime," *The Nation*, April, 7, 1997, pp. 11-20. On employee sabotage, see Mary Curtius, (*Los Angeles Times*), "Employee vandalism gouging companies," *Akron Beacon Journal*, Nov. 8, 1998, pp. G1 and G8. On the costs of private anti-theft measures and the legal industry, see George Winslow, "Capital Crimes: The Political Economy of Crime in America," *Monthly Review*, Nov. 2000, pp. 38-51. On the $300 billion annually lost to tax cheating by the IRS and so fourth, see *Akron Beacon Journal*, May 14, 1978, and Curt Anderson (Associated Press), "Tax evasion scams explode on internet," *Akron Beacon Journal*, April 9, 2001, p. D5.

31) Louis Chevalier, *Laboring Classes and Dangerous Classes in Paris During the First Half of the Nineteenth Century* (New York: Howard Fertig, 1973), pp. 275 ff.

32) Ralph Estes, "The Public Cost of Private Corporations," *Advances in Public Interest*, vol. 6, pp. 337-43. Estes, *Tyranny of the Bottom Line*, pp. 171-89. Michael Satchell and Stephen J. Hedges, "The next bad beef scandal?" *U.S. News and World Report*, Sept. 1., 1997, pp. 22-24.

33) Estes, *Tyranny of the Bottom Line*, pp. 183-84, on unsafe vehicles, p. 95 on advertising.

34) Christopher Lasch, *The Culture of Narcissism: American Life in an Age of Diminishing Expectations* (New York: Warner Books, 1979), p. 396, on the quotation.

35) On unequal education in the United States, see Jonathan Kozol, *Savage Inequalities: Children in America's Schools* (New York: HarperPerennial, 1992).

Chapter Ten: The Mystery of Religion

A) Background

Religion is an important human institution because in almost all instances since civilization to the present, it has been the principal unifying institutional force of alienated society.

The approach here is to present a general view of religion from a contemporary anthropological approach heavily indebted to Marxism, relate the views of Marx/Engels on the subject, trace briefly the struggle between religion and Communism in the Soviet Union as an example of Communist intransigence to religion, observe the views of prominent secular socialists after Marx/Engels, and indicate the progressive and socialist elements among religious groups worldwide, signifying that the 19th and 20th centuries have witnessed an intensification of the class struggle waged by workers and peasants against nobility and capitalists, focusing on leading theologians as representatives of this tendency.

Religion (from the Latin verb *religare*, to bind together) is a complex social phenomenon having socioeconomic, ethical, political, and psychological roots. It is related to some form of dependence on transcendent spiritual power(s) as it attempts to integrate the individual/family to the larger society, and in the process institutionalize codes of social behavior to promote individual/group survival. It is also usually related to some form of hereafter, and through magic/prayer and other such devices, marks the joys and tragedies of life. In the realm of social conflict, either domestic or foreign, it offers an explanation as to *why*. The worship of God(s), according to Emile Durkheim, one of the founders of sociology, expresses the worship of the community, a transcended entity, the sacred, as opposed to the profane, the ordinary.

It is difficult to know when organized religious feeling gripped humanity. Neanderthal man buried his dead 40,000 years ago with food and tools, the body painted with red ocher, perhaps signifying belief in some form of afterlife. The 30,000-year-old cave paintings of Cro-Magnon Man at Lascaux, France, and Altamira, Spain, in which animals are hunted by men, were probably a form of sympathetic magic.

From a broad historical perspective, early religion or magic usually worshipped forces of nature (animism), but with the advent of humanity's greater control over nature or growth of productive force, a theological revolution occurred by the later stages of the Agricultural Revolution, specifically by 4000 B.C. in Mesopotamia/Egypt. This revolution transformed animism into forms of anthropomorphism (often along with animals), allowing humanity to ask for aid from god(s) more sympathetic to its needs than nature. Anthropomorphic religion itself was undoubtedly related to the social psychology involved with ancestor worship, the basis being that children regarded parents/elders as deities/providers.

In association with anthropomorphic deities, gender intervened. About 20,000 years ago, Cro-Magnon statuettes of females, displaying prominent sexual characteristics, may have indicated women's centrality in birth. And during the Agricultural Revolution, earth mothers, alongside animism, predominated; women discovered agriculture, men hunted. But with increasing status and class complexity, more war, and the rise of the state, male gods dethroned the female gods. Among Hebrew herders, for instance, Yahweh, a military male god became the only one; among the Greeks and Romans, male gods enjoyed more power and authority than their female counterparts.

Soon after the advent of civilization in Egypt, with the religion of Aton in the 14th century B.C.E. in Egypt, universal monotheism emerged for the masses briefly, in which the pharaoh Akenhaton and his wife, Nefertiti, worshipped Aton, while the masses worshipped them. Intimately involved with this development of Egyptian religion was an elaborate afterlife system: Egyptian religion may be seen as the first great religion to "cheat" death, becoming the prototype of mystery religion, stressing life after death, the good inheriting paradise, the evil, hell.

The Greek philosopher Euhemerus (c. 300 B.C.E.) formulated a rational/non-supernatural explanation for these and other religious phenomena, observing that the gods of Greek mythology were simply deified mortals, although those of superior social position like kings, their wives, and children. This indicated class-exploitative societies, usually capped by a leader with religious qualities, often a priest/ king.

A key element of religion, as in Judeo-Christianity, was that its higher ideals provided hope to escape present exploitative/alienating societies, with promise for a future life/utopia. Furthermore, the foremost religious prophets proclaimed the need for brotherhood and equality, at least among the in-group. But in the reality of history, of class society under ruling elites, religion itself became another means to alienate, chaining humanity to existing social systems as well as promoting religious conflict: within Protestantism, for instance, between Puritans and Quakers in America, Anglicans and Dissenters in England; between Orthodox Russians and Polish Catholics, Muslim Turks and Orthodox Greeks, Protestants and Catholics in Europe and in America, Christians and Jews in Europe and America, and Jews and Moslems in Palestine related to the establishment of Israel. Indeed, religious bigotry and related violence are usually associated with ethnic-economic rivalry. In this regard, the dominant religion in an area often segregated the minority. One of many examples were the decrees of the Fourth Lateran Council of 1215 in Rome, which required Jews to wear distinctive marks on their clothing and prohibited sexual relations between Catholics and Jews, indeed simply repeating an earlier order of 339. Indeed, the virtual destruction of European Jewry by the Nazis during World War II cannot be understood properly without observing a thousand years of European anti-Semitism.

There was a contradictory aspect of religion: on the one hand it displayed high ideals of social justice, while on the other it reflected the imperfect ethics of class-dominated predatory societies with their penchant for "double-think" – to use an Orwellian term. It accepted exploitative socioeconomic relations, but alleviated them for the in-group through band aid efforts, like charity, while being invariably antagonistic to outsiders.

Traditional religion blended the real-existing world with the phantom-invisible one, uniting the "real", or ephemeral present with the "eternal" supernatural; and in reflecting complex social organization, it is necessarily replete with elaborate hierarchies of invisible/visible beings/symbols, usually related to concerns for the individual's present and future life within some form of communal setting.

The afterlife beliefs of religion are a wonder to behold. They are based as they are on a reward/punishment axis of heaven(s) and hell(s) to reinforce worldly "justice" within the confines of class and caste. Believers of Judaism, Christianity, and Islam, for example, are twice born. Of course there are exceptions, including Ultra-Orthodox Jews believing in reincarnation (Rabbi Ovadia Yosef, leader of the Israeli Shas Party, remarked that Jews murdered in the Holocaust are reincarnated sinners). In Christianity, Origen, second only to Augustine among the Church Fathers, was a proponent of reincarnation – several instances of it being in the Bible – but the Fifth Ecumenical Council in 553, in which Western bishops were scarcely represented, repudiated it.

After death, resurrection is promised in these religions, itself related to final judgment for heaven or hell; there are also intermediate states like purgatory and limbo for Catholics. As for non-believers after the advent of Christ, Christians traditionally relegate them to hell. But Hinduism and its offshoot, Buddhism, allow for many reincarnations before reaching *nirvana* (the Hindu version is attaining sufficient wisdom to end any attachment to the world of materiality; the Buddhist perspective is disinterested understanding of the human condition and its corollary of infinite compassion). Rebirth is related to *karma* or the moral cosmic law of accumulated good/bad actions, involving caste or *dharma* for Hindus and class for Buddhists; good moving the individual up the social ladder, the bad moving down. This locks most individuals into a set of almost unalterable and oppressive socioeconomic and other relationships – predestination.

Not surprisingly, in Hinduism, for instance, the more "virtuous" and powerful are at the higher reaches of socioeconomic and intellectual endeavors: the *Brahmans* (priests) at the top are followed by the *Kshatriyas* (kings, nobility, warriors), and *Vaisyas* (merchants, bankers, artisans, and free workers) – members of the top three castes are at least twice-born. The preponderance of economic power is in the hands of the *Kshatriyas* in large landed estates, although the bankers and merchants also have considerable wealth. The *Brahmans* themselves are quite wealthy, subsisting on fees for religious services and investments on land, in this regard being somewhat economically dependent on the *Kshatriyas* and wealthier *Vaisyas*. The overwhelming majority of the Hindu population is in the *Sudra* caste, of serfs and farm workers, which follows the leading three. At the bottom are those below the castes or *Dalits*, the "untouchables," performing the most unclean and menial work, a fourth of the Hindu world. The caste system itself was legally outlawed in India in 1947, but tenaciously still exists, especially in the countryside.

The many-reincarnations belief of Hinduism and Buddhism allows their believers to taste the various socioeconomic levels of society before being liberated from the temptations of the "selfish body," of not returning to the material world. This seems more compassionate than that of the twice-born religions presenting their adherents to only one chance for eternal salvation or damnation. But the many-reincarnations belief buttresses the status quo by counseling patience to social inequality/oppression.

Traditional Christianity itself, as an example of twice-born religions, has its own variant of the *karma* doctrine in the form of predestination. God, omnipotent and omniscient for His (not usually Her) own reasons, saves some persons (a small minority) for heaven, relegating the others to hell. Why this is so is a mystery known only to God. Signs of election include being a Christian, but each Christian sect traditionally believes that its membership has priority in salvation. Free-will Christians who maintain that they can receive deliverance with the aid of Christ must reconcile this stance with

God being omnipotent/omniscient, who neglects others for varying reasons, including not believing in Christ's divinity.

Salvation also has a class connection. For very early Christianity, the rich were usually condemned to hell, while the poor entered heaven; for later Christianity, sin condemned one to slavery according to St. Augustine; for Calvinists, poverty was surely a sign of sin, a sensible idea if equal egress to the means of production were granted to everyone – which, of course, seldom happened. But for some of 20th century Christianity, under the impress of socialism, the rich and powerful were again seen as oppressors and prime sinners.

The agitator Jesus of Nazareth, a religious revolutionary communist, was related to the ascetic communist Essene Hebrew sect through John the Baptist, who baptized him. Jesus, whose God demanded justice-quality, was crucified by the Romans on the orders of the Sadducees, or Hebrew priests, which the poor-unorganized Hebrew masses could not prevent.

These stances reflected the antagonistic socioeconomic relations of class society and accompanying manifestations of alienation, which included one's social station in an afterlife. Today, most Christian groups grant relatively easy access to heaven, indicating the increasing presence of secularism.

An old social phenomenon related to salvation that is deeply imbedded in the Christian and Buddhist tradition is in collective celibacy/asceticism, or monasticism (Islam also has its mystic Sufis and their orders, some practicing celibacy, and Hinduism, its holy men).

From a humanistic socialist perspective, asceticism may be considered a prime virtue in a world of exploitative socioeconomic and other arrangements because it helps to overcome normal worldly attachments and temptations while often devoting attention to the poor/oppressed. In this sense, asceticism/celibacy, with its stress on the communal/spiritual (it often becomes corrupt) is at once a protest against the traditional world of wealth and power and an opening to a more socially just world, thus to be applauded. To be sure, sublimating the sex drive promotes its own special problems, as encouraging exclusivity and accompanying elitism. Of course, there are instances in which believers can have a closely-knit community and even have multiple sexual intimacies, along with children, prosperity, and promise of heaven, the Oneida experiment in New York in the 19th century being one.

Religion itself over the centuries has been challenged by philosophical materialism and near variants, although the three most prominent of the Greek philosophers believed in god(s). Plato and Socrates in a soul related to one god, while Aristotle in as many as 55, with no concern for humanity. In the East, its principal philosopher, the Chinese Confucius, enunciated a basic materialism interested in ethical/social matters, relegating religion to the marginal: "We do not know life; how can we understand death?"

In the West, the rise of Christianity overwhelmed philosophical materialism. Christian monopoly of education relegated it to the nether world. But with the Renaissance, beginning in Italy, the rise of the bourgeoisie and science, and the Enlightenment of the 17th and 18th centuries, a skeptical spirit developed, including that of traditional religion. Its most audacious thinkers followed the Greeks in their atheism and deism, banishing a personal god from the cosmos. Leading figures in this regard were Henri Bayle, Spinoza, Voltaire, and Diderot. As for Romanticism, its radical side was definitely atheist, as evidenced by Percy Shelly whom Marx admired.

It is this tradition of atheism that Marx/Engels embraced; they were not alone in this for the leading 19th century socialists, including socialist anarchists, were atheists – Owen, Proudhon, Bakunin coming readily to mind.

In the 19th-and 20th centuries, especially with the continued rise of scientific and technological progress and widespread national/secular education, philosophical materialism was at center stage once again, its criticism of religion upheld by leading social philosophers and scientists.[1]

B) Marx and Engels on Religion

As philosophical materialists, Marx and Engels viewed religion from a historical/anthropological perspective involving two primary alienations – the first between humanity and nature, the second among human beings.

The first posited that human beings, although part of nature, were self-reflective, aware of their need to wrest from it their very subsistence. The second comprised antagonistic socioeconomic and other relations among human beings, arising from technological progress and resultant individual, status, and class struggles, especially with the advent of civilization.

In *Anti-Dühring*, Engels presented his and Marx's most comprehensive and general view of religion. He saw that "All religion, however, is nothing but the fantastic reflection in men's minds of those external forces which control their daily life, a reflection in which the terrestrial forces assume the form of supernatural forces." Normally for Engels, because of human dependence on nature, "it was the forces of nature which were first so reflected."

This mindset led to these forces of nature progressively transforming themselves into "varied personifications among the various people," as into various gods and goddesses when "social forces begin to be active – forces which confront man as equally alien and at first equally inexplicable, dominating him with the same apparent natural necessity as the forces of nature themselves." Then, the "natural and social attributes of the numerous gods are transferred to one almighty god who is but a reflection of the abstract man." This view is consonant with that of modern anthropology, of religion progressing from animism to anthropomorphism in its various forms, to universal monotheism. He related this religious development to the "sentimental form of men's relation to the alien natural and social forces which dominate them, so long as men remain under the control of these forces." Finally, he compared the mystery of religion to that of the "capitalist mode of production," whose periodic economic crises engulf those living under it with "bad debts and bankruptcy, nor secure the individual workers against unemployment and destitution."[1]

In an arresting passage in *The German Ideology*, Marx and Engels again delineated the multiple roots of early religion in the psychology/sociology/economics of human survival in a hostile natural environment, including humanity's increasing consciousness of not only being a part of nature like other animals, but apart from it, possessing its own uniqueness:

> At the same time it is consciousness of nature which first appears to man as an entirely alien, omnipotent, and unassailable force. Men's relations with this consciousness are purely animal, and they are overawed by it like beasts. Hence, it is a purely animal consciousness of nature (natural religion) – for the very reason that nature is not yet modified historically.[2]

To better survive, early humanity attempted to better understand and manipulate this nature through religious practices, themselves constituting an early form of science.

With the advent of the Neolithic Age and civilization, with its consequences of class oppression and war, religion also now served as an institution offering solace in an unbearable present. For Marx:

> Religious suffering is the expression of real suffering and at the same time the protest against real suffering. Religion is the sigh of the oppressed creature, the heart of a heartless world, as it is the spirit of spiritless conditions. It is the opium of the people. The abolition of religion as people's illusory happiness is the demand for their real happiness. The demand to abandon illusions about their condition is a demand to abandon a condition which requires illusions. The

criticism of religion is thus in embryo a criticism of
the vale of tears whose halo is religion.[3]

In *Anti-Dühring*, Engels followed Marx's criticism of religion,
of consoling the masses to accept their socioeconomic inferiority
to ruling elites, thus lessening class hostility (To reinforce Engels
here, I present these instances of religion – there are many others
– being inextricably intertwined with the status quo of privilege
and power: traditional Judaism, Hinduism, Islam, and Christianity;
for the last, recall the Orthodox Byzantine and Russian Empires,
Catholic Bourbons and Hapsburgs, Anglican English monarchy, and
Lutheran German Kaiser and Scandinavian kings).

But the centrality of religion itself in alienated societies allowed
for divisions to develop within the religious structures themselves,
with the most progressive side invariably representing the hopes and
aspirations of the broad masses for better and more just societies. In
this picture, Engels focused on the social aspects of religion in two
works, "On the History of Early Christianity" and *The Peasant War
in Germany.*

In "On the History of Early Christianity," Engels presented
a masterful account of the origins and rise of Christianity, in
which Roman oppression of subject people and their response was
central. Thus is was, for him, that the salient fact concerning early
Christians was their being the "lowest strata of population," from
"impoverished free men" in the urban areas, from slaves, including
newly emancipated ones, of "small peasants who had fallen more and
more into bondage through debt." Indeed, for many of these social
layers their golden age was in the past:

For the ruined free men it was the former polis, the town and
the state at the same time, of which their forefathers had been free
citizens; for the war-captive slaves, the time of freedom before their
subjugation and captivity; for the small peasants, the abolished gentile
system and communal land ownership. All that had been smitten
down by the leveling iron fist of conquering Rome. In this world,
Engels observed that among "groups of people whose interests were

mutually alien or even opposed," there "could only be a religious way out" to end their socioeconomic inferiority and degradation in an invincible Roman state system which they could not challenge because of their very separation from one another and its very power. This involved for him these pre-existing religious elements: the belief in a soul surviving the mortal body after death; the millenarian-apocalyptic tradition found in the Bible, of Isaiah, Ezekiel, Book of Enoch, Book of Daniel, and John's "Revelations," the last with its promise of a heavenly kingdom to be ushered in by Christ's return – revolution through the supernatural, indicating the weakness of the divided masses to effect change.

In this respect, Engels quoted from Ernest Renan – the author of *The Origins of Christianity* – who observed that: "If I wanted to give you an idea of the early Christian communities I would tell you to look at a local section of the International Workingmen's Association." This similarity was appropriate from a social-psychological perspective, the imminence of victory over the ruling elites of brutal and exploitative societies. But there was critical difference between the early Christians and the members of the First International as to how revolution would come about: for the former, the class struggle through the supernatural; for the latter, a secular class struggle.[4]

This certainty of imminent triumph over adversaries was an important factor in the rise of Christianity in the early centuries of its existence and of Marxian socialism. Although Jesus of Nazareth has not returned quickly as promised, many Christians believe in his imminent return, as in Fundamentalist Protestant sects. Many Marxists themselves, especially true believers, also foresee the imminent triumph of socialism, although the implosion of Communism in Eastern Europe and the former Soviet Union has dampened this enthusiasm. As for the importance of equality in the early millenarian Christianity, Engels accepted the truism that as a religion of the oppressed, it espoused some human equality ("all were equally born in original sin") and that its "early traces of common ownership...can be ascribed to the solidarity of a proscribed sect rather than to real equalitarian ideas." In any event, he saw the end of this equality with the "establishment of the distinction between priests and laymen."[5] To be sure, Christian socialists would dispute Engels' view that early Christianity was not overly concerned with earthly equality.

In *The Peasant War in Germany*, written in the summer of 1850 in London shortly after the failure of the 1848 revolutionary wave in Europe, Engels reflected on the popular upsurge of German farmers and workers in the early days of the Protestant Reformation: they were emboldened by the split in the German nobility, by economic suffering from the nobility's seizure of the commons because of rising capitalist pressures, as well as by wishing to end serfdom with its onerous burdens of forced labor, rents, and other dues. Popular demands for freedom were "clothed religious shibboleths", concealed "behind a religious screen", as was common to the time.

In his schema of the German Workers' and Peasants' Revolt in the 1520s in Germany, Engels described how religion intersected with the socioeconomic and political struggles of the period. He – and subsequent historical scholarship confirmed this – theorized a three-cornered fight at this time: the struggle between Protestantism and Catholicism was related to the ones between the Catholic Holy Roman Emperor and much of the nobility and their middle class allies in the cities (the party represented by Martin Luther in the religious/ ideological arena), and the large peasant masses, along with workers whose most revolutionary spokesperson was Thomas Münzer.

Luther's attack on Catholicism coincided with his promoting the cause of the rising bourgeoisie in alliance with the nobility, and although Luther was sympathetic to many of the peasant demands for more freedom and equality relative to their socioeconomic superiors, he counseled peasants to be patient. But when Luther had to choose between the revolutionary masses and the revolutionary nobility/ bourgeoisie, he favored the latter. Indeed, he turned on the peasants and workers with a vengeance during the 1525 class war, urging in "Against the Murdering Hordes of Peasants" that the princes "knock down, strangle and stab" the peasantry.

Engels also drew the revolutionary socioeconomic, political, religious, and philosophical views of Münzer: that the Bible demanded a "kingdom of God...without class differences, private property and state authority...foreign, to the members of society"; that Jesus was only a man; that the Bible was not the "only and the infallible revelation," superseded by "reason, a revelation which existed, and still exists, among all peoples at all times," and "through his faith, through reason come to life, man became godlike and blessed"; that "there is no hell and no damnation...no devil but man's evil lusts and greed"; that "heaven is to be sought in this life, and that it is the task of believers to establish this heaven, the kingdom on earth"; that to effect this, a "union...no only throughout Germany, but throughout all Christendom" was needed.

A man not only of theory but also of action, Münzer joined other communists to control the town council of Mühlhausen, but the only reforms enacted, as Engels pointed out, were to democratize its constitution, a "senate elected by universal suffrage and controlled by a forum," and a "hastily improvised system of care for the poor."

Finally, Münzer was the peasant leader in the fateful battle of Frankenhausen in Thuringia in May 1525 between peasants and nobility, where the latter won. He was later captured, tortured, and beheaded by the forces of order. Engels praised him as one of the notable precursors of modern socialism.[6]

Marx's critique of religion was especially acute in "On the Jewish Question" (1843), a work of his youth, in which he castigated religion in general, but particularly the capitalist practices of Jews and Christians allowed by their respective teachers/clergy. Some pertinent background on Jews: in the first decades of the 19th century, two-thirds of Jews in Prussia and "almost all the Jews in Eastern Europe" were "small traders and hawkers."

It was true, Marx asserted, that in separating church and state in civil society, "man emancipates himself politically from religion," but religion still remained as an expression of the *"war of all against all"* and as the "expression of man's *separation* from his *community*, from himself and from other men – as it was *originally*."

In his dissection of Judaism, Marx first divided the *"Sabbath Jew"* from the *"everyday Jew,"* the latter representing secular Judaism involved with *practical* need, *self-interest*, in "huckstering", its "worldly God" being "money." He critiqued the "Jewish Jesuitism... in the Talmud," or the "the relation of the world of self-interest to the laws governing the world, the chief art of which consists in the cunning circumvention of these laws." Thus, for him, "Judaism" represented "a general anti-social element of the present time" and "in the final analysis, "emancipation of the Jews...from practical real Judaism would be the self-emancipation of our time."

This "Judaism" or commercialization, for Marx, was now prevalent among Christians:

> In North America the practical domination of Judaism over the Christian world has achieved as its unambiguous and normal expression that the teaching of the Gospel itself and Christian ministry have become articles of trade, and the bankrupt trader deals in the Gospel just as the Gospel preacher who has become rich goes for business deals.

And, "Christianity sprang from Judaism. It has again merged in Judaism." Or to paraphrase Marx, religion was a practical aid to succeed in business under capitalism and indeed is a business itself, intimately intertwined with it. Or, religion was used by alienated individuals under capitalism to exploit others, God favoring them and their particular religion over others.

To be sure, Marx foresaw the assimilation of the Jews into the general population with the advent of socialism. From a German-Jewish family (Germany has few Jews) that nominally became Christian, Marx was not exposed to the social psychology of Eastern European Jews whose large numbers in concentrated areas was propitious for Zionism. But let's add this: in an increasingly secular world with much intermarriage (in the U.S. in the 90s, half of Jewish men marry non-Jews), the Jewish religious/ethnic connection is becoming ever more tenuous. Now, if Marx's remarks were anti-Judaic/Jewish, they were also anti-Christian/European. Marx simply did not like any religion condoning capitalist practices and scarcely interested in social reform, so true for almost all of them during his lifetime.[7]

Thus, it was not surprising, as Marx pointed out, that middle-class Protestantism and capitalism were synonymous. Indeed, Max Weber's classic *The Protestant Ethic and the Spirit of Capitalism* maintained that the rise of Protestantism provided the genesis of modern capitalism. From a Marxist perspective, he was incorrect for the changing productive forces and new class alignments, especially the rise of the bourgeoisie and its wishes to charge interest and the desire of the German nobility and Henry VIII of England to plunder the lands of the Catholic Church were decisive in the rise of Calvinism, Lutheranism, and Anglicanism. Once established, the Protestant bourgeois ethic did, of course, reinforce capitalism. Catholicism and Orthodoxy also succumbed to the capitalist spirit, but more slowly for their center of gravity was generally in more economically backward areas (many feudal or almost so), of Southern and Eastern Europe, exceptions for Catholicism being the Rhineland and northern Italy.

We should also observe a topic of interest, which without it a viable capitalism favoring the bourgeoisie was impossible. The Old Testament prohibited charging interest among Hebrews, although allowing it with respect to gentiles; also the two highest castes of Hinduism were denied charging it, although the *Vaisyas* could. Christianity and Islam in their early histories, following Judaism, banned the charging of interest to co-religionists, then for everyone.

But, for Christianity as an example, the Protestant revolution in the 16th century saw Calvin allowing for interest, as did Luther, but not more than 5 percent and forgiving payment if legitimate need occurred in the meantime. Earlier, Italian bankers in the Renaissance circumvented the prohibition on interest by calling interest a penalty for not paying a loan on time. Catholic Canon law itself prohibited interest until the 19th century.

Calvin's justification to allow for interest was of a relativist economic and sociological nature, with historical dimensions. He admitted that Deut. 23: 19-20 prohibited Hebrews from charging interest to one another, although allowing its use in dealings with others. Thus, for him, interest was not expressly forbidden, relative to time and place. Ideally, trade and charging interest were reprehensible, rural life allowing that they not be employed, but with the rise of urbanism, interest and trade were necessary for fallen humanity to survive. Indeed, he averred that lending money for interest was preferable to trading.

To return to the subject of Marx's supposed anti-Semitism, Marx clearly distinguished between Judaism as the practicing capitalist religion of Jews and Jews as a persecuted religious-ethnic group. In a *New York Daily Tribune* article in the mid-50s, as background for the Crimean War, he defended the poor and "suffering" Jews of Jerusalem, who, although "despised by the Orthodox and persecuted by the Catholics," were nevertheless capable of stoutly resisting "Muslim intolerance and oppression."[8]

It should also be mentioned that Engels towards the end of his life staunchly fought against anti-Semitism, now viewing Jews "for the first time" as "not identified with capitalism but considered as possible allies in the struggle for socialism." In fact, he praised the work of Jews for socialism, of Marx, Ferdinand Lassalle, Eduard Bernstein, Victor Adler, and Paul Singer. Then, too, at the urging of Marx's daughter Eleanor, he became interested in the struggles of Jewish socialist workers in London's East End, only death preventing his writing the preface of a *Manifesto* edition in Yiddish.[9]

Traditionally, it is difficult to disentangle religion from ethnicity or from community life in general. In the normally totalitarian societies of the past, based on sharp class divisions, general economic scarcity, and brevity of life, religious matters/differences were of great concern, for religion was closely intertwined with all aspects of community life, including the important economic factors and future afterlife. For instance, when the Protestant Revolution succeeded in

Germany, the princes determined the religion of their subjects and dissenters were forced to leave or be persecuted.

The problem of morality, in which religion traditionally is associated with, is of great concern for Marxists. Engels in *Anti-Dühring* presented the most comprehensive analysis of it in the writings of Marx/Engels, situating class itself as the primary base of morality. For him, the "morality preached to us today" consisted of "Christian-feudal morality inherited from the earlier religious times," divided "into a Catholic and Protestant morality, each of which has no lack of subdivisions. Then, "alongside these we find the modern-bourgeois morality and beside it also the proletarian morality of the future." These moralities – of the "feudal aristocracy, the bourgeoisie and the proletariat" – now exist simultaneously, for him, in "the most advanced European countries."

Significantly, for Engels, "ethical ideas in the last resort" came from "the practical relations... of class position...from the economic relations in which they [men] carry on production and exchange." He also formulated that the moralities discussed comprised "three different stages of the same historical background, and for that reason have much in common." Furthermore, for him, "at similar or approximately similar stages of economic development, moral theories must of necessity be more or less in agreement." An example of his was "Thou shalt not steal," not eternal because "in a society in which all motives for stealing have been done away with...only lunatics would ever steal," this posing problems for the "preacher of morals" proclaiming this "eternal truth." In the meantime, this commandment presumably holds true for socialists today. Thus it was, for him, that "a really human morality which stands above class antagonisms and above any recollection of them becomes possible only at a stage of society which has not only overcome class antagonisms but has even forgotten them in practical life."[10]

Indeed, who can argue with Engels that the early Christian principles of equality were subverted by the rise of the Constantinian church in the Roman Empire, reflecting the power of its upper classes over the masses, and that Christianity allowed for the existence of slavery in the "Roman Empire for centuries" and for the "Venetians" later to engage in the "Negro traffic."[11]

In this vein, in a newspaper article in the *Deutsche-Brusseler Zeitung* on September 12, 1847, Marx proposed that the "social principles of Christianity justified the slavery of antiquity, glorified the serfdom of the middle ages, and equally know, when necessary, how to defend the oppression of the proletariat." Furthermore, these principles condoned the "necessity of a ruling and an oppressed class, the former enjoined to be "charitable" to the latter (in a fallen world without the "communism of love" there would remain the residue of charity, of some voluntary or compulsory sharing, never efficacious in erasing the economic differences of class), itself part of a double standard in which "all vile acts of the oppressors against the oppressed to be either the just punishment of original sin and other sins or trials that the Lord in His infinite wisdom imposes on those redeemed."[12]

Indeed, in *Capital*, Marx in great detail recounted the many social horrors perpetrated by the bourgeoisie on the working class in daily life in Europe and the many atrocities committed by their imperialism.[13] Is not this Marxist morality incomparably superior to that of contemporary bourgeois religion?

It should also be pointed out that class-dominated society enslaved women in the capitalist patriarchal family as Marx and Engels observed in the *Manifesto* (this was also true of its patriarchal pre-capitalist varieties). In this complex, sexist religion was instrumental in oppressing women in the family (Islam, Judaism, and Hinduism allowed polygyny, while wives were clearly subservient to husbands in Christianity). Especially was the aggressive or hard side of religion related to this, the one that sanctioned holy war and punishment of social inferiors, of women, children, and those in lower classes.

Ultimately, for Marx and Engels, real/practical religion could not basically escape the socioeconomic and other confines of exploitative societies, pitting individuals, status groups, classes/castes, and nations against one another. Of course, in periods of historical transition, when the class struggle of oppressed classes against their ruling elites intensified, Engels, in particular, noted that the good or progressive side of religion manifested itself. From a broad historical perspective, both held that a fully developed socialist morality could only exist when the balance of class forces/class struggle worldwide favored the working class.

C) Other Secular Socialists

Marx's and Engels' secular socialist analysis of religion has been followed by other socialists, Marxists and others. In this light, we examine the views of Karl Katusky, the leading Marxist theoretician of the Second International, the neo-Marxists, Erich Fromm and Ernst Bloch, and Veblen.

Kautsky creatively employed a Marxian historical materialism to contrast an early communist-oriented Christianity based on mutual aid among the poor and oppressed, with a later one in the hands of the wealthy and powerful interested in "mastery and exploitation." For him, the authentic Jesus of Nazareth was the committed social revolutionary, who not only condemned the wealthy and powerful and expelled the moneychangers from the temples, but urged his followers to arm themselves ("Think not that I come to send peace on earth; I came not to send peace, but a sword."); not the one, transformed after his betrayal to the power structure, who advised that "those using swords will get killed," the pacifist Jesus. He then gave a rational explanation of Jesus as the Messiah of hope for working-class mutual-aid societies of the period, so weak and alienated in their attempts to change society that they transformed their champion into a god who would soon return to destroy the world of wealth and power for one of justice and equality for his believers.[1]

Fromm, a noted psychoanalyst who taught at the National University in Mexico and authored many works, is a humanistic socialist. His Marxism was revealed in many works, one on Marx himself, *Marx's Concept on Man*, upholding Marx's humanistic socialism as expressed in the *Economic and Philosophical Manuscripts*.

In *Psychoanalysis and Religion*, which specifically dealt with religion and its importance as a harbinger to contemporary socialist aspirations, Fromm significantly observed the overarching fact that there were two primary, yet antithetical, streams in the Judeo-Christian tradition, the authoritarian and humanistic: the former stressed the importance of obeying a God of fear and retribution, justifying social and economic inequality by regarding the status-quo as God-ordained; the later emphasized the power of love, joy, and self-fulfillment and recognized that, although human beings had limited powers, they could still change oppressive socioeconomic and other structures, as the Hebrew prophets urged.[2]

Bloch was a philosophy professor in East (Communist) Germany, who, after deprived of his position there for being utopian, lived in West Germany. In *The Principle of Hope*, he traced elementary human yearnings for the good society or utopia in history, even in the confines of brutal surroundings. His journey examined human need for joy and hope as expressed in/by dreams, myth, theater, the great religious prophets, philosophy, and literature, including the many utopian novels and works of Plato, More, Owen, Fourier, and William Morris, but he concentrated on Goethe, Hegel, and Marx. Utopian expressions in history were seen as forerunners of the socialism to come.

In this intertwining the spiritual/artistic side of the human spirit throughout the ages to the concomitant social struggles waged by the masses, including the one now by the proletariat and its progressive allies to emancipate humanity, Bloch combined a Marxist dialectical materialism with spiritual/artistic hope. Like Engels, Bloch was fascinated by the spiritualist/millenarian/communist Münzer, as evidenced by his *Thomas Münzer as Theologian of the Revolution*.[3]

Veblen also approached religion from a humanistic socialist perspective. Although ridiculing religion ("If there is a difference between religion and magic, I have never been able to find out."), he nevertheless recognized its importance in human affairs, insisting on its intimate relationship with the economic and social organization of society, and accompanying social psychology under the impress of ruling groups in which the priesthood was an integral part. For instance, he observed that such Christian attitudes as "non-resistance and brotherly love" (only practiced by the masses) gave way to "pecuniary competition," in daily life when "handicraft" and "petty trade" fractured the socioeconomic bonds of medieval society to usher in capitalism and the natural-rights outlook of the 18th century. This element, for him, representing such traits as "egoism, self-interest, or individualism," was egalitarian and revolutionary, with its emphasis on ownership of private property, subverting medieval social and economic privileges. Ownership itself at this time was still largely consonant with "workmanlike serviceability" and the "instinct of workmanship," with their correlative elements of "mutual aid and serviceability to common good."[4]

But the early period of capitalism, based on small private property and handicrafts because of new technology and new "pecuniary relations," ultimately metamorphosed, for Veblen, into one of large industry and accompanying extensive labor division, in which the spirit of workmanship was not as intimately linked with the product of labor as before, lacking the close connection between "serviceability and acquisition" and the "use of wealth and the common welfare." Instead, the new enterprises were now based on an "impersonal, dispassionate" drive "for profit," a growing cleavage developing between the "natural rights of pecuniary discretion," on the one hand, and "brotherly love" on the other, which either lead to upper-class "ideals of emulation and status" or to a working-class "Christian principle of brotherhood."[5]

Veblen conceptualized religion as operating in two general periods – the barbarian/predatory in a rural/agricultural setting, and the mechanistic/urban since the Industrial Revolution. The first thrived in the milieu of a socioeconomic structure characterized by deep social division, of "superior and inferior, noble and base," which being normally "predatory" or warlike, manifested an attitude of "devoutness,"[6] itself related to underlying elements of "personal wealth" and "invidious distinction."[7] The second, witnessing humanity's progressive mastery over nature, had belief in the

254

supernatural markedly diminishing. Nevertheless, he noted that not only did the leisure class still cling to its religiosity, whose practices reinforced its "conspicuous consumption," but so did many workers and farmers.[8]

Thus it was for Veblen that among Americans, for instance, religion was more ensconced in rural settings and the South than it was in the urban North. Religion was almost universally practiced among the recently arrived and poverty-stricken immigrants from Southern and Eastern Europe – Catholics, Orthodox, and Jews – and by African-Americans. He also saw that artisans or skilled workers and middle-class adult males were less prone than others to attend church, although their wives and children did. Furthermore, as between males and females, more of the latter were "religious" because of their traditional dependency on the former. Then, too, he noted the widespread religious prejudice in America, his example being that of Protestant Fundamentalism, as reflected in the evangelism of Billy Sunday, also opposed to modern theories of evolution ("such-like maggoty conceits are native to the religious fancy").[9] However, he approved that non-conformist Protestants had shorn their ministers of priestly powers and privileges and had erected simple and utilitarian churches devoid of costly waste.

To be sure, Veblen expected that, in the long run, religion would become ever more redundant before the advancing "matter-of-fact" attitudes promoted by the new machine technology, invariably antithetical to magic. Such attitudes would lead the groups most involved and influenced by its scientific views, the industrial workers, technicians, engineers, and scientists, to question the supernatural foundation of religion.[10]

In picturing religion as an institution used by the ruling classes to buttress their power and privileges, Veblen perceived its relationship to waste as reflected in the "consumption of ceremonial paraphernalia," including "shrines, temples, churches, vestments, sacrifices, sacraments, holidays, attire, etc." The clerics themselves as part of the leisure class were thus normally exempt from "vulgar labor," befitting the "servants of an invisible master,"[11] serving chieftain and capitalist in bureaucracies to indicate their power to waste and command.[12]

This waste was intimately involved with both earthly and heavenly hierarchies. For instance, among various Christian sects:

> Beyond the priestly class, and ranged in an ascending hierarchy, ordinarily comes a superhuman vicarious leisure class of saints, angels, etc. – or their equivalents in the ethnic cults. These rise in grade, one above the other, according to an elaborate system of status. The principle of status runs through the entire hierarchical system, both visible and invisible.[13]

Veblen also commented on the close ties between religion and sports/luck/gambling, intimately involved with the "barbarian temperament." The principle aims here were not only to be luckier or more favored by the supernatural than opponents, but through such sterling barbarian qualities like "force and fraud" and "ferocity and astuteness," based on "invidious comparison," to inflict upon them a "more painful and humiliating defeat."[14]

On the whole, Veblen claimed that modern civilization, with its advanced technology based as it is on the principles of science, was corrosive to religion. To this, he added that "the decay of the system of status" or rise of social and economic equality, would also lessen the power of a leisure-class dominated religion.

But Veblen did not underestimate the soft side of religion with its focus on "charity" and "social good-fellowship," equated with the enduring human elements of "human solidarity" and "sympathy." Furthermore, he was aware of religion's "aesthetic" dimensions and its allowing humanity a "sense of communion with the environment, or with the generic life process." In fact, these elements for him imparted to religion a "direction contrary to the underlying principles of the institution of the leisure class as already formulated."[15] These remarks would lead one to believe that, although an atheist, Veblen would have tolerated a working-class religion resting on traditional virtues, as opposed to one based on inequality and exploitation.

D) Relations Between Secular Socialism and Religion in the Soviet Union

Over the centuries, traditional Christianity, as an example of religion, has had stormy relations with secularism, let alone with secular socialists. As part of the governing order, religion obviously attempted to maintain its monopoly on education and in the world of ideas. As observed, the Enlightenment and the bourgeois French and American Revolutions in the 18th century were important events in destroying this religious monopoly, and in the late 19th century the well-known *Kulturkampf* between Otto von Bismarck and the Catholic Church occurred in Germany.

In the 20th century, the main struggle between religion and secularism involved Soviet Communism and the various Orthodox Churches and Catholicism in the Soviet Union and Eastern Europe and between Chinese Communism and Buddhism in China. One example of this conflict that will be presented is that of the Soviet Union.

The Russian Orthodox Church was intimately tied to Russian Czarism. The independence of the Moscow Patriarchy was terminated when Peter the Great established the Holy Synod in 1721, making the church an arm of the state. Its Procurator, who oversaw the Synod, was a layperson appointed by the Czar, in effect the chief of the Orthodox Church, Ceasaropapism. In this vein, the church's catechism enjoined the faithful to obey and give their lives to the Czar, while to disobey him was to disobey God.

With the advent of the Russian Bolshevik Revolution in November 1917 and subsequent civil war in 1918-20, the Russian Orthodox Church under Patriarch Tikhon opposed Communism and excommunicated its followers, while the White armies enjoyed the services of many priests. Under these circumstances, Communists killed many priests and closed many churches. Then, during the

1922 famine, when Communists sold church treasures for food, relations between church and state again worsened. In 1922-23, Soviet trials against leading laypersons and priests resulted in 33 executions; Tikhon himself, after admitting to anti-Soviet activity and confessing, was released. But the Soviets tolerated religion and employed it during World War II in defense of the nation.

Lenin's Marxism largely influenced communist relations with religion. In "The Tasks of the Youth Leagues," a speech delivered in October 1920, Lenin charged that the traditional ruling classes basically utilized religion to further their hegemony over the masses, taught to accept their oppression for a future heavenly happiness. He, then, related morality to class, the highest goal for Communists being to advance the interests of the working class. In *Materialism and Empirio-Criticism; Critical Comments on a Reactionary Philosophy* (1909), the materialist Lenin theorized that the only valid knowledge of the world was tested by human senses/human instruments for scientific knowledge. God, as such, could not be objectively proved.

Thus, in the Soviet Union, members of the Communist Party of the Soviet Union (CPSU) were required to profess atheism, religion itself relegated to the status of a medieval superstition, to be fought through a Communist/scientific education. But religion was tolerated and believers could contribute monies and time to its continuance.

In the meantime, to replace the former influence of religion in marking the significant phases of a person's life like marriage and death, the Soviet state ceremonialized them. Religion itself would disappear when its basic roots were removed, i.e., exploitative socioeconomic relations. This is not to say that the Soviets rejected Christianity totally. In a 1966 article in *Science and Religion*, a leading Soviet atheistic journal, many of Christianity's moral/ethical values were endorsed.[1]

To be sure, Communist morality was powerless to prevent Stalinist brutalities, principally including the elimination of the *kulaks* (richer farmers) as a class, with up to ten million deaths by starvation and up to five million sent to the *Gulag* (labor camps) and the purges within the CPSU in the 1936-38 period, resulting in up to five million members and officials arrested and half a million executed. According to Stephen F. Cohen in *Rethinking the Soviet Experience*, twenty million people were murdered and died by starvation in the 1932-53 period. Nikita Khruschev freed ten or so million people from the Gulag in the 1956-64 period. When the ideals of Communism clashed with an economically and socially backward Russia, forced by historical circumstances to both industrialize and prepare for World War II, the former elements were overwhelmed by the latter reality.

The militant anti-religious stances of Soviet and Chinese Communism were also consonant with Marx's views, who, although tolerant of religion, also wished for its elimination through education and confiscation of religious property that could generate income, as in *The Civil War in France* for the latter element.

E) Reformist and Socialist Religion

As observed, Marx/Engels and other secular socialists recognized that in periods of historical transition religion itself as a major social institution was invariably involved in their socioeconomic and other tension points, for within its institutional structures the forces of change and the status quo clashed. It was, therefore, not surprising that a formidable religious reformist and socialist tradition developed in the last two centuries within the world's major religions, such as Christianity, Judaism, Islam, Hinduism, and Buddhism. In other words, the proletarian class struggle to reform or change capitalism for socialism was reflected in either the reformist or totally socialist morality of individual theologians or parts of various religions, the latter, for instance, represented by Catholic Liberation Theology in Latin America.

The exploration begins with the social doctrines of Catholicism, the largest – indeed central – Christian group, fashioned by Catholicism's long history of being part of the governing order in the West, much of it under the rule of kings and nobility. Thus, its core social doctrines historically were of a conservative nature, based on Aristotle and

Aquinas, defending private property, the male-dominated patriarchal family, and socioeconomic inequality, although generally antithetical to capitalist "usury," unbridled economic individualism, and large trade and industry, signifying the rise of the bourgeoisie.

Catholic social views often longed for a medieval past when everyone knew his/her place in villages/small towns, with their sense of community, the wealthier socioeconomic groups paternalistically looking after their socioeconomic inferiors under the rubric of "Christian charity."

It should also be pointed out that with few exceptions – Belgium, the Rhineland, northern France, and northern Italy – the Industrial Revolution came rather late to Catholic Europe, permitting the mindset of the Middle Ages to continue. Thus, even the more conservative side of Catholicism lodged in the papacy would decry capitalist evils, wishing to mitigate them while still upholding the new inequality ushered in by capitalism.

The landmark papal encyclical on the socioeconomic ravages that capitalism inflicted on the working-class was *Rerum Novarum* ("Of New Things"), issued by the progressive Pope Leo XIII in 1891. (Encyclicals or papal letters are position papers on Catholic views, which, although not binding on Catholics, carry great weight among them. Only in matters of dogma, like the Immaculate Conception of Mary, are popes considered infallible).

To begin, it lamented capitalist destruction of the medieval craft guilds and the present clearly inadequate social services for the working-class, as "workingmen have been surrendered, isolated and helpless, to the hard-heartedness of employers and the greed of unchecked competition." It, then, denounced the evils of usury and the fact that "a small number of rich men has been able to lay upon the teeming masses of the labouring poor a yoke little better than slavery itself." In appealing to Catholic social justice, it urged employers not to see their workers as slaves, but rather that work in itself was honorable, thus to treat them justly and to pay them a living wage, a wage not based on market-place bargaining, to end the brutality of children working in factories, and to lessen the burden of women's factory work and even eliminating it. It approved of the establishment of labor unions, with the right to strike, recognizing that the collective strength of workers was needed to improve their socioeconomic lot, permitting some form of institutional antagonism between labor and capital, but rejected the notion of a general class struggle advocated by socialists, especially Marxists. In this vein, it denounced industrial violence injuring capital, recommending local, state-sponsored arbitration boards to settle industrial disputes over hours of work and working conditions.

Nevertheless, *Rerum Novarum* accepted socioeconomic inequality as part of the natural order of things, for although God granted the earth to humanity, he left it to human institutions to determine its distribution, an approach related to an almost explicit social Darwinism, of natural inequality as a fact of life: "People differ in capacities, skills, health, strength; and unequal fortune is a necessary result of unequal conditions." Thus, a completely just world could never exist on earth. This defense of private property, insisted that without it "nobody would have any interest in exerting his talents or industry." But it also asked that private property heed the pleas of workers and render them social justice based on "Christian charity," quoting Aquinas that those who have goods share them "without hesitation when others are in need." To be sure, it also condemned an atheistic Marxian socialism. The immediate significance of this encyclical was the formation of Catholic reform parties, like the Catholic Center Party in Germany and the Popular Party in Italy.

Rerum Novarum was influenced by the efforts of earlier and contemporary Catholic social activists concerned with ameliorating the lives of workers, like Bishop Emmanuel von Ketteler in Germany and Cardinal James Gibbons in the United States: both favored labor unions – Gibbons, the Knights of Labor, the right to strike, worker-owned cooperatives, and state legislation to aid workers, like reducing working hours and promoting better working conditions.

Rerum Navarum was not only reaffirmed, but broadened in *Quadragesimo Anno* ("On the Fortieth Year" of *Rerum Novarum*), in 1931, when Pope Pius XI repeated Catholicism's commitment to more social justice through profit sharing for workers in industry to promote greater harmony between capital and labor, endorsing various forms of fascism, which through the corporate state sought to insure social peace between them.

In *Populorum Progressio* ("On Progress for the People"), Pope Paul VI, a noted liberal scholar whose ideas were very similar to Pope John's, again declared that private property was not an unconditional right without responsibilities, there being no justification for one to retain "what he does not need, when others lack necessities." Furthermore, he broke new ground in asserting the necessity of "building a world where every man, no matter what his race, religion or nationality, can live a fully human life, freed from servitude imposed on him by other men or by natural forces over which he had not sufficient control," castigating the "international imperialism of money," and decrying the increasing gap between rich and poor nations.

Pope John Paul II (the "Polish Pope") in various encyclicals, continued in this social tradition in works such as *Laborem Exercens* ("On Human Work") (1981) and *Centesimus Annus* ("the One Hundredth Year" of *Rerum Novarum*) (1991), allowing as a last resort for armed struggle against socioeconomic oppression. Although defending private property, socioeconomic inequality, free-market economics, and the profit system under capitalist auspices, he maintained that limits be placed on them, subordinated to social justice and to work itself, which played a central role in human development. In fact, he insisted on the "priority of work over capital," which "places an obligation in justice upon employers to consider the welfare of the workers before the increase of profits," and critical importance of unions in working-class life, to protect the "dignity" of workers, including their "participation in the life of the industrial enterprise so that, with others and under the direction of others, they can in a certain sense work for themselves through the exercise of their intelligence and freedom." Furthermore, in the spirit of human solidarity, he urged society to provide everyone with various social services to insure their well-being, including pensions, health insurance, and workers' compensation. Although the state had a responsibility to bring about social reform, unions also had to be involved in this process. He also criticized a "sinful" and wasteful Western consumerism in a world of great poverty.

These encyclicals were reflected in the United States by The National Conference of Catholic Bishops' pastoral letter in *Economic Justice for All* (1986). It forthrightly declared that, "We feel the pain of our brothers and sisters who are poor, unemployed, homeless living on the edge," and for Catholics to "work actively for social and economic justice." It also affirmed "we judge any economic system by what it does for and to people and by how it permits all to participate in it," and that "all people have a right to life, food, clothing, shelter, rest, medical care, education, and employment." Importantly, it allowed for the "socialization...of certain means of production" and "cooperative ownership of the firm by all who work within it," urging that "full employment is the foundation of a just economy," and insisting that the "highest priority" was to eliminate the poverty of those on welfare and the lowest income groups to end a "social and moral scandal." Then, too, the letter bestowed proper recognition on labor unions and advocated the strengthening of civil liberties and democratic institutions. These measures were to be undergirded by "an unalienable dignity that stamps human existence prior to any division into races or nations and prior to human labor and human achievement."[1]

Key individuals predated this progressive movement toward a full-fledged socialism in Catholicism. A precursor was the French cleric, Félicité Robert de Lamennais (he flourished in the first half of the 19th century), who attacked the privileges of kings/nobility and capitalists, fearing that the Catholic Church's close association with them would cause the masses to leave it. His solution called for Catholicism to disassociate itself from the ruling classes by accepting the separation of church and state and by supporting a democratic and egalitarian society, freeing the workers from their capitalist overlords through cooperative enterprises. For this and other views, he was excommunicated. Another was the socialist Charles Péguy, who was killed in World War I while in the French army. In his epic poem/drama, *Joan of Arc*, dedicated to individuals working for the "universal socialist republic," he synthesized a deep religious fervor with an equally great love for socialism. In his *Socialist City (De la cité socialiste)*, he sketched the outlines for a future democratic and socialist society whose economic parameters featured cooperatives run by workers, clearly in the tradition of Proudhon and revolutionary syndicalism.

Perhaps the most noted Catholic theologian of 20th century, the French neo-Thomist, Jacques Maritain, an intimate of Péguy, became a Christian socialist by the 1930s, inspired by *Rerum Novarum* and *Quadragesimo Anno*. In *True Humanism* (1936), he cogently spelled out the need for a "certain collectivization of ownership" in large enterprises inasmuch as it protected human dignity and solidarity. In citing Proudhon and Sorel, he upheld the principle of economic democracy, involving workers' ownership/management through unions, labor not to be regarded as simply a commodity by capital, socioeconomic arrangements to be so organized that a worker's job was a right. Then, too, the new society would guarantee all of its citizens a comfortably standard of life. These economic imperatives would take place in the context of an open and free democratic society in a "pluralistic commonwealth" of competing ideologies. He disseminated his liberal/socialist ideas in America as a professor at Columbia and Princeton.

Another prime example of Catholic socialism was the personalist (he stressed the primacy of the individual) Emmanuel Mounier, the founder and editor of *Esprit*, the leading French Catholic Journal, from 1932 until his death in 1950. Under Mounier, *Esprit* engaged in a serious dialogue with Marxism/Communism.[2]

Weil was another outstanding example of Catholic socialism, particularly of the anarcho-syndicalist variety; we have already discussed her book on working-class alienation under capitalism. Her influence on the Catholic left in Europe, the United States, and elsewhere was considerable, as on Pope Paul VI. Although never baptized as a Catholic, this upper-middle class French-Jewish professor of Greek at a lycée, after several mystical experiences, one in which she felt the presence of Christ, became a devout Catholic, thoroughly immersed in a Catholic milieu. Earlier, she had supported Communism, but was appalled by Stalinism, turning to revolutionary syndicalism, deeply involved in its Workers' Education Circle.[3]

In the United States itself, there is the well-known Catholic socialist-anarchist movement, The Catholic Worker (CW), founded in the early 1930s by Dorothy Day and Peter Maurin; its monthly journal, *The Catholic Worker*, which began publication on May 1, 1933, is still going strong. Day, born into a middle-class Episcopalian family, joined the American Socialist Party, became a reporter for the socialist *New York Call*, and was involved in the publication of the *Masses* and the *Liberator*. In 1927, she converted to Catholicism. Maurin, born into a poor French peasant family, was a member of the Christian Brothers for nine years, joined the *Sillon* (Furrow) movement favoring workers and unions, farmed in Canada for many years, and went to New York City in 1925 as an unskilled worker, where he eventually met Day. The general socioeconomic views of the CW were heavily influenced by Kropotkin, Tolstoy, Martin Buber, the Jewish religious philosopher who contributed to their newspaper (more on him soon), and the English Distributism of the Catholics Hilaire Belloc and Gilbert K. Chesterton, espousing a return to a medieval-like society of small towns and villages dominated by small producers/property, honoring work, and not charging interest.

Specifically, Day and Maurin called for a decentralized society based on mutual aid whose socioeconomic parameters combined small private property in a communitarian setting of small farms and factories. Tools, land, buildings, and machinery (the last kept to a minimum) were to be held in common, wage labor and assembly lines done away with, and crafts restored, freeing workers from meaningless/alienating work. Furthermore, they would end racism, anti-Semitism, all exploitation, and war. CW members are pacifists, even refusing to fight in World War II. The CW combated poverty with Houses of Hospitality, staffed by volunteers.

The influence of the CW on American Catholic intellectuals and members of the Church's hierarchy should not be underestimated: socialists and peace stalwarts, like Michael Harrington and Fathers Daniel and Philip Berrigan, the last two imprisoned for anti-Vietnam war activities, are closely associated with it.[4]

The importance of socialism today within Catholicism is also well illustrated by the splendid work of the Maryknoll Order among workers and farmers in Latin America and by their outstanding publishing house, Orbis Books, a valuable resource of Catholic Socialism, emphasizing the social struggle in poor nations.

In Latin America, Catholic Liberation Theology, whose doyen is Gustavo Gutierrez, today encompasses a large minority of the Catholic clergy, playing a leading role in establishing more than 200,000 Basic Christian Communities or mutual-aid groups. It was also much involved in the Sandinista Revolution in Nicaragua. Its theology, combining the revolutionary life of Jesus of Nazareth and revolutionary Marxist socioeconomic analysis, envisages a God of the poor and oppressed who encourages them to fight for a better life in the here and now.

An examination of Gutierrez's *A Theology of Liberation* (1973), a leading work of this movement, follows. To begin, Gutierrez categorically proposed a socialist solution to solve the manifold problems of contemporary society, based on the "social ownership of the means of production." In socialism's construction, he quoted Che Guevara on the importance of not only increasing material prosperity, but in transforming the human person for the better.

He also favored Marxian class struggle, which occurred within the "church itself," between the "oppressors" (the wealthy and their allies) and "oppressed" (workers and farmers), many of them living in "material poverty," a "scandalous condition," and in a "subhuman situation." Thus, "class enemies" existed and "it is necessary to combat them." In this regard, he asserted that "to love all men does not mean avoiding confrontations; it does not mean preserving a fictitious harmony." Indeed, the "liberation of the poor and the liberation of the rich are achieved simultaneously.

One loves the oppressors by liberating them from their inhuman condition as oppressors." Anyone denying the existence of the class struggle, for him, including the Church, could only aid the "dominant sectors," there being no neutrality here. He charged the Catholic Church in Latin America with being part of the present capitalist and "alienating" social system, of upholding its "dominant ideology," based on the "worst kind of violence – a situation which pits the powerful against the weak." Only by severing its ties with this power structure, with a "radical critique" of it, could the Church properly fulfill its mission on earth.

In this vein, Gutierrez examined the concept of sin in human history, which he insisted was of an individual/collective nature, i.e., individual sin was related to the larger socioeconomic and other collective sins, to be "regarded as social, historical fact, the absence of brotherhood and love in relationship among men, the breach of friendship with God and with other men, and, therefore, an interior personal fracture." This "sin is evident in oppressive structures, in the exploitation of man by man, in the domination and slavery of peoples, races, and social classes." Sin was, thus, "the fundamental alienation, the root of a situation of injustice and exploitation." Only by overcoming this sin could humanity witness in history the "growth of the Kingdom," but itself is "not the coming to the Kingdom, not of all salvation." Thus, although allowing for the existence of a socialist humanity, he also saw that a supernatural occurrence was needed for complete human fulfillment/liberation.

The ending of class oppression and a classless society, for Gutierrez, was ultimately based on God's love for humanity, which literally demanded that humans love one another, for following the Hebrew prophetic tradition, "man is created in the image of God." Individual/class oppression was thus an affront to God, indicating alienation from Him and the general community, the Bible replete with denunciations of the wealthy oppressing the poor, insisting on a society of general equality and "common ownership of goods," as in Acts, instituting a proper *koinonia* (Greek for "community").[5]

Protestantism, no less than Catholicism, has been progressively involved in the socialist project. In mid-19th century England, the term "Christian Socialism" was first coined by two Anglican ministers, Frederick Denison Maurice and Charles Kingsley (both were professors at Cambridge University, the former in moral philosophy and the latter in history), and J.M. Ludlow, a lawyer. Their periodical, *The Christian Socialist*, condemned a selfish and predatory middle-class ethic for one based on political democracy and worker-run cooperatives.[6]

In the United States, the Protestant Social Gospel movement was especially influential in the 1900-1920 period, during the heyday of American socialism. It continued the earlier Christian utopianism of the first half of the 19th century, although different social and economic settings characterized the two movements: the first thrived in a basically rural milieu and was usually fundamentalist, while the second acted in the urban scene, coping with intense working-class poverty, generally accepting science, and Darwinian evolution.[7]

Two early exponents of this Protestantism were Washington Gladden, a Congregationalist minister from Columbus, Ohio, and Richard T. Ely, a professor of economics at Johns Hopkins, University of Wisconsin, and Northwestern. The former advocated a world without racial and religious prejudice – deeply aware of the plight of African-Americans and the wrongs perpetuated upon them by society and of prejudice between Catholics and Protestants – and took an active interest in alleviating working-class misery, to be remedied by extensive socialization of industry (mines, railroads, telephones and telegraph, gas, electricity, and water), and cooperative ownership of large business: "All people should unite to furnish the capital and direct the work," a view reminiscent of Emerson's dictum uniting labor and capital. The latter, a consistent advocate of labor, supported the eight-hour day, formation of labor unions, abolition of child labor, workers' compensation, and the nationalization of large industry, but allowed small private enterprise.[8]

The foremost proponent of the movement was Walter Rauschenbusch, who after graduating from a gymnasium in Germany, attended the University of Rochester, Rochester Theological Seminary, and the University of Berlin, concentrating on economics and theology; then, he went to London to study industrial relations, meeting members of the socialist Fabian Society.

Thus it was that when Rauschenbusch became the pastor of the Second Baptist Church in New York City, in a slum near Hell's Kitchen to minister to working-class German immigrants, his interest in socialism quickened. (In addition to Christ and the Bible, the other important ethical-intellectual influences on his socialism included Marx, Edward Bellamy's *Looking Backward*, Henry George's *Progress and Poverty*, Leo Tolstoy, and the Fabians). As early as 1900, he supported the Presidential runs of Eugene V. Debs, the standard-bearer of the American Socialist Party (ASP), although he never joined it.

The principle model for Rauschenbusch's socialism was primitive Christianity as practiced in the Book of Acts, buttressed by the belief that God worked in history for the growing perfection of human beings and their collective institutions. In the coming of socialism, he assigned to the working class the principal role because it suffered the most, the goodness-through-suffering theme.

In *Christianity and the Social Crisis* and *A Theology for the Social Gospel*, Rauschenbusch condemned capitalism as the greatest enemy of God, a system spawning great riches and its corollary of great poverty, "inherent in a social system that exalted profit and position above virtue, and an economy that taught us to approach economic questions from the point of view of goods and not of man," of treating people like things or commodities, encouraging a competitive spirit based on covetousness, invariably breeding fear and intolerance, in which the new machine technology, although leading to more economic abundance, also brought the specters of unemployment and ill-distribution of wealth. His remedy proposed a society of general equality, socializing large property under the control of the producers, alongside small private enterprise, to come through democracy and passive resistance; he influenced, for instance, Dr. Martin Luther King, Jr., also a democratic socialist.[9]

The socialist impulse of the Social Gospel extended to the 1930s depression period. One of its leading figures, Reinhold Niebuhr, a disciple of Rauschenbusch and a well-known theologian, joined the ASP, running once unsuccessfully on its ticket for the U.S. House of Representatives. He later became a left liberal, one of the founders of Americans for Democratic Action in 1940.[10] Norman Thomas, the chief spokesperson of the ASP after Debs' death, also entered socialism through the religious route, as a Presbyterian minister.[11] He ran for president in 1928, 1932, 1936, 1940, 1944, and 1948.

Today, the Social Gospel tradition continues in American life through mainline Protestantism and Orthodoxy in The National Council of the Churches of Christ in the United States, comprising progressive elements of both, which enunciates a left liberal, if not a moderate socialist, economic and social orientation. For instance, it envisages the possibility, with the recent, spectacular developments in technology/production, of "a world without hunger, nakedness or human beasts of burden," "participation" of the citizenry in the decision-making process in society, for all people "regardless of employment status" to have "an adequate livelihood," the vital importance of "human rights and freedoms," narrowing the income gap between the rich and the poor nations, and the diminution of the armaments race. It is also acutely aware of the "hazards of great wealth," holding that private property is not an absolute right, and of the dangers of pollution.[12]

In Europe, the two foremost Protestant theologians of the 20th century, Karl Barth and Paul Tillich (both also active ministers), were firmly lodged in the socialist camp. Barth, depicted as the "red" pastor in his native Switzerland, wholeheartedly assisted workers in their fight to establish unions and win higher wages and recognized the importance of politics to achieve socialism, becoming a member of the Social Democrats.

Tillich, author of *Systematic Theology* and a chaplain in the German Imperial Army in World War I, was so utterly appalled by the death and destruction unleashed by the forces of autocracy and capital, that he became a left-wing socialist. In fact, in the work that he was most proud of, *The Socialist Decision*, he emphasized the critical role of Marx in developing a working-class consciousness, realizing that under capitalist economic arrangements, workers were invariably condemned to an inherent inferiority. In the tradition of Marx and Proudhon, among others, he believed that socialism would at once "liberate the workers from having to work for someone else's profit," educate them in understanding the complexities of the new technology, and remove the curse of purely repetitive work through technological innovation. In the tempestuous period after the collapse of Imperial Germany shortly after the war, when Germany was on the brink of a social revolution, he rejected the Communists and reformist Social Democrats, only to endorse the revolutionary Independent Socialists. He also had the rare distinction of being the first non-Jew to lose his professorship at a Germany university with the advent of Nazism. With the aid of Niebuhr, he came to America to continue his teaching.[13]

Count Leo Tolstoy and Nicholas Berdyaev represented the radical Orthodox socialist tradition. Tolstoy, the author of *War and Peace* and *Anna Karenina*, enjoyed the wealth, power, and culture of one born into the Russian nobility in the 19th century, advantages gained at the expense of the peasantry that, until the 1860s, were serfs. In his middle years, Tolstoy experienced a religious conversion to imitate Jesus as a Christian anarchist, practicing an ascetic lifestyle, rejecting individual possessions, and identifying himself with the peasantry. He would change the world through non-violent resistance, by non-payment of taxes, and refusal to serve in the military, actions based on Christian love. The ultimate aim of these pursuits was to establish cooperative communes, devoid of private property, where people live and work together on the basis of equality and solidarity. This pervasive radicalism resulted in his excommunication from the Russian Orthodox Church.[14]

Berdyaev, the outstanding Orthodox theologian of the 20th century, enunciated a controversial theology that reflected an individualist view of religion – a personalist – embedded in a mystical eschatological vision. Since he regarded himself as a member of the

Russian intelligentsia, in the legacy of Tolstoy and Dostoevsky in the religious realm, and of the Westernizer socialists, like Herzen, Belinsky, Chernishevsky, and Bakunin, his thought combined a deep religiosity to a basically Marxist/anarchist perspective; he loathed the authority of the state.

A rebel Marxist youth, Berdyaev repudiated the class of his parents, the nobility, for the working-class and Marxism. Although he later left Marxism for religion, he remained steadfast in his socialist convictions, including the cooperative ownership of the means of production, decentralist patterns to prevent authoritarianism, the abolition of wage labor, and participatory democracy. The end result of his socialism was the creating of a new working-class, akin to the old nobility, in which classlessness would still allow for some status differentiation. Berdyaev was expelled from the Soviet Union in 1922 because he refused to abandon religious activities, migrating to France to become a close friend of Maritain and Mounier.[15]

Principal thinkers of Judaism, Hinduism, Islam, and Buddhism have also embraced socialism. In Judaism, Martin Buber, a professor of religion and social ethics at the University of Frankfurt before spending the last years of his life at the Hebrew University in Jerusalem, was its leading, near-contemporary thinker. An expert on Hasidism, the widespread religious phenomenon gripping the Jewish poor in Eastern Europe in the last few centuries, he analyzed the connection between utopian longings and social misery.

The good society, for Buber, would be a socialist one whose socioeconomic parameters insured a general equality. But for it to flourish, its primary ethical values of cooperation in the spirit of equality and brotherhood must be daily experienced in the personal interactions of its citizenry, otherwise it would lack authenticity. Thus, he rejected the Soviet Communist experience/model for the anarchist-socialist one of Proudhon, Kropotkin, and especially of Gustav Landauer, a German-Jewish social philosopher and socialist who added to the views of the first two, the element of religion, in the sense of its being "a bond of common spirit in freedom."

Buber saw the best example of this good society in the Israeli *kibbutzim*, whose small-scale collectively-owned property allowed for participatory democracy at work and intense social engagement, all under the bonds of a shared historical heritage, of language/ ethnicity, and religious tradition. To be sure, *kibbutzim* personnel play a leading role in the Israel Labor Party today, including the staffing of its top leadership. But *kibbutzim* now are themselves important capitalist enterprises, hiring labor, losing, in the process, their earlier idealism.[16]

Mohandas K. Gandhi is surely one of the giants of our age. Born into an Indian Hindu family in the *Vaisya* caste, he led a life of privilege. His father was an important, local politician. Gandhi was educated in both India and in England, studying law in London and admitted to the bar. While in South Africa, practicing law in the 1890s, he encountered the systematic dehumanization of white racism, which he decided to change through *Satyagraha*, or love-force, a nonviolent resistance to evil.

Deeply influenced by Tolstoy, Gandhi founded Tolstoy farm in 1910, a cooperative village based on the moral foundations of love-force to challenge racist South Africa. This utopian experiment embodied the key contours of his vision of the good society, of free individuals living in self-governing cooperative villages, where the work was of the cottage-industry variety (he opposed the dehumanization of Western industrialism) that would allow for not only full employment but the necessary smallness to promote human solidarity. He would even permit some petty capitalism, but at death, one's estate reverted to the community. In 1915, Gandhi returned to India to fight for its independence from British rule, spending many years in prison for practicing the passive resistance of love-force.

The social ethics of Gandhi, which obviously included his socialism (he once stated that everyone's time was equally valuable), were firmly based not only on the Hindu classics like the Bhagavad-Gita, but on the Bible and Koran, which he read daily. Under the inspiration of the love-force, he also became a determined champion of the *Dalits*, whom he called *harijans*, or "Children of God." In 1948,

Gandhi was assassinated by a Moslem zealot whom he forgave as he fell to the ground.[17]

Islamic societies, no less than those of other religions, have also been active participants in the modern socialist project: to be sure, secular socialism in its Marxist form has not influenced their peasant masses, although it has had some impact in urban areas among workers and middle-class intellectuals. Early Islam, like Christianity, attempted a radical reorganization of society, with its precepts of a fraternal and generally egalitarian community based on social justice, with no interest on loans.

Recent Islamic socialism has both a fundamentalist or theocratic bent (under the Ayatollah Ruholla Khomeini in Iran), and a generally secular current under Gamal Abdul Nasser in Egypt, Mu'ammar Qaddafi in Libya, the ruling Ba'th socialist parties in Syria and Iraq, and in the governing parties of Algeria and Tunisia. Its hallmarks are widespread nationalization of industry and banking, cooperatives in the countryside, and extensive social welfare. Concerning women, the Iranian radical fundamentalists have championed the veil or traditional sexism, although the Libyans, the Ba'th group and the Algerian and Tunisian socialist have a liberal position toward them.

The most thoroughgoing socialist party in the Islamic world – in fact the most authentically socialist one in the contemporary world – was that of Libya under Qaddafi, which has socialized the means of production and exchange, with people's committees running society, resulting in a pervasive egalitarianism so intense that any business outside of small family has employees who are partners. To promote women's equality, Qaddafi and the left of the revolution have also consciously and successfully integrated women into economic life outside the home, even attempting, without success, to let them serve in the military.

The handbook of this revolution is Qaddafi's *Green Book*, a fiercely anti-capitalist and pervasively socialist tract. Examples: "No individual has the right to carry out economic activity in order to acquire more...wealth than is necessary to satisfy his needs, because the excess amounts belongs to other individuals"; "Whoever works in a socialist corporation is a partner in its production"; and, "Whoever works for a wage has no incentive to work."

This tract challenges the traditional conservative Moslem clerics, or *ulama*, for a socialist Islam based on the communal/egalitarian scriptures of the Koran, disregarding the *hadith* or narratives of Mohammed, in agreement with some Islamic and many Western scholars who question its authenticity, akin to Moslem *Shii* views.

The success of this revolution was based on the support of the impoverished Libyan masses whose Bedouin egalitarianism and sense of individuality within the communal boundaries of family, clan, and tribe are proverbial. Furthermore, a weak bourgeoisie and large oil revenues aided in the generally weak resistance to socialism associated with modernity. Then, there was the key influence of the anti-imperialism and socialism of Nasser on Qaddafi and the revolutionary youth of his generation. The official name of Libya is the Socialist People's Libyan Arab *Jamahiriyyah*; the last word denotes "people's democracy." But Qaddafi became dictatorial and was deposed.

Another outstanding Islamic socialist was the Iranian intellectual/ teacher, Dr. Ali Shariati, one of the principal inspirers of the 1979 Islamic Revolution in Iran. His education, including studies at the Sorbonne in Paris, synthesized traditional *Shii* concerns for social justice, as embodied in the return of the Twelfth Imam to usher in the definitive era of social justice, with world socialist thought. He was an enthusiastic supporter of the Cuban and Algerian socialist revolutions and admirer of the now-legendary Third-World-revolutionary Communist, Che Guevara.

To be sure, Shariati was an ardent proponent of the centrality of the class struggle in history waged by the masses (peasantry and workers) against their governing elite (landlords and bourgeoisie), and within this model opposed Western imperialism, along with its junk consumerism and racism. Furthermore, like Rauschenbusch and Gutierrez in their studies of Christianity, he contrasted early revolutionary Islam under Ali, one of equality and brotherhood, with the later one of the Savafid dynasty, of sharp class divisions and concomitant socioeconomic oppression.

A final remark on political Islam: Jon Obert Voll, an authority on the subject, noted that its radical fundamentalist current has both a "long-term durability" and ability to "inspire revolution." [18]

Buddhism was founded by Siddhartha Gautama (563-483 B.C.), called the Buddha or Enlightened One. The religion of Buddhism is yet another philosophy/religion compatible with socialism. The Buddha, a prince from the *Kshatriya* Hindu caste and from what is now Nepal, renounced family, wealth and power after observing the great disparities between his privileged life and the socioeconomic misery of the masses. In attempting to understand why the elite enjoyed wealth and power, while the masses suffered, he became an ascetic for six years, living in a forest, but eventually concluding that this did not lead to wisdom in changing society. His solution called for a peaceful social revolution, of nonviolence or *ahimsā*, rejecting the Hindu caste system, but still adhering to its reincarnation cycle.

The Buddha conceptualized a deep dichotomy in the human condition, of injustice and strife, but also goodness that promised liberation. On the one hand, life was pervaded by general suffering, physical illness, death, and psychological anguish/alienation from thwarted desires and disappointments in seeking wealth/power to gratify the senses, related to individual-social selfishness. On the other hand, there also existed a strong desire for justice and equality within the human condition, to be attained through the "four noble truths," "eightfold way," and compassion and loving kindness for all living creatures.

Thus it was that the Buddha established *sangha* chapters, akin to Christian monasteries, admitting even *Dalits* to practice a communist poverty and celibacy in equality. The Buddha himself was ultimately a communist, calling nothing his own, and in anticipating the early Christians, deemed begging meritorious, encouraging the first general strike of the masses against their wealthy exploiters. Furthermore, he viewed great wealth as wicked, the only decent thing being to give it to the poor, thus indicating his abhorrence of wealth and power.

Early Buddhism today is best represented by its *Hinayana* or *Theravada* form (strong in Southeast Asia, Sri Lanka, Myanmar, Cambodia, Thailand, and Vietnam), which regards the Buddha as a great human reformer, denies the existence of a personal and omnipotent/omniscient god/force, including one creating the universe, and rejects the immortality of the soul. But there is still a transcendent and all-powerful supernatural force permeating the universe, which judges, as already observed, human and other living beings according to their *karma*.

The *Mahayana* version of Buddhism, which continues in India, China, Tibet, Taiwan, and Japan, regards the Buddha as a god-like figure and believes in *bodhisattvas*, human beings achieving moral perfection returning to Earth to further everyone's salvation.

Buddhism itself suffered greatly in India and China where it was once strong. In India, the invasions of the White Huns in the 6th century and Turkic Moslems in the 11th century, in addition to the Hindu counterattack, terminated Buddhism as a viable force. But it survived as part of Hinduism, the Buddha becoming one of the avatars of the god Vishnu. Recently, Buddhism gains strength there, especially among the *Dalits*. In China, Buddhism had many adherents, but waned in strength when the emperor Wu-Tsung in the 9th century, fearing the growing power of the tax-exempt *sangha* chapters, abolished many of them.

Buddhism, like other religions in their accepting the patronage of kings, implicitly reinforced the status quo of class and attendant oppression, in the process of which *sangha* chapters became corrupt. This state, in turn, was often related to focusing on individual salvation, tending to minimize or ignore the broader socioeconomic causes contributing to individual-social alienation. Indeed, only *sangha* members could generally escape the deadly grip of real-existing life, of brutal exploitation of the many. Not surprisingly, Buddhism often magnified the small sins of the poor, while the large individual and collective socioeconomic ones of the ruling elite were often downplayed, indicating their hegemony.

The *karma-nirvana* doctrine (in some degree related to family *karma* and even beyond in some Buddhist texts) ostensibly rewards the rich and powerful while condemning the poor for former-life sins: in Tibet, prior to their liberation by Chinese Communism, slaves of the feudal aristocracy and monasteries were told by them that this was the why of their lowly status. Furthermore, are the people of the First World more virtuous than those of the Second and Third? But from the perspective that members of the *sanghas* attempt to escape exploitative/alienating society – this can never be done completely – the *sangha* counterculture is potentially revolutionary.

Buddhism along with other major religions today emphasizes the importance of the socioeconomic element in the makeup for some happiness, itself in Buddhism texts and in recent Buddhist lay movements, like the *Soka Gakkai* ("Value Creation Society") in Japan, with its more than one million well-organized followers (this is a tightly-knit mutual-aid society): A formidable force in contemporary Japanese politics, it firmly endorses a form of a this-world paradise, its followers urged to strive for wealth and all that goes with it, like good health and many friends.

To be sure, Buddhism, along with other religions mentioned, has now many socialist adherents. Sri Lanka, a predominantly Buddhist nation, has a powerful Buddhist socialist tradition, leading to extensive nationalization of the productive forces undergirded by democracy. Its official name is Democratic Socialist Republic of Sri Lanka. In Myanmar, organized Buddhism is the principal force bringing about its socialist character, of large-scale nationalization of commerce, industry, and land, undergirded by peasants' and workers' councils. This nationalization for U Nu, a Buddhist and former prime minister, was in accordance with Buddhist principles: "Property is meant not to be saved, not for gains. It is to be used by men to meet their needs in their journey to Nirvana." But he rejected state socialism for one in which workers and peasants actively participated in running the economy.

Regarding the key question involving relations between Marxism (and Soviet and Chinese Communism) and Buddhism, the views of

D.C. Vasayavardhana (*The Revolt in the Temple*, 1953), a prominent Sri Lankan Buddhist intellectual, are representative. He noted the many similarities between the aims of Marxism and Buddhism, like human brotherhood and equality, international peace, and their shared rationalism, but disapproved of Marxian class struggle and dictatorship of the proletariat, opting instead for an evolutionary road to socialism through "discussion, cooperation, agreement." Buddhism itself suffered greatly under a militantly atheist Chinese Communism, but the Chinese government has now restored many previously destroyed Buddhist temples and monasteries.[19]

To be sure, Marx's prophecy of traditional religion's becoming progressively irrelevant, predicated on the increasing importance of science/technology, itself associated with the rise of the city and mass secular education, is partly correct. The following in percentages for contemporary regular church attendance on any given Sunday: the United States, 44; Ireland, above 50; 5 or under in Germany and Scandinavia; 27 in the UK; 21 in France; and 40 in Italy. In former Communist Eastern Europe/Soviet Union, 2 in Russia, but more than 50 in Poland. Outside these areas, Communist China is officially atheist, but India is very religious. Indeed, as already observed, in the Islamic world, Catholic Latin America, and in Hindu and Buddhist nations, where religion is important, it itself must become ever more socialist to survive.

Other statistics on religion are in order: on acceptance of life-after-death for selected nations in percentages: the U.S. and the two Irelands, 80; Italy, 65; Poland, 60; West Germany, 55; former East Germany, 12; UK, 50; Israel, 42. As for belief in God (not only a theistic one), for selected nations in percentages: the U.S. leads with 94, followed by Italy, the two Irelands and Poland, from the mid-80s to low 90s; UK and Israel, 70; West Germany, 65; East Germany, 32; Norway, 60; Russia, 54. Belief in traditional Christianity in the U.S. varies widely, highly correlated with the amount of general education, socioeconomic status and region. For instance, in a survey after World War II, among four denominations, in percentages: on belief in Jesus as God's divine son – Congregationalists, 40;

Methodists, 54; Catholics, 86; Southern Baptists, 99. On belief in life after death – Congregationalists, 36; Methodists, 49; Catholics, 75; Southern Baptists, 97. And on the belief in the definite second coming of Jesus – Congregationalists, 13; Methodists, 21; Catholics, 47; Southern Baptists, 94.[20]

In discussing the major religions, we observed their double standard with respect to worldly wealth and power: Although their prophets had high ideals, once they become well ensconced in the world they increasingly reflected the views of ruling elite. For instance, they allowed their average adherents to engage in war and to succeed in business, thus permitting the economic exploitation of labor, including the employment of slavery – although Buddhists were admonished not to engage in the slave trade – and were not too kind to unbelievers or members of other religions, invariably condemning them to the fires of hell or to deferred salvation. Thus, it is neither surprising that when members of different religions wish to marry one another and have children, "religious" disputes typically follow, nor is it surprising that various religious-social associations themselves invite conflict in business and other areas of life as they usually favor their co-religionists at the expense of others, nor that religiously-inspired warfare among and within religious groups, is a common occurrence.

Penultimate remarks on religion in the U.S.: the progressive elements of it have been catalogued, but the Catholic Church's position on abortion and sexuality is still reactionary, although 85 percent of Catholic couples use contraceptives and many approve of abortion, especially in the first trimester.

There is also a conservative white Protestant fundamentalism, most of whose adherents are from the white working and lower-middle classes, which is highly racist, homophobic and sexist, opposition to abortion belonging to the last category. They staunchly resist civil rights for blacks and other minorities. Their leading conservative ministers, all Republicans, include Pat Robertson, Jerry Falwell, and Donald Wildmon. The Reverend Billy Graham does not endorse Presidential candidates, but he gave an unofficial nod to George W.

Bush in the 2000 election. To be sure, the many Black Protestant fundamentalists are on the left of the main political spectrum; Dr. Martin Luther King Jr. was a democratic socialist and many others are near socialists. The historically sharp socioeconomic differences between the two groups explain their respective politico-religious orientations.[21]

Will alienated institutional religion escape its exclusiveness, with its bigotry and parochialism (the Unitarian Universalist Association has), and even unite to establish a world which the great religious prophets were pointing towards a worldwide fraternal society of general equality, fraternity, and liberty based on pervasive democratic norms? Perhaps, but only if they become more spiritual, which includes embracing more tolerance and more socialism.

Notes

A) Background

1) On religion in general, see Marvin Harris, *Culture, People, Nature: An Introduction to General Anthropology* (New York: Harper and Row, 1988), pp. 447-81, for an anthropological approach. Shepard, *Sociology*, pp. 433-57, for a sociological view. Bronislaw Malinowski, *Magic, Science, and Religion, and Other Essays* (Garden City, NY: Doubleday Anchor Books, 1948), pp. 17-148, for instance, on the similarities and differences between magic and science, along with other matters, as fear of death and its ties to religion, religion and community solidarity, and so forth. Sigmund Freud, *The Future of an Illusion* (Garden City, NY: Anchor Books, 1964), pp. 1-92, indicates that religion is an "illusion," its antidote being science. Erich Fromm, *Psychoanalysis and Religion* (New Haven, CT: Yale Univ. Press, 1950), pp. 1-119, is a superlative commentary by a humanistic socialist and psychoanalyst on the components of religion – more on him later. Emile Durkheim, *The Elementary Forms of Religious Life* (New York: Free Press, 1995), p. 236-41 and 418-48, on the connection

between "religious evolution" and "social conditions," justifying existing social structures, society itself being the source of religion. On religion and invention, see David. F. Noble, *The Religion of Technology: The Divinity of Man and the Spirit of Invention* (New York: Alfred A. Knopf, 1997), chapter 1. On reincarnation in Judaism and Christianity, see Jack Katznell, "Rabbi's statement causes furor," *Akron Beacon Journal*, Aug. 7, 2000; and Joseph Head and S.L. Cranston, eds., *Reincarnation: An East-West Anthology* (New York: Julian Press, 1961), pp. 25-43. On the primary religious source emphasizing reincarnation, see K.M. Senn, *Hinduism* (Baltimore, MD: Penguin Books, 1961), pp. 27-31 on the problem of caste and reincarnation. On Marx's quotation in "Toward the Critique of Hegel's Philosophy of Law: Introduction," see Easton and Guddat, *Young Marx*, p. 250.

B) Marx and Engels on Religion

1) Frederick Engels, *Anti-Dühring: Herr Eugen Dühring's Revolution in Science* (Moscow: Progress Publishers, 1975), pp. 374-76 on the quotations.
2) Marx and Engels, *The German Ideology* in *Young Marx*, p. 422.
3) Karl Marx, "Toward the Critique of Hegel's Philosophy of Law: Introduction," in Easton and Guddat, *Young Marx*, p. 250.
4) Friedrich Engels, "On the History of Early Christianity," in Feuer, *Marx and Engels*, pp. 168-94.
5) Engels, *Anti-Dühring*, p. 125.
6) Friedrich Engels, *The Peasant War in Germany*, in Feuer, *Marx and Engels*, pp. 413-37. An excellent work on millenarianism is by Norman Cohn, *The Pursuit of the Millenium: Revolutionary Messianism in Medieval and Reformation Europe and its Bearing on Modern Totalitarian Movements* (New York: Haper Torchbooks, 1961), pp. 251-71 on Münzer. The Judeo-Christian-Islamic tradition is deeply millenarian.

7) Karl Marx, "On the Jewish Question," *Marx/Engels Collected Works* (vol. 3 ; *Marx and Engels, 1843-1844*), pp. 146-74. On Jews being small traders in Prussia, see Enzo Traverso, *The Marxists and the Jewish Question: The History of a Debate, 1843-1943* (Atlantic Highland, NJ: Humanities Press, 1990), p. 20. Max Weber, *The Protestant Ethic and the Spirit of Capitalism* (New York: Charles Scribner's Sons, 1958), pp. 95-183 on "religious foundations of worldly asceticism" and "asceticism and the spirit of capitalism." On Calvin and his approving of capitalist entrepreneurship and charging of interest, see Ernst Troeltsch, *The Social Teachings of the Christian Churches* (New York: Harper Torchbooks, 1960), II, 641-52; Harold J. Grimm, *The Reformation Era, 1500-1650* (New York: Macmillan, 1954), p. 350.

8) Traverso, *Marxists and Jewish Question*, p. 30.

9) Ibid., pp. 26-27.

10) Engels, *Anti-Dühring*, pp. 113-15.

11) Frederick Engels, *The Origin of the Family, Private Property, and the State* (New York: International Publishers, 1942), pp. 136-37.

12) Karl Marx, "The Communism of the Paper Rheinischer Beobachter" (Excerpt), *Deutsche-Brusseler-Zeitung*, Sept. 12, 1847, in Feuer, *Marx and Engels*, pp. 267-69.

C) Other Secular Socialists

1) Karl Kautsky, *Foundations of Christianity* (New York: Russell and Russell, 1953), pp. 235, 309-23. Matthew 10:14 ff., for instance.

2) Fromm, *Psychoanalysis and Religion*, pp. 10-63.

3) Ernst Bloch, *The Principle of Hope*, 3 vols., trans. by Neville Plaice, Stephen Plaice, and Paul Knight (Cambridge, MA: MIT Press, 1986), I, 51-77 on basic human drives and Sigmund Freud, Carl Jung, and Alfred Adler, 77 ff. On daydreams and night dreams, 249 ff., on Marx's "Eleven Theses on Feuerback," 287 ff.; II, 471-624 on "social utopias."

4) Joseph Dorfman, *Thorstein Veblen and His America* (New York: Viking Press, 1935), p. 489 on the religion-is-magic quotation. Thorstein Veblen, "Christian Morals and the Competitive System," *International Journal of Ethics*, Jan. 1910, pp. 178-79.
5) Veblen, "Christian Morals," pp. 179-80.
6) Thorstein Veblen, *The Theory of the Leisure Class*, intro. By C. Wright Mills (New York: Mentor Book, 1953), pp. 197 and 215.
7) Ibid., pp. 199-200.
8) Ibid., pp. 215-16.
9) Thorstein Veblen, "Dementia Praecox," in Thorstein Veblen, *Esays in Our Changing Order*, ed. Leon Ardzrooni (New York: Viking Press, 1934), pp. 430-31 ff. The quotation is on p. 431 – Veblen ties the renaissance of Protestant Fundamentalism to World War I, one of its manifestations being a resurgent Ku Klux Klan activity. Also, see Veblen, *Leisure Class*, p. 213-14.
10) Veblen, *Leisure Class*, p. 215.
11) Ibid., pp. 204-10.
12) Ibid., p. 202.
13) Ibid., p. 207.
14) Ibid., pp. 181-82 ff.
15) Ibid., pp. 217-18.

D) Relations Between Secular Socialism and Religion in the Soviet Union

1) On the relations of Communism and the Russian Orthodox Church in the Soviet Union, see John Shelton Curtiss, *The Russian Church and the Soviet State* (Boston: Little, Brown and Co., 1953); chapter 3, for instance, presents the Church's animosity to Communists in the Civil War; chap. 9 highlights the drama of the Church's relations with the Soviet State. This work is not unfriendly to the Soviet State. V.I. Lenin, *Materialism and Empirio-Criticism: Critical Comments on a Reactionary Philosophy* (New York: International Publishers, 1927), chapter 1, for instance. On religion and socialism, see the special issue

of Monthly Review, *Religion and the Left*, July-August, 1984, vol. 36, no 3 – p. 36, for instance, on the 200,000 base Christian communities of Catholicism in Latin America.

E) Reformist and Socialist Religion

1) On Catholicism: On the encyclicals mentioned, see E.E.Y. Hales, *The Catholic Church in the Modern World: A Survey from the French Revolution to the Present* (New York: Image Books, 1960), pp. 193-212 on "Rerun Novarum" and "Quadragesimo Anno." And, Michael Novak, *Freedom with Justice: Catholic Social Thought and Liberal Institutions* (San Francisco: Harper and Row, 1984), pp. 108-82, with much commentary by this conservative on Catholic social conservatism. He never once mentions Jesus of Nazareth or other Hebrew prophets. National Council of Catholic Bishops, *Economic Justice for All* (Washington DC: National Council of Catholic Bishops, 1986), pp. v-xvi, 6-33, 65-105, 147-52. Also, for some of the more recent encyclicals issued by Pope John Paul II, see *In These Times*, Aug. 21- Sept. 3, 1991, p. 2; *Akron Beacon Journal*, March 1, 1995, p. A9.

2) See Peter N. Stearns, *Priest and Revolutionary: Lamennais and the Dilemma of French Catholicism* (New York: Harper and Row, 1967). Marjorie Villiers, *Charles Péguy: A Study in Integrity* (New York: Harper and Row, 1965). Jacques Maritain, *True Humanism*, trans. M.R. Adamson (London: Geoffrey Bles: The Centenary Press, 1938), pp. 156-204 as an example of his socialism. John Hellman, *Emmanuel Mounier and the New Catholic Left, 1930-1950* (Toronto: Univ. of Toronto Press, 1981), pp. 200 ff. on sympathy for Marxism.

3) On Simone Weil, see Simone Pétrement, *Simone Weil: A Life*, trans. from French by Raymond Rosenthal (New York: Pantheon Books, 1976). See also Simone Weil, *Oppression and Liberty*, trans., from French by Arthur Wills and John Petrie (Amherst, MA: Univ. of MA Press, 1973), pp. 83-108 on her good society, basically a socialist-anarchist one. Simone Weil, *The Need for*

Roots: Prelude to a Declaration of Duties Toward Mankind, trans. by Arthur Wills with a preface by T.S. Eliot (Boston: Beacon Press, 1960), pp. 34-184 on her basically socialist-anarchist society.

4) On the Catholic Worker, Dorothy Day and Peter Maurin, see Dorothy Day, *The Long Loneliness: The Autobiography of Dorothy Day* (New York Curtis Books, 1972), pp. 193-316 on her Catholic Worker experiences, including her encounters with Maurin. Dorothy Day, *Loaves and Fishes* (New York: Harper and Row, 1963), is on the journal *The Catholic Worker* and the movement in general; pp. 28-41 on "Houses of Hospitality"; pp. 42-59 on "Communitarian Farms"; pp. 103-117, on Ammon Hennacy another key member of the movement. Arthur Sheehan, *Peter Maurin: Gay Believer* (Garden City, NY: Hanover House, 1959), pp. 90 ff on his meeting Day and so forth.

5) Gustavo Gutierrez, *A Theology of Liberation* (Maryknoll, NY: Oribs Books, 1973), pp. 111 ff on necessity for socialism in Latin America; pp. 236-37 on Guevara; 272 ff. on the class struggle; 265 ff. on the Church being part of the traditional power structure; 175 ff. on sin; pp. 287 ff. on Bible's denouncing wealth, power, and privilege of the few at the expense of the many. Also, see the brilliant work of José Porfiro Miranda, *Communism in the Bible* (Maryknoll, NY: Orbis Books, 1987), pp. 1-85. For a Protestant view similar to Gutierrez's and Miranda's see C.M. Kempton Kewitt, "The Marxist Jesus of Nazareth," in Louis Patsouras and Jack Ray Thomas, eds., *Essays on Socialism* (San Francisco: Mellen Research Univ. Press, 1992), pp. 299-343. See also William K. Tabb, ed., *Churches in Struggle: Liberation Theologies and Social Change in North America* (New York: Monthly Review Press, 1986), with its many excellent articles, in which the similarity of interests between Marxism and religious socialism is evident.

6) See O.J. Brose, *Frederick Denison Maurice, Rebellious Conformist* (Athens, OH: Ohio Univ. Press, 1971). Brenda Colloms, *Charles Kingsley, The Lion of Eversley* (London: Constable, 1975).

Peter N. Stearns, *Priest and Revolutionary: Lamennais, and the Dilemma of French Catholicism* (New York: Harper and Row, 1967).

7) See Donald Gorrell, *The Age of Social Responsibility: The Social Gospel in the Progressive Era* (Macon, GA: Mercer Univ. Press, 1988).

8) Robert T. Handy, ed., *The Social Gospel in America: Gladden, Ely, Rauschenbusch* (New York: Oxford Univ. Press, 1966), pp. 33-169, on Gladden; pp. 184-250 on Ely.

9) On Rauschenbusch, see Dores R. Sharpe, *Walter Rauschenbusch* (New York: Macmillan, 1942). See, for instance, *His Christianity and the Social Crisis* (New York: Macmillan, 1914), pp. 44-92, in which Jesus of Nazareth is portrayed as a socialist.

10) On Niebuhr, see Gabriel Fackre, *The Promise of Reinhold Niebuhr* (Philadelphia: J.B. Lippincott, 1970), pp. 20-21. June Bingham, *Courage to Change: An Introduction to the Life and Thought of Reinhold Niebuhr* (New York: Charles Scribner's, 1961), pp. 163 ff.

11) On Thomas, see W.A. Swanberg, *Norman Thomas: The Last Idealist* (New York: Scribner's Sons, 1976), pp. 43-179, for instance.

12) See National Council of Churches of Christ in the United States of America, *A Policy Statement* (1966), 5 pp.

13) On Karl Barth, see Thomas C. Oden, *The Promise of Barth: The Ethics of Freedom* (Philadelphia: J.B. Lippincott, 1969), pp. 25 ff. on his socialism. On Paul Tillich, see his *The Socialist Decision*, trans. Franklin Sherman from German, intro. John Stumme (New York: Harper and Row, 19710, pp. 61 ff., 117 ff., and 157 ff. Wilhelm and Marion Pauck, *Paul Tillich: His Life and Thought* (New York: Harper and Row, 1976), I, 67, ff., on Tillich's socialism.

14) Henri Troyat, *Tolstoy*, trans. from French by Nancy Amphoux (New York: Doubleday, 1965), especially pp. 373-584 on Tolstoy's religious/anarchist quest.

15) Nicolas Berdyaev, *Dream and Reality: An Essay in Autobiography* (New York: Macmillan, 1951). Nicolas Berdyaev, *The Realm of Spirit and the Realm of Freedom*, trans. Donald A. Lowerie (New York: Harper and Brothers, 1952), pp. 57-63 on socialism. Nicolas Berdyaev, *Slavery and Freedom,* trans. from Russian by R.M. French (New York: Charles Scribner's Sons, 1944), pp. 200-22 on his socialism.

16) Laurence J. Silberstein, *Martin Buber's Social and Religious Thought: Alienation and Quest for Meaning* (New York: New York Univ. Press, 1989), pp. 193-98 on Buber's religious/socialist decentralized society. Also, see Martin Buber, *Paths in Utopia*, trans. R.F.C. Hall, intro. Ephraim Fischoff (Boston: Beacon Press, 1958), pp. 7 ff., 24 ff., 38 ff., 46 ff., and 139-49. For proper human relations, see Martin Buber, *I and Thou*, trans. and prologue by Walter Kaufmann (New York: Charles Scribner's Sons, 1970), pp. 92-100.

17) Mohandas K. Gandhi, *An Autobiography: The Story of My Experiments with Truth* (Boston: Beacon Press, 1957), p. 137, on his being "overwhelmed" by Tolstoy's *The Kingdom of God Is Within You.* C.F. Andrews, *Mahatma Gandhi's Ideas: Including Selections from His Writings*, intro. Horace G. Alexander (London: George Allen and Unwin, 1949), pp. 202-17 on Tolstoy Farm. Louis Fischer, *The Life of Mahatma Gandhi* (New York: Harper and Row, 1964).

18) For an excellent view of the various currents of Islamic or Arab socialism, see John Obert Voll, *Islam: Continuity and Change in the Modern World* (Syracuse, NY: Syracuse Univ. Press, 1994), for instance, pp. 173 ff., 289-373; 313 for the brief quotations. On the Arab left, socialists and communists, the former being particularly important in Arab life, see Albert Hourani, *A History of the Arab Peoples* (New York: MJF Books, 1991), pp. 397-410; and John L. Esposito, *Islam: The Straight Path* (New York: Oxford Univ. Press, 1991), pp. 156-86 on Islamic socialism. On Qaddafi and the Libyan Islamic Socialist Revolution, see David Blundy and Andrew Lycett, *Qaddafi and the Libyan Revolution*

(Boston: Little, Brown, and Co., 1987), pp. 57-68, 84-129. Dirk Vanderwalle, ed., *Qadhafi's Libya, 1969-1994* (New York: St. Martin's Press, 1995). The various articles by well-known writers in the field are excellent. On the Green Book, see Muammar al-Qadhafi, Part II: *The Solution of the Economic Problem, Socialism* (London: Martin Brian and O'Keefe, 1978), pp. 19-20 on the quotations. On the Iranian Islamic Revolution, including its extensive nationalizations, banks, large industry, insurance companies, and so forth, see Martin Kramer, ed., *Sh'ism, Resistance and Revolution* (Boulder, CO: Westview Press, 1987): articles by Marvin Zonis and Daniel Brumberg, "Shi'ism as Interpreted by Khomeini: An Ideology of Revolutionary Violence," pp. 47-66; Mangol Bayat, "Mahmud Taleqani and the Iranian Revolution," pp. 67-94; Shaul Bakhash, "Islam and Social Justice," in Iran," pp. 95-116. On Ali Shariati, see Esposito, *Islam*, pp. 178 ff.

19) For a general view of Buddhism, see Richard H. Robinson and Willard R. Johnson, with assistance from others, *The Buddhist Religion: A Historical Introduction*, 4th ed. (Belmont, CA: Wadsworth Publishing Co., 1997), pp. 218-19, 238-40, 301-09, on Buddhism's social activism, with new emphases on changing the present world. Edward J. Thomas, *The History of Buddhist Thought* (New York: Barnes and Noble, 1967), is excellent; pp. 11-26, for instance, on "The Ascetic Ideal," the Sangha life-style. Peter A. Pardue, *Buddhism: A Historical Introduction to Buddhist Values and the Social and Political Forms They Have Assumed in Asia* (New York: Macmillan, 1968), indicates the complex interplay between Buddhism and political and social forces; for instance, pp. 27-30, on asceticism for lay Buddhists, while economically exploiting others, including slaves, although slave-trading is prohibited. Larson, *Religion of the Occident*, pp. 126-54, presents the best short description of the Buddha's socioeconomic and other views that I know. On Buddhist Socialism and the differences and similarities between Marxism (and 20th century Communism) and Buddhism, see Ernst Benz, *Buddhism or*

Communism: Which Holds the Future of Asia? (London: George Allen and Unwin, 1966), pp. 95-124. on the "Social and Political Teachings of Buddhism," is of great interest. The quotation from U Nu is from here. "The Buddhist Critique of Communism," pp. 217-34, is a masterpiece; it features Vijayavardhana's *The Revolt in the Temple.*

20) On traditional religion's general decline, although it appears to be slightly gaining in Eastern Europe and the former Soviet Union with the fall of Communism, with statistics, see *Time*, Aug. 9, 1976 (Gallup Poll); David Briggs, "Religion Enjoys a Revival," *Akron Beacon Journal*, May 22, 1995, p. A6; P. Ehrensaft and A. Etzioni, *Anatomies of America: Sociological Perspectives* (New York: Macmillan, 1969), pp. 272-85. Gordon Wright, *France in Modern Times: 1760 to the Present* (Chicago: Rand McNally, 1960), p. 557, "The Dechristianization of Rural France." H. Stuart Hughes, *Contemporary Europe: A History* (Englewood Cliffs, NJ: Prentice-Hall, 1976), p. 290, on Communism's destruction of Orthodox Christianity in Russia. *Akron Beacon Journal*, Jan. 16, 1998, p. A9 – a recent poll in Russia has 46 percent of respondents as atheists.

21) On Christian conservatism in America, see Sara Diamond, *Not by Politics Alone: The Enduring Influence of the Christian Right* (New York: Guilford Press, 1998). Clark Morphew, "Conservative Christians back Bush," *Akron Beacon Journal*, Jan. 13, 2001, pp. A14 and A16. On the democratic socialist Martin Luther King Jr. see David J. Garrow, *Bearing the Cross: Martin Luther King Jr. and the Southern Christian Leadership Conference* (New York: William Morrow, 1986).

Chapter Eleven: Imperialism

A) Background

That imperialism, "the policy of extending a nation's authority by territorial acquisitions or by the establishment of economic and political hegemony over other nations," is of major importance in written history is to state the obvious.[1] Empire building has been associated with the "great" personages of history, including Alexander the Great, Julius Caesar, Peter the Great, Frederick the Great, Napoleon Bonaparte, and Adolf Hitler. The consequences of imperialism themselves are mass death and destruction and more oppression for the losers.[2]

Imperialism itself is so deeply ensconced in the human condition that it even forms an integral part of its religious systems. In the Judeo-Christian-Islamic tradition, crusades against unbelievers are common. In the Old Testament, a militaristic Yahweh commanded the Hebrews to extirpate their enemies without mercy, like King Sihon and his subjects, "including the women and babies."[3]

Christianity and Islam have followed in this tradition, with the crusade and *jihad* respectively, victory or defeat being dependent on God's will. Not surprisingly, religion, interwoven with nationalism, is still a significant force in 20th century warfare (including guerrilla activity), as between Hindu India and Moslem Pakistan; the Judaism of Israel and Islam of the Arab states; Croatian Catholics, Orthodox Serbs, and Bosnian Moslems in Bosnia-Herzegovina; and Catholics and Protestants in Northern Ireland. The last continues religious conflict between Catholics and Protestants, endemic since the Protestant revolution in the 16th century. Furthermore, there is the longstanding Christian animus against Jews, resulting in many slaughters and deportations in the last thousand years, an element of the Holocaust perpetrated by Nazi Germany during World War II.[4]

In the founding Western civilization, the Greek, its prototypical *Iliad* well portrayed the mindset of an imperialist society in which an insult to one of the ruling elite (the abduction of Helen, wife of King Menelaus of Sparta, by the Trojan prince Paris) was sufficient excuse for war. As Weil asserted in the "Iliad, Poem of Might," "the true hero of the *Iliad* is might," a force "which makes a think of anybody who comes under its sway," including not only those whom it killed or subjugated, but the conquerors themselves whose hierarchy of power further subordinated underlings to superiors. Furthermore, imperialism, for her, inimical to human solidarity and balance, led the Greek aggressors to no less an object in mind than "all the riches of Troy, all the palaces, the temples and the houses as ashes, all the women and children as slaves, all the men as corpses."[5]

In Thucydides' *The Peloponnesian War*, Greek civilization was torn asunder by the rival imperialisms of Athens and Sparta, in which treachery and massacre were the norms in a world deifying force. A leading Athenian unflinchingly informed his fellow citizens that:

> You should remember that your empire is a despotism exercised over unwilling subjects, who are always conspiring against you; they do not obey in return for any kindness which you do them...but in so far as you are their masters; they have no love of you, but they are held down by force.[6]

And, we should not neglect the importance of imperialism in Roman Civilization that unified the various and discrete groups of Europe to bring about Western Civilization, with its resultant of widespread slavery.

In the last five hundred years, imperialism has been an integral part of capitalism. Its early variety could be seen in the Commercial Revolution from the 15th to the 18th centuries, in which the state was under the rule of a king-and-nobility complex with capitalist commoners often playing a secondary role in Spain, Portugal and France. But in England and the Netherlands, capitalists entrepreneurs (the great ones being members of the nobility in England) were clearly in the ascendancy by the 17th century. With the rise of the Industrial

Revolution in the 18th century and rise of finance capitalism and international cartels in the 20th century, capitalism continued its earlier imperialism under new forms.

It was during the Commercial Revolution that most of the early inhabitants of the Americas were either worked to death in the silver and gold mines and plantations or slaughtered in revolts or died from disease brought by Europeans, necessitating slavery. In a related note, Native American populations were decimated by the Spanish conquest; on the Island of Hispaniola, there were a quarter million people in 1492, five hundred in the 1540s; in the Aztec-dominated areas, from nine to fourteen million in the 1530s, and half a million in the 1630s.

Thus it was that African slaves came to America to work for the Portuguese, Spanish, Dutch, English, and French entrepreneurs in the first great international money crop – sugar, and later, cotton; from ten million for Philip Curtin, to seventeen million for Ferdnand Braudel, to fifty million for Basil Davidson between 1500 to 1800. The many centuries of African slavery in the Americas is the principal seedbed of modern racism.

In this light, many of the prominent thinkers of liberalism either accepted slavery or owned slaves, although acknowledging it as immoral: Locke, the author of the *Fundamental Constitution for the Carolinas* (1669), representative of the former, Jefferson, the latter. But Smith opposed empire, and by extension, slavery, with its concomitant economic theory of mercantilism, stressing the importance of colonies for wealth. He argued that free trade was less costly and more efficient than empire and interminable wars in creating wealth.[7]

But even before written history or civilization, imperialism/war is not unheard of. There is an argument today between anthropologists as to the prevalence of war before the Neolithic/Mesolithic Ages, or approximately 10,000 years ago. According to Lawrence H. Keeley (*War Before Civilization*), there is ample evidence that even before this time, primitive societies engaged in fighting, as in the Upper and Late Paleolithic Age in what was Czechoslovakia as early as

24,000 to 35,000 years ago and in Gebel Sahaba in Egypt from 12,000 to 14,000 years ago. These early wars or skirmishes can be attributed to economic reasons, like control of land areas to furnish food. Keeley opposed the views of mainstream liberal and socialist anthropologists, like Montagu and Marvin Harris who averred that war only occurred in the Mesolithic/Neolithic Age over property and its extensions, but not too frequently before that time, and that it was with the advent of near civilization that war and its train of enslavement and exploitation became norms in human affairs. All three assigned various levels of socioeconomic complexity for organized war, Keeley allowing small groups to be more warlike than Montagu and Harris.[8]

B)

Marx and Engels followed the fortunes of European imperialism very closely, especially its British variety, but did not neglect those of the Dutch, Spanish, Portuguese, and French, as well as non-European varieties, like those of the Moguls in India and the Manchus in China. They delineated the contours of modern capitalist imperialism (Marx in *Capital* calls it the "colonial system") in its first two phases, that of the Commercial Revolution (1500-1750) in which agricultural and merchant capital predominated, followed by the Industrial Revolution (1750-1900) in which the great capitalists were industrialists. Although they did not live to see the rule of finance capital in the 20th century, they were acutely aware of its importance, of bankers of one nation investing in others, the Medicis and Fuggers being obvious examples.

Marx's and Engels' writings on imperialism and its consequences might be divided into four basic periods: the first brief allusion to it in the *Manifesto*; the second, of many articles in Horace Greely's New York Daily Tribune in the 1850s; the third in *Capital*, I, which drew largely from the second, with some mention of it in *Capital III*; and the fourth in articles and letters.

In the *Manifesto*, Marx and Engels in a Eurocentric vein pointed out that the bourgeoisie tied to the great European empires forced "all nations, even the most barbarian, into civilization," and that "free trade" in a "world market" would diminish "national differences and antagonisms between peoples" that were "vanishing gradually day by day," a process accelerating with the "supremacy of the proletariat"; this at a time when basically only the British bourgeoisie favored international free trade in the 1840s, when England's industrial, commercial, and financial supremacy was hindered by protectionism.[1] There was an element of hope here that universal bourgeois hegemony might usher in world peace, itself strengthened by the rise of the proletariat and socialism, but it was dashed by national capitalist rivalry in which a warlike nobility played a prominent role in fomenting, resulting in murderous wars, especially two world wars in the 20th century. But after World War II, which considerably weakened international capitalism while correspondingly strengthening Communism and social democracy, capitalism embarked once again on a free trade/world market mode to prevent war and stop socialism through regional and continental-wide organizations and international banking and regulatory institutions.

Soon after the *Manifesto*, Marx and Engels became close students of imperialism in general, not only interested in imperialism within Europe, like that of the British in Ireland, but in European conquest/ meddling in the rest of the world. This was well observed in their writings from August 1851 to March 1862 as British correspondents for the *NYDT* – many under Marx's name are written by Engels – about British and European affairs, a substantial number on imperialism. (Greeley, one of the great American newspaper editors, who founded the NYDT, was a political activist supporting progressive causes, including utopian socialism.)

Their articles in the NYDT on imperialism focused primarily on its British variety, especially in India and China, but also in Greece, but did not neglect others like French imperialism in Algeria and Russian intrigues in Persia. Some of their titles include, "The British Rule in India," "The East India Company – Its History and Results," "War in Burma," "The Revolt of India," "Lord Canning's Proclamation and Land Tenure in India," "The British Quarrel with

China," "The Opium Trade" (two articles), "The Anglo-Chinese Treaty," "The New Chinese War" (four related articles), "Revolution in China and Europe," "Algeria," and "Questions of the Ionian Islands."[2]

Marx's many articles on British imperial practices in India indicated his keen concern for non-Europeans. From a long-run perspective, Marx, who regarded imperialism as a policy resting on "brute force" – viewed the British conquest of India as a progressive step toward socialism, which can only come from a developed capitalism. This would primarily involve the English destruction of the Indian "Asiatic mode of production," in which collective village property was taxed by the state/ruling class. This position would presumably lead to the rise of a working class and the possibility for socialism, in the process of which the "Hindus themselves shall have grown strong enough to throw off the English yoke altogether." In this progression, he was aware of the great social misery endured by the Indian masses.[3]

Among the other cardinal observations of Marx on India were the rapacity and brutality of the British East India Company and Britain's systematic destruction of the indigenous Indian textile industry. He recounted the successive British legislative acts, which excluded Indian exports, especially cotton, in which India was renowned, to maintain a favorably balance of trade. Thus it was, for him, that British cotton exports to India would lead to the destruction of cotton manufacturing in India. Marx's analysis here clearly contradicted his observation that India would industrialize under English auspices, for the textile industry was a key area of early English industrialization, as it would have been for that of India. This example is one of many in Marx on how imperialism normally benefited the imperialists at the expense of the conquered.[4]

In 1856, Marx wrote an article, "English Ferocity in China," which recounted the incident of the supposed British ship the "Arrow", manned by an English captain, boarded by Chinese authorities who removed twelve Chinese crew members, charging them with piracy against a Chinese ship. But when the British consul protested this incursion on a "British" ship, the Chinese released nine of the twelve suspects whom the consul did not accept as freed. But, as Marx pointed out, the "Arrow" was built and owned by Chinese nationals who had unlawfully registered it as British to cover up their smuggling. The result of this incident led the British to peremptorily bombard Canton and capture its forts. Thus it was, for him, that a "peaceful country, without previous declaration of war, for an alleged infringement of the fanciful code of *diplomatic etiquette* [italics mine], is attacked by imperialists."

In the course of reporting on China, Marx also commented on the Taiping Rebellion from 1851 to 1864, a great uprising led by a disgruntled Chinese teacher, Hung Hsiu-ch'uan who lived in the Canton area. Under the influence of Baptist missionaries, Hung saw himself as heavenly king and younger brother of Jesus. His new religion stressed the Old and New Testaments, but also accepted Buddhist reincarnation, although ferociously anti-Buddhist. Its radical social philosophy called for the end to foreign Manchu rule, women's equality with men, and cooperative economic arrangements, including the sharing of harvests. This rebellion, which resulted in the deaths of up to 40 million people, undoubtedly became the most significant revolutionary event of the 19th century. It indicated the increasing importance of protosocialist ideas in China as its traditional power structure was weakened by Western and later Japanese imperialism.

In an article with a global outlook, one appropriate for today, "Revolution in China and in Europe," Marx suggested that the Taiping Rebellion was facilitated by England's victory in war over China, eroding the Chinese emperor's patriarchal authority, China's unfavorably trade balance with British India because of the opium trade, resulting in much silver leaving China, as well as opium's corrosive, corruptive effect, which "had entirely demoralized the Chinese state officers in the southern provinces," and the penetration of English textiles, causing Chinese "spinners and weavers" great hardship.

It was in this article that Marx, in a vision of a possible worldwide popular/socialist revolution, asserted:

> that the next uprising of the people in Europe, and their next movement for republican freedom and economy of government, may depend more probably on what is now passing in the Celestial Empire – the very opposite of Europe – than on any other political cause that now exists – more than even on the menaces of Russia and the consequent likelihood of a general European War. But yet it is no paradox, as all may understand by attentively considering the circumstance of the case.

Marx here in Hegelian manner exclaimed that China's political disintegration, aided by British imperialism had resulted in revolution, which, in turn, might inspire revolutionary forces in Europe. To be sure, he still believed in the early 1850s that a socialist revolution was imminent in Western Europe.[5]

In this regard, recall the impact of the Chinese Communist Revolution on the world and its audacious attempt to usher in a communist society in the backdrop of extreme poverty/underdevelopment. The People's Communes phase in the late 1950s and the Great Proletarian Cultural Revolution in 1966-69 were the furthest left that a large-scale peacetime socialism has ever progressed to.

In *Capital*, I, Marx fully developed his critique of Western imperialism, which already during his lifetime had largely carved out the world for itself. Is it not of great interest that Marx concluded his masterwork critiquing the economic inner workings and dynamism of capitalism and its exploitative human relations by commenting on its inherent aggressive imperialism?

As already observed, Marx regarded the Middle Ages as the spawning ground for banking or "usurer's Capital" and "merchant's capital," the seedbeds of modern capitalism, in whose development he focused on the importance of usury or interest in consolidating the economic supremacy of capitalists over the underlying population.

In time, for Marx, with progressive dissolution of feudalism, "with the expropriation and partial eviction of the country population" and by going outside the municipalities where the guilds were strong, "at sea ports" or in "inland points," banking and commercial capital established bridgeheads of the newest form of capital, the industrial.

In the development of capitalism, Marx emphasized the importance of imperialism in promoting its growth during the Commercial Revolution:

> The discovery of gold and silver in America, the extirpation, enslavement and entombment in mines of the aboriginal population, the beginning of the conquest of the East Indies, the turning of Africa into a warren for the commercial hunting of black skins, signalized the rise of the era of capitalist production. These idyllic proceedings are the chief momentum of primitive accumulation. On their heels treads the commercial war of the European nations, with the globe for a theatre.

And:

> The colonies secured a market for the budding manufactures, and, through the monopoly of the market, an increased accumulation. The treasures captured outside of Europe by undisguised looting, enslavement, and murder, floated back to the mother-country and were there turned into capital.[6]

Marx, then, named the early European imperialist nations, "Spain, Portugal, Holland, France, and England."

In England "by the end of the 17th century", capitalist "primitive accumulation" or early development was already made up of these related elements: "The colonies, the national debt, the modern mode of taxation, and the protectionist system," which "employ the power of the State," hastens the "transformation of the feudal mode of production into the capitalist mode." In this scenario, he – Marx – observed that war or "force...is itself an economic power."[7]

Marx, of course, was describing the rise of Mercantilism, a capitalist economic doctrine during the Commercial Revolution that eschewed free trade for state intervention in economic affairs, like subsidizing industry through grants and high tariffs. Mercantilists as ardent imperialists advocated that colonies provide the mother country raw materials for manufacturing, along with gold and silver, while serving as buyers of manufactured goods – all of this for a favorable balance of trade to foster national prosperity and power.

Marx commented extensively on this mercantilism: One example was France under Louis XIV in the 17th century, when Colbert, his finance minister, granted "state subsidies to private persons." Another was on the economic thought of Thomas Mun, a 17th century English economic thinker whose *England's Treasure by Foreign Trade* emphasized the critical importance of a favorable trade balance to increase national wealth and power. And yet another were the various Navigation Acts of England, like those of 1651, 1660, and 1673, involving the monopoly of colonial products, including tobacco, sugar, and so forth, providing manufactured goods to the colonies, and compelling foreign manufactured goods to first go to England. Mercantilists feared foreign finished products as they were more expensive than raw materials, hindering domestic manufacturing.[8]

Marx himself was more than aware that imperialism under the mercantilist label impeded the growth of industry in conquered nations as "England did with the Irish woolen manufacture." Indeed, he again averred that, "Colonial system, public debts, heavy taxes, protection [tariffs], commercial wars, etc., these children of the true manufacturing period, increase gigantically during the infancy of Modern Industry." Rising industrialization was the key to the increase of commercial wealth – "Today industrial supremacy implies commercial supremacy."[9]

In his description of imperialism and trade in connection with the rise of capitalism, including "Modern Industry," Marx presented several examples. The first was the English East India Company (1600-1874), which ruled India for most of this period, a state within a state as its charter allowed it to purchase land, make alliances with local rulers, hire troops, declare war and peace, issue money, and possess judicial authority. A profit-making machine for most of its existence, the company's annual profits were from 20 to 40 percent, and when it ceased to be profitable, the English government assumed rule over India; its higher staff, however, still enriched itself through high salaries and business opportunities.

As Marx pointed out, this company had "exclusive monopoly of the tea-trade, as well as the Chinese trade in general, and of the transport of goods to and from Europe," and the "coasting trade of India and between the islands, as well as the internal trade of India... the monopoly of the higher employees of the company." Furthermore, the company enjoyed "the monopolies of salt, opium, betel, and other commodities," in which the "employees of the company themselves fixed the price and plundered at will." Also, "between 1769 and 1770, the English manufactured a famine by buying up all the rice and refusing to sell it again, except at fabulous prices."[10]

The close connection between capitalist imperialism and development of capitalism in the metropolis was tellingly examined by Marx in his description of it in the seaport of Liverpool: "Liverpool waxed fat on the slave trade," leading to "primitive accumulation" of capital, quoting from an English writer how this trade "'occasioned vast employment for shipping and sailors, and greatly augmented the demanded for manufactures of the country.'" He noted the relationship between slavery and supposedly free labor, both under the capitalist umbrella:

> Whilst the cotton industry introduced child-slavery in England, it gave in the United States a stimulus to the transformation of the earlier, more or less patriarchal slavery, into a system of commercial exploitation. In

fact, the veiled slavery of the wage-earners in Europe needed for its pedestal, slavery, pure and simple in the new world.[11]

Ever the moralist, Marx recounted many of the crimes committed by the European capitalist Christian imperialists. Although Christianity condemned slavery in general, it permitted it. In fact, in the American South, Protestantism was a staunch defender of slavery, quoting appropriate passages from the Bible, favorable to it, like Paul's admonition for slaves to obey their masters.

Marx's many examples of capitalist-imperialist savagery included that of the Dutch in the East Indies, where slaves were secured and areas in Java were depopulated; of the British inducing famine in India (already commented upon); and of New England Puritans enacting legislation to pay for the scalps of Indian men, women, and children.[12]

In *Capital*, Marx also examined the British conquest of Ireland and impoverishment of its people. The English conquest allowed 7,000 English landlords (the "Protestant Ascendancy") to own 93 percent of the land. In this conquered nation, Catholics, the overwhelming majority of the population, could neither vote nor serve in the military and civil services, nor even attend universities. The vast majority of the Irish became tenant farmers working on one to two acre plots, with no tenure security, able to be evicted at a moment's notice.

Marx observed the terrible Irish famine of 1846 in which about one million starved to death, with the consequent mass exodus to the United States, but asserted that living standards for remaining tenant farmers and workers still fell because in this agricultural nation there was a critical difference in employment with that of an industrialized England:

> But the difference is that in England, an industrial country, the industrial reserve army recruits itself from the country districts, whilst in Ireland, an agricultural country, the agricultural reserve recruits

itself from the towns, the cities of refuge of the
expelled agricultural laborers. In the former, the
supernumeraries of agriculture are transformed into
factory-operatives; in the latter, those forced into
the towns, whilst at the same time they press on the
wages in towns, remain agricultural labourers, and
are constantly sent back to the country districts in
search of work.

Thus it was that an economically backward nation devoid
of industrial capital could not properly exploit its workforce to
industrialize.[13] Marx here exclaimed how imperialist powers
"forcibly rooted out, in their dependent countries, all industry" –
like the English extirpation of "the Irish woolen manufacturers."[14]
This accurately delineated the differences in employment between a
developing/dynamic capitalism and of stagnant agricultural nations
today whose workforces are still mostly underemployed/unemployed.

Furthermore, in an April 1870 letter to S. Meyer and A. Vogt,
Marx stated that the English aristocracy and bourgeoisie had a
"common interest...in turning Ireland into mere pasture land which
provides the English market with meat and wool at the cheapest
possible prices."[15] Thus, agricultural Ireland helped to foster English
industry by providing it with inexpensive agricultural products/raw
materials. Under these conditions of underdevelopment, Ireland could
not hope to become industrialized as there were no protective tariffs
against British manufactured goods.

A question arises here: Does successful Western imperialism
allow for higher living standards among Western workers than
among the conquered? The answer, from a broad perspective, is yes.
To be sure, the advantages of imperialism, for instance, were greater
for England and Holland than for Spain and Portugal for a variety
of reasons, as in degree of commercial/industrial development and
fortunes of war. British successes in colonization undoubtedly aided
British industrial development, while this did not occur for Spain
and Portugal. But where industrialization did happen, as in England,

allowing for a large working class to develop, its class struggle against the bourgeoisie, in addition to the rise of science and improved technology, dramatically raised its living standards, as opposed to generally stagnating ones in poorer Western-dominated nations. Let us not forget this "time" preference and its long-run results. Engels often referred to the advantages accruing to the English proletariat, especially its upper stratum, from successful English imperialism.

Marx's analysis of English industrial development being aided by imperialism does not imply that other routes for industrialization do not exist. For instance, U.S., German, and French industrialization depended much less on a successful imperialism than the English example. But, would American industrialization have been as rapid without its meeting weak Native American resistance to practically virgin areas possessed of great resources – rich farmland, iron ore, coal, and oil? Then, too, recall the impetus to German industrialization when Germany defeated France in 1871, acquiring the iron-ore and potash deposits of Alsace-Lorraine. French imperialism itself was much less lucrative than the English one.

Marx's analysis of imperialism also noted that capitalists, constantly plagued by falling profit margins at home, needed more trade and foreign investment to arrest their general decline:

> Capitals invested in foreign trade are in a position to yield a higher rate of profit, because, in the first place, they come in competition with commodities produced in other countries with lesser facilities of production, so that an advanced country is enabled to sell its goods above their value even when it sells them cheaper than the competing countries.[16]

And:

> Capitals invested in colonies, etc., may yield a higher rate of profit for the simple reason that the rate of profit is higher there on account of the backward

development, and for the added reason that slaves, coolies, etc., permit a better exploitation of labor.[17]

Marx also discussed the role of finance capital in the expansion of the capitalist mode of production, noting that the banking capital of an economically declining Venice "formed one of the secret bases of the capital-wealth of Holland," which, in turn, in the 18th century lent "enormous amounts of capital, especially to its great rival England." England, in turn, invested much capital in the United States. Marx saw that declining industrial states employed their banking capital to finance that of rising industrial ones.[18]

In capitalist development, Marx argued that the public debt itself, related to banking, was a powerful lever, which provided its investors with a risk-free environment. The Bank of England, formed in 1694, lent money to the government at 8 percent a year, while "empowered by Parliament to coin money out of the same capital, lending it again to the public in the form of bank-notes."[19]

C) Imperialism after Marx and Engels

After the deaths of Marx and Engels, imperialism has continued to flourish. The intention is to now note leading critiques of it by socialists, like Veblen, selected Marxists, and even conservatives.

Imperialism was a major concern for Veblen. Not only did he write two well-regarded works in which imperialism was the leitmotif – *Imperial Germany and the Industrial Revolution* (1915) and *An Inquiry into the Nature of Peace and the Terms of Its Perpetuation* (1917) – but also articles, including "An Early Experiment in Trusts" (1904) and "Outline of a Policy for the Control of the 'Economic Penetration' of Backward Countries and of Foreign Investments," (1917), as well as a review of J.A. Hobson's *Imperialism*.

In *Nature of Peace*, Veblen traced the genesis of imperialism to the New Stone Age when humanity reached the necessary technological level to insure the survival of relatively large organized groups with a sufficient economic surplus to allow for "individual ambitions and gains." For Veblen, this presupposed some unspecified pre-existing unequal socioeconomic relations (probably slight) that invited "invidious distinction"; then, with the advent of civilization, this inequality became, for him, pervasive and steep.[1]

Veblen's early interest in the intricacies of modern imperialism was cogently revealed in a sympathetic review of J.A. Hobson's *Imperialism: A Study* (1902) in the March 1903 issue of the *Journal of Political Economy*. (Hobson, a liberal/socialist, espoused the nationalization of only certain key economic sectors.) On the whole, Veblen agreed with Hobson that the taproots of the new imperialism (that of the late 19th century when the great European powers carved out for themselves most of Africa) were related to capital's drive to find outlets for new investments. But he disputed Hobson's thesis that the under-consumption of goods by workers forced capital to seek profit elsewhere, holding that capitalists formed combinations, like trusts, to prevent a ruinous competition over the price of goods, squelching overproduction.

He then heartily applauded Hobson's characterizing imperialism as a "social pathology" that favored particular "business interests," as well as furnishing careers for the "military, clerical, academic, and civil-service circles" that economically drained imperialist nations with higher taxes. He also approved of Hobson's attacking the imperialist mindset for being antithetical to "popular government," and to "liberty and equality," and agreed with him that "Darwinian-jingo" justification of the "higher" white groups in conquering their non-white "inferiors" was based on a specious racism promoted by a crass economism and malevolent patriotic propaganda.

The review finished on a pessimistic note, recognizing that since "the motive force of imperialism is a militant sentimentality guided by the business interests of a small class," there could be no "appeal to the common sense of the community," for it was impossible under present circumstances to "gain a wide hearing."[2]

Soon after, in 1904, Veblen continued his study of imperialism in the cogent "An Early Experiment in Trusts," a well-delineated exposition of an early Viking business organization, very much patterned on the model of the modern "trust" to control output of production to maximize profits by eliminating competition.

The Viking "trust" in the Baltic Sea area was not the product of spontaneous development. In the beginning, the Vikings performed their usual practices, engaging in the twin practices of "piracy" and the "slave trade," aided by technological factors and ample labor reserves. In the technological area, better methods of "shipbuilding, navigation, and the manufacture of weapons" were utilized, while excess "freehold farmers" supplied available recruits.

By the 6th century, there were loosely-knit Viking business combinations with some control over business traffic, which by the 10th century, under the enterprising robber-merchant, Palnatoki, now having more than six hundred ships, established a "trust" to regulate trade for optimum profit. As a matter of course, the trust was drawn into the dynastic politics of the area, being decisive in the "Danish conquest of England", but disintegrated when it attempted to incorporate Norway with Denmark.

This account admirably illustrated how in the course of trade Viking business evolved from small to large scale operations, inevitably becoming entangled with dynastic machinations, including imperialist ambition, the fusion of economics with politics being deftly explored.[3]

The most extensive critique of imperialism by Veblen was *Imperial Germany and the Industrial Revolution*, in which he drew the principal elements of a German imperialism leading to World War I, blaming it more so than others. He located this pathology in uneven economic development resulting in this domestic and international class dynamic: Prussian dynastic/Junker aggressive militarism, relying on the new power unleashed by rapid industrial development after 1871, competing with British and French imperialism, still dominated the strengthened social formations of new industry, the bourgeoisie and pacific proletariat represented by socialism unable to prevent their rulers from launching war.[4]

Preparation for war itself dictated German economic autarky, "a self-contained industrial community," that, although supposedly less economically efficient than the more accepted free-trade model, enhanced war potential. (Short-term economic sacrifice would lead to long-term economic gain through conquest). Veblen's description of this nexus between the military and industry is today's "military-industrial complex," its ultimate aim being nothing less than economic/military/political supremacy.[5]

Veblen related imperialism to the power of the rulers over their subjects. Successful war, for instance, reinforced an "enthusiastic subservience and unquestioning obedience to authority."[6] Indeed, he anticipated George Orwell's *1984* in stating: "What is military organization in war is a servile organization in peace."[7] And, he traced this slavishness to the Junkers' strategy of inculcating the masses, beginning with early formal education, with such sentiments as "romantic loyalty" and a "militant patriotism,"[8] based on "solidarity of prowess," to ensure Germany's "place in the sun."[9]

It was in this volume that Veblen observed two diametrically opposing social forces in the years just before World War I: On the one hand, an imperialist and war-like leisure class representing the various oppressive institutions,[10]; on the other, the masses, workers and farmers who, despite their "flunkeyism," were now subjected to the new industrial patterns fostered by "machine technology" and its "mechanistic conception" of social reality making socialist ideals possible, maybe leading to revolution and subsequent return to primeval archetypes featuring equality and "free and popular institutions."[11]

In *An Inquiry into the Nature of Peace and the Terms of Its Perpetuation* (1917), Veblen continued the socialist themes so prominent in *Imperial Germany*. Along with Hobson and the influential work by Lenin, *Imperialism: The Highest Stage of Capitalism*, whose second revised edition appeared in 1917, Veblen situated modern imperialism in the context of a dynamic and aggressive capitalism. Veblen's analysis of imperialism in this work was somewhat different than Hobson's and Lenin's because it placed less emphasis on under-consumption, that workers' wages inevitably lagged behind output, thus allowing for an excess of goods and profits to spill into foreign trade and investment, encouraging imperialism. But along with Hobson and Lenin, Veblen again envisaged imperialism as being largely driven by an economic nationalism under the ruling groups already described. The three also agreed that, although imperialism furthered the careers/interests of select ruling group members/ institutions, including those of business, in the national ledger of profit and loss, military and administrative expenses often exceeded any profit.[12]

In this work, Veblen divided the leading imperialist nations into four categories: The very aggressive new to a world-scale imperialism, Germany and Japan; those that would fight if provoked, France, Great Britain, and perhaps the United States; those following the lead of more industrialized and stronger allies, Austria-Hungary; and those, presumably deficient in dynamic industrialization, Russia – the last two, doubtful aggressors.[13] Furthermore, he did not see any basic differences between the imperialism of authoritarian monarchies (German and Austria-Hungary) and democracies (France and Great Britain), but admitted that in the former nations it was much more difficult for anti-imperialist forces to dissent than in the latter.[14] This analysis also involved the balance-of-power principle.

Again, Veblen deftly sketched the connection between nationalism and imperialism when he decried the persistence of "patriotism," described as "a sense of partisan solidarity in respect of prestige," and "a spirit of particularism, of aliency animosity between contrasted groups of persons."[15]

Prophetically, Veblen saw Germany and Japan as the two likeliest nations to precipitate the next great war, or World War II.[16] For him, only the rise of socialism could prevent this holocaust:

> The peoples of the quondam Imperial nations must come into the league (League of Nations) on a footing of formal equality with the rest. This they can not do without the virtual abdication of their dynastic government establishments and a consequent shift to a democratic form of organization.[17]

Or nothing less than the destruction of monarchy, the military, and large private capital formations through the abolition of "property" and the "price system" to come from a socialist revolution stemming from a "cleavage between those who own [property] and those who do not."[18]

War for Veblen was inimical to the realization of socialism because it invariably reinforced a feudalistic/capitalistic mindset based on "suspicion, duplicity, and ill will." Its antithesis, associated with modern technology and its "matter of fact" view prevailing over personal and class domination, was equated with socialism.[19]

In his "Outline of Policy," Veblen again related "commercial enterprise" with "national ambitions," "economic penetration" and "investment in foreign parts," and to obviate them, advised – tongue in cheek – nations not to support their investors in foreign ventures. Furthermore, he continued in a Marxist manner by declaring that:

> Investment is made in the foreign country to get a
> higher rate of profits than at home; which draws a part
> of the available means of industry out of the country,
> or keeps up the rate on home investments, by keeping
> the productiveness of the country's industry down;
> which enhances or keeps up prices, and the cost of
> living.

These conditions, for him, only benefited the "interested business concern," involved in foreign investment, with any corresponding cash flow going to the coffers of the "well- to-do," employing it for more conspicuous consumption, which necessarily "limits the production of goods to meet the ordinary needs of the community."[20]

Lenin's *Imperialism: The Highest Stage of Capitalism* (1917) was a popular work, drawing much from Hobson's *Imperialism*, Hilferding's *Finance Capital*, and Nikolai Bukharin's *Imperialism and World Economy*. Basically, for Lenin, monopoly capitalism was now intertwined with big-power rivalry and war:

> Imperialism is capitalism in that stage of development
> in which the dominance of monopolies and finance
> capital has established itself; in which the export of
> capital has acquired pronounced importance; in which
> the division of the world among the international trusts
> has begun; in which the division of all territories of
> the globe among the great capitalist powers has been
> completed.[21]

For Lenin, monopoly capitalism allowed for the "concentration of production" in "cartels, syndicates and trusts" in the economically developed nations, their "capture of the most important sources of raw materials", the role of banks or finance capital, the carving out of Africa by some of the great imperialist powers and the export of capital from the developed capitalist nations to colonies and weaker nations in search of higher profits through inexpensive labor and cheap raw materials. This pattern was part and parcel of a "parasitic or decaying capitalism," resulting in war – World War I was already underway – to be presumably followed by working-class revolution.[22]

A principal thesis of this work, of the capital of the advanced capitalist nations increasingly going to colonies and underdeveloped areas, was disputed by many observers, like William L. Langer, a well-known American historian who argued that much more capital was invested by the leading capitalist nations among themselves than their colonies and other underdeveloped areas in the early 20th century.[23] This, of course, was true, but less so today. But he failed to point out that capital invested in underdeveloped areas contributed to their economic malformation as they were usually condemned to be either producers of raw materials or agricultural products, or low-wage platforms of selected manufactured goods, resulting in their being more subject to price fluctuations and economic downturns than those in the First World. Furthermore, he did not include the injurious economic role of their comprador elites whose economic and political interests intermeshed with foreign imperialists. Thus there was the anomaly of large foreign debts incurred by poor nations to rich nations, while their elites deprived them of scarce capital by investing large sums of money in the advanced nations for safekeeping. Exceptions to this model in the late 20th century were Taiwan and South Korea that became industrial powers with American aid in its fight against Communism, which incidentally also forced reforms, as in agriculture, and in the case of South Korea, largely nationalized banking and heavy-industry sectors.

A large-standing debate among socialists was whether capitalism and war were synonymous. For Rudolf Hilferding in *Finance Capital* and Kautsky in his theory of "ultra-imperialism" in 1914, economic rationalization through oligopoly/monopoly and international cartels, despite decline of free trade, allowed the possibility for more international capitalist cooperation. But they insisted that this possibility had to contend with powerful imperialist/militarist forces in the leading nations equated with an anti- humanistic authoritarianism, infinitely stronger than liberal capitalist democratic elements.[24]

Even more certain than Hilferding and Kautsky that capitalism would lead to war was Lenin, who theorized that the totality of national capitals overrode those of its international variety; his *Imperialism* unerringly predicted World War II, basically begun by the imperialism of the Axis powers. But he himself approvingly quoted from Hobson of a "European Federation" under a capitalist elite dominating "tame masses." His account of imperialism was largely analogous to Veblen's in focusing on the ever-growing concentration of finance capital over the industrial variety whose profits endlessly were attracted to underdeveloped areas.[25]

In following Engels, Lenin maintained that the more favored sections of the working-class in some nations were able to somewhat partake of the fruits of imperialism in the form of higher wages. In this vein, he mentioned an Oct. 7, 1858 letter from Engels to Marx, which held that "the English proletariat is becoming more and more bourgeois," and "for a nation which exploits the whole world this is, of course, to a certain extent justifiable."[26]

Another question arises as to what degree is the export of capital due to the underconsumption of the workers in the developed world, thus allowing excess funds to be profitably used outside the home nation. To be sure, there is an endemic problem of underconsumption by workers under capitalism, the term excess profits is meaningless. Profits are simply channeled where returns on capital are the highest.

Today, this line of thought is confirmed by Harry Magdoff in *Imperialism: From the Colonial Age to the Present*: "Export of capital, like foreign trade, is a normal function of capitalist enterprise." Furthermore, "capital exports…become an important prop to the export of goods," thus capitalists profit doubly. In investing in poorer nations, because of inexpensive labor and various concessions – as in not paying taxes for many years – higher profits are not uncommon.[27]

George Lichtheim, a distinguished 20th century scholar of socialism, also agreed with Marx in his work *Imperialism*, specifically Marx's fusion of nationalism and imperialism, which held that the chief proponent of Western imperialism (where there is a social-class relationship) was the chauvinistic bourgeois press. But the problem was more complex for him. Like Veblen, he associated war and militarism with the traditional "more primitive, aggressive, and warlike impulses" that inhabited the "frontiers" of the West. The social groups anxious to fight were the "landed gentry" and the "rural population" generally, while the basically pacific groups were "middle-class burghers and industrial workers." Although he balanced this view with one that the German bourgeoisie and even many workers had a strong martial nature. But we know that the most avid supporters of Nazism were in upper- and lower-middle classes, and the Nationalist Party, led by the Junkers, was a close Nazi ally. Finally, he agreed with Lenin that the world was divided "among the great internationals trusts," as in the period between the two world wars.[28]

A pertinent question was whether wars spawned by 20th-century imperialism have aided or hindered socialism? From a broad perspective, insofar as war machines buttress the existent social and other relations in any society and create great chasms between victors and losers – in this following Veblen – they are inimical to socialism. But since modern war especially is injurious to the institutions of economically backward nations under assault, like China and Russia, in conjunction with the class struggle, it does aid in brining about the deformed socialism of the former Soviet Union and the current one of China. War itself certainly accelerated the march of industrialization and invention, especially in war-prone societies, like Germany and Japan, but even a supposedly more pacific Great Britain had its iron and steel and other industries benefit from government military contracts.[29]

In a manner closely following socialist views were those of *Imperialism and Social Classes* by Joseph Schumpeter, a well-known conservative Austrian-American economic and social commentator who asserted that the rising capitalist class grafted itself upon the older warlike dynastic/feudalistic power structure, thus making it a bearer of a capitalist imperialism:

> Nationalism and militarism, while not creatures
> of capitalism, become "capitalized" and in the end
> draw their best energies from capitalism. Capitalism
> involves them in its workings and thereby keeps them
> alive, politically as well as economically.

As for the forces that opposed nationalism/imperialism, Schumpeter believed that they revolved around socialism:

> Socialists...exclude nationalism from their general
> ideology, because of the essential interests of the
> proletariat, and by virtue of their domestic opposition
> to the conservative stalking force.[30]

Even the great conservative sociologist Max Weber, in examining imperialism, emphasized its association with the exploitation of land and labor and its being favored by big industry, military machines, and elite groups in general who hungered after prestige and honor.

He then affirmed that imperialism's most resolute opponents were workers, except for those directly employed in war industry.[31]

In the late 20th century, imperialist rivalry and war – which have often fueled social revolution – have not only been the greatest of all destroyers but have poisoned the domestic politics of nations in the guise of military-industrial complexes that consume enormous amounts of resources. Since World War II, for instance, American military spending has hovered from 3 to 15 percent of GDP. In the late 1980s in annual dollars, world military expenditures were almost $900 billion, but declined slightly since the end of the Cold War, to $785 billion in 1998.

World military spending in 2015 is about $1 trillion. The U.S. share alone is more than a third of it, many times more than Russia's and China's.

Although the Cold War is over, the U.S. annually needs $90 billion to defend Europe and twelve aircraft groups, costing $2 billion each to operate. The military-industrial complex still employs 5 or so percent of full-time workers, many highly skilled, wishing to accelerate spending on an intercontinental ballistic missile defense system. Overall, about half of the federal budget, including interest payments from past wars and veterans' benefits, is eaten up by the military. Total American military expenditures since the Second World War easily exceeded $10 trillion, $4 trillion alone spent for the development of nuclear weapons.

It should be pointed out that the military-industrial complex in America, which consumes more than a third of the world's military expenditures, intimately involves leading political and military figures. Examples follow: Retired General Alexander Haig, former NATO commander, has served as President Nixon's chief of staff, President Reagan's secretary of state, president of United Technologies, is a member of the board of many corporations, including Chase Manhattan Band and Texas Instruments, and has represented defense firms, like United Technologies, McDonnell Douglas, and Boeing. In addition, he represented foreign governments in business deals with American companies and government. Former President Bush, the elder, is a key adviser to the Carlyle Group, a leading military contractor, including representing it with foreign governments, and is reimbursed for his services with stock in the company. Former President Bush was president on the board of directors of Carterair, a subsidiary of Carlyle, and when as governor of Texas, appointed the board of the Texas teachers' pension fund, which invested $100 million in Carlyle. Others to be included in this military-industrial scenario of government-business relationships include Frank Carlucci, secretary of defense under President Reagan and current president of Carlyle, and William Kennard, former chairperson of the Federal Communications Commission, also now employed by Carlyle. From a larger than a military-industrial perspective, there is the after-government employment of Henry Kissinger, former secretary of state under President Nixon and national security advisor under President Ford, now with his consulting firm to corporations dealing with governments; he is also on the board of directors of many corporations. These relationships are not of a conspiratorial nature, but rather the norm for a class-based capitalist-bureaucratic society dominated by large corporations.

Rival imperialism and civil wars in the 20th century have killed at least 150 million civilians and military personnel: In the two major wars alone – World War I and II – about 13 million and 75 million were killed half in the latter being civilians (double the amount for the wounded), including Nazi racist imperialists systematically murdering Jews and Gypsies, as well as Russians and others. Millions were killed in the Holocaust. Since World War II, the epidemic of war and its train of oppression has continued, as anyone who reads the daily press can attest to. As for the material costs of 20th century war, in 2000 dollars, they are probably in the many-trillion-dollar range. The perils of war today also involve thermonuclear destruction that has receded with the end of the Cold War; however, this may only be brief interlude, as the underlying causes making for war still exist.[32]

D) American Imperialism: A Case Study, with a Prologue of Its Soviet Variety

It is axiomatic that the foreign policies of the two superpowers – the former Soviet Union and the United States – closely reflect the concerns of their ruling elites, of an absolutistic bureaucracy pertaining to the former Soviet Union and a conservative corporate capitalist one for the United States, the latter fearful of any opening to the left, especially in the poorer nations whose polarized class structures, of small ruling bourgeois and/or nobility elite facing impoverished and brutalized masses, favored either a right or left alternative in domestic and international policies.

Before examining American foreign policy, the former Soviet Union will be examined and shown as similar and different. But before embarking on a brief exposition of Soviet imperialism in Eastern Europe, the existence of the Soviet Union was an important factor in the rise of Chinese Communism and consequent decolonization in Asia (Indonesia, India, and Vietnam), Africa (Kenya, Algeria, Zambia, Mozambique, Angola) and in the Americas (Cuba).

Soviet imperialism itself was associated with the Soviet Army's advance during the final stages of the Second World War into Poland, Hungary, Romania, Bulgaria, and East Germany. In Yugoslavia, under Tito (Josip Broz), the Communist-led partisans reflected a successful indigenous Communism. After a brief period of cooperation with opponents, socialists and others, for several years in the "People's Democracy" phase, the Communist parties of these nations (except for Yugoslavia which proceeded to Communism rapidly on its own) consolidated their positions to becoming, for all intents and purposes, single-party states. They nationalized industry and collectivized agriculture, the latter's intensity and success being varied; in Poland, for instance, collectivization never proceeded far, although it did so in Bulgaria and Romania. Furthermore, in challenging the traditional religious structures, with their usually reactionary mindset, Communism aided progressive change, encountering much more opposition from a disciplined and international Catholicism than the discrete national churches of Eastern Orthodoxy.

In the realm of popular support, Communism especially in Bulgaria, East Germany, independent Yugoslavia, and Czechoslovakia (in free elections in the last, its Communist party garnered 38 percent of the vote, emerging as the largest party), enjoyed much popular support, but less so in Romania, Poland and Hungary. After Communism imploded in 1989-1991, renamed Communist parties in Eastern Europe, usually using the name "socialist," did very well in every one of the nations mentioned, heading governments or being the main opposition parties.

On the whole, the Communist legacy in Eastern Europe has contributed to increasing the strength of socialism by modernizing an economically underdeveloped region, which included destroying its traditional large landowner/military elites, invariably disdaining democracy and civil liberties. The exceptions to this generality were Czechoslovakia, with its industry, democracy, and large working and middle classes, and East Germany whose large working class was strongly Communist before the rise of Nazism, although there was also some industry in Poland and Hungary with at least some semblance of a working class. In addition, Communism promoted mass education, extensive social-welfare systems, like socialized medicine and old-age pensions, increased women's freedom, and promoted much socioeconomic equality. The institutionalization of Communism as governing entity also contributed to the socialist project in influencing Western European social reform and massive nationalizations in industry and banking, prodded by two large Communist parties in Italy and France and other socialist formations.

The repressive and brutal aspects of Soviet Imperialism are not discounted: It was anti-democratic and anti-civil libertarian, very harsh in dealing with the old regimes/elites, and, if need be, with workers, defeating the Hungarian Workers' revolt in 1956 with great loss of life, repeatedly interfering with Polish workers' struggles, particularly the Solidarity Union, and in squelching the "socialism with a human face" in1968 Czechoslovakia. Nevertheless, there was always movement and change in these nations and when Communism expired there, it was replaced peacefully outside of Romania.[1]

For the United States, its basic foreign-policy conservatism was best expressed by George F. Kennan – of diplomatic history fame, key advisor to the State Department, and ambassador to the Soviet Union – who bluntly affirmed that a rich America would unstintingly protect its power and privilege with alliances not based on the "luxury of altruism and world-benefaction," or "unreal objectives such as human rights, the raising of living standards, and democratization."

This view, however, must be modified, for the United States would defeat Soviet Communism for control of an economically advanced Western Europe, with a strong working class and socialist tradition, by raising its living standards ravaged by the devastation of World War II (the Marshall Plan) and supporting its democratic/civil libertarian tradition, contrasting them with the lack of democracy/ civil liberty and lower living standards in the Soviet Bloc. (Without the Marshall Plan, a left-wing socialist Western Europe was a distinct possibility.)

From a national/bourgeois perspective this was a rational foreign policy for objectively Soviet Communism, even much more so than an economically marginal Communist China, was the principal opponent of American capitalism. Soviet hegemony would signal the demise of the upper-bourgeoisie, its large property expropriated by the state. This thesis followed the one of William Appleman Williams, a distinguished American diplomatic historian who held that the main contours of American foreign policy fashioned by its capitalist elite were in its early history based on territorial expansion, and later in opening the world to American trade and investment.[2]

A brief background on American imperialism before World War II is necessary before observing it afterward to indicate its continuity. From its earliest history, the United States has been an expansionist nation: As an extension of a modern and aggressive Western European capitalism, it subjugated Native Americans, easily defeated Mexico, abolished slavery in the Civil War, and by the end of the 19th century became a world power thanks to its pre-eminent industrial strength, great natural resources, and large population. Then, with the advent of the Spanish-American War in 1898, it annexed the Philippines and Puerto Rico and imposed a protectorate on Cuba.

It was during this period that the views of Admiral Alfred Thayer came into vogue; in *The Influence of Sea Power Upon History*, and other works, he theorized that the future greatness of a large-island America would rest on sea power to protect its commerce and colonies, providing it with markets and raw materials. This manifested itself in the early 20th century, particularly in the Caribbean and Central America, as three "progressive" Presidents – Roosevelt, Taft, and Wilson – sent American troops there repeatedly to protect American power/investments. In World War I, United States entry allowed Great Britain, France, and Italy to defeat Germany, Austria-Hungary, and Turkey, while preserving the safety of American loans to the Allies. In World War II, again, with the Soviet Union and Great Britain, the United States was instrumental in defeating the Axis powers (Germany, Japan, and Italy).

Several examples of American intervention in the internal affairs of other nations will be given to indicate its general nature before concentrating on its involvement in Vietnam and Latin America, where it is most apparent: It massively supported the reactionary Kuomindang regime in China representing the landowners and comprador capitalists in their fight against Chinese Communism in the 1945-49 period. In Europe, it provided the Greek right, ensconced in the upper bourgeoisie and military, the necessary economic and military assistance to defeat the Greek Communists in the 1947-49 civil war. In 1953, in Iran, the CIA was instrumental in aiding its generals to stage a coup d'état against the legitimate government of Mohammed Mossadegh after it nationalized the Anglo-Iranian Oil Company. In 1953, the CIA was also an accomplice in the assassination of Patrice Lumumba, the first premier of the liberated Congo and a socialist. In 1965, when President Achmed Sukarno of Indonesia veered leftward (he probably supported the Indonesian Communist Party's unsuccessful attempt to rid the army of conservative generals),

General T.N.J. Suharto, with the aid of the CIA, murdered hundreds of thousands of Communists, and soon afterward became president.[3]

The most dramatic example of American imperialism after World War II was in Vietnam. The fall of Vietnam to Communism – the "domino theory" – might lead to that of the surrounding states, including Indonesia. Vietnam, part of the French colonial system before World War II, was under Japanese rule during the conflict. After the war, the Vietnamese, like the rest of Western Imperialism's subjects, attempted to liberate themselves. But the French refused to leave and, with massive American economic assistance, held on until their defeat at Diem Bien Phu in 1954 by the Vietnamese Communists led by Ho Chi Minh.

With the French defeat, the United States directly intervened to prevent Communist annexation of South Vietnam through elections. Its basic thrust was to prop up a small ruling class, the mandarins, who owned about half the land, and a middle-class in the urban areas opposed by Communist-led guerrillas supported by most of the peasantry and North Vietnamese.

Perhaps as many as one-fourth of the South Vietnamese were allied with the Americans, who literally bought them off through massive assistance to a large South Vietnamese army and government and by the consumer purchases of the American army whose peak strength there was 575,000 in 1968.

This war, which also spilled into Laos and Cambodia, resulted in high human and material losses as Americans dropped a greater tonnage of bombs on Indochina alone than all combatants did in World War II on one another, employing extensive use of Agent Orange, a cancer-causing chemical used to destroy vegetation, which still pollutes the countryside. This horrendous war killed 3.8 million Vietnamese and 600,000 in Cambodia, with many millions being injured. American losses measured 58,000 killed and 300,000 wounded. The material costs to the Vietnamese people were in the many billions of dollars, while for the Americans, including veterans' benefits and interest on the national debt, they stood at $676 billion by the mid-90s.

American imperialism in Latin American, as observed, was of long duration. Nevertheless, from the 1930s to the early 1970s, populist and even moderate socialist movements in Latin America had some success against the economic penetration of American big business. Instances of this include President Lazaro Cardenas of Mexico nationalizing some large industry in the 1930s, including the oil fields. In Argentina, in the 1946-55 period, President Juan D. Peron followed an anti-U.S. imperialist stance, nationalizing large sectors of the economy.

After a successful social revolution in Cuba led by Fidel Castro and Ernesto "Che" Guevara, which rapidly turned to a Communist solution to counter United States intransigence, the U.S., breaking international law by interfering in the internal affairs of another sovereign nation, openly aided Cuban exiles in the ill-fated Bay of Pigs invasion of April 1961. Then, a possible nuclear holocaust was averted in the summer of 1962 when Soviet nuclear missiles sent to Cuba at Fidel Castro's request were withdrawn when President Kennedy threatened to destroy them.

The obsession to destroy the Cuban Revolution has been a principal aim of American foreign policy, lest it spread throughout Latin America. There have been numerous attempts by the CIA to assassinate Castro, even working with American Mafia, which lost its gambling casinos and brothels in Cuba. In early 2015, President Obama, along with high-ranking officials including Pope Francis, negotiated what became peaceful co-existence with Cuba.

In 1964, when the Brazilian President João Goulart was intent on making far-ranging socioeconomic reforms, the United States aided a successful coup d'etat of generals against him by sending the Sixth Fleet off the Brazilian coast on the grounds of stopping increasing Communist influence within his government.

In Chile, where a large democratic socialist movement was in place for decades, a democratic socialist, Salvadore Allende, led a popular front electoral coalition, including Communists, to victory in 1970. His program called for the nationalization of the American-owned Anaconda Copper Company and a social-welfare package to improve the living standards of the working class. Allende was opposed by the Chilean bourgeoisie and it ancillary military component.

President Richard M. Nixon and Secretary of State Henry A. Kissinger were determined to topple Allende from power as they stopped economic assistance and insisted that foreign loans be promptly paid, but continued aid to the Chilean military and with the covert assistance of the CIA and other American agencies encouraged the Chilean military to destroy Allende's government in 1973. Kissinger, in 1970, on Allende and his socialist coalition, stated, "I don't see why we need to stand by and watch a country go Communist because of the irresponsibility of its own people."

American meddling in Central America is of long-standing duration. In Guatemala, after President Jacobo Arbenz in 1953 wished to expropriate lands of the United Fruit Company, the CIA, with aid of Guatemalan army officers, attacked his government from Honduras, forcing him to resign. This action led to four decades of civil war between the left and right, resulting in 200,000 deaths, more than 80 percent of them committed by right-wing CIA-backed death squads. In 1963, when General Rafael Trujillo fell and was replaced by the popularly elected President Juan Bosch, the United States invaded the Dominican Republic to forestall his reforms. From 1980 to the early 90s, El Salvador was in the throes of civil war, resulting in 75,000 deaths, pitting left against right, the CIA intimately allying itself with its wealthy conservatives and military. In 1989, the United States invaded Panama with massive military force to dislodge General Manuel Antonio Noreiga from power.

In Nicaragua, after the Sandinista National Liberation Front overthrew the dictatorship of Anastasio Somoza in 1979 backed by the United States for many decades, the United States once more stepped in. As in the other instances, this interference was predicated to stop a bogus Communist threat, for the Sandinistas, left-wing socialists and not Communists, were supported by the Socialist International, composed of democratic socialist parties, including the French, German, Spanish, and Swedish.

From the very beginning, President Reagan was determined to destroy this "Communist" revolution by imposing a trade embargo on Nicaragua and ordering the CIA to form a counter- revolutionary force of "Contras" to destabilize it. The CIA itself was caught in mining the harbors of Nicaragua, an illegal act of war. When the World Court ordered the U.S. to pay for this crime, Reagan refused its jurisdiction. Ultimately, the Sandinistas lost power in a narrow electoral defeat, the basic reason being the wish of many Nicaraguans to simply end a murderous guerrilla war financed by America, resulting in the deaths of many tens of thousands.

Every one of these actions in Central America by the U.S. was against accepted norms of international law as it not only armed its client states there and trained their leading officers, but repeatedly intervened to buttress their right-wing rulers, either through the CIA agents advising their military in their daily operations, which included deliberate mass murder of civilians, or, if all else failed to stop popular forces, directly intruded with massive military force to defeat them.

As Ralph et al., in *World Civilizations* (a typical college textbook) affirmed, President Reagan's policy in Central America rested on the premise that American interests there "would take precedence over treaties, conventions, and international law."[4]

Notes

A) Background

1) *The American Heritage Dictionary*, 2nd College Edition (Boston: Houghton Mifflin Co., 1982), p. 645.
2) Veblen, *Leisure Class*, pp. 22 ff., in which warriors and priests are the key members of the traditional leisure class; and pp. 192-216 on "Devout Observances."
3) On the quotations, see Numbers 33:53, Deuteronomy 7:7, 7:16, 2:33-36, and 3: 6-7.

4) On consequences for disobeying God, see Deuteronomy 28:15 and other parts of 28.
5) George Panichas, ed. *The Simone Weil Reader* (New York: David McKay, 1977), pp. 153-83, "The Iliad: Poem of Might."
6) Thucydides, *The Peloponnesian War*, trans. Benjamin Jowett, intro. H. Baldwin and Moses Hades (New York: Bantam Books, 1965), p. 174.
7) See Michael Beau, *The History of Capitalism, 1500-1980* (New York: Monthly Review Press, 1983), p. 19, which maintains that much of mercantilism is built on large, not small, capital. On the number of slaves and slavery, see Ferdnand Braudel, *Civilization and Capitalism*, vol. III, *The Perspective of the World* (New York: Harper and Row, 1984), p. 440. Philip Curtin, *The African Slave Trade: A Census* (Madison, WI: Univ. of Wisconsin Press, 1969). Basil Davidson, *The African Slave Trade* (Boston: Little, Brown, 1961). Also, see Russell Thornton, *American Indian Holocaust and Survival* (Norman, OK: Univ. of Oklahoma Press, 1987).
8) Montagu, *Man*, pp. 105-06; Montagu, *Human Aggression*, pp. 256 ff. And 270-71; Marvin Harris, *Culture, People: An Introduction to Anthropology*, 5th ed. (New York: Harper and Row, 1988), p. 361; Lawrence H. Keeley, *War Before Civilization: The Myth of the Peaceful Savage* (New York: Oxford Univ. Press, 1996), pp. 25-39 and 111-41.

B)

1) *Manifesto*, pp. 10 ff.
2) Karl Marx and Frederick Engels, *On Colonialism: Articles from the "New York Tribune" and Other Writings* (New York: International Publishers, 1972). Shlomo Avineri, ed. and Introduction, *Karl Marx on Colonialism and Modernization: His Dispatches and Other Writings on China, India, Mexico, the Middle East and North Africa* (Garden City, NY: Doubleday and Co., 1968), pp. 2-28 for an excellent introduction.

3) *Capital,* I, 823 on "brute force." Marx and Engels, *Colonialism,* pp. 35-42.

4) Ibid., pp. 42-53.

5) On China, ibid., pp. 112-119 and 231-49.

6) Ibid., pp. 823 and 826 on the two long quotations.

7) Ibid., pp. 823-24.

8) In America, an outstanding mercantilist is Alexander Hamilton whose *Report on Manufactures* and other writings envisage a partnership between government and business.

9) *Capital,* I, 830 and 826 on the quotations.

10) Ibid., p. 825.

11) Ibid., p. 833.

12) Ibid., pp. 824-26.

13) Ibid., pp. 767-83 on Ireland.

14) Ibid., p. 830.

15) Marx and Engels, *Colonialism,* pp. 336-38.

16) *Capital,* III, 278.

17) Ibid., p. 279.

18) *Capital,* I, 829-830.

19) Ibid., pp. 827-828.

C)

1) Thorstein Veblen, *An Inquiry into the Nature of Peace and the Terms of its Perpetuation* (New York: B.W. Huebsch, 1917), pp. 31-76.

2) Thorstein Veblen, Review of J.A. Hobson's *Imperialism: A Study, Journal of Political Economy,* March, 1903, pp. 311-14.

3) Thorstein Veblen, "An Early Experiment in Trusts," *Journal of Political Economy,* March, 1904, pp. 270-79.

4) Thorstein Veblen, *Imperial Germany and the Industrial Revolution,* intro. Joseph Dorfman (New York: Augustus M. Kelley, 1964), pp. 258-59.

5) Ibid., pp. 242 ff.

6) Ibid., p. 65.

7) Ibid., pp. 81-82.

8) Ibid., p. 253.

9) Ibid., pp. 258-59.

10) Ibid., p. 269.

11) Ibid., pp. 268-69.

12) Cf. Veblen, *Nature of Peace*, pp. 26 and 72 ff. with Hobson, *Imperialism*, pp. 11-12 in Harrison M. Wright (ed.), The "New Imperialism"; Analysis of Late Nineteenth Century Expansion (Boston: D.C. Heath and Co., 1961); and V.I. Lenin, *Imperialism: The Highest Stage of Capitalism* (New York; International Publishers, 1939), pp. 117-18.

13) Veblen, *Nature of Peace*, p. 79.

14) Ibid., p. 156.

15) Ibid., pp. 22, 31-76 are on patriotism. The quotation in this paragraph are respectively on pp. 31, 38, 39, and 45.

16) Ibid., pp. 77-117, for instance.

17) Ibid., p. 241.

18) Ibid., pp. 362-67.

19) Veblen, *Imperial Germany*, pp. 268-69.

20) Thorstein Veblen, "Outline of a Policy for the Control or the 'Economic Penetration' of Backward Countries and of Foreign Investments," in *Essays in Our Changing Order* (New York: The Viking Press, 1934), *pp. 361-82.*

21) Lenin, *Imperialism*, p. 89.

22) Ibid., pp. 62-63 and 124-25.

23) William L. Langer, "A Critique of Imperialism," *Foreign Affairs*, XIV, (October, 1935), 102-15.

24) Rudolf Hilferding, *Finance Capital*, edited and Introduction by Tom Bottomore (London: Routledge and Kegan Paul, 1981), pp. 311-36 on "The export of capital and the struggle for economic territory," 337-63 on "Finance capital and classes," and 364-70 on "The proletariat and imperialism." This work was first published in 1910.

25) Lenin, *Imperialism*, pp. 103 and 119.

26) Ibid., p. 107.

27) Harry Magdoff, *Imperialism: From the Colonial Age to the Present* (New York: Monthly Review Press, 1978), pp. 120-21.

28) George Lichtheim, *Imperialism* (New York: Praeger, 1971), pp. 81-87 and 119-20.

29) Eric J. Hobsbawm, *Industry and Empire: An Economic History of Britain since 1750* (London: Weidenfeld and Nicolson, 1968), pp. 10-39.

30) Joseph Schumpter, *Imperialism and Social Classes* (Cleveland, OH: Meridian Books, 1961), pp. 95-96.

31) Max Weber, *Economy and Society: An Outline and Interpretive Sociology,* ed. by Guenther Roth and Claus Wittich, 3 vols. (New York: Bedminster Press, 1968), II, 913-21.

32) On military spending, see *U.S. News and World Report*, March 6, 1995, p. 68; Robert L. Borosage, "All Dollars and No Sense," *Mother Jones*, Sept/Oct., 1994, pp. 41-44. On waste in military procurement, see A. Ernest Fitzgerald, *The High Priests of Waste* (New York: W.W. Norton, 1972), pp. 282-332. On the wasteful and obsolete aircraft-carrier groups and ninety billion dollar annual cost to defend Europe, see Borosage, "All Dollars and No Sense," p. 3. On the cost of nuclear weaponry, see *Akron Beacon Journal*, July 13, 1995, p. A4. On jobs and the military-industrial complex; the annual expenditures of the CIA ($3 billion and $10 billion for the NSA), see *The Nation*, Oct. 6, 1999, p. 5-6. *Akron Beacon Journal*, Oct. 16, 1997, p. A3.: total annual spending in the mid-1990s on clandestine-intelligence operations is about $26.6 billion; the CIA is forced to reveal this in October, 1997 by a lawsuit. On civilian and military deaths in the 20th century, see Gabriel Kolko, *Century of War: Politics, Conflict, and Society Since 1914* (New York: The New Press, 1994), pp. 103, 207-08, 315; Hobsbawn, *Age of Extremes*, pp. 34-35. Arlene Levinson, "20th is century of death," *Akron Beacon Journal*, Sept. 17, 1995, p. A2., estimates that two hundred million people have been killed in the 20th century in massacres/omniocides, politically-induced famines, as in China, in the 1960s, starvation, and so

forth. On genocide, see Jonathan Schell, *The Fate of the Earth* (New York: Avon Books, 1992), pp. 17-91, especially.

D) American Imperialism: A Case Study, with a Prologue on Soviet Imperialism

1) On Soviet Imperialism in Eastern Europe and Eastern European Communism, see H. Stuart Hughes, *Contemporary Europe: A History,* 4th ed. (Englewood Cliffs, NJ: Prentice-Hall, 1976), pp. 381-98 and 509-18. On the fall of Eastern European Communism, see Eric Hobsbawn, *The Age of Extremes: A History of the World, 1914-1991* (New York: Pantheon Books, 1994), pp. 461-99, entitled "End of Socialism." Also, see *Dissent*, Spring 1990, whose cover is "Revolution in Europe."

2) William Appleman Williams, *The Tragedy of American Diplomacy,* 2nd ed. revised and enlarged (New York: Delta Books, 1972), pp. 19-89 on imperialism and the American character; p. 313 calls for an end of American imperialism based on frontier expansion and Open Door Policy on the basis that it "no longer bears any significant relation to reality." On American imperialism in the early 20th century, see Dana G. Manro, *Intervention and Dollar Diplomacy in the Caribbean, 1900-1921* (Princeton, NJ: Princeton Univ. Press, 1964), pp. 160-216, for instance, on Nicaragua. On Kennan's remarks in 1948, see Noam Chomsky, *What Uncle Same Really Wants* (Berkeley, CA: Odonian Press, 1993), p. 9. On the reactionary policies of American imperialism, resulting in mass slaughter and disregard of human rights, see Noam Chomsky and Edward S. Herman, *The Political Economy of Human Rights*: Vol. I, *The Washington Connection and Third World Fascism*; Vol. II, *After the Cataclysm: Postwar Indochina and the Reconstruction of Imperial Ideology* (Boston: South End Press, 1979), 1-40 is a "Summary of Major Findings and Conclusions." This work is a clear and convincing indictment of United States foreign policy throughout the world, including Vietnam, Iran, Indonesia, East Timor, and Cambodia.

3) On Vietnam, see Gabriel Kolko, *Anatomy of War: Vietnam, the United States and the Modern Historical Experience* (New York: Pantheon Books, 1985). On the total human and material costs of the war for the United States alone, see *The Nation*, Dec. 24, 1990, p. 793, and Feb. 18, 1991, p. 184. on the anti-Vietnam War movement, see Lawrence Lader, *Power on the Left: American Radical Movements Since 1946* (New York: W.W. Norton, 1979), pp. 195 ff. On the college teach-ins which began at the Univ. of Michigan in March 1965. On massive public resistance to the war and the usual government duplicity on the war, see Howard Zinn, *Declaration of Independence: Cross-Examining American Ideology* (New York: Harper Perennial, 1991), pp. 123-46.

4) On United States imperialism in Latin America, see: For a typical college textbook, Philip Lee Ralph, et al., *World Civilizations: Their History and Their Culture*, 8th ed. (New York: W.W. Norton, 1991), II, 781-87. It includes U.S. complicity in overthrowing Allende and intervention against the Sandinistas; p. 810 on U.S. disregard for international law. On Kissinger's remarks on Chile, see *In These Times*, July 4-17, 1990, p. 4-5. On recent U.S. involvement in Central America, see Walter LaFeber, *Inevitable Revolutions : The United States in Central America* (New York: W.W. Norton, 1983), pp. 5-18, 29-58, 64-92, 164-302. LaFeber, a distinguished historian of American foreign policy accurately indicates the reactionary meddling of the American elite in this region. Noam Chomsky, *Turning the Tide: U.S. Intervention in Central America and the Struggle for Peace* (Boston, MA: South End Press, 1985), pp. 85- 170, again, well portrays U.S. imperialism here. On CIA involvement with mass murder in Nicaragua, see Allan Nairn, "C.I.A. Death Squads," *The Nation*, April 17, 1995, pp. 513 ff. On American determination to crush the Sandinista Revolution in Nicaragua, see William I. Robinson and Kent Norsworthy, *David and Goliath: The U.S. War Against Nicaragua* (New York: Monthly Review Press, 1987), pp. 9-172. William M. LeoGrande, a Congressional staff member of the Democratic Party, in *Our Own Backyard; The United States in*

Central America, 1977-1992 (Chapel Hill, NC: Univ. of North Carolina Press, 1998), covers events particularly in El Salvador and Nicaragua and U.S. Presidential and Congressional maneuvers pertaining to them in great detail, blaming President Reagan and Congressional Republicans more so than the Democrats for much of the carnage there. P.x, Ultimately, for him: "For good or ill, Central America's fate during this crisis depended fundamentally on decisions made in Washington – decisions over which Central Americans themselves had little influence." On CIA and foreign policy, see Bob Woodward, *Veil: The Secret Wars of the CIA, 1981-1987* (New York: Simon and Schuster, 1987). A prescient work on American imperialism from the 1970s to 1990s is by Michael T. Klare, *War Without End: American Planning for the Next Vietnams* (New York: Alfred A. Knopf, 1972), pp. 3-28, 88-240. On the economic figures involving the North's pillage of the South, see Tom Athanasiou, *Divided Planet: The Ecology of Rich and Poor* (Boston: Little, Brown, and Co., 1996), p. 214.

Chapter Twelve: The Women's Question

A) Background

After we present a brief background on the women's question throughout the ages, we explore the views of Marx and Engels on the subject before bringing it to the present via key socialist thinkers and pertinent statistics. While not an exhaustive study, this chapter relies on representative and impressionistic examples.

Since human males and females are humanity, relations between them are of primary importance in understanding the human condition. Indeed, in the socialization process of human beings, gender relations within the crucible of the nuclear/extended family are interwoven with those of status/class to form the individual's social horizon. In this light, gender relations, as part of the class struggle, not only reflect its progress for socialism, but are a reliable general index in measuring the level of technological development.

To what degree have men and women throughout history been equal? According to contemporary anthropology, throughout most of human history, stretching back to hundreds of thousands of years and beyond (most of it in the Paleolithic Age or "savage" period of hunting/gathering), in which humanity usually lived in small groups or bands numbering less than a hundred, the sexes were more than likely equal or almost so. But certainly in the Neolithic Age or "barbarian" period, with the advent of the agricultural revolution, including domestication of animals, with general organized warfare and beginning of class society, the position of men over women over time became well established. Men were larger and stronger than women, making better warriors. The women, meanwhile, were more vulnerable in social relations than men because of child-bearing. (But in the early stages of the Neolithic Age, with women's discovery of agriculture, women actually enhanced their already high position relative to men as evidenced by many female goddesses, only to rapidly lose it). But their inequality was relative, for in many

Neolithic groups, women had a high social position, more so among sedentary agriculturalists than herders, as determined by matrilocal/patrilocal and matrilineal/patrilineal proportions. It was during the later Neolithic Age that polygyny definitely became established.

By the time of early civilizations, women were generally in a subordinate position to men, but, again, in Egypt and with the Minoans, women had a high social position, and among the latter might have been men's equals. Polygyny among the wealthier men was now common in some societies, like the Hebrew, with Solomon, for instance, having seven hundred wives and three hundred concubines. The earlier Hebrew herder patriarchs, like Abraham, were also polygynous. And, in the *Iliad*, the Greek conquerors enslaved Trojan women not only to satisfy their sexual appetites, but also to enrich themselves.

In the classic Greco-Roman world, women continued to be subservient to men. Among the Greeks, with the exception of Sparta whose girls trained alongside boys, women were secluded in the home. But the position of Roman women was much higher, for, although unable to hold political office, they could join their husbands in outside-of-home activities, at "respectable parties, games, shows, and even political gatherings," and have "access to money and power."

The general oppression of women in civilized societies is invariably intertwined with religion, the traditional unifying institution. Notable examples include Hindus, where polygyny was permitted and women were excluded from the sacred learning, strictly subject to fathers and husbands, taught to regard them as veritable gods, and encouraged to commit suttee upon a husband's death; among Christians, they were ordered to obey their fathers and husbands, and be silent in church (they could not be priests) because of excessive carnality, thus tendency for evil; among Moslems, they were subject to polygyny and concomitant subordination, the Koran allowing men four legal wives who can be divorced.

A brief historical background of women's oppression, complementing the traditional religious one, follows. In China, for instance, women's inferiority was indicated by polygyny, brides being forced to live with their husbands' families. In this patrilineal/ patrilocal arrangement, women usually were regarded as being, especially without sons, as not much higher than servants. For wealthy Chinese men, there was access to many women, their sensual pleasures being fulfilled by concubines and prostitutes. Furthermore, foot-binding, the crippling of women that made them more fully dependent on men (erotic playthings), was common among them. Where Islam is dominant, the custom of purdah often prevails, which is the sequestering of women at home and veiling them. In sub-Sahara Africa, polygyny still reigns today with its usual patrilineal/ patrilocal arrangements. The exceptions here are among the Igbo and Yoruba in West Africa where women are equal to men, both genders having parallel power structures, capped by a dual monarchy for the Igbo. Female infanticide, still prevalent in India and other parts of the world, is yet another expression of women's inferiority. And, of course, the double-standard of sexual behavior still often continues – infidelity being an egregious sin for wives but not for husbands; women were also to be chaste before marriage, but not men.

In the West, patrilineality and patrilocality have also been the norms. Women's subordination, for instance, was well indicated in the early 19th century Napoleonic Code in which, unless special arrangements were made, a wife's property belonged to her husband, and in the English practices – from about 1750 to 1850 – of selling unfaithful wives in the marketplace, usually purchased by lovers. For most of the 19th century in the U.S., women neither voted nor held property if married, nor could they protect themselves legally if beaten by their husbands, nor could they easily initiate divorce proceedings, nor speak before mixed gatherings, nor receive a good education. (The first woman to admit to higher education was at Oberlin College in Ohio, in 1837.

But women's equality or near equality is not a new idea: Socialist utopians have championed it throughout the ages. Plato's *The Republic* had women being generally equal to men in the guardian class, with the exception of the top generalship. In More's *Utopia*, women did not have absolute equality, but could vote and have access to equal education. In Campanella's *City of the Sun*, the family was abolished, universal suffrage and co-education existed, although women could not be magistrates.

In 19th-century utopian socialism, flourishing in the United States in the first half of the 19th century, gender equality, for instance, was at center stage. The Shakers, founded by Anne Lee Stanley, who believed that God was both male and female, practiced a celibacy and communism based on sexual equality. Owen's New Harmony in the mid-1820s proclaimed sexual equality, as did Brook Farm and the religious Oneida Community (1848 to 1880) whose Bible Communism included complex marriage, allowing men and women to love and procreate with other members of the community. Even the Icarians of Cabet in the 1850s and later, although regarding the father as the head of the family, urged gender equality for work and education. [1]

Two significant works of women's liberation by socialists are Mary Wollstonecraft's *Vindication of the Rights of Women* (1792) and John Stuart Mill's (one of the fathers of British socialism) *Subjection of Women* (1869).

The first, a landmark work, presented a detailed exposition for women's emancipation, insisting that gender equality be realized in all avenues of activity – economic, social, political, and cultural – present inferiority being based on oppressive institutions, not nature. In her far-ranging criticism of present society, Wollstonecraft was well aware of the pernicious influence of private property and the resultant unequal social divisions that made for a corrupt leisure class that, among its other failings, contributed to the enslavement of women – "Destructive, however, as riches and inherited honours are to the human character, women are more debased and cramped... than men" because of their yet lowlier position in society. She also boldly opposed the "legal prostitution" of marriage that condemned many supposedly happy women to intense alienation – "the most respectable women are the most oppressed" – and favored women "who can enter any profession and industry, from which would flow a more loving relationship between the genders, resulting in a happier humanity," for "the state of war which subsists between the sexes should end to the advantage of all concerned." [2]

The second work argued for gender equality in marriage, education, employment, suffrage, indeed in all aspects of life. Mill, acutely aware of the unequal power relations between men and women throughout the ages, held that to undo this mistakenly "natural" condition would be difficult, but not impossible. In this, he contrasted Aristotle, who proclaimed the normality of the few ruling the many, including women, with Plato, who was impressed by the high social status of Spartan women. [3]

As for marriage, Mill maintained that wives silently endured the harshness of their husbands, one sanctioned by law and custom, and added that the unequal relations between the genders had men wishing "the women most nearly connected with them" to be "not a forced slave but a willing one, not a slave merely, but a favorite." For him, that this state was accepted by most women indicated the power of traditional social conditioning. He would replace this nightmare by the "justice" of equality. [4]

The enormity of women's oppression was so great for Mill that he compared it to that of "unenlightened societies" in which "colour, race, religion, or in the case of a conquered country, nationality, are to some men, sex is to all women; a preemptory exclusion from all honorable occupations." It was so deep that:

> Sufferings arise from cause of this nature usually
> meet with so little sympathy, that few persons are
> aware of the great amount of unhappiness even now
> produced by the feelings of a wasted life. [5]

The great reputation of Mill in intellectual circles was an important catalyst to the women's movement, not only in England, but also in the U.S. Among the many prominent individuals whom Mill influenced to champion women's rights was the outstanding English socialist (a brilliant mathematician, philosopher, and historian), Bertrand Russell. [6]

Two significant events signaled the rise of the women's movement in the United States. The first was the women's rights convention, organized by Elizabeth Cady Stanton and Lucretia Mott, at Seneca Falls, New York in 1848, which drafted a "Declaration of Sentiments and Resolutions," unequivocally calling for equality with men in all spheres of life. The second, in 1890, organized by Susan B. Anthony, Stanton, Mott, and others, was the founding of the American Woman Suffrage Association, instrumental in the passage of the 19th Amendment to the Constitution in 1920, federally granting women the right to vote, the decisive political happening for gender equality.

Modern socialism itself has continued to play a proper role in the women's movement throughout the world. In the United States, for instance, in addition to utopian-socialist contributions, Florence Kelley, was a prime example of an activist in both socialism and feminism in the early 20th century. Also of note was that American feminists often employed the threat of becoming socialists if their demands for equality were not promptly heeded, as by Stanton at the International Council of Women in 1888.

In the Second Socialist International, socialist women forcefully fought for gender equality, a significant element being the suffrage. Socialist feminism during this period was especially strong in the United States, Germany, and Austria. Although many socialist women, including Clara Zetkin and Rosa Luxemburg, urged postponing the women's right issue until after the revolution, many, like Emma Goldman and Alexandra Kolantai, fused it with the struggle to achieve socialist itself. [7]

The first nations to grant women the general suffrage were New Zealand in 1893 and Australia in 1902; between 1918 and 1920, Great Britain, Germany, and the United States came aboard, and by 1945 and 1946, France and Italy did so, as did Switzerland later. It is safe now to assert that women have formal legal equality with men, including the vote in the economically advanced nations, as well as in many of the poorer ones, although, because of the oppressive past, women have yet to achieve full economic and other equalities with men.

B) Marx and Engels and Later Socialists on Women

Marx and Engels took a keen interest in the women's question. In the *Manifesto,* they clearly spell out their program for women's liberation, boldly calling for the "abolition of the family," specifically of the bourgeois variety whose foundation rests "on capital, on private gain." Indeed, they saw that the nuclear family existed basically only among the bourgeoisie in the cities, but scarcely so "among the proletarians." [1]

Apropos of this, Marx and Engels observed working-class children "transformed into simple articles of commerce and instruments of labor," aware of the prevalence of child labor, only one of the horrors of 19th-century British working-class life already described. They also attacked the patriarchal-capitalist head of the family who "sees his wife a mere instrument of production," thus normally exploiting her. They, then, decried the hypocritical double-standard of bourgeois society involved in extra-marital affairs, as bourgeois men "take the greatest pleasure in seducing each other's wives," as well as frequenting prostitutes. In advocating a "community of women," Marx and Engels stated that it was already here so why the hypocrisy in upholding the sanctity of the family or sexual faithfulness? [2]

We now observe the anthropological views of Marx and Engels on the why of women's oppression by men, the key work in this regard being Engels' *The Origin of the Family, Private Property and the State* heavily influenced by Lewis Henry Morgan, an American anthropologist who closely studied the Iroquois Indians. His historical schema of savagery/barbarism/civilization/ in *Ancient Society*, approved by Marx and Engels, confirmed their historical materialism.

Engels formulated that early human cultures were characterized by communist arrangements in which sexual intimacy occurred in the "primitive horde" or group marriage – indiscriminate mating – there being neither a distinct family as now known nor private property;[3] later, however, sexual mating excluded close relatives. He also held that, although during the savage and early barbarian periods, women were socially superior to men; with the increasing importance of hunting, men assumed this superior position. [4] The great reversal for women, according to him, came with the "overthrow of mother-right" with the domestication of animals and rise of war and attendant slavery, allowing men, now armed, an economic surplus from cattle and slaves. Thus it was that in marriage, women belonged to men, signifying patriarchy, the economic explanation being primary.[5] But now, under an advanced capitalism challenged by socialism, Engels foresaw that the emancipation of women would come about:

> When women can take part in production on a large social scale, and domestic work no longer claims anything but an insignificant amount of her time. And only now has that become possible through modern large-scale industry, which does not merely permit of the employment of female labor over a wide range, but positively demands it, while it also tends towards ending private domestic labor by changing it more and more into public industry.[6]

It should also be added that Marx/Engels were aware that the first two labor divisions within early humanity were "caused by differences of sex and age, a division...based on a purely physiological foundation," which led to other divisions with the "expansion of the community, by the increase of population...conflicts between different tribes, and the subjugation of one tribe by another."

There is a recent theory, however, proposed by anthropology professor at Harvard, Dr. Richard Wrangham, that suggests pair bonding between individual males and females as early as a million or so years ago, in the Homo Erectus period, in connection with cooking tubers and other roots, women cooking them protected by men. This conflict-oriented view may have some merit, but early and later primitive groups could only survive by intense mutual aid within the group in the context of early technology; humans are neither as swift nor as strong as most animals.[7]

On the whole, Engels' position on gender relations are now somewhat dated, but remain valid from an overall perspective. Indeed, Engels' work is a significant source for contemporary socialist-feminist theoreticians, including three key examples to be explored – of Simone de Beauvoir, Shulamith Firestone, and Ann Ferguson.

A landmark 20th-century work on women, which deftly employed the insights of Marxian historical materialism, existentialism, and Freudianism, is Simone de Beauvoir's *The Second Sex*. Its aim was to understand women in the multifarious aspects of their lives, in the family, at work, in religion, myth, and in literature under the impress of class society.

A socialist and existentialist, De Beauvoir believed that the ultimate liberation of women and of humanity could only come about with a socialist society in which men and women maintained their separate identities under a common fellowship:

> When we abolish slavery of half of humanity, together
> with the whole system of hypocrisy that it implies,
> then the 'division' of humanity will reveal its genuine
> significance and the human couple will find true
> form. [8]

In the why of women's inequality, De Beauvoir particularly accepted the insights of Engels' *The Origin of the Family:* that the agricultural revolution engendered an increasing economic surplus and concomitant labor division, spawning private property, war, slavery, the state, and women's subjugation. Furthermore: "Maternity dooms woman to a sedentary existence, and so it is natural that she remain at the hearth while man hunts, goes fishing, and makes war."

To the insights of Marxism, De Beauvoir added those of existentialism to the encounter. Importantly, this included the dimension of the "alterity" or the "other" between two unequal partners: Man, being physically stronger and more active than woman, dominated her as "a sexual partner, a reproducer, an exotic object

– and Other through whom he seeks himself"; But with the advent of modern technology, differences in physical strength between the genders would become meaningless. [9]

A most important feminist-socialist critique of the 1970s by Shulamith Firestone, *The Dialectic of Sex*, asserted that socialism must be linked to feminism to achieve ultimate human liberation. She respected the work of Marx and Engels in propounding a historical materialism emphasizing the class struggle, culminating in the final one between the bourgeoisie and the proletariat, and gave due recognition to Engels' *The Origin of the Family* for noting that the

> Original division of labor was between man and
> woman for the purposes of child breeding; that
> within the family the husband was the owner, the
> wife the means of production, the children the labor;
> and that reproduction of the human species was an
> important economic system distinct from the means
> of production.

Then, following in the footsteps of De Beauvoir's *The Second Sex*, Firestone developed the concept of "sex-class," of women themselves constituting a separate class because of their biological servitude involving the bearing and rearing of children. Her socialism had women having "full control of human fertility, including both the new technology and all the social institutions of childbearing and child rearing.[10] Her vision of socialism also welcomed a Marcusian "cybernetic industrial state," to eliminate "drudgery," with wages becoming obsolete, work evolving into an informative and life-enhancing experience. [11]

The final socialist feminist to be examined is Ann Ferguson, a philosophy professor, whose *Sexual Democracy* again called attention to Engel's *The Origin of the Family* as a beginning reference for women's liberation. Then, presumably following Firestone, she enunciated her basic reading of present social reality under the rubric of "sex class," in which social class was expanded upon to include its female component. For example, every social class, like working class and lower-middle class, would have a parallel female side attached to it.[12] The class alignments themselves, undergirded by the "capitalist patriarchal nuclear family" (CPNF), the basic socioeconomic and cultural unit of capitalism that subtly and otherwise exploited and oppressed women through an unequal exchange relationship of labor in the various family duties – "domestic maintenance, children nurturance, and sexuality," embedded in lower wages for women than for men. [13]

Although aware that in the past women had not been able to forge a common bond to transcend class lines, Ferguson believed that present socioeconomic and cultural trends were chipping away at the traditional CPNF, like high divorce rates, the necessity for women to work outside the home, usually at low wages, more relaxed sexual mores, and rise of state welfare systems maintaining poor/ divorced women. She furthermore asked for women's empowerment through progressive social legislation, inexpensive abortion, national childcare, national health insurance, ownership of property, and the vote. In fighting for these reforms throughout the world, she claimed that women, now the lower part of the working class in industrialized nations, would necessarily opt for socialism.[14] Capitalism itself, for her, opposed working-class women because it required an inexpensive work force and reserve army of unemployed, including minority and increasingly white men. But she neglected to point out that socialism demands an alliance between working class men and women as a categorical imperative.[15]

The formulations of Firestone and Ferguson on "sex class" were not novel. Marx and Engels viewed each class as composed of a male and female part, each representing its own particular social psychology and concomitant codes of dress, work, and behavior, basically set by the power relations exercised by the dominant class. In the final analysis, Marx and Engels and other mainstream socialists had class overriding gender, insisting that males and females of the same class had more in common with those of other classes.

In this vein, I agree with Teresa L. Ebert, a feminist and socialist, who affirmed that "Red feminism...insists on the priority of production and class struggle in the emancipation of women and reaffirms the solidarity of humanity on the basis of shared needs." This view did not deny the double oppression borne by women, of sex and class, but posited that human liberation was the task of both working-class men and women, with other allies, to effect socialism that by definition would end the age-old divisions between the sexes. In this progression, any advance to ameliorate the position of women with respect to men was a step toward socialism. To combat sexism, women now have a bevy of organizations, like Nine to Five, The National Organization of Women, and Emily's List.[16]

The theoretical views just discussed should be seen in the light of these recent American statistics: Women, in 2015, make up almost half of the market workforce, including 72 percent of married women, two principal factors contributing to this: The drop in real wages among most men since 1973 has literally forced more women into the paid work force, as has their desire for more or full independence from men. But women's earnings today are still three-fourths of men's, despite the fact that their real earnings have actually risen in the past twenty years. There is also the sexual revolution in the 1960s, with its more permissive attitudes toward premarital and casual sex, itself signifying women's greater equality. These elements, in turn, have increased divorce rates – doubling in the industrialized nations from 1970 to 1995. In 1995, for instance, the divorce rate in the U.S. is 54 out of 100 marriages; in Sweden, 41; England/Wales, 41; Canada, 38.3; and France, 31.

Social class intersects with sexual revolution/women's greater autonomy and economic downturn to savage the working class in higher rates of fatherless children – a fifth of white and two-thirds of black children at birth, largely from the lower part of the working class. A half of black, a quarter of Hispanic, and sixth of white families are headed by women, half of which are poor – thus the "feminization of poverty."

This growing fatherless-family poverty is related to existential problems, especially faced by poor female teenagers whose families cannot provide them with sufficient support. Many come from abusive homes with male predators or live in the streets seeking the protection of older males simply to survive, who usually get them pregnant and then abandon them. Tragically, their only traditional hope and purpose in life or for a tolerable socioeconomic survival is to have children and a mate.

From a socioeconomic perspective, a majority of women are in the lower part of the occupational structure. It is a truism that in women's occupations, like clerical work, nursing, and primary and secondary education, earnings are lower than men's in industrial work, transportation, engineering, law, business management, and medicine, an economic disparity exacerbated by divorce (a year after divorce, men's standard of living goes up by 10 percent, women's down by 27 percent). Married women often usually have a non-career track of low-wage, part-time or full-time work to supplement their husband's income, usually the principal one for the family.

If work is measured by the new concept of "comparable worth," which holds that wages should approximate the intrinsic worth of the job, many low-paid clerical jobs invariably held by women should pay as much, if not more, than assembly-line/factory or building-trades work in which men predominate. Most men oppose this concept for it would impinge on their earnings and social power.

The work place itself has been hellish for women, about half reporting losing jobs – peremptorily discharged or leaving of their own volition – because of sexual harassment. In 1995, the Equal Employment Opportunity Commission, a watch-dog for affirmative action, was besieged by more than fifteen thousand complaints from women charging sexual harassment at work, twice the number filed in 1991. In 1996, in a well-known case, the commission charged Mitsubishi Motor Manufacturing of American for allowing egregious sexual harassment of about two-thirds of its nine hundred women work force in its Normal, Illinois plant. Then, too, widespread sexual abuse in the military is now in the news. Women's socioeconomic inferiority continues into old age, their retirement income being generally insufficient, only three-fifths to that of men, forcing many to work until they die.

Middle-class women are making economic gains: Of recent college-degree recipients, two-fifths in law and a third in medicine are women, as well as more than half of BA's and MA's. Furthermore, in the top five hundred corporations, women hold 40 percent of executive/administrative positions, although only about 2 percent of those in top management and less than 5 percent serve on boards of directors.[17]

Notes

A) Background

1) On women in primitive societies, the Neolithic Age, and in civilization, see the general picture in Harris, *Culture, People, Nature*, chapter 20. Also, see Barbara Watterson, *Women in Ancient Egypt* (New York: St. Martin's Press, 1991). Sarah B. Pomeroy, *Goddesses, Whores, Wives, and Slaves: Women in Classical Antiquity* (New York: Schocken Books, 1975), pp. 57-119 on Athenian women; pp. 149-226 on Roman women, p. 189 on the quotation. For modern women, see Donald Meyer, *The Rise of Women in America, Russia, Sweden, and Italy* (Middletown, CT: Wesleyan Univ. Press, 1987). Almost any college textbook on general history now covers the role of women in society.

2) Mary Wollstonecraft, *A Vindication of the Rights of Woman* (London: Source Books Press, 1971), pp. 173-84 on the malevolent influences of private property and class society on women; on "legal prostitution"; and, on women leading active productive lives; p. 206 on the battle between men and women.

3) John Stuart Mill, *Subjection of Women*, intro. Robert Carr (Cambridge, MA: MIT Press, 1972), pp. 13-14. Written in 1861 and first published in 1869.

4) Ibid., pp. 16-18 ff. And p. 80.

5) Ibid., p. 100.
6) Ibid., p. xxiv. Bertrand Russell, *Autobiography, 1972-1914,* 3 vols. (Boston: Little, Brown, 1967-69), I, 233.
7) On socialism and feminism, see Meyer, *Rise of Women*, pp. 83-90. Ellen Carol DuBois, "Woman Suffrage and the Left: An International Socialist-Feminist Perspective," *New Left Review*, no. 186, March/April, 1991, pp. 20-45.

B) Marx, Engels, and Recent Socialist Feminists on Women

1) Marx and Engels, *Manifesto*, pp. 26-27.
2) Ibid., pp. 27-28.
3) Frederick Engels, *The Origin of the Family, Private Property and the State* (New York: International Publishers, 1942), pp. 28 ff.
4) Ibid., pp. 40 ff.
5) Ibid., pp. 47 ff.
6) Ibid., pp. 147-48.
7) On the quotation in the preceding paragraph, see *Capital*, I, 386. On Dr. Wrangham's views, see Mark Derr, "Of Tubers, Fire and Human Evolution," *New York Times*, Jan. 16, 2001, p. D3.
8) Simone de Beauvoir, *The Second Sex*, trans. and ed. by H.M. Parshley (New York: Vintage Books, 1974), p. 814.
9) Ibid., pp. 35-36, 66, 58-66, and 77 on the quotations and general views.
10) Shulamith Firestone, *The Dialectic of Sex* (New York: Morrow Quill Paperbacks, 1970), pp. 5-11.
11) Ibid., p. 266.
12) Ferguson, *Sexual Democracy*, pp. 167-69 and 194.
13) Ibid., pp. 42-46.
14) Ibid., p. 163.
15) Ibid., pp. 164 ff.
16) Anderson, *The Movement,* pp. 312-317, on discrimination of women among the Left. Roger S. Gottlieb, *History and Subjectivity; The Transformation of Marxist Theory* (Atlantic

Highlands, NJ: Humanities Press, 1993), chap. 9, "Socialist-Feminism," asserts that Marxists did not stress the women's problem. Teresa L. Ebert, "Toward a Red Feminism," *Against the Current*, Nov./Dec., 1996, p. 27.

17) On statistics and events discussed, the local/daily press and mass weeklies are good sources.

Chapter Thirteen: Capitalist Hegemony 1945 to circa 2000

This chapter not only catalogues the growth of capitalism after World War II but also delves into its continuing contradictions and consequent class struggles whose only solution is socialism. They include the expansion and further concentration of capital, indeed to the phenomenon of transnational corporations (TNCs), which now span the world, itself related to the truism that technology is becoming ever more sophisticated (witness the computer revolution), the ever increasing numbers of the world's working class and emptying of the countryside with the extension of the industrial revolution to the poorer nations of the world, and the continued absolute or relative impoverishment of the working class as the standard of life for most of the American and world's people is decreasing (this includes continuing high levels of real unemployment).

But the accumulation of wealth by the world's capitalist elite is growing, leading to increasing class polarity, especially between the wealthy and upper-middle class (the principal supporters of great wealth), and the working class/lower middle-class combination, on the other. Add to this the continual economic downturns of capitalism and machinations of capitalist speculator-criminals to skirt laws or to work within them to accumulate large sums of money, including the influencing of legislation against the public's interest.

Also, there is now the specter of worldwide pollution, itself intimately related to the capitalist quest for immediate profit and cheapening the cost of labor. Then, too, there are the new demographic trends, of an aging population in the first world and an increasingly young and angry one everywhere. Furthermore, there is the drama of increasing poverty among the peoples of the poorest nations, which, in conjunction with the communications revolution of cheap electronic gadgets (television, radio, and so forth), is rapidly exposing their poor masses to the technological wonders and relative high living standards of the First World.

The dominance of American-led capitalism over Soviet Communism after World War II has been the result of successful U.S. efforts; primarily involved in its early phases was Western European economic recovery and cooperation – thus, the formulation of the Marshall Plan in 1947 to rebuild a war-torn Europe, the formation of the European Coal and Steel Community in 1952, comprising France, Germany, Italy and the Benelux nations, broadened as the European Economic Community in 1957; in 1965 it became the European Community with more nations, which in 1991 metamorphosed into the European Union (EU), comprising most of the European nations of Europe, a community of free trade and evolving common institutions. Militarily, under U.S. leadership, the North Atlantic Treaty Organization (NATO) was formed. Other free-trade blocs formed included the North American Free Trade Agreements (NAFTA), founded in 1994 by the U.S., Canada, and Mexico.

In tandem with these and other trade blocs was the fostering of international free trade under the rulership of the TNCs. Its first step was the Breton Woods Conference in 1994 that established the IMF to lend money to debt-ridden nations, and the WB to lend money for long-term development – both under the auspices of the United Nations (UN), with the U.S. playing the primary role. In 1948, the UN, again under U.S. leadership, established the General Agreement on Tariffs and Trade (GATT), which through various rounds has greatly reduced tariffs worldwide to where in 1999 the average for farm products was 50 percent, but for manufactured goods from 4 to 10 percent.

In the early 1980s, following the U.S. lead, most trade/financial barriers were removed, as in Germany in 1981, France in 1984, and by the EU as a whole in 1988. Only Japan and the East Asian nations had severe trade restrictions but are now relenting towards more free trade with the economic crises of the late 1990s. In 1995, GATT established the World Trade Organization (WTO), which, along with the IMF and WB, is now the principle capitalist weapon enforcing privatization and free trade or rule of the TNCs. (The WTO, which in 2002 includes 130 nations and all the major economic powers, has wide authority to allow the unfettered rule of TNCs against national impediments to markets, granting its members "most favored nation" status, all having equal egress to entrance of goods).

With the end of World War II, capitalism in the West (U.S. and Western Europe) and Japan experienced a period of unparalleled economic growth from 1947 to 1973, a "Golden Age" for the historian Eric Hobsbawn. In this picture, a partial socialism is important only in Western Europe which saw high economic growth rates outside of Great Britain, of 5 percent annually, fueled by the Marshall Plan, mass production methods, new technologies, and economic integration.

This rapid economic growth literally changed the nature of much of the Western European labor force, while creating a labor shortage. Its large agricultural labor sector of the workforce in France and Italy, for instance, shrank from a third and two-fifths, just after World War II, to 5 and 7 percent today. Conversely, the number of industrial service and white-collar workers increased. The labor shortage itself was overcome by more women entering the paid work force and immigrants from Southern Europe, Turkey, and North Africa.

As living standards rose, mass consumerism became widespread in the advanced capitalist world as average working-class families now purchased stoves, refrigerators, television sets, automobiles, and other "luxuries," once only enjoyed by the middle classes and wealthy. Capitalist apologists would now boast of capitalism's superiority to Communism, burdened by an inherited and much lower capital/technological level.

The golden years of capitalist growth, however, were followed by relative economic stagnation with recessions in the U.S. in 1974-75, 1979-82, early 90s and in 2001-02. In the 1990s and early 2000s alone there have been economic slumps in Japan, South Korea, Indonesia, Thailand, the Philippines, Brazil, Argentina, Mexico, and Russia, among others. The EU itself, while maintaining economic growth, has had an average unemployment rate of about 10 percent. In the meantime, the poorest nations have had from zero to negative economic growth in the last two or more decades.

To these economic developments confirming the insights of Marx we add those of Robert Brenner, a contemporary Marxist economic historian, whose "The Economics of Global Turbulence" focused on the economic history of the three principal economic superpowers after World War II – U.S., Japan, and Germany. Brenner's primary thesis held that the general economic stagnation of capitalism since the early 1970s was related to a falling profit rate in manufacturing, resulting from intense national competition in an economic environment of uneven development (Japan and Germany at first benefited from lower labor costs and newer technologies, the older being destroyed by World War II), with its corollary of over-production/over-capacity in search of more profit. But he then proposed that the U.S. in the 1990s gained the economic advantage over its two rivals because of lower labor costs, with the weakening of unions and restructuring of the older industries, new technology, and dollar devaluation. This analysis unequivocally asserted that despite the rise of trade blocs and more free trade, capitalist nation-states still competed against one another economically, each one attempting to gain advantage over the others.

Brenner's cogent analysis was in the context of ever more free trade and the increasing concentration of capital/production, the ever-increasing tendency to oligopoly that tends to restrict output and raise prices, thus lowering consumption and increasing unemployment. But with state intervention to prop up military spending and to restart falling economies by huge tax cuts to business and deficit spending, conspicuous consumption, planned obsolescence of commodities, and export of capital to low-wage nations to keep profits up capitalism still survives. [1]

We now examine some discrete trends of contemporary capitalism, beginning with Marx's thesis of an ever-growing concentration of capital, with the U.S. as an example. Economic concentration in the U.S. is of old vintage. The Pujo House Committee of 1911-12 traced the threads among business: They principally included the House of Morgan whose two major banks through holding companies and interlocking directorates controlled three large insurance companies,

U.S. Steel, GE, and various large railroads. They were opposed by the Rockefeller group in control of Standard Oil Co., two large banks and nine railroads. By the 1907-13 period, the two combinations penetrated one another, resulting in control of 112 banks, insurance, manufacturing, public utility, and transportation companies in a grand economic design.

In *The Private Corporation and Private Property* (1932), Adolphe Berle Jr. and Gardiner C. Means contended that the largest two hundred American manufacturing corporations controlled about half of the industrial corporate wealth with a split in ownership between their owners and managers. Nevertheless, top executives of American corporations, exercising their stock-option provision of their total compensating packages, are large holders of their company's stock: According to *Business Week*, April 15, 2002, the amount is 15 percent. This indicates the power of the few at the top.

Currently, the largest six hundred American corporations generate at least 80 percent of sales revenue, the remaining 22 million businesses (a third are part-time, another third are one-person operations), the remainder. As for the market value of publicly traded American companies, the Standard and Poor's 500 (consisting of the leading five hundred corporations) holds 85 percent of it. In manufacturing, the top two hundred corporations had 48 percent of the sales in 1950 and 60 percent in 1980 and of total assets in manufacturing they owned 53 percent in 1955 and 61 percent in 1983.

This great economic concentration of capital was based on the inexorably drive of capital to expand its horizons, itself related to rising costs for research and development and some savings of economies of scale related to mass markets, and of course to the merger mania of the last two or so decades. During the Reagan and elder Bush presidencies, leveraged buyouts (LBO) number 44,158 at $2.17 trillion and for the Clinton presidency to June 2000, 78,811 at $6.66 trillion, 80 percent among U.S. corporations, the remainder between them and foreign ones. Foreign acquisitions and mergers by TNCs worldwide in 1999 alone were $720 billion and more than a trillion dollars in 2000.

Large mergers/acquisitions from 1998 to 2000 in billions of dollars (some involving foreign corporations) included (the acquired company comes second): Vodafone AirTouch with Mannesmann, $203 billion; America Online with Time Warner, 106; Pfizer and Warner Lambert, 90; Exxon with Mobil, 86; GlaxoWellcome with Smith Kline Beecham, 78. In the auto industry in billions of dollars, there were Daimler-Benz with Chrysler, 40; Renault to control Nissan Motors, 5.4; Ford purchasing the automobile-making part of Volvo for 6.5; General Motors acquiring a fifth of Subaru for 1.4; and Daimler Chrysler purchasing 34 percent of Mitsubishi Motors. In banking, mergers include First Union with CoreStates, Chase Manhattan with Chemical Bank, NationsBank with Bank of America, Bank One with First Chicago, Citicorps with Travelers Group (the latter comprised Travelers Insurance and the investment firm of Salomon Smith Barney; this merger has made the Glass-Steagall Act of 1933, separating commercial from investment banking, obsolete), and J.P. Morgan with Chase Manhattan.

Capital concentration was aided by federal deregulation of corporations in the last twenty years, supposedly to foster more competition. For economists, monopoly competition, of administered pricing in which price competition is minimal, results when four companies have at least 40 percent of domestic sales and at least five companies do so with at least 50 percent internationally.

In the domestic market today, usually in fractions or as percentage of sales revenue by number of companies: seven telephone companies have most of the domestic sales; four airlines, two-thirds; four appliance makers, more than 90 percent; three computer software firms, half; twenty in insurance, half; three in mass merchandising (Wal-Mart alone with 60 percent), three-fourths; four drugstore chains, almost half; ten in pharmaceuticals, including foreign, with most; two grain exporters, half; in food processing, three in beef, almost 80, four cereal companies, 85, and four milling flour, 60; for farms, one percent with 38; in hospitals, once chain alone with 10.

Small business is now becoming ever less viable by the capital-technology nexus. In the sphere of auto dealerships, although there are now twenty thousand, consolidation in the form of super-dealerships is now on the scene and automakers are attempting to abolish dealer franchise laws making it illegal for automakers to sell directly to the public through the internet and company-owned dealers. Sales commissions of independent insurance agents have been halved by insurance companies, their numbers falling by 37 percent between 1987 and 1999, and travel agencies have had their commissions cut by half as travelers contact airlines and hotels directly through the internet. In the grocery business, there were 530,000 outlets in 1950, but 126,000 in 1998, with five companies now controlling 30 percent of the market. In the restaurant business, national fast-food chains, like McDonald's and regional outfits like Bob Evans, now dominate. In assets, the top ten to fifteen companies in banking have half in 2000, and by 2005, it should be 90 percent; for gas and electric firms there were 150 in 1995, a hundred in 2000, and by 2010 "a couple of dozen."

This economic concentration masks even a greater one with interlocking directorates: Inside directors carry on daily business while outside ones represent a larger perspective, as of business in general, having numerous relations with others in the elite business community. Thus, it is that in the larger corporations, common broad policies are arrived at through these directors serving on other corporate boards simultaneously. Not surprisingly, banks and insurance companies are key players here. Holding companies, which control other companies, especially in the public utilities area, also heighten this concentration. [2]

Globally, increasing capital concentration is through the aegis of TNCs and international banking, stock, bond, and currency markets. TNCs are the unifying productive element here, having plants in two or more nations, with at least from a fourth to a third of their profits coming from outside the parent location. Of U.S. TNCs, 55 percent of their industrial output is from plants abroad.

The international economic giants are the largest 500 TNCs, which, in 1998, conducted 70 percent (40 percent of it intra-firm) of the $3.2 trillion world trade. Indeed, the leading 350 alone have more than a fourth of the world's productive assets and comprise a third of the GDP of economically advanced nations. In 1999, of the top 500, 244 are from the U.S., 173 from the EU, and 46 from Japan; and of the top 100, 70 are from the U.S., 26 from the EU, and 4 from Japan.

Three-fourths of TNC investment is in the First World, the remainder in developing nations; in the late 1990s, however, new capital flowed to the latter were 40 percent of foreign direct investment – worldwide its total is $3.5 trillion in 1997. The import/export complex itself on average worldwide is 20 percent of national GDP, slightly higher in the U.S. at 25 percent, but much more so at 50 percent for France, Germany, and the U.K.

With the now large international stock and bond flows, nations are ever more economically intertwined. In the U.S., for instance, foreigners bought 30 percent of new stock purchases (7 percent in 1998) and 40 percent of new bonds, including federal (20 percent in 1998). Another instance of this is the French stock market, in which American and British investors through pension funds own between 30 and 40 percent of it. In the realm of industrial stock alone, foreigners own a fourth of the French and up to two-fifths of the British. In plants and other installations, American and EU TNCs have invested about a trillion dollars in each others' markets.

The TNCs are so huge that the largest ones have sales exceeding the GDPs of many nations: the leading twenty-five alone have annual sales topping $25 billion or more by the early 90s. The largest five in percentage of sales now have a monopoly advantage in these key sectors: consumer durables (70), automobiles and trucks (60), airlines (55), aerospace (55), electrical/electronics and components (50 plus), and steel (50); and not far from it in oil (40 plus), personal computers (40 plus), the media (40 plus), chemicals (35), and insurance (25).

The power of the TNCs and large banks is so pronounced over national governments that the last shred of national sovereignty over TNCs is now proposed by the Organization for Economic Cooperation and Development (OECD), made up of the leading thirty-four nations, with the cooperation of the IMF. Its economic package, the Multilateral Agreement on Investment (MAI), would offer a *carte blache* to TNCs in purchasing, selling, and moving companies without regard to national laws. Furthermore, under MAI rules, nations would neither subsidize their domestic industries nor demand that foreign corporations abide by national guidelines for economic development. Capital now would be truly globalized, making national boundaries largely superfluous. Near-term consequences of this would include weakening of labor unions and environmental protection. Because of socialist and other opposition, MAI talks have stalled, but for how long?

Indeed, Chapter 11 of NAFTA allows corporations to sue nations for "damages from governments" when their laws impinge on "future profits" (seventeen or so cases in litigation involve environmental laws); this is undermining the democratic processes of the nations involved, allowing an MAI-like solution.

In 2001, more than $3 trillion dollars daily circles the globe, of which 15 percent is in the form of capital funds and commodity trading, the remainder in currency and other complex forms of speculation, like hedge funds. Trading is conducted through giant computer networks, the largest being the New York Clearing House Interbank Payment System (CHIPS), made up of eleven private banks that offer their services to 142 other banks globally; it interacts with smaller similar networks, like the Society of Worldwide Interbank Financial Communications (SWIFT) in Belgium, linking a thousand or banks, and a few other smaller computer complexes.

This almost uncontrolled computer/electronic system has encouraged tax havens in the Bahamas, Cayman Islands, Bermuda, Hong Kong, Isle of Man, and elsewhere; in the Grand Cayman Island alone 575 banks and trust companies handle $500 billion in assets. Of course, laws permit this squirreling away of money. It is estimated by Merrill Lynch that in 1998, $6 trillion is deposited by the world's wealthy (two-fifths held by U.S. citizens) with U.S. tax losses alone at $70 billion annually.

One expert on money movements, Anthony Ginsberg, estimated that about half the stock of the industrialized world was associated with tax havens. William Mulholland, the CEO of the Bank of

Montreal, informed a Canadian parliamentary committee that "I can hide money in the twinkling of an eye from all the bloodhounds that could be put on the case." (Some of the $200 billion annually made from illegal drugs was part of this money laundering).

The Securities and Exchange Commission, in a well-known finding, allowed that "off-the books transactions, bogus transfers, and double sets of accounts" were consistent with "reasonable and standard business judgment," that circumvent "currency regulation" and "tax laws." Obviously, the line between the legal and illegal is so blurred here that normal law is almost inoperative as it has been transcended by secrecy and speed: There are recent revelations of Russian money laundering in the many billions of dollars by government insiders and their accomplices.

There is also the specter of a relative de-industrialization affecting the U.S. as manufacturing facilities are moved to low-wage nations like Mexico, China, and Indonesia. Thus it is that of manufactured goods produced domestically, it was 86 percent in 1969, but only 62 percent by the 1980s. This condition is because of such factors as a strong dollar, less expensive foreign goods, relatively high wages (lower than that of some European nations), and lack of an industrial policy to protect much of industry from foreign incursion related to WTO free trade.

Since 1976, the U.S. has run trade deficits ($369 billion in 2000), its cumulative Net International Investment Position (deficit in trade investment to other nations) now alarmingly high: in 1999, it totaled $1.5 trillion or a sixth of a 9.3 trillion GDP, and by the end of 2000 has risen at least a few percentage points. Ultimately, rising foreign debt bodes ill for the American economy, as in forcing a dollar devaluation, which, in turn, increases inflation and interest rates. As for internal debt, the personal one in 1998 was $1.3 trillion or an eighth of GDP, while the corporate one was at about $4.6 trillion or 46 percent of a $9.97 trillion GDP in 2000.

Some perspective on globalization of capital: In the 1860s and 70s, the world witnessed much free trade, high tariffs coming later. Capital movements abroad as percentage of GDP in the late 1990s were lower than those in the late 19th century when the wealthy of England and France heavily invested in Australia, Canada, New Zealand, and the U.S.

After World War I and during the Great Depression, international investment and trade dropped drastically as autarky reigned, but after World War II they rose again. But, while international investment before was of the long-range variety (as in railroads and manufacturing), today much of it is in international assembly lines making manufactured goods and in short-term stock, bond, and currency funds, highly leveraged and speculative. Indeed, with the instant electronic technology of today, the herd mentality easily leads to economic crises. Worldwide, in the last twenty years, there were ninety major bank crises, while from 1870 to 1913, only one led to a crisis in currency exchange rates.

With the increasing importance of global mutual funds in stocks and bonds, in conjunction with the new powers of the GATT/WTO complex, any democratic socialist success, as in France, is hostage to international capital and to regional economic integration requirements like those of the EU. Indeed, global monopolization of the TNCs, and their attendant economic and political power is forcing nations and various states in the U.S. to grant them favorable subsidies and tax breaks simply to operate there. This development compels smaller companies beholden to TNCs, economically, to ruthlessly compete with one another for their contracts, either lowering wages and benefits for workers or causing higher unemployment, thus the race to the economic bottom for workers, including the savaging of unions.

These economic phenomena, of an ever more internationalized capitalism, have made for the lessening of trade wars among nations, although they still persist, as by the U.S. recently to force Russia, Japan, and Brazil to curtail steel exports to it and the EU's preventing U.S. TNCs to being subsidized with monies from off-shore tax havens.

The viability of capitalism – indeed its matrix – resides in the sacrosanctity of private property, an important segment of which is corporation stock. The rise of Communism in the Soviet Union, Eastern Europe, and China signified the advent of state capitalism there. With the collapse of Communism in the Soviet Union and Eastern Europe, nationalized industries were privatized aided by the IMF, representing international capitalism. This led to the establishment of a new capitalist kleptocracy in Russia. In China, the rise of Deng Xiaoping led to the institutionalization of capitalism there; in 2002 private industry furnished a third of economic output. Increasing privatization has also occurred among the nationalized industries of Western Europe, as in Spain, France, Britain, and Italy, and of Latin America, as in Argentina, Chile, Bolivia, Brazil, and Mexico. International capitalism has now definitely stopped socialism in its various forms. [3]

In *Capital III*, Marx observed that capitalism's "new financial aristocracy" or "parasites in the shape of promoters, speculators and nominal directors," was involved in a "system of swindling and cheating by means of corporate promotion, stock issuance and stock speculation." Examples include the S&L debacle under the Reagan and Bush presidencies, which began with the deregulation of the Savings and Loan (S&L) industry in 1982, which instead of only lending money for homes also was allowed to do so for office buildings, junk bonds, and so forth to increase earnings, interest rate ceilings being removed. The debacle occurred with the assistance of a Democratic Congress (whose cost to the taxpayers was $250 billion). These developments caused a wild, speculative frenzy, leading to fraud in appraising real estate (Reagan drastically reduced the number of auditors), outside auditors permitting questionable practices, with S&L officials awarding tainted loans to family members and associates, often receiving kickbacks in return. According to legal experts, fraud cases are difficult to prove, requiring mountains of evidence to distinguish between poor management and fraud.

The crash occurred in the late 1980s, and by 1991, two thousand S&L's were declared insolvent. William Seideman, the former chairperson of the FDIC, estimated that fraud was involved in three-fifths of the bankruptcies, the primary cause in half of them. In the 1990s, the Justice Department tried twenty-one thousand fraud cases, thirteen hundred of the major variety. Many S&L failures were inevitable, with S&L's unable to overcome the high inflation of the 1970s as their fixed-rate home-mortgage loans forced them into speculative frenzies and illegalities to survive.

LBOs are another financial device to make money rapidly. In a typical case, two-thirds of the capital to acquire a company is borrowed by corporate raiders, like Carl Ichan and Boone Pickens, at high interest rates, which are tax write-offs from lending institutions. This capital is, then, converted into "junk bonds," added to the debt of the acquired company as the raiders sell off various divisions at high profit. These financial maneuvers have sharply increased corporate debt.

Another example are the financial machinations of George Soros, a notorious international speculator, chief of the Quantum Fund, based in the Netherlands Antilles, which deals in the risky and arcane areas of highly leveraged hedge funds in options, futures, and derivatives, sheltering profits in various tax-avoidance maneuvers. In a particularly brazen and successful venture, the Soros investment group drove down the English pound in September of 1992, in the course of which they made a $2 billion profit while the British government lost $6 billion. Soros blithely admitted to this economic rape, made possible by his large economic muscle, causing some of his wealthy cohorts some embarrassment. He, of course, is hailed as a philanthropist and courted for advice by heads of state, including President Clinton.

Then, there are the hedge funds, highly leveraged capital pools (approximately three thousand of them exist in the U.S. in 2000), operating secretly and unregulated. The typical one has a leverage of about thirty to one as opposed to twenty-seven to one for the five largest investment banks and fourteen to one for the five largest commercial banks, the last two regulated by federal agencies. The "hedge" applies to the practice of betting that two forms of investments will rise and fall at the same time. To participate in hedge funds, minimum amounts may range from a hundred thousand to millions of dollars.

One such fund was Long Term Capital Management, a limited partnership demanding a minimum of $10 million from each investor, private and corporate, to join its privileged circle. Its leading operatives were John M. Meriwether, a well-known Wall Street player, and two Nobel Prize laureates in economics, Myron S. Scholes and Robert C. Merton.

Specifically, this fund invested monies in government bonds, of the U.S. Treasury, European nations, including Russia (the latter defaults), and developing nations, many of which in 1998 were in an economic free fall, and in bonds for mortgages. In fact, the fund's prophecy that U.S. Treasury Bonds would fall in price proved to be incorrect as the economic crash in Asia, Russia, and fall of stock prices in the U.S. invited investors to them.

This fund leveraged its initial $2.2 billion capital to about $125 billion through borrowing on it, then, employed the latter amount as collateral to purchase $1.25 trillion worth of various exotic investments in many complex derivatives. When one of its already stated plan misfired, it was faced with running out of capital to pay short-term obligations, thus facing bankruptcy.

In this juncture (1998), the Federal Reserve Bank of New York intervened to save this fund from bankruptcy, arranging that banks and brokerage houses, some of which had lent it money in addition to being its partners like J.P. Morgan and Co., Merrill Lynch, Morgan Stanley, Dean Witter, to buy most of it for $3.5 billion. Without this bail-out, knowledgeable opinion held that it would have triggered large bank failures domestically and, ultimately, worldwide.

Finally, an energy shortage has gripped the U.S., which for part of 2001 was of crisis proportion for consumers. In oil, the international oil monopoly, Organization of the Petroleum Export Countries (OPEC), was reducing oil output; in natural gas, in which the nation has huge reserves, relatively low prices and relative over-supply again discouraged investment. Thus, low investment, lack of government oversight to insure conservation (low-mileage sports utility vehicles now proliferate as the auto lobby is triumphant), and government failure to force regulated companies, like electric utilities, to increase investment to keep up with demand, conspired to set the stage for the energy crisis.

Now, it was within this backdrop that deregulation occurred in natural gas and recently in electric power (in the last by twenty-four states by 2001) supposedly to foster more competition and lower prices. But these utilities are natural monopolies, or become oligopolies, like natural gas, with attendant monopolistic competition. Utilities themselves, because they are natural monopolies, were regulated by the states by the early 20th century to allow them a fair profit and consumer price stability.

In California, in which there were rolling blackouts, deregulation was supported by both major political parties, the utilities, and large business on the basis that it would lower their energy costs; some electric companies had lower prices as they mainly did not rely on expensive nuclear energy. But for deregulation to proceed, consumers also will have to pay "stranded costs" or fixed costs incurred by poor electric company investments mostly in nuclear-energy, approximately $200 billion nationally.

But these simultaneous developments have brought about steeply rising prices: The building of fewer plants because regulatory profits, although more than fair, are not high enough to attract sufficient investment. Market manipulation by rival companies, which may somewhat lower the price until a few dominate, occurs. Short-term power manipulation by electric companies through convenient power outages because of "repairs" also happens.

The plan to deregulate involves this "shell game." Electric power companies sell their power plants to energy companies furnishing the power, the electric companies simply becoming the transmission belts retailing it to the public. The producers are not limited to any one geographical area, thus allowing them to further manipulate the market for highest possible returns. Not surprisingly, profits are up for the producers, but the carriers are going bankrupt as they are still somewhat regulated. To be sure, the transmission and energy companies themselves are part of large conglomerates.

In the electric power area alone, prices are so very high in California that its Democratic governor Gray Davis is now proposing the establishment of a state energy board to again impose price regulation, including state purchase of generating plants from private companies and to even build new state-owned ones. Ultimately, the lack of planning in this economic scenario fleeced California consumers in the 2000-02 period of more than $45 billion in higher rates.

In connection with the gross overcharging of rates in California and other Western states, poetic justice occurred when a major culprit of this outrage, Enron, a large energy and trading company, imploded by late 2001. Once a company whose stock value in 2000 reached $90 billion, making it the seventh largest corporation in the S&P 500, by December 2001 its stock sold for pennies. Its demise was because of its being plundered by its principal officers who created a web of intricate financial arrangements, including partnerships based offshore in the Cayman Islands that allowed the hiding of company debt, while netting enormous profits. Enron was investigated by many Congressional committees and the Justice Department. Enron itself made enormous profits from the deregulation of energy, especially in the electricity segment in California, controlling a significant share of that market, being exempt from any oversight by the Commodity Futures Trading Commission. Its CEO, Kenneth Lay, alone earned $205 million in stock options in the last four years of his office. The consequences of the Enron implosion included huge losses for its employee retirement accounts, for banks, like J.P. Morgan Chase, and for the stock market. Lay was sentenced to prison.

Since the implosion of Enron, a plethora of American companies were soon exposed as being involved with fraudulent practices which led to overstating profits, thus keeping their stock prices artificially up: When fraud was discovered, it quickly led to their bankruptcy. They include WorldCom, who overestimated its profits at $3.85 billion in a little more than a year in the 2001-02 period. It employed a simple accounting trick in this deception: Instead of deducting current expenses as a cost of doing business, it listed them as "capital expenditures," allowing their cost to be spread over a number of years. Its CEO, Bernie Ebbers, borrowed $366 billion in the last thee years of his reign and was compensated $183 million, $163 million of which was in stock options.

As for Adelphia, it was looted by its founder John Rigas and his family, who borrowed $2.3 billion from it. In the case of Global Crossing, its CEO, Gary Winnick, enriched himself with $735 million in stock options as the company was imploding. With respect to Tyco, Dennis Kozlowski, received $345 million in stock options in the last three years of being CEO, again personally contributing to its demise.

Corporate fraud itself was abetted by laws permitting CEOs and other executives to gain income through stock options, whose value is tied to stock prices; they are not regarded as company expense, thus raising profits from 20 to 30 percent, which inflated stock prices. To make stock options more lucrative, companies would lend money to top executives who, in turn, would purchase more of them; this device again was not listed as an expense. Furthermore, companies would go into more debt to banks in repurchasing their stock in the market, the aim here being to again raise stock prices and the value of stock options. In short, while these companies were going bankrupt (hiding their losses through illegal accounting practices) their top executives as insiders would sell their stocks at high prices, knowing that they would soon fall, enriching themselves by billions of dollars.

The enormity of these economic disasters cannot be underestimated. For instance, WorldCom's demise saw its stock fall from a high of $64.5 a share to less than a dollar within three years, costing investors more than $175 billion. To be sure, tens of thousands of employees lost their jobs because of these scandals.

In some of these fraud cases, the Arthur Andersen accounting firm was involved in "cooking" their books: Although serving as auditors of these companies, it was also involved in devising accounting practices to manufacture higher profits. This company, which paid a $110 million civil-settlement fine for accounting malpractices in the collapse of Sunbeam, also audited the books of Enron and WorldCom. It is now fined again by the government for the Enron scandal and is now going out of business. [4]

*

In the mid-90s, annual federal corporate welfare costs in billions of dollars run from 53 for Common Cause, 167 for the liberal Nader's Center for the Study of Responsive Law; and 87 for the conservative libertarian Cato Institute (Spencerites). However, these statistics do not include 100 or so billion dollars granted annually to business by local and state governments in the form of industrial revenue bonds, tax abatements, and tax-increment financing, the last reimbursing business for taxes collected from it to aid in its building costs. Some of the larger annual dollar costs in billions in the 90s include 18.3 for the S&L debacle; 9 and more lost in taxes for mergers and acquisitions; from 8 to 29 in subsidies to farmers (in 2000, half of farm income); more than 12 to oil companies as write-offs for royalties to other nations; 30 and more in excessively high depreciation allowances for corporate plant and equipment (many leading corporations pay no corporate tax in any given year – Cisco Systems, Enron, and Microsoft, for instance, did not in 1999 – and stock options for corporate CEOs is a business expense; a minimum of 25 for TNCs shifting expenses and revenues to other nations through "creative accounting"; 29 for business meals and entertainment, including call girls; half a billion for non-payment of royalties for mining on public land, and 4.1 to subsidize corporations doing business abroad by establishing offshore tax havens for them, terminated in 2000 because of EU objections. Recently, the government gave a $70 billion handout to the media giants to use the public digital spectrum on the airwaves for many years.

But there is more, for it is the federal government that plays a vital role in fostering technological change through the Department of Defense and other government agencies, developing atomic energy and the internet with its hardware/software. The Pentagon's

Manufacturing Technology Program is instrumental in modernizing manufacturing, combining the latest techniques of automation and computer technology. Indeed, the role of the government in subsidizing and protecting new technologies is apparent in the instances of the transistor and computer. The transistor's (it was invested in the laboratories of American Telephone and Telegraph) commercial viability was greatly facilitated by initial government purchases of it. Also, the early domestic computer industry was protected by high tariffs on less expensive and superior Japanese computers.

Government tax breaks to corporations might be seen in this larger perspective concerning share of federal taxes: For corporations, it was 33 percent in the late 1940s, but only 8 percent in the early 2000s; this while the individual tax burden increased from 44 percent in the 1940s to 73 percent in the 1990s; excise and other taxes comprised the remainder.

Corporations are also notorious tax dodgers in selling subsidiaries. General Motors (GM), for instance, avoided paying taxes when Hughes Electronic, a GM subsidiary, sold DirecTV, which it owns, to Echo Star for $22 billion. In this transaction, a Reserve Morris tax trust tax break is consummated by GM's subsidiary, in effect becoming an independent company, which, in being sold to Echo Star, would allow by a complicated series of maneuvers Hughes' stockholders to retain a majority stock ownership in the enlarged Echo Star. The end result is a tax-free sale, saving GM $5 billion. The tax-law labyrinth is another key index in indicating the power of big business in influencing Congressional legislation. [5]

In the late 1990s, world capitalism experienced economic crises in South Korea, Thailand, the Philippines, Indonesia, and Russia, while Japan is mired in a no-growth mode. By 2000, with the exception of Japan and Indonesia, the other nations, especially South Korea, have resumed economic growth. We now examine several nations involved.

There is an East Asian economic model in which, although nations have their own discrete variations, certain distinct patterns emerge: Economically, the state is the general coordinator of activity, operating in a climate of usually private ownership of production in giant export-driven trusts, heavily subsidized by the state through low-interest/guaranteed loans. With a high savings rate, low wages (unions are either non-existent or weak), strict state supervision of capital and consumer markets prevents foreign economic domination, a model that has led to rapid economic growth.

The current economic crisis in East Asia is destroying this paradigm, principally allowing foreign capital to buy East Asian capital assets cheaply – with exceptions, notably Japan. This development is related to the advanced capitalist world now in a stage of relative economic stagnation, with high levels of unemployment/ underemployment and/or lower real wages from productive over-capacity, thus not being able to as readily absorb as before the products of East Asia.

Background regarding the East Asian crash consists of China's devaluing its currency by a third in 1994, making its exports more competitive against those of other Asian nations, and, in 1995, the U.S. and Japan agreed on an economic tradeoff; the yen would depreciate against the dollar, helping to rescue a lagging Japanese economy by boosting its exports to the U.S., the *quid pro quo* being continued Japanese export of capital to the U.S., importantly in the form of purchasing its treasury bonds, keeping U.S. interest rates low to aid economic growth. These events adversely impacted South Korea and Southeast Asia, for the currency of these nations is tied to the dollar: Thus, as the dollar rose in relation to the yen, so did their currencies and prices of export goods, both countries' export growth to the U.S. falling to zero by 1996. The corporate debtors of these nations covered this deficit by short-term/high-interest loans from Japan and the West; but when they no longer met interest payments on them, foreign speculators, anticipating an approaching economic crisis, fled these nations, forcing the value of their currencies and stock markets to plummet rapidly, further endangering repayment of their foreign debts.

Foreign capital itself has been an important factor in the economic growth of these nations (again with the exception of Japan and South Korea in the last few decades). For instance, Japanese banks, awash with money in a relatively stagnant domestic economy, expanded their sphere of economic penetration in Southeast Asia and South Korea, lending them $265 billion and investing a $100 billion.

The economic debacle of South Korea occurred in the eleventh largest economy in the world, the result of a state partnership with the *chaebols*, or large conglomerates, which successfully penetrated international markets for decades. Unlike Thailand, Indonesia, and the Philippines, South Korea at first largely fueled its economic development from internal sources, but now its banks must repay about $66 billion of $160 billion owed to outside banks (foreigners have about $50 billion invested there), but more than $50 billion are "non-performing" or cannot be repaid.

This development is caused by a rising trade deficit with Japan as South Korean corporations, in failing to sufficiently upgrade internal research and development, were forced to rely on advanced Japanese technology, and a trade surplus of $6 billion in 1988 with the U.S. turned to an $11 billion deficit by 1996.

South Korean banks, encouraged by foreign ones to borrow money from them, lent money to domestic industry, leading to over-expansion of facilities and speculation in Asian and Russian securities. In the meantime, currency speculators, like Soros, sensing the coming economic downturn, quickly made large profits by driving the won down by half relative to the dollar in 1997, which, although lowering the price of exports, made debt repayment too high, seven *chaebols* falling in 1997.

To "rescue" South Korea economically, the IMF-led group lent its banks $57 billion to repay debts to Japanese and Western banks, which because of the yen's devaluation, were twice as burdensome. The South Korean government itself assured repayments with government-guaranteed bonds and submitted to these creditor demands: Not only to reduce its spending, increase taxes, and relax import restrictions to control inflation, but to allow international capital to have more than 50 percent of its national corporations, including banks, and to gain access to its internal markets.

Indonesia, the world's fourth most populous nation with a population of more than 200 million, is still in an economic free fall after sustained growth in the last three decades: From July 1997 to January 1998, the *rupiah* plunged 75 percent against the dollar. Its stock market in 2001 remains in shambles. Basic food prices are now rapidly rising while more millions are unemployed, with many tens of millions of its people subsisting on the equivalent of a dollar a day.

Why the immediate crisis? About a third of the $130 billion external Indonesian debt (half by government, half by several hundred private capitalists) could not be repaid on schedule. Thus the IMF-led coterie lent Indonesia $43 billion to allow for debt repayment, forcing the repressive government of Indonesia's President Suharto in a cul-de-sac; If it accepted the IMF's money and demands (similar to the South Korean ones), economic austerity might topple it, non-compliance shutting off foreign credit, again doing so. The large domestic private debt itself will be paid by the people at large through higher taxes. Suharto has been recently forced to relinquish the presidency.

The IMF bailouts themselves will allow for Japanese and Western banks to be reimbursed by debtors while simultaneously purchasing the highly devalued assets of Indonesian capitalists, forcing them to a secondary position. The magnitude of the economic disaster for South Korea and Indonesia is large, the GDP of the former rapidly falling by half, the latter by four-fifths.

In addition to the U.S.-Japan role, already observed, the more obvious causes for the Asian economic crash included intimate relations between leading politicians and capitalists or family/crony favoritism and corruption. The Suharto family in Indonesia and their friends, the best example, acquired a multitude of enterprises, many now on the brink of or in bankruptcy. The Suhartos in the late 90s were worth $16 billion according to *Forbes*, their close allies – 50 families or so – another $30 billion.

Another reason behind the crash includes financial machinations, like disregarding normal accounting methods, tax evasion, and reckless speculation in real estate, currency, and stock markets, as well as international currency speculators, like Soros, hastening the fall.

Thus it is that the IMF, representing the interests of Western/Japanese capital/speculators, has established a system of economic control over poorer/debtor nations in which their short-tern economic imbalances trigger immediate crises, resulting in massive withdrawals of capital, leading to the collapse of their stock and currency markets, and consequently more borrowing, while selling more of their assets.

The economic nationalism of the "Asian tigers," in which the state plays a *dirigiste* role in promoting development has now been largely shattered in some of them. The consequences of this debt restructuring and sharp currency devaluation has economically devastated their working classes, with higher unemployment, lower wages, and destruction of any social safety net.

The global in the early 2000s that engulfed capitalism has led even some conservative economists to regard IMF-imposed solutions as destructive to capitalism itself: Friedman and George Schultz, the latter Secretary of State under Reagan, among others, asked for the IMF's abolishment on the grounds that it led to ruinous speculation. Others, like Joseph Stieglitz, the chief economist at the WB, urged that speculation be curbed by international control of unrestricted capital movements; yet others advocated something similar to a central international bank to prevent wild swings in national currencies to insure some price stability. Are not these proposals Keynesian?

The Japanese model of capitalism, in which large conglomerates comprising banks, industrial and other companies, cooperated with government in a mercantilist export-driven mode to promote rapid economic growth, was highly successful. Although Japan was heavily bombed in World War II, it was already an advanced industrial nation and with U.S. assistance (the U.S. Japan as a counterweight to Communist China in Asia) it recovered rapidly.

Japan itself, with its large loans and investments in China, Southeast Asia, and South Korea, was especially vulnerable to the economic malaise there. This was sharpened by its domestic economic stagnation related to excess profiteering by its wealthy resulting in collapsed speculative bubbles in domestic real estate and stock market – the former falling by about 10 percent annually in the 1990s and the second as seen in the Nikkei 225 index plummeting from 40,000 in December 1989 to near 10,000 in late 2001. This has led to the destabilization of the banking system (the government taking over many failing banks) as bank investments in stocks dropped, with bank debts at a trillion dollars.

Furthermore, corporate profits and wages have been falling and unemployment has reached 5 percent in 2001 as deflation reigns, while export-driven Japanese corporations are increasingly setting up plants in China to compete globally. These developments are occurring in a nation with a sixth of the world's GDP and its principal exporter and importer.

To overcome the economic slump, the Japanese government has been employing Keynesian tactics: It has sharply reduced taxes to increase consumer demand, lowered the interest rate to essentially zero percent to stimulate investment and embarked on a $1.1 trillion program since 1993 in expensive and often wasteful public works to increase business activity and employment. As a result, total government debt in 2001 is a third more than GDP, the highest of economically advanced nations.

These palliatives have not arrested Japan's economic fall because they have not basically corrected the imbalance between investment and consumption (made worse by a public's refusal to spend much of its income for fear of unemployment), of a private property system whose productive and financial systems are now heavily globalized by TNCs and heavily internationalized stock and bond markets. The only way out of this stagnation and to still retain capitalism is for the government to inaugurate a program of inflation (to print ever larger amounts of money) to force consumers to increase spending. But the socioeconomic danger of that is that with zero interest rates, it would wipe out of the savings of workers and lower-middle class. Internationally, this would force Japanese creditors to sell off their assets, further causing economic worldwide chaos. [6]

The U.S. has been in a relatively robust economic expansion from 1991 to 2000, with an annual GDP growth of 3.2 percent (but if one factors in the 1 percent increase of annual population growth, the figure changes to only 2.2 percent), as against the average of 4.7 percent of the previous eight periods of expansion since World War II. For the sake of comparison with other nations, this growth is lower than that of contemporary Germany.

This upturn is basically fed by three elements: Increased consumer spending (two-thirds of GDP is in this form), much of it indulged in by the wealthiest tenth, and rising consumer debt, up a fourth in real dollar terms since the 1980s, rapid rise of the stock market, and more investment/higher productivity.

This economic progress is partly fueled by new technologies, like computers, communications, automation/robotics, making possible instantaneous communication for lean production and just-in-time techniques to extract ever more surplus from workers. But by 2001-2 economic stagnation has set in with stocks falling sharply and unemployment rising to 6 percent. In this economic scenario, the new technological revolution should be factored in. New technologies lead to more unemployment. Although low-wage labor continues to be plentiful, witness the large influx of immigrant Hispanics and other ethnic groups into the U.S.

Some of the wondrous new technologies reducing the work force include, in communications, telephone-answering and voice-recognition machines and other innovations, which replace live operators. Thus it is that American Telephone and Telegraph processes half again as many telephone calls as before with about half as many workers. In commercial banking, with the advent of automatic teller machines, there are now 40 percent less tellers than before. In the fast-food sphere, labor-saving techniques utilize automation and computer-driven technology through innovations, like voice/touch order screens and automated cooking methods. McDonald's is now in the midst of almost automating the ordering of fast food with computer-monitored food preparation and delivery systems. In agriculture, gene-splicing, cloning, and the coming food-producing systems of biomass and enzymes to produce tissue-culture pulp, itself transformed to mimic various traditional crops, will make the few farmers in the First World and the many in the Third ever more superfluous, accelerating the emptying of the countryside.

The first to suffer here are blue-collar workers: For instance, United States Steel produced about the same amount of steel in 1980 and 1990, with 120,000 workers on the first date, but only 20,000 in 1990; this trend similarly affects the automobile, rubber, mining, and other industries. But white-collar workers are then quickly affected by the computer/electronics complex, reducing office-work time and paper handling by about half. An example of this loss of blue-collar and lower-white-collar workers is General Electric, tripling its worldwide sales from 1988 to 1993, but reducing its work force by two-fifths.

Indeed, it is now possible to markedly reduce the number of weekly work hours, especially under socialist arrangements, by eliminating planned obsolescence and luxuries. Jeremy Rifkin in his book, *The End of Work*, certainly makes a convincing case that the proliferation of new technologies will generally make formal work ever more superfluous. His solution is more community work and a shorter work week. This model does not apply to poor nations that need a fully-mobilized population for early capital/technological accumulation. [7]

An analysis now follows of inequality in income and wealth in the U.S. between the capitalist elite and upper-middle-class on the one hand, as opposed to the lower-middle class and working class on the other.

In the realm of income, the average factory worker in 1999 earned $23,712 per year; all other workers in general earned $31,000 per year. At the top of income stream were the chief executive officers (CEOs) of corporations who in 1999 in the largest 350 corporations earned $12.4 million in salary, stock options, and so forth, this being about five hundred to one disparity between them and factory workers. As late as 1980, the top CEOs earned forty-five times the income of average workers. From a wider perspective, in after-tax family income from 1977 to 1999, the top 1 percent gained 115 percent, the top fifth of the population gained 43 percent, the four fifth 14 percent, the middle or third fifth 8 percent, the four fifth 1 percent, and the bottom fifth lost 9 percent. In income for 2001, the lowest fifth garnered 3.0 percent, the middle fifth 13 percent while the top fifth, 56 percent; the richest 1 percent alone garnered 17 percent of it, whereas from 1940 to 1980, it was 8 percent.

As for wages: At the bottom are about 5 million of the workforce earning a minimum wage or less, 41 percent full-time workers; $1 per hour in 1956, $3.80 in 1986 and $5.15 from 1997 to the present, or 2003. From 1968 to 2000, worker productivity rose 60 percent, while in real purchasing power the minimum wage decreased by 35 percent. The majority working at minimum wage are women over age twenty-five with children; they are part of the lower third of the workforce which earns under $15,000 per year – the working poor. Wages themselves have fallen over long periods of time. In the mid-1990s, there were 17 million unemployed and underemployed workers alone. From 1973 to 1995, the bottom 80 percent of the workforce (non-supervisory personnel) saw a decline of 18 percent of their weekly earnings; in the 1989 to 1997 period, the wage decline was 5 percent. There are many factors contributing to this decrease, notably the lower union density in the workforce (from a third in the 1950s to an eighth in 2002), the increasing use of computers and automation resulting in downsizing, the exodus of jobs from high- wage areas to low-wage ones (as in the South and abroad), competition for jobs, especially among the unskilled with immigrants – 12.1 million jobs in 2001 are held by immigrants. The top 20 percent of the wage earners, basically the college-educated, saw their real earnings rise 29 percent between 1978 and 1990.

In the realm of wealth, there is obviously a correlation between income and wealth as the propensity to consume falls with higher incomes. Added to the income, however, is inherited wealth, whose income, of course, is added to work income. It is estimated that for the wealthy or top 1 percent, inherited wealth contributes to about two-thirds of their wealth. There is, of course, much wealth inequality in the U.S. A recent study suggests that in 1998, the top 1 percent of the people have 40.1 percent of total wealth; the next 4 percent, 21.9 percent; the following 5 percent, 11.2 percent; the following 10 percent 11.4 percent; the following 20 percent 10.7 percent; the following 20 percent holding 4.4 percent and the bottom 40 percent, 0.5 percent. In 1972, for the sake of comparison, the top 1 percent in wealth had about 32 percent of it.

At the top of the wealth chain in 1997-98, there were about 170 billionaires, 3,000 to 5,000 centi-millionaires, and about 240,000 deca-millionaires, followed by about 4.8 million millionaires. In terms of the family background of the richest 400 households, 42 percent came from older wealthy families, like the Rockefellers and du Ponts, 6 percent from great wealth, from families with more than $50 million, 6 percent from families with large companies, 7 percent from families which had medium-sized businesses or received help from wealthy family members, and 14 percent from professional families. In comparison, in terms of ethnicity for 1995 in median wealth, including equity in housing, the white median family had $61,000, black family $7,400, and a Hispanic one $5,000.

As for the increase of wealth, from 1976 to 1990, the wealthiest 1 percent saw their wealth almost double, while for the bottom 80 percent it rose 1 percent. We may add that in the important area of stock and bond ownership, the wealthiest 1 percent have about half of privately owned stock and three-fifths of bonds. [8]

Yet another topic to be discussed is the current unemployment problem, an endemic aspect of capitalism inasmuch as it views labor as a market commodity, subject to its demands. In this capitalist perspective, economic efficiency decrees the normality of unemployment, holding that command socialist societies are economically inefficient in employing excess or redundant labor. But this assertion neglects that the specter of unemployment has devastating results on the psyche of the unemployed, removing them from the cycle of normal life, including excluding them from the economic circuit that allows them to participate in society as productive members, conferring upon them an indisputable dignity. Thus it is that in the U.S., the unemployed experience a 30 percent rise in divorce rates, as well as higher rates of spousal and child abuse. Indeed, any economic inefficiency resulting from unemployment is more than offset by ending the waste of conspicuous consumption of the wealthy classes and wasteful planned obsolescence of goods for the sake of profit, itself a variant of conspicuous consumption.

Currently, from an overall world perspective, about a third of the worlds workforce of approximately three billion is either jobless or underemployed; especially are these rates applicable to poorer nations, the wealthier nations enjoying lower ones, although still quite substantial. Officially, unemployment now is at about 6 percent (double for blacks) in the U.S. and more than 10 percent in the European Union. In poorer nations, like Russia, Argentina, and Mexico, unemployment now is in the 20 percent range or more. In Mexico alone, out of workforce of thirty-six million in 1994, ten million are unemployed, fifteen million underemployed, like unlicensed street vendors, with ten million having jobs. The unemployment problem is most acute in sub-Sahara nations, about 50 percent. In the U.S., the official unemployment rate does not include discouraged workers who have simply given up trying to find a job, part-time workers who wish full-time employment, and the two million incarcerated; if it did, the unemployment rate would be about 2.5 times higher.

As for unemployment compensation, it generally does not exist in poor nations, Mexico being an obvious example, although some nations have severance packages, like China. In the economically advanced nations, unemployment compensation varies according to the strength of the labor movement and social democracy: In the U.S., where they are weak, workers receive about half of their wages for twenty-six weeks, whereas in France they are 58 percent for two years, in Germany 36 percent for five years, and in Britain 21 percent for five years.

Unemployment contributes to lower wages for workers procuring new jobs, especially for older workers. In the U.S., for instance, older workers often retire, or take steep wage cuts of about 15 percent, with reductions for professionals as high as 25 percent. As for gaining re-employment for the unemployed in the U.S., as an example, about three-fourths are successful, but 14 percent, usually over the age of fifty-five, retire. Overall, 11 percent of the unemployed were still without work after two years, with unemployment rates among blacks and Hispanics being especially high – 18 percent for the former, 19 percent for the latter. [9]

Perhaps we have now reached a stage of historical development in which capitalist power unifies globally to better control labor and prevent imperialist rivalry leading to world war and socialist revolution. These developments now favor capitalism in the short run, but peace among the great powers should strengthen socialism in the future because of these additional contradictions/problems inherent in the global capitalist system:

1. The continuing globalization of capital in financial markets (stocks and bonds in mutual funds and currency) and credit system or borrowing, with accompanying imbalances, is leading to wild swings of their valuations, exacerbated by speculative hedge and other funds, threatening to bring about financial and accompanying economic chaos. This itself is related to capitalism's inherently uneven economic development, resulting from imbalances in the complex of investment, profit, production, consumption complex.

2. The emptying of the countryside under the impetus of the "green revolution," including new genetically engineered seeds by Monsanto, Du Pont, and others, and continuing spread of capitalism, with its insatiable need for inexpensive labor. In 1950, 70 percent of the world's population lived in rural areas; today it is just over half. For instance, under NAFTA, inexpensive U.S. corn is destroying a rural corn-based way of life in Mexico, displacing small subsistence

farmers economically forced to migrate to the cities as a large reserve labor army for capital; invariably unemployed/ underemployed, their human situation is tragic as the mutual aid of family/village is destroyed by the urban slum, which, however, in time, the class struggle will resurrect. In Mexico and other poor nations, these usually "unofficial" new residents live in indescribably primitive conditions of poverty and squalor, lacking even minimal housing, health care, sanitation, food, schooling, and transportation. The estimated population of selected cities in millions in 2000, including their outer slums – Mexico City, 16.4; Sao Paulo, 17.8; and Bombay, 18.1. By 1990, fifty-four city complexes worldwide have populations of more than five million people. Wherever international capital penetrates poorer nations, its market relations makes ever more of their people as part of the reserve army of capital, obviously a condition exacerbating social tensions.

3. The communications revolution (inexpensive newspapers, radio and television, videos, movies, and computers) allows the peasantry and working class to become ever more aware of socioeconomic conditions outside of their immediate ones. Even if most of the media are capitalist controlled, their stress on consumerism cannot but increase class struggle as most of the people are unable to feast on the consumerist cornucopia of the wealthy.

4. The continuing waste of the world's military-industrial complex (two-fifths of which is spend by the U.S.) itself eats into the scarce resources of social welfare.

5. Socioeconomic tensions should intensify by the increase of the world's population, especially in urban areas, although the birthrate (births per woman) is itself declining rapidly, from six to three in poor nations and from three to under two in rich ones from 1950 to 1995. But with the declining birthrate, an aging population requires higher economic surpluses for support, either to come by taxing the wealthy more, or raising

taxes in general, or higher productivity – the last, a long-term solution. The welfare issue pits European socialism – favoring more – against European conservatism, proposing major cuts on the basis of free market "competitiveness."

6. With lower birthrates and women increasingly working outside the home, the traditional patriarchal family will progressively lose its influence.

7. Spreading pollution, with accompanying lower living standards.

8. Since the rise of neo-liberalism (the IMF/WTO combination), income and wealth gaps between the rich and others, especially the poor in the developed and poor nations, are rising, with the addition of higher taxes for the masses. For instance, in the U.S., the income disparity between the top and bottom fifths of the people between 1979 and 1997 increased from nine to fifteen times, while real median wages declined by at least 10 percent from 1973 to 2000. Its regressive federal tax and social-security system has a two-wage earner median income family in 1997 paying 40 percent on a $55,000 income, triple the amount of 1955 adjusted for inflation.

In many poor nations, there is even much more inequality. But in some areas of inequality, like income differentials between the average and that of the bottom fifth, it is just as large in the U.S. and Britain as in the poorer nations of Brazil and Guatemala, in which the income of the bottom fifth is only a fourth that of the average one. In fact, globally, class polarity widened from 1960 to 1991 as the richest 20 percent of the people increased its share of income from 70 to 85 percent.

From a worldwide perspective, inequality among nations now continues to the point where in the mid-90s, in respective percentages, the economically advanced ones, with 20 percent of the population, have 84.7 of GNP, 84.2 of trade, 85.5 of domestic savings, and 85 of domestic investment.

Circa 2000, half the world's six billion people live on less than two dollars per day, with almost half of this segment subsisting on less than a dollar per day or in poverty; the wealth of its richest 200 families (all billionaires) at a trillion dollars equals the annual income of the world's poorest two-fifths.

Some specificity now on the horrendous poverty in selected nations, obviously exacerbated by very sharp class polarities; one of which, Brazil, has a relatively high per-capita GDP, in 1999 being $6,200. In Brazil, out of 160 million people, 108 million are considered poor by Brazilian standards, 40 million of whom are extremely so, including 12 million *abandonados*, children without parents roaming the streets, while the richest 10 percent have about half the income and more than seven-tenths of the wealth. Of India's population of a billion, two-fifths subsist below the poverty line, half of whom live in abject poverty, not able to eat a full meal daily; a seventh of the families own up to 80 percent of the land, while three-tenths do not have any, this in a society that is predominantly rural, with half the people illiterate. Of Indonesia's 220 million people, more than a third is mired in poverty and half the children are malnourished. Of Pakistan's 140 million people, the poverty rate is 40 percent, with an illiteracy rate of 80 percent. In Sub-Sahara Africa (it does not include The Republic of South Africa), most of its more than half billion people are in dire poverty. To be sure, Communist North Korea has recently experienced famine and more than 40 percent of its people are poverty-stricken; and in Communist China, the partial return to capitalism has caused much socioeconomic hardship, as has the collapse of Communism in Eastern Europe and former Soviet Union.

The working class in both the economically advanced and poorer nations expects higher living standards from capitalism, but global capitalism's downsizing, seeking ever-less expensive wage-platforms and employing technology to cheapen and make labor ever more redundant, is savaging labor generally through lower real wages for most workers, speed-ups, and higher unemployment; variants exist like less unemployment with lower wages (the U.S. model) or higher unemployment with wages still aging somewhat (the EU model).

Official unemployment in the U.S. and EU in 2003is 6 percent and 10 percent.

Indeed, while these long-run trends of working-class immiserating occurred, economic downturns, from 1945 to the present, have periodically rocked the capitalist world, as in the U.S., Russia, Japan, South Korea, Indonesia, Turkey, Mexico, Brazil, and Argentina, while the EU itself is in a mode of slow economic growth.

Increasing economic misery has resulted in rising working-class activity. Since 1995, general strikes have erupted in France, Italy, Spain, Belgium, Greece, Canada, South Korea, Argentina, Brazil, and Columbia, more so than in any other time. Working-class consciousness has also increased; for instance, in polls in Britain on whether the class struggle exists, the affirmative answer was 45 percent in 1964 and 81 percent in 1995. In the U.S. on supporting strikes, the yes was 34 percent in 1964 and 46 in 1996. [10]

That living standards are falling while the GDP is rising is the thesis of such progressive economics as Herman E. Daly and John B. Cobb Jr. in *The Common Good*, as well as for Ted Halstead and Clifford Cobb in "The Need for New Measurements or Progress". For instance, Daly and Cobb Jr. affirmed that after factoring such environmental costs as air and water pollution (with their damage to the physical and living worlds, like soil erosion, depletion of scarce natural resources, and illness), needless advertising, automobile accidents, time lost in commuting, and so forth, which they deduct from the GDP, the standard of life actually dropped. Per capita income in the U.S. more than doubled from 1950 to 1986, but in Daly's and Cobb Jr.'s "index of sustainable economic welfare, which takes into account the above and other rising costs, the real standard of life increased a fourth, reaching its peak years from 1968 to 1979, then declining a tenth.

Halstead and Cobb also maintained that the GDP is also an inaccurate guide in measuring living standards as it does not measure the economic losses incurred by "family breakdown and disease," like divorce, with its high legal fees and maintaining two separate households, and illness, which enrich lawyers, physicians, and hospitals while impoverishing clients and patients. Such income transfers, from one part of society to another, do not contribute to higher living standards. Income inequality itself adds to the misallocation and waste of resources and labor through the conspicuous consumption of especially the wealthy and upper-middle class.

Then, too, there is the planned obsolescence of commodities related to the status/class complex, which again is inherently wasteful. The GDP also counts military and homeland expenditures as pluses, whereas, again, they consume scarce productive and natural resources. Furthermore, the GDP does not measure the social misery of unemployment and underemployment and diminution of leisure time as the work week increases. In addition, the economic costs of such alienated acts as smoking tobacco, drinking alcohol, and various forms of crimes necessitating and expanding court system and prisons are simply added to the GDP, not subtracted from it; these phenomena indicate social breakdown, not economic growth. It should be added that monopoly competition raises prices, adding another tenth or so to the GDP.

As an alternative to the GDP model, Ted Halstead and Clifford Cobb in "The Need for New Measurement of Progress," advocate a Genuine Progress Indicator, or GPI, which measures such elements as the costs of "pollution," "changes in leisure time," "unemployment and underemployment," "income distribution," and so forth – all which lead to a lower standard of life, although "housework and nonmarket transactions would increase the standard of life." [11]

From December 2007 to June 2009, the U.S. was mired in the Great Recession, the most severe economic downturn since the Great Depression of the 1930s. It hit the working class hard as unemployment rose to 10.1 percent (up to 30 million workers unemployed/underemployed/ceased looking for work, a fifth of the workforce); even in 2013, after the Great Recession ended, the U.S. unemployed still numbered 24 million, a sixth of the workforce, in an anemic economic recovery. As for industrial production, it dropped by a third; in 2013, a fifth still not used. The Dow Jones Industrial average plunged more than half, from 14,153 on October 9, 2007 to

6,547 on March 9, 2009. Median household wealth and housing prices decreased by a third.

The following factors caused the Great Recession:

1. Deregulation of the financial system by the Financial Services Modernization Act of 1999, which repealed the 1933 Glass-Steagall Act, now allowing commercial banks to act like investment banks, initiate initial public offerings for new corporation, sell stocks, bonds, derivatives, and, as before, lend money to businesses. This law abetted financial speculation.

2. The Commodity Futures Modernization Act of 2000 deregulated the derivatives market. Derivatives are bets on future commodity prices, like on oil and wheat. This law allowed banks to hedge (insure) bets on derivatives and to make bets on derivatives themselves by many degrees (synthetic derivatives). By 2008, this market was valued at $700 trillion, aided by credit agencies like Moody's Investor Services, which, to earn high commissions, gave triple-A ratings to risky derivatives which included many subprime home mortgages held by mostly the poor, hedged by American International Group (AIG). When the home subprime market collapsed, synthetic derivates investments greatly lost value, freezing interbank lending, causing a Wall Street panic as some banks declared bankruptcy, further destabilizing Wall Street, affecting the entire credit system made insolvent with bonds, stock, and other markets. Economic disaster now looming, this was the immediate cause of the Great Recession.

3. Capitalist fraud, as already observed, was a major contributing factor causing the Great Recession and is part and parcel of business. Three economists – Luigi Zingales, Adair Morse (both of the University of Chicago), and Alexander Dyck (of the University of Toronto) claimed that in any given year, from 11 percent to 13 percent of American corporations,

committed business fraud. Another report by economists Paul Romer and George Akerloff stated that in banks too-big-to-fail, their executives inevitably pillaged them.

4. Decreasing worker's wages/consumption: A number of statistics on the increasing economic misery of U.S. workers, buffeted adversely by free trade, technology changes (computerization, automation, robotics, anti-union legislation (Taft-Hartley Act), and unfriendly National Labor Board decisions: From 1973 to 2006 US labor productivity increased 83 percent, but average hourly workers' wages in 1982 constant dollars were $8.46 in 1970 and $8.27 in 2009. Middle-income workers (75 – 150 percent of median income) as percentage of the workplace, 61 percent in 1970, 51 percent in 2011.

5. This rising economic inequality between labor and capital by super exploitation of workers explains the increasing financialization of the economy in finance, insurance, and real estate (FIRE). Thus it is that in the 1970s, the richest 1 percent had 8 percent of income and 18 percent of wealth; the difference in 2012 was drastic, rising to 22.5 percent of income and 40 percent of wealth. The richest 10 percent had a third of income in the 1970s, and half in 2012.

6. Financialization itself is related to tens of trillions of dollars circling the globe for quick profit and then leaving for greener pastures – an important destabilizing element (More on this later).

7. Debt: By 2008, personal, corporate, government debt was 350 percent of GDP, or $48 trillion – the world's highest debt. The credit system was at a breaking point.

Thus it is that despite the consumer spending spree of the wealthy (more on this later), and military deficit spending Keynesianism, the Great Recession occurred, aided by this salient fact, consumer spending of the working class had reached its outer limit. Consumer debt was the major underlying cause of the Great Recession.

In late 2007 and 2008, the federal government intervened to stanch economic disaster, under Presidents George W. Bush and Barack Obama and Congress. It nationalized AIG (later re-privatized), paying ailing banks their insurance fully ($180 billion); further rescued banks with $340 billion in stock purchases in them; purchased $80 billion of General Motors and Chrysler stock (nationalizing them) to prevent bankruptcy (both later re-privatized); secretly lent $16 trillion at low interest rates to crippled corporations in and outside the US; granted $260 billion to prop up municipal and state finances to maintain their workforce; aided small business by tax breaks in the tens of billions of dollars; had the Federal Reserve Bank through Quantitative Easing (QE) purchase $4 trillion from US banks in treasury-backed bonds and mortgage securities (many subprime) from 2009 to 2013 (the program principally aiding rich bondholders/stockholders) continuing at least to 2014; cutting Social Security taxes; extending unemployment benefits to 99 weeks (later reduced); initiating a $100 billion program to rebuild part of the infrastructure; and lowering interest rates, still at 0.25 percent in 2014.

These government measures prevented a Second Great Depression. They stabilized the financial system, partly stimulated the economy, reduced unemployment (in the mid-6 percent level in 2014), and even permitted anemic GDP growth, 5.9 percent for 2008-12. (In 2013, GDP increased a miniscule 1.7 percent). GDP losses because of the Great Recession, according to the Congressional Budget Office, by 2017 will be $7.5 trillion.

Although workers' economic misery suffered greatly in the 2008-13 period, pre-taxed corporate profits rapidly recovered to record highs: from $1.38 trillion in 2008 to $1.85 trillion in 2011, to $2.19 trillion in 2012, to over $2 trillion in 2013, in a 2013 GDP of $17 trillion.

One of Marx's dictums is that as capitalism develops, the larger capitalist enterprises envelop the smaller ones, subsequently creating a greater economic concentration. Examples include: in the critical banking sector, the ten largest banks had 10 percent of assets in 1990, 60 percent in 2008. In 2012, 15 percent of S&P corporations garnered

60 percent of profits, much less before. As percentage of business income, the richest 1 percent had 17 percent of it in 1979, 43 percent in 2007. Also, the largest 200 corporations increased their share of total gross profits of the economy from 13 percent in 1950 to 30 percent in 2008. Large companies, more than 500 workers, employ half the workers and have 57 percent of payroll. The percentage of companies with annual incomes between $10,000 and $10 million have only 17 percent of total business income. Globally, the largest 500 corporations had 19 percent of the world's GDP in 1960, 32 percent in 2008.

This rapid concentration of capital is leading for Paul Krugman, (Nobel Laureate in economics and a New York Times columnist) to state that the US is becoming a "society with a hereditary aristocracy of wealth," a third of the largest 50 fortunes are inherited and another third will soon be. To avert this condition, he recommends high estate taxes; I recommend a socialist society.[12]

EU Economic Malaise and Continuing Inequality

The US financial crisis rapidly spread to the 28-nation EU and its 18-member euro zone of common currency sector because US and EU banks have much interbank lending.

Several examples of EU bank failures: In Ireland, because easy credit to some of its corporations could not be repaid, government assumed debt. In Spain, after a speculative frenzy in housing collapsed, government again paid for the losses. When rich speculations fail, their losses are socialized via government.

In Greece, its banks, on the verge of collapse, were rescued by the European Central Bank, the European Commission, and the IMF. The shortfall of government taxes, forcing the government to borrow excessively, was caused by wealthier classes paying lower taxes by tax avoidance, employing bribery of tax collectors, and other tax avoidance measures. A Greek government default (many loans from French and German banks) might have led to the collapse of the European banking system. (The BRICK nations, Brazil, Russia, India, and China escaped the economic downturn in the US and EU.

The economic downturn in the EU and its Euro zone in the 2008-12 period was deep, the Euro zone's GDP, for instance, falling by 4 percent. We first note GDP decline selected euro zone nations in this period. France, second largest (Germany, the largest), 1 percent; Italy, third largest, at 6 percent; Spain, fourth largest, 4 percent. Others falling include Greece, 25 percent; Portugal, Ireland, Belgium, and the Netherlands. Great Britain in the larger EU also experienced economic decline. Even the EU/euro zone economic powerhouse, Germany, had anemic economic growth, reporting 0.5 percent in the last two quarters of 2013.

The EU economic downturn has led to higher national debt as percentage of GDP. Examples, circa 2012-13; Greece, 170; Italy, 130; Portugal, 130; Ireland, 124; France, 90; Spain, 90; Germany, 80; US, by comparison, just above 100.

Economists argue whether government debt of over 100 percent is harmful to the economy. Japan's national debt today of over 200 percent of GDP, for instance, has led to anemic economic growth, at about 0.5 percent annually since 2000. National debt itself is largely owned by bondholders, the wealthier class, indicating rising wealth inequality. But Keynesian economic stimulus via government deficit spending, especially in World War II, solved the US depression of the 1930s.

The EU economic downturn has resulted in high unemployment in 2013, early 2014, percentages in selected nations: Greece, 28; Spain, 27; Portugal, 18; Ireland, 13; Italy, 12; France, 11; Britain, almost 8; Germany, 5.4. Overall, 12.2, or 26 million from a workforce of about 245 million. For youth, unemployment (ages 15-24) is higher, again in percentages: Greece, 62.5; Spain, 56; Italy, 40; Portugal, 39; Ireland, 28, France, 26; Germany, 10.

More than half of the unemployed are still so for over a year in Greece, Spain, Italy, Portugal and Ireland, 44 percent in Germany, 41 percent in France; EU overall, 48 percent.

Regarding EU new jobs, more than half are low-paid, replacing permanent ones with expensive social benefits, often not paying a living wage. Indeed, many employed workers in Greece (800,000), Spain, Italy, and Portugal have not been paid for a month or longer. Overall, EU unemployed received reduced social benefits and when they run out after one-two years, its soup kitchens and family assistance, for economic survival; some are homeless.

Indeed, it is appealing that the unemployed are treated so shabbily. In Greece, they even lose health insurance after a year's unemployment. Even the strong social welfare system in France, healthcare and other social services, have been reduced while, to stimulate the economy, business taxes have been cut.

A socialist solution for high unemployment is a government job program, which socialist governments in Spain, Portugal, and France, for instance, did not initiate. Reasons for this principally include EU economic austerity measures to please wealthy bondholders to ensure low inflation, to be later examined.

It now appears that EU social democracy, buffeted by deep economic downturn, with high unemployment and lower wages for workers, is also reducing the social welfare sector. Workers are the principal losers in this scenario.

Higher unemployment/lower wages has led to increasing socioeconomic inequality in EU nations between the richest 1/10 percent of the people and the remainder, especially the lower half. In Germany, for instance, the richest 10 percent of households had 26 percent of income in 1991, 31 percent in 2010, while the income of the lower half fell from 22 percent to 17 percent.

If income (and wealth) inequality is increasing in a relatively prosperous Germany, it certainly is so in the rest of the EU mired in depression in the last six years. This is also borne out by comparing the income share of the richest 1 percent in 1980 and 2008-12 in percentages in selected EU nations: Britain, 6. 12; Italy, 7, 9.4 ; Sweden, 3.5, 7; France, 8, 8.1; Spain, 8, 8.2; Denmark, 6.2, 6.4.

The richest 10 percent in the EU have also increased income percentage from the 1960s/70s to 2010: Britain, 28, 41; Germany, 30, 36; France, 32.1, 32.2 – U.S., by comparison, 33, 49.

Regarding how many times the average income of the richest 10 percent exceeded the income of the poorest 10 percent in selected nations from about 1985 to 2010: US, 11, 16; Italy, 7, 10; Britain, 7, 10; Germany, 5, 7; Sweden, 4, 6.

Increasing income/wealth inequality is also indicated by the value of private capital as percentage of national income in selected EU nations and US comparing 1970 to 2010: Britain, 300, 500; Germany, 200, 400; France, 300, 580; US, 330, 400, although 500 in 2007, dropping because of the stock market crash. The greatest share of the private wealth goes to the richer classes.

Technological innovation alone is another factor leading to worker impoverishment – higher unemployment resulting in lower wages. The percentage loss in labor share of income in every decade from 1975 to the present in selected EU nations: Germany, 2.6; Italy, 2.3; France, 2.2; US, by comparison, 1.3.

The super exploitation of US and EU labor by capital may also be observed in the more than $30 trillion in tax havens in the US, Cayman Islands, Bermuda, and so forth. Circling the globe ("hot money"), rapidly entering/leaving nations, inevitably promoting economic instability.

After a six-year economic slump for the EU and its euro zone, the European Commission projects a 1.2 percent GDP growth fro the euro zone in 2014 and 1.8 percent for 2015; for the EU, 1.4 percent and 2 percent in 2015. Even Greek GDP growth in 2014 will increase 0.6 percent, but Greek unemployment rate will still hover at 26 percent. Spain's GDP will increase 1 percent in 2014, but unemployment will still be at 26 percent. The EU jobless rate in 2014 will remain at 12 percent, dipping slightly to 11.7 percent in 2015. Technological advances allow for higher economic growth, but continued high unemployment.[13]

Regarding global wealth, the richest 1 percent have 40 percent, according to Oxfam International. Furthermore, 85 of the world's

1,682 billionaires (US, 417) in 2013 have as much wealth as the world's lower population half. Also, there are 167,000 households in the world worth more than $30 million in 2013. They are the world's economic, social, and political masters. [14]

An interesting article on worldwide income/wealth distribution growth, including the US from 1986-88 to 2008, by Eduardo Porter, a New York Times economic columnist, and employing statistics by Branks Miloanovic, formerly of the World Bank and now at the Graduate Center of City University of New York, and observations by Damon Silvers, policy direction, AFC-CIO, as well as the International Labor Organization (ILO), reveals the following:

Because of free trade and large investments by TNCs of wealthy nations like the US and Japan in poor/developing nations like China, 1) workers' salaries in the latter have risen while those in the former have remained stagnant (in China, for instance, rising wages have lifted a half billion of its billion from abject to mere poverty); 2), worldwide income differentials between rich and poor nations have lessened – still considerable; 3), overall, as in the EU, US, and China, wages lag behind productivity gains, causing workers' income share of GDP to fall, increasing income/wealth inequality between workers and the wealthy.

These observations have been buttressed by an exhaustive study by Thomas Piketty, a French economist and scientist, and his many collaborators in Capital in the Twenty First Century.

Its basic assertion is that wealth was six times more than national income before 1914 (World War I began), slipping to two times up to the mid-1970s (Great Depression, World War II, rise of communism/ socialism), but since then wealth has resumed its earlier six to one advantage worldwide.

With the fall of Communism in the Soviet Union, rise of capitalism in communist China, and the weakening of labor/socialism in the west, the capitalist class now rules a world of increasing income/ wealth for them and correspondingly less income/wealth for the working class, a trend which will continue unless higher income and also wealth taxes by working class political action is imposed on capitalists. I, along with Piketty, believe that this tax reform in the near term in unlikely.[15]

Finally, ending this study, I return to Keynesianism covered in Chapter 6, an attempt to save capitalism by preventing severe economic downturns and concern for workers through expanded social services. In essence, it is a humane capitalism, while ensuring capital's hegemony over labor.

Keynesianism in the west reached its apogee in Western Europe after World War II, as in Britain, France, Germany, Scandinavia, Italy, under the impress of social-welfares Catholic/liberal secular, Communist and social democratic parties, allowing for expanded social welfare, some nationalization of banking/industry and government intervention to soften economic downturns.

In the US, Keynesianism, under the Democratic Party, saw government intervene to nullify the ravages of economic downturns and expand social welfare. It was less successful than in Western Europe.

Why? Because the US working class has usually been fractured by successive immigrant waves until the present, divided by ethnicity/religion, and the curse of slavery and Jim Crow, as evidenced by the 11 million undocumented Hispanic immigrants alone. These realities have resulted recently in a conservative white blue-collar workforce, two-thirds voting for the Republican John McCain in 2008.

Although EU economic policies, like free trade, free labor movement and keeping annual budget deficits as close to 3 percent, have led to lower wages and higher unemployment for workers, social democratic parties have difficulty to pursue Keynesianism to overcome these obstacles, like initiating government job programs or more nationalizations because of capital flight increasing economic downturn. So far the working class has accepted increasing economic misery, but I suspect that before long it will fight back, leading to a resurgent socialism. My socialist solution? Leave the EU/euro zone and return to unfettered national planning.

The weakening of the socialist project in the EU has led to the rise of xenophobic right-wing nationalist parties, like the National Front in France whose platform is against IMF, EU, immigrants, especially Muslims, and favors economic protectionism, re-industrialization, more social welfare, but only for French citizens. In a society of high unemployment/low economic growth, these policies should have broad popular support, especially among workers. But up to now this party is still politically weak.[16]

Despite economic downturn and economic austerity in the EU, labor/socialist parties have succeeded in most instances to protect extensive social welfarism – universal healthcare, four-six week vacations, generous maternity leaves, adequate disability pensions, lower old-age retirements, and so forth than its US counterparts.

In the US, the Keynesian compromise has been hampered by the rise of conservatism, beginning with the Reagan Revolution in the 1980s.

This is starkly indicated in a Social Progress Index formulated by Michael E. Porter, a Republican business school professor at Harvard, and collaborators in a two-year study measuring "livability."

They observed a plethora of social-welfare and other programs, as in education, heath, ecological progress, tax policies, social mobility, personal safety, speech, press, religious freedoms, and so forth in 132 nations. Overall, the US is ranked number 16, behind European democracies like Norway, Sweden, Denmark, Switzerland, Netherlands, France, Germany, and Britain. Specifically, the Index measured the US as no. 39 in basic education, 70 in health, 34 in access to water and sanitation, 31 in personal safety, and 69 in protection the ecostructure, among others.

In comparing, for instance, economic progress as it relates to its social counterpart between the US and France in the 1975-2006 period, the Index reported that economically the US did better than France, but that "99 percent of the French population actually enjoyed more gains…than 99 percent of the American population." [17]

On balance, in the last 30 or so years, capitalist parties have considerably weakened the Keynesian compromise especially in the US and EU. With the fall of the Soviet Union and rise of capitalism in China, capital now has a definite advantage over labor.

In the meantime, the bourgeoisie are enjoying the largest part of the consumerist cornucopia in the US; the richest 5 percent consume about 40 percent of it, the richest 10 percent, 60 percent.[18]

Notes

1) On general economic and other developments discussed in this section, see Eric Hobsbawm, *The Age of Extremes: A History of the World, 1914-1991* (New York: Pantheon Books, 1995), pp. 257-319. For an excellent economic history of this period focusing on the U.S., Germany, and Japan, see Robert Brenner, "The Economics of Turbulence: A Special Report on the World Economy, 1950-98," *New Left Review*, no. 229, May/June, 1998, entire issue.

2) On economic concentration see Adolf A. Berle Jr. and Gardiner C. Means, *The Modern Corporation and Private Property*, rev. ed. (New York: Harcourt, Brace, and World, 1968), pp. ix-x and 18-46 (first published in 1933). William Dugger, *Corporate Hegemony* (New York: Greenwood Press, 1989), p. 17. Steven Brouwer, *Sharing the Pie: A Disturbing Picture of the U.S. Economy* (Carlisle, PA: Big Picture Books, 1991), pp. 14-16. Walter Adams and James B. Brock, *Dangerous Pursuits: Mergers and Acquisitions in the Age of Wall Street* (New York: Pantheon Books, 1989), pp. 12-15 ff. David C. Korten, *When Corporations Rule the World* (West Hartford, CT: Kumarian Press, 1995), pp. 221 ff. On bank concentration, see Consumer Reports, March 1996, pp. 10-15. On public utilities concentration, see *The New York Times*, Dec. 18, 2000, p. C6. On interlocking directorates, see G. William Domhoff, *Who Rules America? Power and Politics in the Year 2000*, 3rd ed. (Mountain View, CA: Mayfield Publishing CO., 1998), pp. 33-49. On the Pujo Subcommittee, see Arthur S. Link, *American Epoch: A History of the United States Since the 1890's* (New York: Alfred A. Knopf, 1958), pp. 51-52. On increasing concentration of capital in the retail and other fields mentioned and greater squeeze by big business on small

business, see *New York Times*, Sept. 14, 2000, p. A27, and *Akron Beacon Journal*, July 16, 2000, pp. A1 and A10.

3) On transnational corporations, see William Greider, *One World Ready or Not: The Manic Logic of Global Capitalism* (New York: Simon and Schuster, 1997), pp. 211-22 on the leading transnational corporations. Richard J. Barnet and John Cavanaugh, *Global Dreams: Imperial Corporations and the New World Order* (New York: Simon and Schuster, 1994), pp. 385-402 on the globalization of trading stocks, bonds, and currency, with scant or non-existent government supervision, resulting in widespread tax-fraud and evasion. Edward S. Herman, "Globalization in Question," *Z Magazine*, April 1997, pp. 8-11, affirms that under present arrangements, any single national control of international money movements is impossible because of international capital flight. On the six trillion dollars in off-shore tax havens, see Alan Cowell and Edmund L. Andrews, "Undercurrents at a Safe Harbor," *New York Times*, Sept. 24, 1999, pp. C1 and C14. On holdings by Americans abroad and foreigners in the U.S., see Dough Henwood, *Wall Street: How it Works and for Whom* (London: Verso, 1998), p. 61. On foreign stock ownership, for instance, in France, see Craig R. Whitney, "Anxious French Mutter as U.S. Envoy Tries to Sell Globalism," *New York Times*, Dec. 2, 1999, p. A10. On U.S. bonds and stock owned by foreigners, see Robert Brenner, "The Boom and the Bubble," *New Left Review*, Nov./Dec., 2000, pp. 28-29. On the greater internationalization of capital in the late 19th century than in the 1990s, see Nicholas Kristoff, "At This Rate, We'll Be Global in Anther Hundred Years," *New York Times*, "Week in Review" section, May 23, 1999, p. 5. On privatization, see *New York Times*, July 30, 1998, pp. C1 and C4; Jan. 16, 2001, pp. C1 and C8, March 13, 2002, p. A3. *Economist*, Sept. 14, 2002, pp. 3 ff. Centre for Co-Operation with the Economies in Transition, *Mass Privatization: An Initial Assessment* (Organization for Economic Co-Operation and Development, 1995).

4) On the Savings and Loan debacle, see Jeff Gerth, "A Blend of Tragedy and Farce," *New York Times*, July 3, 1990, pp. C1 and C6; Jerry Fricker and Stephen Pizzo, *Inside Job: The Looting of America's Savings and Loans* (New York McGrawHill, 1989). On Soros, see Connie Brück, "The World According to Soros," *New Yorker*, Jan. 23, 1995. On hedge funds, see John Cassidy, *New Yorker*, July 5, 1999. On the energy crisis and collapse of Enron, see Larry Everest, "California's Energy Crisis," *Z Magazine*, April 2001, pp. 33-39. Robin Blackburn, "The Enron Scandal and the Pension Crisis," *New Left Review*, no. 14, Mar/Apr 2002, pp. 26-51. On the WorldCom debacle, see Daniel Kadlec, "WORLDCOM," *Time*, July 8, 2002, pp. 20-26. On these and other corporate implosions and shenanigans in 2002, the events are well covered in the *New York Times*.

5) On government giveaways to corporations, see Common Cause Newsletter, March 1996. Robert L. Borosage, "The Politics of Austerity," *Nation*, May 27, 1996, pp. 22-24. Noam Chomsky, "Power in the Global Arena," *New Left Review*, no., 230, July/August 1998, pp. 13-18. Neil deMause, "To the Highest Bidder," *In These Times,* May 31, 1998, pp. 11-13.

6) For an overview of the East Asian crisis in the late 1990s, see Robert Wade and Frank Veneroso, "The Asian Crisis: The High Debt Model Versus the Wall Street-Treasury-IMF Complex," *New Left Review*, no. 228, March/April 1998, pp. 4-23. Also, see the article in *New York Times*, June 12, 1998, pp. A1 and C6 on the precipitous economic fall of East Asia in the late 1990s. On Japan, see Brenner, "The Economics of Turbulence," in *New Left Review*, May/June 1998; and articles in *New York Times*, March 1, 2000, p. W1 and March 12, 2000, pp. A1 and A5, and Paul Krugman's column of Aug. 31, 2000. These are only a small fraction of the many articles in *New York Times* on East Asia and Japan.

7) Jeremy Rifkin, *The End of Work: The Decline of the Global Labor Force and the Dawn of the Post-Market Era* (New York: G.P. Putam's Sons, 1995), pp. 3-58, for instance; one section of

a most valuable book which has significantly influenced the writing of this section. Rifkin, following Engels, avers that technological advances under capitalism are making ever more workers superfluous. Also, see William Wolman and Anne Colamosca, *The Judas Economy: The Triumph of Capital and the Betrayal of Work* (Reading, MA: Addison-Wesley, 1997), a work with a plethora of useful statistics. Again, *New York Times, Nation, Z Magazine, New Yorker,* and *New Left Review* have provided most of the material for this reporting.

8) On income and wages: *Nation*, July 23/30, 2001, p. 26. *Akron Beacon Journal*, April 23, 1996, p. A8 and April 25, 1996, p. C3. Alexander Cockburn column, *Nation*, Nov. 17, 1997, p. 9. R.C. Longworth (*Chicago Tribune*), "Those Fabulously Wealthy CEOs...," *Akron Beacon Journal*, Sept. 11, 2000, p. A11. Holly Sklar, "Booming Economic Inequality, Falling Voter Turnout," *Z Magazine*, March 2000, pp. 37 ff. Ray Boshara, "The $6,000 Solution," *Atlantic Monthly,* Jan/Feb., 2003, p. 94. On Wealth: Holly Sklar et al., "The Growing Wealth Gap," *Z Magazine*, May 1999, pp. 47-52. Doug Henwood, "The Nation Indicators," *Nation*, April 9, 2001, p. 8. *Economist*, 30 May, 1998. *Nation*. Oct. 20, 1997, p. 7. *Z Magazine*, Dec. 1998, p. 47.

9) On unemployment, I have utilized sources from newspapers and magazines. For instance, see Robert J. Samuelson, "Are Workers Disposable?" *Newsweek*, Feb. 12, 1996. P. 47. *New York Times*, May 9, 1999, p. WK5. Ray Marshall, "A World Out of Work," *Akron Beacon Journal*, Oct. 15, 1995, pp. G1 and G3. Donna St. George, "Families Cope," *Akron Beacon Journal*, Jan. 28, 1996, PP. A1 and A4.

10) The statistics in the section concerning hope for a socialist future are culled from the *New York Times, Nation, Z Magazine, U.S. News and World Report.*

11) Herman Daly and John B. Cobb Jr., *For the Common Good: Rediscovering the Economy Toward Community, the Environment and a Sustainable Future* (Boston: Beacon Press, 1989), pp. 1-84 and 401-54. Ted Halstead and Clifford Cobb, "The Need

for New Measurements of Progress," in *The Case Against the Global Economy*, eds. Jerry Mander and Edward Goldsmith (San Francisco: Sierra Club Books, 1996), pp. 197-206.

12) On the US Great Recession, see Jack Rasmus, Epic Recession: Prelude to Global Depression (London: Pluto Press, 2010). Don Peck, Pinched (New York: Crown Publishers, 2011). Joseph E. Stiglitz, Freefall (New York: Monthly Review Press, 2012). Many The New York Times articles, abbreviated hereafter as NYT. On US corporate economic concentration, see John Bellamy Foster, "Monopoly and Competition in Twenty-First Century Capitalism," Monthly Review, vol. 62, no. 11, April 2011, pp. 1-39. On income/wealth inequality, Robert Reich, "Inequality in America," The Nation, July 19/26, 2010, pp. 13-15. Steven Rattner, "The Rich Get Even Richer," NYT, March 26, 2012 p. A21. Annie Lowrey, "Top 10 % Took Half of U.S. Income in 2012," NYT, Sept. 11, 2013, pp. B1 and B3. Gary B. Nash et al., The American People, 3rd ed. (New York: HarperCollins, 1994), pp. 1053-58. On capitalist fraud, NYT, June 6, 2012, p. B4. Matt Taibbi, "The People vs Goldman Sachs," Rolling Stone, May 26, 2011, pp. 41-46. On corporate profits, Jack Rasmus, "The Great Corporate Tax Shift," Z Magazine, Dec. 2013, p. 36. On rising business income, Paul Krugman, "Wealth Over Work," NYT, March 24, 2014, p. A19. On a probable hereditary U.S. wealth aristocracy, Paul Krugman, "America's Taxation Tradition," NYT, March 28, 2014, p. A23. On higher productivity/stagnant workers' wages in the US since the 1970s, Steven Greenhouse, The Big Squeeze: Tough Times for the American Worker (New York: Anchor Books, 2009), p. 39, 2011, The New York Times Almanac, ed. John W. Wright (New York: Penguin Books, 2010), p. 349.

13) On unemployment/economic downturn: Michael Schuman, "The Jobless Generation," Time, April 16, 2012, pp. 46-47. Jack Ewing, "For Tepid European Economy, A Lost Decade Looms," NYT, Aug. 17, 2012, pp. B1 and B5. Julia Werdigier, "Jobless Rate... Forecasts," NYT, July 17, 2013, p. B2. On growing socioeconomic

inequality in the EU, see Eduardo Porter, "American Labor Policy is Spreading in Europe," NYT, Dec. 4, 2013, pp. B1 and B4. Matthew Schofield, "Richest 85 have as much as half the world," ABJ, Jan. 21, 2014, p. A5. On economic growth in the EU for 2014-15, Associated Press, "Expectations For Growth in Europe Are Increased," NYT, Feb. 26, p. B3. On up to $34 trillion in tax havens worldwide, according to Citizens for Tax Justice, see Thom Hartmann, Free Speech TV, July 19, 20, 2012. On weakening EU social welfare, see Asbiorn, "European Labor," Monthly Review, vol 65, Jan. 2014, pp. 36-57. On recent EU unemployment/new jobs, Liz Alderman, "Europe's Weak Recovery Snubs Jobless," NYT, April 9, 2014, pp. B1 and B4. Eduardo Porter, "A Relentless Widening of Disparity in Wealth," NYT, March 12, 2014, pp. B1 and B4. On income disparity of top 10 percent/bottom 10 percent, Eduardo Porter, "A Search...inequality," NYT, March 26, 2014, pp. B1 and B8. On loss of worker income because of technological innovation, see Eduardo Porter, "Tech Leaps, Job Losses and Rising Inequality," NYT, April 16, 2014, pp. B1 and B8.

14) On the world's rich: Corinne Grinapol, "How the Rich Get Richer," The Nation, Feb. 17, 2014, p. 8. On the $30 billion Wealth Group, Julie Creswell, "If the Very Rich Were Like Wine..." Vintage," NYT, March 5, 2014, p. B3. Matthew Schofield, "Richest 85 have as much as half of world," Akron Beacon Journal, Jan. 21, 2014, p. A5.

15) Eduardo Porter, "A Global Boom, But Only for Some," NYT, March 19, 2014, pp. B1 and B13. Interview of Thomas Piketty on Capital in the Twenty-First Century in New Left Review, "Dynamics of Inequality," no. 85, Jan./Feb/ 2014, pp. 103-116. These studies confirm Marx's view that capitalism, unless prevented by the working class, inexorably leads to more capitalist income/wealth at the expense of workers.

16) On the French right-wing National Front, see Cecile Alduy, "The Battle for the Soul of France," The Nation, March 24, 2014, pp. 11-21.

17) On US lagging behind advanced EU and other Western European Nations, see Nicholas Kristoff, "We're Not No.1! We're Not No. 1!" <u>NYT,</u> April 3, 2014, p. A 25.
18) On consumer consumption by the US wealthy, see "Even Marked Up Luxury Goods Fly Off the Shelves," <u>NYT,</u> Aug. 4, 2011, p. A3. Jack Rasmus, <u>Z Magazine</u>, July/August, 2011, p. 29, <u>NYT,</u> Feb. 3, 2014, pp. A1 and A11.

Chapter Fourteen: American/Western European Socialism

As a revolutionary nation founded by the American Revolution of 1776-83 within a frontier environment, in which land was inexpensive and allowed for rampant socioeconomic equality, the U.S. invited many communistic religious and secular utopias, especially in the 19th century.

A noteworthy utopia was New Harmony in Indiana, founded by utopian socialist Robert Owen in 1825. Another similar society was Brook Farm, near Boston, which remained in existence from 1841-47. Brook Farm's identity and structure closely mirrored Transcendentalism, which was the primary religious-philosophical current among the New England intelligentsia in the mid-19th; its members included the novelist Nathaniel Hawthorne and editor/writer Charles A. Dana. Visitors included Ralph Waldo Emerson and Horace Greeley. Other well-known utopias included the Shakers, Oneida, and the Icariens founded by Etienne Cabet.

It was Emerson, America's great sage of the 19th century, who proclaimed the essentials of socialism: "The union of labor and capital in the same individual through the cooperative principal." In connection with socialism are those three well-known utopian novels: Looking Backward (1888) by Edward Bellany; A Traveler from Altruria (1894) and Through the Eye of the Needle (1907) by William Dean Howell, an outstanding novelist and editor of periodicals, especially Harper's Monthly, 1900-1920. The first novel was very popular: 162 clubs carried its socialist message under the rubric of "nationalism."

In the American radical-socialist tradition, a principal father is the indomitable Radical Republican Thomas Paine, whose 1776 revolutionary pamphlet Common Sense helped spark the American Revolution. He was an arch-democrat, representatives served only short terms. An enemy of kings and aristocracy, he promoted state social services for the unemployed, universal education to age 14, maternity benefits, old age pensions and a graduated income tax. Importantly, he asserted in a socialist vein that wealth beyond personal individual effort "is derived to him by living in society." Or, great wealth comes from using/exploiting others. Nevertheless, he accepted some socioeconomic inequality.

An outstanding early American socialist pioneer was Wendell Phillips, a wealthy Harvard graduate. In his youth, he was an ardent abolitionist and insisted that government provide emancipated blacks with land to guarantee their new freedom. After the Civil War, he became involved in socialist activity. His good society included cooperatives run by workers, equalization of property and education, and ending the invidious wage system pitting workers against one another. His socialist ideas were similar to Marx's. He was an ardent supporter of the 1871 Paris Commune. He ran unsuccessfully for governor of Massachusetts in 1870 on the Labor and Prohibition Party ticket. His socialist newspaper was The National Standard.

The most important socialist after Eugene V. Debs in U.S. history is Daniel De Leon, a Marxist after 1890 who led the Socialist Labor Party (SLP), founded in 1877; in 1898, it had a membership of 80,000. De Leon attended European universities and was a graduate of Columbia University's Law School. He also led the Socialist Trade and Labor Alliance, the industrial union arm of the SLP, and was one of the founders of the syndicalist Industrial Workers of the World (IWW) in 1905.

Debs is the most well-known American socialist. A worker by the age of 15, he quickly engaged in union activity. He became president of the American Railway Union, leading it in the successful strike against the Great Northern Railroad; was involved in the 1894 Pullman Strike; was imprisoned and, while incarcerated, read Marx and became, ultimately, a socialist. He was one of the founders of the Social Democratic Party in 1898, which became the Socialist Party (SP) in 1900.

Running on the SP ticket for the U.S. presidency in 1900, 1904, 1908, and in 1912, Debs received 900,000 votes, or 6 percent, of the total, the highest percentage received by a socialist. He opposed U.S. entry into World War I; was tried under the 1917 Espionage

Act and jailed, but later pardoned by President Warren Harding in 1921. He was also one of the founders of IWW in 1905, but he soon left it because he opposed its direct action tactics. He advocated socialism to be run from the bottom up, for participatory-democracy; not surprisingly, he was a fierce opponent of bureaucracy.

By circa 1914, the SP had over 40,000 dues-paying members, 31 mayors, and 1,200 lesser offices in 340 towns and cities; also two members in the U.S. House of Representatives, Victor Berger from Milwaukee and Meyer London from New York City. In the 1912 AFL Convention, the socialist Hayes Max received a third of the vote for the presidency running against Samuel Gompers. A socialist periodical, The Appeal to Reason, had a circulation of 300,000.

An important socialist periodical, The Masses, 1911-17, with a circulation of up to 20,000, was read by socialist intellectuals, activists, writers, and so forth. It featured articles on politics, art, literature and science. After 1912, it shed its democratic socialist stance for revolutionary action against capitalism. It was barred from U.S. mails when the U.S. entered World War I in April 1917, and its editor Max Eastman and staff were tried under the October 1917 Espionage Act. The case was eventually dropped by the government.

The Masses eventually continued as The Liberator, 1918-23. Among its contributors were Eastman, John Dos Passos, Carl Sandburg, John Reed, Mabel Dodge (from the rich Dodge auto family), Arturo Giovannitti, Upton Sinclair, Edmund Wilson, Bertrand Russell, George Bernard Shaw, Amy Lowell, Floyd Dell, Maxim Gorky, Roger Baldwin, and Stuart Chase.

"Gas and Water" Socialism, the municipal ownership of utilities, natural gas, street cars, water works, etc., was advocated in the 1890s and early 1900s in Toledo by Samuel Jones and in Cleveland, Ohio, by Newton Baker. Baker was successful in socializing water works, the Cleveland Transportation System and Muni Light, which provided electric power.

We should also note the importance of socialism in the early 20th century among reformers, intellectuals, and writers of the Intercollegiate Socialist Society (ICSS), founded in 1905 by the novelist Upton Sinclair, and whose first president was the novelist Jack London. It included such luminaries as Paul H. Douglas (later a U.S. senator from Illinois), Walter Lippmann, Randolph Bourne, Norman Thomas, A.J. Muste, Florence Kelley, Stuart Chase, Vida Scudder, Roger Baldwin, John Dewey, Selig Perlman, and John Sprago, among others.

The ICSS favored evolutionary democratic socialism, of public ownership of large industry/banks but allowing for privately owned small business. After World War I in 1918, the ICSS called itself the League for Industrial Democracy.

In addition to the preceding socialists (some later became progressives), others included outstanding economists, novelists, dramatists, and composers like Veblen, Ernest Hemingway, Maxwell Anderson, Clifford Odets, Eugene O'Neil, Arthur Miller, Aaron Copeland, and Leonard Bernstein, among many others.

American Socialism suffered a heavy blow with U.S. entry into World War I, with Germany as the primary enemy. This led to much discrimination against German-Americans, many of whom were socialists and viewed as un-American. Furthermore, Russian Communism was portrayed as dictatorial, against democracy and also un-American.

After the death of Debs in 1926, Norman Thomas assumed leadership of the SP. A graduate of Princeton Union Theological Seminary, he was a Presbyterian minister until 1931. He ran as U.S. president on the SP ticket in 1928, 1932, garnering 880,000 votes, the highest he ever received. A democratic socialist like Debs, he opposed communism, fascism and American capitalism.

In the 1930s, known primarily as the Great Depression period, the SP did stellar work organizing, establishing mass unemployment councils, and fighting for black equality.

The successful Russian Communist revolution in 1917 and a series of strike actions by American workers in 1919 brought about the First Red Scare of 1919-20. It was led by the Democratic Attorney General A. Mitchell Palmer in the Palmer Raids, which saw "Reds" everywhere, arresting more than 5.000 radicals and deporting 600 aliens. It aided the conservatism of the 1920s.

The 1917 Communist Revolution in Russia eventually led to the formation of the American Communism Party (CP). It was closely aligned to the Soviet Union, basically worker-centered, intimately involved in union activity, especially in the Congress of Industrial Organizations (CIO) with its membership of unskilled and semi-skilled industrial workers. In fact, during the Second Red Scare, the CIO in 1949 expelled all 11 of its CP-dominated unions.

The heyday of the CP was during the Great Depression of the 1930s as it was involved in union organization (half of its membership did so). It was also active in leading black sharecroppers in the South, forming councils for the unemployed and evicted tenants and fighting for improved government relief which resulted in large mass demonstrations in New York City, Chicago, Detroit and Chicago, inevitably battling police. It also aided Mexican farm workers in California and was instrumental in fighting for black civil rights and economic equality, even supporting a separate black nation in a caste-dominated south. The outstanding black leader, W.E.B DuBois, was a communist, and the black actor, singer, and activist Paul Roheson was closely aligned with the CP.

The CP attracted many intellectuals, writers and artists to its ranks as evidenced by its journal, The New Masses. Also, many immigrant workers were either members of sympathetic to the CP's workerism. It fared poorly, however, in presidential elections: William Z. Foster in 1932 garnered about 100,000 votes, the most ever by a CP candidate. CP membership was never large: 75,000 in 1938, 80,000 in 1947 and 17,500 in 1985. CP leaders included Earl Browder Foster, Jay Lovestone, and Gus Hall.

As already noted, the CP played a major role in the 1930s; its influence among the masses should not be underestimated.

American socialism in the 1920s was involved in perhaps the most noted criminal case in American history: Bartolomeo Vanzetti and Nicola Sacco – known as Sacco and Vanzetti. These two Italian immigrant and anarchists were accused of killing two men in a robbery in May 1920 near Boston. They were soon tried, convicted, and sentenced to death for not only the murders but for their anarchist beliefs and the prevalent anti-foreign sentiment that was so prevalent and influential in the 1920s.

American liberals/socialists, including many in the artistic and literary community, fought to exonerate them. Upton Sinclair's novel Boston and Maxwell Anderson's plays, Gods of the Lightning and Winterest, addressed the case and its aftermath; the latter work, which takes place after the executions on August 22, 1927, had Dante Sacco as the main protagonist. Edna St. Vincent Millay, the brilliant poet, also wrote a sonnet for Sacco-Vanzetti. Exactly 50 years after the executions, Michael Dukakis, the Democratic governor of Massachusetts and presidential nominee, exonerated them, declaring their innocence.

The apogee of American social democracy was the 1944, second Bill of Rights Speech of FDR advocating for all the right's a job, home ownership and a comfortable retirement.

With the extension of Communism to Eastern Europe and China soon after World War II, the Second Red Scare of 1945-54 occurred against American Communism. It include the earlier Smith Act (1940) and the McCarran Internal Security Act (1950), spy cases of Julius and Ethen Rosenberg (both executed), and Alger Hiss, a prominent New Dealer and assistant secretary of state. Then there were the Truman Loyalty Program, the "Hollywood Ten" trial of alleged Communist writers, eleven Communist leaders tried and imprisoned, 2,700 Communists losing their jobs and blacklisted, and the CP losing legal status until the 1960s. Then, the Joseph R. McCarthy hearings occurred in the early 1950s in the Senate in which Communists were said to be in and hold offices within the United States government. McCarthy would overreach and discredit himself.

The two Red Scares were basically orchestrated by the conservative corporate elite, or groups of hysterically anti-communist members that smeared not only communists but also socialists and progressives who wished to reform American society. The Communist threat was a fiction, a mirage like the McCarthy hearings.

While the Second Red Scare was developing in the 1948 elections, the CP supported Henry A. Wallace, FDR's Vice President in 1940-44. Wallace was in the extreme left of the Democratic Party espousing peaceful co-existence with the Soviet Union, which was spreading Communism to Eastern Europe, ending Jim Crow in the south, and expanding New Deal reforms to include universal healthcare, a guaranteed government job program and so on.

To the immediate right of Wallace's Progressive Party was the Americans for Democratic Action (ADA) whose pro-labor and pro-Civil Rights platforms and aims worked for black equality. Its members included Eleanor Roosevelt and Hubert Humphrey, among others. They accused Wallace of being a communist dupe. Wallace received 1.15 million votes, mostly in New York State.

The ADA, socialists and other progressives did not wish to cooperate with an expansionist Soviet Communism, which was seen as anti-democratic and totalitarian. This view took precedence over Communist destruction of the nobility and capitalists in Czarist Russia and Eastern Europe and establishment of a society of general socioeconomic equality and extensive social welfare programs.

The rise of the new left in the Students for a Democratic Society (SDS) in the 1960s occurred as living standards were rising – part of the post-war economic expansion in the midst of the Civil/Voting Rights Acts granting full citizenship to blacks in the south, all while the unpopular war in Vietnam raged. Also, women and other oppressed groups were mounting movements for liberation, a topic to be covered later.

Most SDS members were white middle-class students having a broadly socialist orientation. At its height in 1970, the SDS had about 100,000 members in more than a hundred colleges. It evolved from the older student league for Industrial Democracy, a democratic socialist organization opposed to the authoritarian communism of the Soviet Union.

SDS aims are encapsulated in the "Port Huron Statement" (1962), written by Tom Hayden, and "America and the New Era" (1963). They include ending materialistic, alienating, war-obsessed and authoritarian capitalism for a decentralized socialist society based on participatory democracy which would eliminate sexism, racism, and discrimination against LGBTs. Furthermore, it would end the manual-mental labor dichotomy with integrated labor combining both as quickly as possible. The end result would be a society of educated people living in a milieu of general socioeconomic, cultural, and political equality. Also, it called for a quick end to the Vietnam War.

The student movement against the Vietnam War began in earnest with "Free Speech" actions at the University of California, Berkeley, in which students occupied the administration building and fought police. As many as 700 students were arrested, leading to a student strike.

In April 1968 at Columbia University in New York, SDS-inspired students occupied the library and other buildings to protest the Vietnam War and the university's unsatisfactory relations with the nearby black community. After skirmishes with police, 800 students were arrested.

Another signal event against the war occurred at the August 1968 Democratic Convention in Chicago, where pro-war Hubert Humphrey was elected as its presidential candidate. Ten thousand SDS/leftist youth students converged on the convention, fighting 10,000 police, 6,000 National Guardsmen, and 1,000 FBI agents in a bloody melee. Hundreds were injured and arrested. A government report characterized the event as a "police riot" because police attacked not only students but bystanders.

The strong SDS chapter at Kent State University at Kent, Ohio, protested President Nixon's widening the war in Southeast Asia by invading Cambodia. The protest resulted in four students killed at the university and nine wounded when members of the Ohio National Guard opened fire on a student demonstration on the campus on May 4, 1970. A few days later at Jackson State (a black college) in Mississippi, two black students were also killed in dormitories by police bullets.

These events triggered the greatest mass student strike in American university history: the closing of almost all universities by millions of students for months to protest the slaughter of students and the continuing Vietnam War. In Europe, French university students began the 1968 May events, whose aim was a new socialist-anarchist society.

In a 1969 SDS split, its left wing – the Weathermen, soon Weatherpeople – embarked on direct action to topple capitalism. Led by Bill Ayers, Mark Rudd and Bernadine Dohrn, its principal event was in "Days of Rage" in Chicago on Oct. 8, 1969, when 600 of them charged police, resulting in hundreds of injured but no deaths.

The cops won.

By 1970, the Weatherpeople had launched 423 attacks against police stations and 101 against military bases, with bombings also in Seattle and Madison, Wisconsin. These actions are similar to anarchist "propaganda by Deed," to waken the masses against capitalism.

A Fortune poll in 1968 indicated that 20 percent of college students were favorable to the New Left.

The Black Liberation struggle in the 1960s, especially in the South, witnessed much violence: 37 churches were bombed, resulting in the deaths of many blacks, including children, thousands beaten and arrested. Also there were black city riots in New York, Detroit, Cleveland, and Los Angelas, among others.

These are some of African American organizations that participated in the struggle for justice and equality in the turbulent 1960s: the Southern Christian Leadership Conference of clergy whose chief spokesperson was Dr. Martin Luther King Jr., a democratic socialist; the National Association for the Advancement of Colored People; the Congress of Racial Equality composed of blacks and whites; the leftist student nonviolent coordinating committee which worked closely with SDS; the CP whose member Angela Davis was very active.

There was also the Nation of Islam and the indomitable Malcolm X who left it, and the Hispanic fight for justice led by Cesar Chavez of the Farm Workers Union, among others.

Native Americans, too, fought for greater rights under the banner of the American Indian Movement led by Dennis Banks and George Mitchell. By the end of the 1970s, Indians won many lawsuits to recover lands under earlier treaty rights. It was also in the 1960s that Gay, Lesbian, Bisexual, Transgendered (LGBT) liberation began in earnest.

Today, SDS and many of the other groups mentioned continue the struggle for more equality and justice. The Occupy Wall Street movement, which erupted in September 2011 with sit-ins in many cities. Its views and aims were socialist, and its message drove home the shibboleth of "We are the 99 percent."

Closely allied to the New Left is the counterculture "hippie" movement of mostly young people who have dropped out of the capitalist rat races. They live a life of personal liberation/nonconformity in dress, sexual behavior and values, and expression; they live outside of marriage, live in communes, and are immersed in music, art and illegal drugs.

Today, the large center-left is comprised of the Democratic Party House Congressional Democratic Caucus of 80 or so members whose electorate is largely from large cities, including blacks and Hispanics. It supports free state college tuition, a government job program, raising taxes on the rich and corporations, universal healthcare, increased social welfare benefits for the poor, ending endless wars, and clean energy.

The Green Party has a platform very similar to that of the House Congressional Democratic Caucus but focuses on the importance of clean energy. It has elected many local officials. The American Democratic Socialists and Communists still continue as do various anarchist groups. While their numbers are small, their activity cannot be underestimated.

Why has Socialism up to now been politically weak in America? First, slavery and Jim Crow have deeply divided black and white voters. In the South today, Republicans are the white party, blacks the Democratic Party. The racism of white workers allows for much conservative politics. Second, sharp class/status divisions among skilled and unskilled workers related to successive immigrant waves, compounded by ethnic and religious divisions, have also weakened working class unity. Third, relatively high wages/living standards compared to other nations, allowing until recently for some upward social mobility. Fourth, labor reforms via the ballot have led to less radicalism. Fifth, capitalist control of the media extolls capitalism while neglecting labor/socialist activity. Sixth, the class power flow in capitalist societies in which the subaltern workers wish to improve their socioeconomic circumstances, forces them to admire/emulate their class superiors as much as possible, again dampening their class struggle against capital. And of course, declining social mobility in the present age exacerbates the class struggle.

To be sure, underneath the American shibboleths of "democracy," "freedom," and "free enterprise," there is the authoritarianism/ totalitarianism of the economic whip of socioeconomic inequality at whose apex is a small capitalist oligarchy.

Today, interest in socialism in American society is widespread, especially in the age 18-29 category, a group that either favors socialism over capitalism or are equally divided over the merits of capitalism and socialism in opinion polls, as noted in: NYT, Jan. 19, 2012, p. A21; and The Nation, June 11, 2012, pp. 18-22.

Western European Socialism, 1945 to the Present

The Industrial Revolution brought about a large working class in Western Europe by the last quarter of the nineteenth century, with many workers embracing socialism beliefs and aims.

By 1914, labor/socialist parties in Western Europe were important politically, led by the German Social Democratic Party which garnered more than a third of the vote in 1912. In France, at this time, socialists received a sixth of the vote; in Italy, a fifth; Belgium, a third; Sweden, Norway, Denmark, a third; Finland, almost half; Britain, 7 percent.

World War I brought about the 1917 Bolshevik Revolution and the rise of Communism in the former Russian Empire – and, subsequently, the later existence of the Union of Soviet Socialist Republics, the first socialist nation in history.

In 1919-39, before the outbreak of World War II, there were labor/socialist governments in Britain under James Ramsay MacDonald; Leon Blum in France under a Popular Front of Socialists, Communists, and Radicals; in Germany, under Friedrich Ebert; in the 1936-39 Spanish Civil War, in a Popular Front of Socialists, Communists, liberals, and even anarchists briefly, under Francisco Largo Caballero. The rise of Fascism in Italy and Nazism in Germany in the 1920s and 30s destroyed the Socialist and Communist parties in these nations.

With the defeat of Germany and Italy during World War II, Socialism and its Communist variant advanced rapidly after 1945. Soviet occupation of Eastern Europe and Communist triumph in Yugoslavia saw Eastern Europe becoming Communist – Yugoslavia, Poland, East Germany (German Democratic Republic), Romania, Hungary, Bulgaria, and Albania.

The pain and destruction of World War II saw the rapid rise of labor, socialist and communist parties in almost every non-communist European nation. At this time, communist parties captured a third of the vote in Italy and a fourth in France.

In the communist states, all capitalist property was confiscated; in democratic Western Europe, the capitalist class was greatly weakened by extensive nationalizations, leading examples to be examined.

In France, Socialists, Communists, Catholic MRPs, and Gaullists untied to nationalize Renault automobiles, coal, gas/oil, electricity, merchant fleet, Bank of France (the central bank), four largest deposit banks, largest insurance companies, (armaments and railroads were nationalized in the 1930s).

In Britain, the labor government after assuming power, nationalized the Bank of England (the leading bank), iron and steel, coal, electricity, trucking, gas/oil, and railways.

The third Western European nation to embark on extensive nationalization at this time was Austria, while the fourth was Italy, first begun by the Fascists under Mussolini in the 1930s with the Institute for the Recovery of Industry, which, under the impress of Christian Democrats, communists and socialists, became the largest employer, controlling iron and steel, gas/oil, telephones, broadcasting, and a fourth of bank deposits.

To be sure, with the rise of conservative parties, denationalizations happened. In Britain, the conservatives de-nationalized the railways, coal, trucking, iron and steel. In France, although more nationalizations occurred under the socialist Mitterrand in the 1980s, subsequent right wing governments engaged in some de-nationalizations.

An important accomplishment of the Western European left and of the communists in the Soviet Union and Eastern Europe was extensive social-welfare legislation, which included universal healthcare, retirement, disability benefits, accident insurance, free college tuition (generally speaking), increasing the years of general education, and maternity leave benefits – all of which were significantly more extensive and generous than in the U.S.

Another significant gain for labor/socialism in Western Europe after World War II was worker/union participation in running industry. In this area, German socialism/labor is the most successful. Thus, almost half of the boards of directors of large German corporations represent unions (co-management). French, Swedish, and Norwegian unions are also involved in varying degree in management decisions.

Unions, or primary centers of working class power, are generally stronger and further to the left than those in the U.S. Some important ones are in the socialist left/communist camp. They include the Confederation Generale de Travail (CGT) in France; the Confederation of Trade Unions (GDB) in Germany; and the British National Union of Rail, Maritime and Transport Workers.

To be sure, the capitalist counteroffensive after 1980 destroyed the communism of the Soviet Union/Eastern Europe and weakened the strong social democracy in Western Europe. But viable social welfare systems are still in place, some nationalizations remain, and state regulation of the economy is extensive to protect a moribund capitalism. This allows European states to have large state economic sections of the GDP, generally in the 40-50 percent range, as opposed to the U.S.'s low 30 percent.

Why the drift to the political center-right in Western Europe? Although recently socialists rule in France and Italy, and are now again in Sweden; as a coalition government in Germany, and very strong in Serbia and Greece, among its other nations. Among the various factors involved include, for many workers, rather high living standards in a consumerist culture, fear of immigrants (mostly of Muslims), generous social welfare benefits, continuing status difference involved with wage differences, and continued bourgeois hegemony over them, led many of them to identify themselves with the capitalist status quo.

These conditions have led to increasing socioeconomic inequality because there are no EU capital controls and severe restrictions on government deficit spending to stimulate the economy, resulting in Eurozone recession in 2008-12 and continued economic stagnation to the present. The result? Workers have been savaged with lower/stagnant wages, lower social welfare benefits, and high unemployment.

The future promises a socialist upswing.

A) American Socialism

Hubert Gutman, Founding Director et al., Who Built America? Working People and the Nation's Economy, Politics and Society, Vol. I: From Conquest and Colonization Through Reconstruction and the Great Uprising of 1877; Vol. II: From the Guilded Age to the Present (New York: Pantheon Books, 1989, 1992). (1329 pages)

Lawrence Lader, Power on the Left, American Radical Movements Since 1946 (New York: W.W. Norton, 1979). George R. Vickers, The Formation of the New Left: The Early Years (Toronto: D.C. Heath, 1975). Nancy Zaroulis and Gerald Sullivan, Who Spoke Up? American Protest Against the War in Vietnam (New

York: Hold, Rinehart and Winston, 1975). Theodore Rozak, <u>The Making of a Counter-Culture</u> (New York: Doubleday, 1969). Gary B. Nash et al., <u>The American People: Creating a Nation and Society</u>, 3rd ed. (New York: Harper Collins, 1994). Oliver Stone and Peter Kuznick, <u>The Untold History of the United States</u> (New YorkL Gallery Books, 2012). Articles in <u>The New York Times</u>, <u>The Nation</u>, <u>Z Magazine</u>, <u>Monthly Review</u>, <u>New Left Review</u>.

B) The basic work on the European left is by Donald Sassoon, <u>One Hundred Years of Socialism: The Western European Left in the Twentieth Century</u> (New York: The New Press, 1996). <u>The New York Times</u>, <u>New Left Review</u>, <u>Monthly Review</u>, <u>Z Magazine</u>, <u>The Nation</u>

Chapter Fifteen: Soviet Union / Russia

The aim now is to examine the first of two great revolutions and their aftermaths led by Marxist socialists in the twentieth century: the Russian (Chinese the other) in 1917. It was conducted in a nation led by a Czar/nobility ruling class, with a relatively small working class and weak bourgeoisie.

The November Communist Revolution in Russia was preceded by the March 1917 one in which workers in Petrograd and Moscow reacted to rising food and fuel shortages and the incompetence of Czar Nicholas II in conducting the war (World War I) against the Central powers, resulting in high casualties and deep German and Austrian/Hungarian penetration of Russian territory. Within a brief period, this revolution allowed a reformist socialist government under Alexander F. Kerensky to hold power, but its insistence that the war continue brought to the fore a Communist Revolution.

The Communist leader was Vladimir I. Lenin, a brilliant tactician of revolution as well as an outstanding intellectual. Several months before the Communist Revolution, he wrote *State and Revolution*, which called for a democratic and egalitarian socialism, a position which reversed the one in *What is To Be Done?* (1901), viewing workers as not rising much about trade-union consciousness.

Although Lenin's vision was largely contingent on the Western European working class also making a socialist revolution begun by Russian workers, it optimistically believed that Russian workers could quickly be "educated" not only to perform their work democratically, but also to participate in democratically running an egalitarian society with full civil liberties for all except for the nobility and bourgeoisie, the elite classes.

In following Marx, Lenin pictured the state as "an organ of class domination, an organ of oppression of one class by another." Thus, the new socialist state, an alliance of peasants and workers, would first destroy the old police forces, military, and bureaucracy by a "dictatorship of the proletariat," composed of the "armed people," to bring about new and democratic institutions to reflect its pervasively democratic quality. He would also reject parliamentary democracy, equated with the rule of the bourgeoisie, quoting from Marx's *The Civil War in France* that the Paris Commune of 1871 established a government that was "a working, not a parliamentary body, executive and legislative at the same time." For him, this specifically signified that all officials were "elected and subject to recall at any time, their salaries reduced to "'workingmen's wages.'" In insisting on a general wage equality and recall of officials, Lenin's aim was clear: to prevent the rise of a bureaucratic socialist class that would thrust itself above workers and farmers. As for the fear among many socialists that inequality of functions based on prevailing labor division might catapult mental labor over the manual, and thus establish a bureaucratic socialist elite, Lenin, like Marx, thought that a pervasive democracy, a direct one for all practical purposes, would prevent this.

But this was not to be, as will later be observed, when the Communist Party of the Soviet Union (CPSU Party) eschewed democracy, but retained much socioeconomic equality. In the latter vein, Marx, in *The Critique of the Gotha Program*, did assign higher salaries to mental over manual labor, but never stated its extent; moreover, it was not too steep. Until 1931, the Soviet Communist Party's Partmax—Party Maximum—forbade members to earn more than skilled workers.

Furthermore, Lenin, again echoing Marx's (*The Civil War in France*) "united cooperative societies," had the "united workers themselves who hire their own technicians, managers, bookkeepers, and pay them *all*, as indeed, every 'state' official, with the usual workers' wage." He qualified this socialist democracy and egalitarianism with the caveat that "with human nature as it is now," "subordination, control," and "managers" were still necessary. He also called for free speech. These views prompted George Lichtheim, a leading 20th-century commentator on socialism/Marxism to label Lenin's *State and Revolution* as "quasi-anarchist." Lenin's thesis here is that mere nationalization of industry is not its socialization whose control is under the aegis of the workers themselves, as Marx proposed in *Grundrisse*, p. 833.

The March to November period of 1917 was momentous in world history. In March, revolution in Russia toppled the Czar. In April, the United States declared war on Germany to preserve the international balance of power and to protect its large loans to the Allies, principally Great Britain and France. In November, the Red Guard of twenty thousand armed workers, with the support of the Kronstadt sailors, launched the first successful socialist revolution in history in Petrograd, toppling the government of Kerensky, himself a moderate socialist who ruled with the support of the middle class. The Bolsheviks or left-wing socialists who led this revolution were determined to take advantage of the chaotic economic and military conditions that followed the end of Czarism.

In quick order, the Bolsheviks enacted a sweeping socialist program that confiscated the land of the wealthy and nationalized the factories that were put under the control of workers' committees, but the land of the small peasantry (those who tilled their own land) was left undisturbed.

The question normally arises as to the extent of popular support enjoyed by the Bolsheviks in the former Russian Empire. The answer is not difficult. In the November 25, 1917 Constituent Assembly elections, which most observers hold to have been relatively open and honest, the Communists received 25 percent of the vote and the deeply divided Social Revolutionary Party (SRP), basically the party of the peasantry, 58 percent, but its left wing, from about one-third to one-half of it, allied itself with the Bolsheviks. The Bolsheviks themselves prorogued the Assembly, and with good reason: SRP representatives had been picked before the radicalization of the peasantry, and, thus, did not accurately represent their constituents. There is no doubt that the Bolshevik-Left SR alliance had about half of the votes. Nevertheless, it should be pointed out that soon after the revolution, Communists became the minority in many Soviet elections and soon subordinated them and the unions to the Party apparatus, relegating Lenin's *State and Revolution* to the dustbin of history.

Despite the anti-democratic nature of Soviet Communism, its profound economic and social changes—nationalization of industry, laws to protect women, promise of extensive social insurance, and stress on equality—won its many supporters in Russia and among revolutionary workers and intellectuals throughout the world.

The Bolshevik success in the former Russian Empire, coupled with the defeat of Germany and Austria-Hungary, opened the possibility for Communist revolution in Europe. In Germany, the Marxist Social Democratic Party (most of which was reformist) and the Independent Socialists (who urged an immediate nationalization of industry), held the reins of government, and the latter with the Spartacists (the German Communists) demanded a left-wing government not dissimilar to the one in Russia. In Italy, during the summer of 1920, hundreds of thousands of workers seized six hundred factories. And in France, in 1919-1920, the National Confederation of Labor conducted a series of strikes that involved hundreds of thousands of workers, and the French Socialists veered leftward as the majority of them voted to join the new French Communist Party. It was also at this time that the Bolsheviks successfully overcame their internal and foreign opposition, and resumed a military counter-offensive in Poland whose aim was to spread the revolution to the rest of Europe. For a brief period, it seemed that Germany, and even France and Italy, might become part of the red tide. But the old order withstood these revolutionary assaults, isolating Communism to what became the Soviet Union.

The seedbed of Communism's authoritarian structure was the Civil War Period of 1918-21 where the Red Army under Leon Trotsky defeated the reactionary White armies representing the old order, the rule of the nobility and bourgeoisie; in this struggle the Menshiviks, democratic socialists, often sided with the old order, itself aided by the U.S., Britain, and France.

Millions were killed in the Civil War, and agriculture and industry suffered grievously as the contending armies fought each other, with famine conditions widespread. True, the Red Army won by 1921, but Russia was in ruins.

In 1921, there occurred the mutiny of the revolutionary socialist Kronstadt sailors at their base outside Petrograd, which called for new elections in the soviets, free speech and assembly, and end of forcible grain requisitioning from the peasantry. It was crushed by the Red Army under Trotsky. During 1921, there were also peasant uprisings in the countryside and workers' strikes in the cities against the Communists. If elections were held then, the Communists would have lost (Figes, pp. 751-72.)

It was at this time, 1921-22, that a famine also gripped Russia because of drought, resulting in the deaths of three million, which could have been more than ten million without the aid of the Vatican, the U.S., and others.

It was under these conditions/events that Lenin proposed the New Economic Policy (NEP), 1921-28, allowing for a more private enterprise and a free market in agriculture. But this economic relaxation ran parallel to Communists outlawing all parties, including the SRP and the socialist Mensheviks.

Furthermore, the Party ultimately imposed (1) tight control (censorship) of intellectual/artistic life, the schools and media closely supervised; and (2) a secret police to impose conformity, which allowed a privileged Soviet elite to emerge. These manifestations were a caricature of Marx's thought. But in the socioeconomic arena, following Marx, there was to be much equality. These developments occurred in a poor nation whose agricultural (1924-25) and industrial (1927) outputs reached pre-World War I levels.

In the midst of the preceding disasters and accompanying socioeconomic and political tensions, there was in 1921 a momentous Tenth Party Congress which decided the fate of Soviet democracy. The Workers Opposition within the Party led by Alexander G. Shlyapnikov and Alexandra Kollontai demanded that unions not only directly represent workers, but that they plan and manage national economy, acting as a counterweight to the Party/state bureaucracy, thus preventing a bureaucratic absolutism. In this fight, Trotsky rejected the demands of the unions on the basis that they represented their narrow interests as against that of the Party representing the workers' broader ones. But Lenin and Stalin, the majority, opted for limited union independence. The defeat of the Workers Opposition inevitably led to the rise of a bureaucratic/authoritarian party to be led by small Party cliques.

After Lenin's death in 1924, the two leading contenders vying for power were Trotsky (War Commissar and leader of the Red Army, the number two person after Lenin) and Joseph Stalin, the number three—Trotsky's great enemy—who by 1922 was General Secretary of the Party's Central Committee which coordinated the other principal organs. Principal others included Gregory Zinoviev, Chairman of the Petrograd Soviet and first chief of the Third or Communist International (Comintern); Lev Kamenev, Chairman of the Moscow branch of the Party and Lenin's chief deputy in many areas; and Nicholai Bukharin, the editor of *Pravda*, leading theoretician of the Party and leader of the Comintern from 1926 to 1929.

In a series of intra-party power struggles, Trotsky was eliminated from his top position by the troika of Stalin, Kamenev, and Zinovioev in 1924-25. Then in 1925-27, Stalin, Bukharin, and others dueled Trotsky, Zinoviev, and Kamenev—the last two fearing Stalin now allied themselves with Trotsky. The first combination favored a moderate policy for industrialization to maintain a worker-peasant alliance and was cautious for world revolution, while the latter proposed more rapid industrialization and world revolution.

In 1928, Stalin and Bukharin emerged victorious. But in 1929, Stalin and Bukharin clashed: the former called for rapid industrialization and rapid collectivization of agriculture; the latter favored continuing NEP and a slower pace for industrialization. Stalin won, emerging as the preeminent leader of the Party.

These maneuvers/disputes occurred within the leading political organs of the Party, the Central Committee, and the more exclusive Politbureau.

Peasant resistance to collectivization was fierce, especially among the kulaks or richer peasants, the Party responding by encouraging a civil war between them and poor peasants. Along with bad weather and resultant famine, several million kulaks perished, the few million survivors sent to labor colonies. Soviet agriculture never fully recovered from this disaster. Meanwhile, about twenty or so million peasants migrated to the cities as unskilled workers to help build the infrastructure and industry of the early five-year plans. Both rapid collectivization of agriculture and industrialization further depressed already low living standards.

In the meantime, a series of laws further eroded working-class power: a 1927 one forbade strikes and slowdowns, penalties for this being from one to twenty years in prison; a 1932 one denied workers the right to change jobs or move without permission; in 1934, workers' councils in factories were abolished, further insulating management from working-class interference, and collective bargaining was terminated; the latter was revived in 1947, but not for wages.

The rapid collectivization of agriculture related to rapid industrialization, beginning with the first five-year plan in 1929 and subsequent ones, brought many millions of excess peasants to the cities to work as unskilled labor, living in overcrowded housing. Then, German-Nazi rearmament in 1933-34 by sworn enemies of the Communist Soviet Union forced it to increase military expenditures. These developments further lowered already low living standards, with consequent rising sociopolitical tensions within society and the Party; Stalin resolved them within the Party by unleashing terror within it against imagined enemies. In 1936 and 1938, Stalin and his cohorts conducted bloody Party purges killing up to 500,000 Communists, including most of the Old Bolshevik leaders, like Bukharin, Zinoviev, Kamenev, A.I. Rykov, and G.Y. Sokolnikov; Trotsky was assassinated later by a Stalinist agent in Mexico. In 1937, between these two eruptions, Stalin decimated the top army command and officers who might have been plotting to overthrow him, many tens of thousands being slaughtered and imprisoned.

The murder and imprisonment of Communists, the destruction of the Kulaks and resettlement of many minority populations in labor camps were part and parcel of the Gulag which involved many millions of people, with about 3.8 million sentenced for counterrevolutionary crimes, up to 800,000 shot to death, and many millions dying of horrid labor camp conditions. By 1939, 2.9 million individuals were in prison, labor camps, special settlements, and so forth. The secret police (NKVD and OGPU) now became important in Party affairs.

These developments reinforced the rise of an administrative party-state elite, transforming the CPSU into an authoritarian organization, like a capitalist corporation. Under Stalin, it was governed solely by him, and after his death by small cliques in the key decision-making bodies, like the Politbureau and Secretariat. Party democracy was limited in that from the district level and upward, all party-state officials were answerable to the top party organs that decided who was to be elected to all offices, the *nomenklatura*, authoritarian-bureaucratic, numbering 400,000, with 800 to 1,800 individuals occupying its highest echelons, the Party/state/managerial/military/educational/scientific/security agencies elite. They assumed power after Stalin's death in 1953, their descendants viewing themselves as superior to workers and farmers; it terminated the terror, but continued to disregard elementary civil liberties and participatory democracy. The Party membership itself fairly represented a cross-section of Soviet society: in 1981, 44 percent were manual workers, 44 percent non-manual, and 12 percent collective farmers; in 1989, the Party had 19.5 million members.

The most horrendous trauma suffered by the Soviet people was the 1941 invasion, which penetrated deeply into Soviet territory, to the gates of Moscow and the Caucasus, inflicting huge human losses (16 million civilians and 9 million military were killed) and material ones (1,700 towns, 30,000 industrial plants, and 98,000 collective farms or 25 percent of the 1940 capital assets were destroyed.)

The Soviet Union ultimately beat the German invaders and their allies because it had greatly industrialized thanks to the first three Five-Year Plans. When the Germans advanced deeply into Soviet territory, Soviet industry massively (1360 major plants) moved to the East—almost half to the Urals, a fifth to Central Asia, a fifth to Siberia, and a sixth to the Volga Region.

American material aid to the Soviets also aided victory over the Germans, though it was hindered at first by Stalin's military blunders in the early years of the war. Ninety percent of the German military in World War II were killed on the Russian Front.

Despite huge human and material loss, Soviet economic recovery after the 1945 victory was very rapid. The fourth Five-Year Plan of 1946-50 by 1947 equaled 1940 industrial production and by 1950 national income was two-thirds higher than in 1940.

The following Five-Year Plans saw rapid Soviet economic growth, among the world's highest to 1980 by which time it was a predominantly urban society with a well-educated workforce and advanced social welfare system, with ever-rising living standards for its people, and a leader in science and technology. The extensive social welfare system included maternity and child benefits, socialized medicine, low rents and utility bills in state housing, inexpensive meals at work and school, free education, including college, subsidized vacations, low-cost public transportation, unemployment insurance (rarely used because of a job guarantee), and old-age pensions.

Most of these benefits were via the workplace, the aim being to retain a restive labor force with economic rewards. (Nevertheless, in the decades following World War II, 30 percent of workers would change jobs annually.)

Consumer goods production also increased rapidly: in 1960, 50 percent of families owned radios, 10 percent television sets, and 4 percent refrigerators; in 1985, 100 percent in the preceding categories, their technical quality inferior to that of the West.

Despite the erosion of working-class power in the workplace in the economically stressful drive to industrialize in the five year plans of the 1930s and World War II period of 1941-45, the Party afterward granted workers extensive rights at work: (1) guaranteed employment; (2) difficulty to dismiss workers: only for work incompetence or not following factory discipline. Only the trade union committee could discharge worker(s) and then by a two-thirds vote. If the worker retained his/her job, management could not appeal this union decision. If technological change made workers redundant, the enterprise would have to retrain them. Furthermore, the work pace after World War II became leisurely. To be sure, trade unions were also involved in enterprise production planning. Also, enterprise managers (99 percent were CPSU members) were chosen by the trade unions from a list of candidates drawn up by higher Party organs. Unions also determined piece rates and bonuses of workers, handled all social matters, like insurance, housing assignments, and vacation time (three weeks by the 1970s). By the 1970s there was a forty-two hour workweek consisting of six seven-hour days.

After 1975, the Soviet Union's economic dynamism lost momentum, falling behind the U.S. Economic practices allowing for early rapid growth would lead to later problems inherent in a mature economy demanding greater flexibility and efficiency. They principally included: (1) Over-centralization in planning, generally cumbersome, thus, in a continual crisis (the expected hoarding of raw materials by plant managers allowing for a semblance of economic order); (2) utter disregard of price mechanisms to determine actual costs and economic efficiency, economic indices being based on tonnage and quantity, not necessarily on quality and use, wasting much production; in the early stages of industrialization this did not impose an undue burden on the economy, but did so with industrial maturity; (3) neglect of new technological development—only 2 percent a year being devoted to replacing old plant/equipment—resulting in a precipitous drop in productivity; (4) a very wasteful military buildup during the Cold War; and (5) lack of authentic participatory democracy at work made workers apathetic—on the last, see Lebowitz, pp. 57ff.

A CIA report in 1982 indicated that the Soviet Union had an annual GDP growth rate of 4.7 percent from 1950 to 1980; but its 1976 to 1988 annual GDP growth of 2.1 percent compared unfavorably to the 3.1 percent of the U.S. and 2.7 percent of Western Europe. Even so, the $8,700 per capita of the Soviet Union in 1987 was not far from the 10,000 dollar one of the UK and the 12,000 dollar one of France.

As Soviet society became ever more urbanized, wealthier, educated, and complex, its people, including those within the ruling elite, favored changes to restructure industry, democratize society, and establish civil liberties along Western European lines. But there were these realities that posed problems for change. Alongside the nationalized sector, there was a growing illegal private one which accounted for about a seventh of the economy by the early 1980s, conducted by state managers of enterprises utilizing state property as their own, government officials in key state agencies, overtly corrupt, bribery as a way of life, characterizing the rule of Leonid I. Brezhnev, first secretary, then general secretary of the CPSU from 1964 to 1982 and also president of the USSR. Not surprisingly, this class sprang mainly from the well-educated elite or Communist *nomenklatura*, the most privileged sector of Soviet society (more on their favored position later).

It was within this general elite that emerged the most determined opponent of Soviet socialism, their aim being to consolidate their power position with large property, becoming like the Western-European capitalist elites whom they admired and wished to emulate. In a representative sample of its Moscow segment in 1991, for instance, 77 percent favored capitalism, 13 percent democratic socialism, and 10 percent Communism or nationalism. This disenchantment was replicated, in varying degree, by the lower socioeconomic levels of the population, especially their upper half.

The antithesis to this new capitalist class or power elite in the 1980s was the working class, eighty-one million or 62 percent of the workforce, about half being skilled or very skilled, the remainder being semi- and unskilled. Other classes/workforce sectors: a sixth in agriculture, more than half being manual workers; a lower-middle class of specialists between a fourth and a fifth (14 percent of the workforce were college graduates); and an upper-middle class of 5 percent in the higher reaches of the economic and other complexes.

In 1985, Mikhail Gorbachev became general secretary of the CPSU and promptly inaugurated *glasnost* or "openness" (democratization and implementing civil liberties) and *perestroika* or "restructuring" of the top-heavy and increasingly inefficient central economic planning. *Glasnot* ended Party censorship in intellectual/artistic life, including media censorship and so forth. Before this change an underground press (*zamistdat*) of dissident intellectuals existed.

Within the Party itself there was acrimonious debate about the contours of Soviet history. For Gorbachev and those favoring a mix of state ownership and capitalism, the NEP was the ideal time when the state held the commanding heights of the economy but yet allowed the existence of small private enterprise; they also preferred Burkharin's relatively slower tempo to industrialize as opposed to Stalin's quick one which alienated many of the peasants and workers with its brutality and iron discipline. Khrushchev himself accepted Stalinist rapid industrialization but decried Stalin's purges. These debates put into question the validity of Communist rule after Lenin.

Gorbachev further loosened the Party's grip on power when he abolished its secretariat and replaced it with a democratically elected Congress of People's Deputies. In the 1989 elections, Communists received the majority, but also granted 100 seats outside the electoral process.

Some background on consumer consumption/goods. First, the Soviet military had high quality equipment and it consumed more than a sixth of the GDP because of the Cold War. On the other hand, consumer goods were of low quality and there were perennial shortages of them, shoppers having to take extra bags in case of goods appearing unexpectedly which they would then hoard. Gorbachev wished to reform this glaring defect of Soviet society.

In 1988, Gorbachev was instrumental in enacting *Perestroika's* Law on State Enterprises which promoted the decentralization of the economy, increased marketization (companies competing with each other for market share), and greater worker participation in individual companies with the establishment of Labor Councils to play an important role in deciding wages, work discipline, technical training, and electing/removing management.

Also, laws were passed to allow for cooperatives in retail trade, small industry, banks, and exporting goods, the last run by members of the party-state elite who greatly enriched themselves. Many of the cooperatives were actually purely capitalist enterprises, owners hiring workers, further aiding the capitalist offensive. By 1988, 2.9 million people were in the corporate sector.

In August 1990, Gorbachev and Boris Yeltsin formulated the 500 Day Plan which would privatize 70 percent of industry into joint-stock companies, established private banks and a private securities market—furthering the rise of a capitalist class. In October 1990, in the Presidential Plan, Gorbachev would extend the 500 Day Plan over a longer period of time. (This plan would be overtaken by later events.) Then in July 1991, Gosplan, charged with overall economic planning, and Gosnab, which managed supply relations among enterprises, were abolished, signifying the end of the central planning/ allocation of resources. Furthermore, in the same month, Gorbachev applied for Soviet membership in the International Monetary Fund and World Bank, the mainstays of world capitalism. For Gorbachev, state economic activity would only encompass "defense, healthcare, education, science, and culture." Is not Gorbachev now a social democrat?

The end result of these *Perestroika* changes led to higher wages than normal for workers, emptying store shelves of goods, causing "shortages," lower capital investment for future growth, and reduced state taxes, producing higher tax deficits, finally causing lower economic output as GDP fell 2.4 percent in 1990 and 12.8 percent in 1991. *Perestroika* failed economically.

In a May 1991 poll in European Russia just before the Russian Federation presidential elections, only 10 percent approved the existing socialist system and 36 percent wished for a more democratic socialism (46 percent for socialism), 17 percent favored an American/ German type of capitalism and 23 percent for a Swedish form of capitalism (40 percent for capitalism), and 14 percent had no opinion.

Then, only 30 percent viewed the Party favorably, 60 percent did not. But only 10 percent favored privatizing heavy industry and only 20 percent of industry producing consumer goods. This poll indicated great dislike of the Party, but against the privatization of industry.

In this divided opinion, the critical group supporting Yeltsin were many of the party-state elite occupying many important positions in society, whose aim was to enrich themselves in a capitalist Russia. (Kotz, pp. 115-41 on the polls and Russian elite.)

The majority of the intelligentsia also opposed the Party and favored capitalism (95 percent of the economists did so). Communist censorship of the media before Glasnost was an important factor in alienating the intelligentsia from "actual socialism."

Gorbachev's competitive market system for the sake of efficiency and greater economic growth betrayed socialism. To begin, competition is wasteful economically because the market is often fickle and unsuccessful companies lose much or all their capital and workers become unemployed, many for long periods of time or permanently. To obviate this state of affairs, there is the Marxist socialist principle, as already observed, of united workers' cooperatives working together on a common plan that also allows for continuing economic openness and flexibility. Furthermore, these cooperatives would work closely with cooperative consumer societies to produce products priced fairly with proper cost in mind. This schema allows for the optimization of capital/labor inputs— technology/materials goods. Incidentally, even in capitalist America large corporations are engaged in oligopolistic competition, controlled price competition to keep prices artificially high. Ultimately, cooperative socialism is less wasteful than the capitalist model which also distorts distribution of goods by conspicuous consumption of especially the rich. But as already observed, workers themselves subverted Gorbachev's competitive model by awarding themselves higher wages as normal relative to productivity and so forth. Under the socialist cooperative principle, the preceding imbalances would not have occurred. Centralized Soviet planning did ultimately lead to slower economic growth, but never in the negative territory, although free market *Perestroika* inexorably led to economic downturn.

Does centralized planning, which is very successful in concentrating economic resources to build up infrastructure/heavy industry, necessarily fail to cope with economically advanced/ sophisticated economies tracking hundreds of thousands of items/ transactions daily? No, because computers can quickly process/track myriads of products/transactions while also allowing some economic indeterminacy. This, the Soviet Union failed to do.

I, myself, oppose a centralized computer system for running the economy because I fear centralized power in any of its forms— economic, political—as inimical to general equality in its many forms, this train of thought conditioned by my study of history. I emphasize economic and political patterns in which workers' councils, using computers, cooperate together to plan the national economy in its various levels, while also allowing a central national center some economic autonomy to correct any economic imbalances and project future economic growth.

Thus, for me, Gorbachev's *Perestroika*, which increased workers' power in the workplace, was laudable, but its allowing for a growing private-property/market capitalist sector in the economy could not but have strengthened a rising capitalist class which ultimately swept away any working class power which existed in the "actual socialism" of the Soviet Union.

Glasnot led to the free elections in June 1991 in the Russian Federation for the presidency, resulting in Boris Yeltsin's decisive victory over five opponents, including the Communist one.

Yeltsin, supported by the Russian elite, attacked their privileges deceptively, especially those of the *nomenklatura*, endorsed massive privatization/marketization of the economy, workers an economic share of their workplace, private ownership of apartments, and end of the Russian Federation's economically subsidizing the remainder of the Soviet Union.

Let us add that many manual/mental workers who voted for Yeltsin did not approve of the perquisites of the *nomenklatura*, were not averse to owning their apartments, and so forth; they were unable to foresee that Yeltsin's near future massive division of state property among the people ad marketization would enrich a kleptocratic capitalist class mainly from the party-state elite who would enrich themselves while plunging Russia into economic catastrophe, impoverishing most of its people.

Yeltsin then challenged Gorbachev's power to issue decrees or make laws as president of the Soviet Union; Gorbachev had added this position to his secretary generalship of the CPSU. This internecine struggle within the Russian Republic encouraged nationalist movements in the other republics (the Ukraine, the Baltic ones, and some others) to break away from the Soviet Union. Gorbachev attempted to save the Soviet Union in March 1991 by a Union Treaty that granted greater powers to the various republics, but retained a common currency, military, foreign policy, and economic coordination. He simultaneously announced the end of Marxism-Leninism as the official ideology of the Soviet Union.

Gorbachev's actions so angered traditional Communist leaders and their followers in the military, state administration, security agencies, and majority of Party committees, that they launched a coup d'état against both Yeltsin and Gorbachev in August 1991. It detained Gorbachev, but Yeltsin with twenty-thousand bourgeois demonstrators defied them. At this critical juncture, two generals leading the army units to arrest Yeltsin defected, allowing Yeltsin to remain free. They probably did not wish to provoke a fight with unarmed civilians.

Yeltsin seized the opportunity to exploit the failed coup d'état: He suspended the activities of the Party, forced its Central Committee and Gorbachev its leader to resign, called for the end of the Soviet Union, and formation of a loose Commonwealth of Independent States comprising Russia, Ukraine, and Belorussia. On Dec. 25, 1991, Gorbachev resigned as President of the Soviet Union, which itself expired on Dec. 31, 1991.

Gorbachev could have saved Soviet socialism by adopting the program of the Worker's Opposition.

The Communist society that Yeltsin and his capitalist cohorts overthrew, despite its many deformities, was very egalitarian in comparison to capitalist societies. In 1988, its Gini coefficient (zero equals absolute economic equality, one, absolute inequality) was 0.24, like Sweden's, an advanced social-democratic nation. In fact, the income disparity in the 1989 Soviet Union was about 8 to 1 between the average income of an industrial worker of 250 rubles a month, to 1,200-1,500 rubles a month for Politbureau members (the primary governing political organ), to the 2,000 rubles a month for the highest generals. To be sure, this elite had many perquisites related to their position, like better housing, special stories for consumer goods and better access to leading schools for their children but, compared with the wealth and luxuries of Western elites, the Communist one was of poor paupers. By 1993, the Russian capitalist Gini coefficient was 0.48, like that of the Philippines, a poor nation of great inequality; by 2007, it was 0.44, still one of much inequality. This great income inequality may be partly measured by the increasing income gap between managers and unskilled workers, 1.7 times as much under 1960s Communism, to 3.9 times as much in a 2007 capitalist Russia. (Wood, "Iceberg Society," pp. 21 ff. and Kotz, p. 112.)

Another way to measure this steep socioeconomic inequality circa 2005-10: one estimate in 2005 had 30 percent of the people with an income of more than 150 percent of the national median, 40 percent from 62.5 percent to 150 percent of the median, while 30 percent at 65 percent below the median or in poverty.

Russia and the U.S. have more income inequality than other economically advanced nations. Income differentials in Russia between highest to lowest tenths of the population are twenty-three to one, very similar to poor nations. An extreme example of this inequality: Board members of Gazprombank in 2010 earned $2.9 million, 350 times more than the median wage of under $8,000.

In 1992, with the overwhelming support of the Russian Dume and the advice of Jeffrey Sachs, a Harvard economist and disciple of Friedman, Yeltsin embarked on a "shock therapy" program to privatize the Russian economy. But Just before doing so, price controls were lifted, causing hyperinflation which wiped out the savings of most of the people within a matter of weeks, ensuring that once privatization began, the shares workers received would be quickly sold to speculators for almost nothing.

Opposition to Yeltsin's aggressive capitalist stance was centered in the Russian parliament whose majority elected in the 1990 elections was solidly Communist, of old-line types and many Gorbachavites, opposing the lifting of price controls and massive privatization: These proposals occurred as the economy continued to deteriorate. In fact, Parliament launched attacks against Yeltsin which almost succeeded. Yeltsin then struck back in late September 1993 by declaring the Parliament dissolved and calling for new Parliamentary elections. But the Parliament defied Yeltsin and voted to impeach him, appointing Vice President Alexander Rutskoi to replace him as president, barricaded themselves in the Parliamentary building and called for a national strike to support them. Ten thousand anti-Yeltsin demonstrators supported Parliament. Yeltsin replied by sending tanks to bombard the Parliament, killing 100 and arresting its leaders—this was the last chance for a democratic socialism.

In December 1993 elections, Yeltsin rammed through a new Constitution narrowly approved by the voters (there was widespread voting fraud) which gave him powers akin to a czar.

Thus, in 1994 massive privatization occurred. It granted 51 percent of a company's assets to workers and managers (20 percent gratis to workers and 5 percent to managers, who together could purchase another 26 percent), 29 percent to the public in vouchers (151 million for every person in Russia at seven dollars each), with the remaining 20 percent in government hands to be sold later. In 1995, this scheme was coupled to "loans for shares," private banks lending money to a bankrupt government giving away the national resources (factories and so forth) for almost gratis; $200 billion sold for $7 billion. This privatization resulted in a horrendous plunder of state property, involving tens of billions of dollars in state assets in the oil, gas, and metals sector to powerful insiders in the government. By

1995, 80 percent of Russian state industry was privatized. (Medvedev, *Post-Soviet Russia,* p. 147.)

The new rich were mainly from the party-state elite (in the key Moscow area two-thirds were managers), bankers of state banks and functionaries in strategic party/state sectors able to use their positions to become rich; 85 percent were members of the *nomenklatura;* 70 percent had a higher education; 40 percent admitted to engaging in illegal activity (Medvedev, *Journey Through the Yeltsin Era,* pp. 183 and 200.)

They enriched themselves rapidly thus: (1) Acquiring low-interest state loans through normal bureaucratic networks to purchase stock of newly privatized enterprises, making rules allowing them to appropriate much of the stock for nothing, while obtaining scarce raw materials and delaying payment of wages; (2) bankers retaining a part of interest on loans for themselves; (3) open theft of company assets by being in a power position to do so; (4) establishing private shell companies alongside still-existing state ones, allowing the former to purchase commodities from the latter at low prices, then selling them at higher world market prices in the West, squirreling most of the profits there; (5) the state's granting favored capitalists' monopoly status to export oil and other products or to import tobacco without paying taxes; (6) government banks, lending money to private ones below the inflation rate, which, in turn, would lend money much above it; later these private banks would lend money at high interest rates to the government whose collateral were some of the nation's richest companies under the rubric of "loans for shares"; with government default, these banks promptly acquired the companies. Of course, to participate in this wholesale robbery, access to Yeltsin was imperative.

The richest of the Russian kleptocrats was Boris Berezhovsky, from an educated Russian-Jewish middle-class family. A brilliant student, he received a Ph.D. in applied mathematics in 1983 and was involved for twenty-five years in research, becoming a member of the prestigious Academy of Sciences.

After being involved in 1989 in a company, Logovaz, selling Russian automobiles, Berezhovsky successively became owner with others of an international finance company, Forus; the principal Russian television station, ORT; Sibnet, a large oil company; a bank which went bankrupt; and other ventures. He became a multi-billionaire principally because of his close association with Yeltsin after 1993, instrumental in re-electing him president in 1996 and 2000; he was also closely tied to gangsters. As Paul Klebnikov writes in *Godfather of the Kremlin*: "Berezovsky took control of the men who ran the government and forced the state to feed his business empire," and "he and crony capitalists produced no benefit to Russia's consumers, industries, or treasury," as the companies under his control "stagnated or declined." He later fled Russia to avoid arrest for illegal activity.

It should also be pointed out that organized crime or the Russian Mafia was firmly ensconced in the ruling capitalist class. It largely comprised privatized former KGB (security agency) networks and other mobs, using the gun for extortion or "protection" of 80 percent of business, controlling a fourth of the banking system and thousands of companies, including many still state-owned ones.

Thus it is that within six years of privatization, at least half of the Russian GDP was controlled by a small coterie of capitalists: Berezovsky claims that he is one of seven (six are Jewish, reinforcing anti-Semitism) tycoons owning half of it; this is disputed by another one of them, Vladimir Potanin, who asserts that about thirty own that much. The magnitude of this plunder is unparalleled in modern history, the American Robber Barons being a distant second.

Privatization itself led to a much lower government share of GDP, from about half in 1991 to a third after 1993, and free markets, including open monetary rates and lower tariffs—half of Russia's consumer goods (Russian industry was not formulated to produce inexpensive domestic products) and half of its food are now imported. (When the U.S. was building its industry in the late 19th/early 20th centuries, high tariffs excluded cheaper foreign goods.)

To compound the whole economic malaise is the salient fact of the kleptocracy's engaging in capital flight: from 1991 to 2001, from $200 to $350 billion left Russia abetted by hyperinflation, which also forced the robber-capitalists to send money abroad to protect its value, as they stripped the assets of their newly acquired companies. (In this economic malaise foreign capital was afraid to invest, having only 0.5 billion dollars in direct investment in 2000.) It was accomplished largely through false contracts (four-fifths from this source), payment for non-existent imports, and outright theft by leading government officials and gangsters with the aid of bank officials in Russia, the U.S., and elsewhere. Or a company would export goods, usually raw materials, at low prices to an offshore shell company, which, in turn, sold them at high profit deposited in foreign banks. As for graft by high officials and cooperating banks, it was estimated that a third of $31 billion of IMF loans to Russia were siphoned off to the West.

Now, with the flight of foreign capital and continuing one of the domestic variety, and with the government's not being able to collect much in taxes from a poor economy, it was a forced to borrow ever more money from Russian and foreign banks at high interest rates. The Russian ruble itself became more superfluous because to lessen foreign debt the government was forced to let the ruble float, reigniting inflation.

These developments left the Russian banking system in shambles, the government's central bank being forced to acquire other large private banks that lost money on speculation in government bills losing value rapidly! As the government allowed the ruble to fall through inflation, the working class, including most of the farmers, lower-middle class mental labor, and pensioners became further economically marginalized, with wages and pensions lagging significantly behind rising food and other costs. By 1995, Russians held up to $20 billion, the $100 bill very prevalent.

The kleptocracy itself was divided on inflation, depending on their major investments/interests, those lending money to the government for stock in some remaining government-owned assets would gain, while those whose banks went bankrupt would lose.

To be sure, as during the early 1920s when the Weimar Republic experienced a very high inflation, those possessing assets, i.e., the rich and speculators in currency made fortunes. But even if the present inflation were checked, the underlying systemic economic crisis continued in deindustrialization and capital flight. Not surprisingly, the Russian Government as of the summer of 1998 was in default to its international creditors. In light of robberies and economic disasters, Joseph E. Stiglitz, the World Bank's chief economist until 1999, unequivocally stated that the Russian government should renationalize privatized industry, then re-privatize it in an orderly fashion.

Other distressing economic statistics: the majority of the workforce itself either received its wages late or was reimbursed in kind—with two-fifths not paid last months' wages, a fourth three months in arrears, and an eight paid in kind. Government revenues themselves were falling rapidly, unable to collect most of the taxes owed to it. More than half the wages were unreported, as well as 90 percent of business income. Furthermore, the majority of large private enterprise itself was now bankrupt, obviously unable to pay taxes; in fact, the government, to avoid economic chaos, was obligated to subsidize these companies, in the process further enriching the new wealthy entrepreneurs. The parasitic nature of this capitalism had wages as percent of GDP falling from 47.5 in the early 1990s to 36 by 1997, whereas in the U.S. they were 58 percent. Not one major productive facility was built from 1991 to 2000.

Other results of robbery/privatization: by 1999, GDP fell by half as per capita income from 1991 to 1999 decreased from $8,700 to $4,200, and capital investment collapsed by 90 percent as production in industry plummeted by half, oil by the same amount, electricity by a fifth, and gas by an eighth. From half to three-fourths of the economy was conducted through barter and IOUs, a third-to-half in the black market. Then, too, the scientific community was severely decimated, reduced from 3.4 million in 1990 to 1.3 million in 2000. As for the real unemployment rate circa 2000, it was between 20 and 25 percent, and to avoid starvation, 40 percent of the domestic food supply was grown in private gardens. Largescale agriculture itself was in collective farms, but de-collectivization would have made food even scarcer as small farms could not afford mechanization.

The lack of food circa 2000 to maintain decent health was of serious concern for most Russians: according to the World Health Organization, the average one daily ingested 2,100 calories (15 percent are starving) less than the 2,200 minimum required by it, as opposed to 3,400 in the 1980-85 period. Thus, the tuberculosis rate, a good indicator of social deprivation, per thousand was 80 as opposed to 68.6 for poor nations in general and 35.1 in East Asia; and infant mortality rate per thousand live births was 26, approaching that of Latin America and the Caribbean at 32 (it was 7 in the U.S.). Not surprisingly in 2008, 30 percent of the Russian population would not reach age 60, the same as in India, while the average age of death for Russian males at 61 was lower than in India and Egypt. Epidemics in cholera and typhus were widespread, and most tragically, up to 80 percent of the children were undernourished with accompanying physical and mental disabilities. A once good social welfare/health system was now in shambles.

In the midst of the economic malaise, a critical 1996 presidential election occurred in the Russian Federation (the last chance for a probable Communist return) between Yeltsin and the Communist Gennady Zyuganov, with the former winning 53.7 percent, the latter 40.4 percent.

Yeltsin prevailed because the economic malaise was not as bad as it would become, with many voters being attracted to the voucher system encouraging individual ownership in factories and housing. Even so, the voting results reflected these facts: Yeltsin had an almost unlimited campaign budget, while Zyuganov's was very limited; Yeltsin controlled the state and private media which permitted Zyuganov scant exposure; in control of public funds, Yeltsin dispensed economic largesse, allowing workers to be paid back wages. Furthermore, the 97,000 polling sites and the regional electoral commissions were in the hands of the government, allowing it to manipulate final voting results. Indeed, if Yeltsin would have lost the election, he probably would not have relinquished his office (Service, p. 548). Apparently, the seventy years of Communist indoctrination in the schools and media failed to win a majority of votes.

Then, the economic downturn from 1989 to 1999 further made workers more economically fearful, and tied to their workplace; managers themselves in a paternalistic manner kept as many workers as possible employed. Indeed, sheer economic survival dampened working-class resistance to capitalism. According to the International Labor Organization, 85 percent of Russians were below the poverty line in 1992.

The class structure of Russia, circa 2013, is one of great socioeconomic inequality. Its richest 1 percent in 2011 is led by 101 billionaires worth $433 billion, having 29 percent of Russia's $1,479 billion GDP, the highest concentration of OECD nations. (In the U.S., 413 billionaires in 2011 worth $1,518 billion have 10 percent of a $14,582 billion GDP.) Underneath them are thousands of mere millionaires: the rich are followed by an upper-middle class in the 5-10 percent range, part of a middle class of about 25-30 percent of better-off workers and petty entrepreneurs, followed by about 70 percent of average-to-poor workers. Poverty, officially, is still widespread: 29 percent in 2000 (actually, as already noted, much higher) and 17 percent in 2007.

In December 2000, the capitalist oligarchs replaced Yeltsin (who became an alcoholic incompetent) with Vladimir Putin, a former Lieutenant Colonel in the KGB (the security agency), then director of its successor, the FSB. This appointment indicated the importance of the *siloviki*, the security and military personnel.

In the 2000 election, Putin won the presidency and his United Russia Party the majority of seats in parliament. This party was supported by the capitalist oligarchs and the media under its control. Nevertheless, a relatively strong Communist Party in opposition now emerged.

From 2000 to today (2013), the capitalist United Russia Party has ruled Russia. Its pre-eminent leader is its President Vladimir Putin, followed by his handpicked Prime Minister, Dmitri Medvedev; in 2008, they exchanged positions as they also did in 2012. It should be added that Putin suppressed the business gangsterism of the Yeltsin period.

To be sure, from 1999 to 2013, except for the 2009 depression, the Russian economy has grown at a fairly rapid pace of 5-7 percent annually, powered by a strong hydrocarbon sector (30 percent of the economy). By 2007, the GDP reached 85 percent of its 1989 level and by circa 2010 at 100 percent of it—twenty-one years of lost time/growth.

In 2012, automobile ownership in Russia is 250 per 1,000 people (543 in Germany). Generally, this 250 group comprises the wealthier elements of Russian society and is also an indication of Russian productive wealth; Russian per capita income in 2013 is at $18,000 (half that of Western Europe), but, as already observed, the median per capita in 2010 at $8,000, indicates great income inequality.

Russia today features a modern and relatively prosperous Moscow, St. Petersburg, and a few other large cities, but most of the residents in small cities and rural areas live in relative poverty and dilapidated infrastructure, which needs an infusion of $2 trillion to become modern. As for taxes, the personal income one is 13 percent for everyone, highly regressive; the corporate one is 24 percent, much of it evaded.

The relative poverty today of most Russians is shown by the fact that 70 percent of adults do not have a savings account. But the rich and upper-middle class play in the financial markets: 9 percent in foreign currency, 7 percent in stocks, and 3 percent in mutual funds.

Despite capitalist oligarchic rule, popular pressure has forced Putin to continue pensions and strengthen socialized medicine. The pension age for workers is 55 for women and 60 for men in the private sector; for government workers, 60 for women, 65 for men. There is also disability insurance.

As for the Russian healthcare system, it collapsed with the fall of the Soviet Union and subsequent economic catastrophe. Living standards fell, and unemployed increased, and lack of healthcare, with increased alcoholism and smoking, more heart attacks, mental depression, and suicide. But from 2004 life expectancy increased: in 2009, 62.77 years for men, 74.67 years for women, ten years less than in the EU and U.S., much of it caused by excessive use of smoking and alcohol.

In 2011, the healthcare system was strengthened by additional government revenues in socialized medicine, but a small private-insurance sector also exists.

The kleptocratic Russian capitalists have continued to send their ill-gotten gains abroad, registering their corporations in Cyprus, Britain, and the Netherlands, among other nations, fearful of losing it in the uncertain political-economic climate at home. An estimate by Ben Judah in *The New York Times* ("Did Putin sink Cyprus?" Ap. 3, 2013, p. A23) asserts that in the 2008-12 period, $350 billion left Russia, much of it re-circulated to it as a protected foreign investment. This robbery comes from the surplus value extracted from the Russian working class. It should have been employed to better compensate workers and to rebuild a crumbling infrastructure that would have occurred if Russia were a socialist state.

The Putin reign, 2000 to the present, as already observed after 2001, has been generally characterized by rapid economic growth but has stalled recently, falling to an anemic 0.5 percent in 2013. To be sure, corruption continues unabated. One estimate circa 2005 has corruption totaling in the hundreds of billions of dollars annually, greater than the revenues of the Russian federal budget; it is fuelled by cliques and nepotism at the apex of the economic/political pyramid.

There is also increasing governmental bureaucratization as the Putin/government is tightening authority over the underlying population. This is shown by the rapid increase of its functionaries, numbering 1.3 million circa 2007, twice as many as in the Soviet period; this increase also consolidates the wealth of the capitalist elite, ruling in partnership with leading figures in the military and security agencies.

The instability of Russian society is illustrated by its high murder and crime rates: Circa 2007, the former is triple that of the U.S. and tenfold that of Western Europe; the latter increased dramatically after the fall of the Soviet Union. Then, too, the war in Chechnya has been brutal, tens of thousands of Chechens killed.

If socialism is to revive in Russia, its core is in the unions, 45 percent of the workforce. The Communist Party of the Russian Federation is the principal party challenging United Russia. In the 2012 presidential elections, Putin received 64 percent of the vote, the Communist Gennady Zyuganov, 15 percent. Also, the 25 percent of the workforce employed by government is a potential state-socialist voting bloc. Furthermore, half of the workforce outside the home comprises women whose lower pay than men's causes discontent. Lastly, the 40-hour week won by Russian workers may embolden them to seek more concessions, like a shorter workweek, higher wages, and more workplace control. Lastly, dismal GDP growth lately should lead to a more restive workforce.

The Putin-Medvedev duo, representing the capitalist oligarchy, faced by increasing working-class resistance, have allowed wages to outstrip productivity, causing inflation and making Russian products less competitive in world markets. This economic dynamic in 2013 has led to GDP dipping to the 1-2 percent range and inflation rising to the 5 percent area. These economic realities have resulted in lower living standards for workers and their intensifying the class struggle against the capitalist oligarchs.

Endnotes

See, for instance, on early Bolshevism, L.H. Haimson, *The Russian Marxists and the Origins of Bolshevism* (Cambridge: Harvard Univ. Press, 1955). T.H. Hammond, *Lenin on Trade Unions and Revolution, 1893-1917* (New York: Columbia Univ. Press, 1957). On Lenin's utopianism just prior to the Communist Revolution, see Lenin, *State and Revolution*, pp. 32-85. On socialization of industry see Karl Marx, *Grundrisse*, translated Martin Nicolaus (New York: Vintage, 1973), p. 833. On Communist Revolution, see E.H. Carr, *The Bolshevik Revolution, 1917-1923*, 3 vols.

(Baltimore, MD: Penguin Books, 1966). Eric Hobsbawm, *The Age of Extremes; A History of the World, 1914-1991* (New York: Pantheon Books, 1994), pp. 54-84 on the impact of the Russian Communist Revolution. On Lenin, see Louis Fischer, *The Life of Lenin* (New York: Harper Colophon Books, 1964). On Stalin, see Issac Deutscher, *Stalin; A Political Biography* (New York: Vintage Books, 1961). On Trotsky, see Issac Deutscher, 3 vols.; I: *The Prophet Armed, 1879-1921*; II: *The Prophet Unarmed, 1921-1929*; III: *The Prophet Outcast, 1929-1941* (New York: Oxford Univ. Press, 1954, 1959, 1963). Donald C. Hodges, *The Bureaucratization of Socialism* (Amherst, MA: Univ. of Mass., 1981), pp. 78 ff. and 119-20 on Soviet wages. On the monstrosity of Stalinism and its deformation of socialism, see Roy A. Medvedev, *Let History Judge: The Origins and Consequences of Stalinism* (New York: Alfred A Knopf, 1971), pp. 152-257, for instance. Roy A. Medvedev, *On Socialist Democracy* (New York: Alfred A. Knopf, 1975), pp. 108-47, on the lack of democracy within the communist party; pp. 225-26, on the steep salary differentials between workers and elite, including perquisites, on the order of 50/100 to 1; pp. 227-28, on the special privileges of the elite; pp. 164-209, on the lack of speech and press freedoms. Moshe Lewin, *Russia/USSR/Russia: The Drive and Drift of a Superstate* (New York: The New Press, 1995), p. 73, by 1928, the Bolsheviks become a bureaucratic-hierarchical-administrative party; pp. 185-208 on the rise of the Stalinist bureaucracy which in the course of industrialization subordinated the workers to it; pp. 311-32, on Stalinism being replaced by "bureaucratic absolutism." On Soviet society, see Moshe Lewin, *The Gorbachev Phenomenon: A Historical Interpretation* (Berkeley, CA: Univ. of CA. Press, 1988), pp. 43-56, on urbanization and new work force. On the dissolution of the Soviet Union/Communism, including causes of, as hierarchical and authoritarian work relations, steep labor division, and lack of democracy: see David Kotz with Fred Weir, *Revolution from Above: The Demise of the Soviet System* (London: Routledge, 1997), pp. 34-61, on perestroika and fall of communism; pp. 63-72, on the intelligentsia; pp. 109-55, on the party-state elite and political struggles; pp. 157-99, on shock therapy and its aftermath; p. 115 on the Moscow elite's favoring capitalism. Also on privatization: Rose Brady (a *Business Week* editor), *Kapitalizm: Russia's Struggle to Free its Economy* (New Haven, Yale Univ. Press, 1999), pp. 44-154 and 212-16. Although supporting Russian capitalism, she presents many of its unsavory aspects. Stanislov Menshikov (A Russian economist), "A Ruling Class Destroys its Own Regime," *Monthly Review Press*, vol. 49, no. 5, Oct. 1997, pp. 49-57; he also presents much material on the social origins of the new rich and avers that most of mental labor (university and other teachers, engineers, and so forth) support socialism. Daniel Singer, *Whose Millennium? Theirs or Ours?* (New York: *Monthly Review Press* 1999, pp. 29-43, presents much material. On Potanin and Sidanko, see Neela Banjeree, "A High Cost for BP Amoco's Investment in Oil Concern," *New York Times*, Aug. 13, 1999, pp. C1 and C17. John Lloyd, "The Russian Devolution," *New York Times Magazine*, Aug. 15, 1999, pp. 34-41 principally. On the fall of Communism/Soviet Union, see, for instance, Mészáros, *Beyond Capital*, pp. 622-62; Hobsbawm, *Age of Extremes*, pp. 461-99; Jonathan Steele, "Why Gorbachev Failed?," *New Left Review*, no. 216, April/May 1996, pp. 141-52—there is also much material on privatization. On the 1996 Russian elections, see, for instance, *New York Times*, July 4 and 5, 1996; and David Remnick, "The War of the Kremlin," *New Yorker*, July 22, 1996, pp. 40-57. On recent economic statistics on Russia, see Fred Weir, "Robbing Russia Blind," *In These Times*, Jan. 11, 1998, pp. 21-23, and *New York Times*, May 26, 1998. pp. A1 and A6; and May 28, 1998, pp. A1, A11-12 and A28; Aug. 28. 1998, pp. A1, A10, and C17; Sept. 2, 1998, pp. A1, and A12-13; Sept. 3, 1998, pp. A1 and A11. Stanisla Menshikov, "Russian Capitalism Today," *Monthly Review*, vol. 51, no. 3, July/August, 1999, pp. 81-99. On the horrendous poverty and its consequences catalogued in The Silent Crisis by the European's Trust—an NGO in Eastern Europe—see Ian Phillips, "Tens of millions of children threatened in eastern Europe," *Akron Beacon Journal*, Oct. 12, 2000, p. A20. On Stiglitz, see Louis Uchitelle, "World Bank Economist Felt He Had to Silence His Criticism or Quit," *New York Times*, Dec. 2, 1999, p. C1 and C6. On the 1996 election, see Jerry F. Hough, Evelyn Davidheiser, and Susan Goodrich, *The 1996 Russian Presindential Election* (Washington, DC: Brookings Institution Press, 1996), 123 pages. On the fortunes of post-Soviet Russian communism, see Joan Barth Urban and Valerii D. Solovei, *Russia's Communists at the Crossroads* (Boulder, CO: Westview Press, 1997), pp. 97-120 on Zyuganov's views. Other works consulted: Roy Medvedev, *Post-Soviet Russia; A Journey Through the Yeltsin Era* (New York: Columbia Univ. Press, 2000). Orlando Figes, *A People's Tragedy; The Russian Revolution, 1891-1924* (New York: Penguin Books, 1996). Robert Service, *A History of Modern Russia; From Nicholas II to Vladimir Putin* (Cambridge, Mass.: Harvard Univ. Press, 2003). David Preistland, *The Red Flag: A History of Communism* (New York: Grove Press, 2009), István Mészáros, *Beyond Capital: Towards a Theory of Transition* (New York: Monthly Review Press, 1995). This work details the processes involved which led to the fall of the Soviet Union, importantly the rise of the bureaucracy at the expense of workers' power in running the economy that ultimately led to the rise of capitalism. On healthcare in Russia, see http://en.wikipedia....., 3/16/2013. On pensions, see http://www.pfruf...., 3/16/2013). Vladimir Popov, "Russia Redux?" *New Left Review*, no. 44, March/April 2007, pp. 37-52. Tony Wood, "Contours of the Putin Era," *New Left Review*, no. 44, March/April, 2007, pp. 53-68. Robert V. Daniels, *The Rise and Fall of Communism in Russia* (New Haven: Yale Univ. Press, 2007). Sheila Fitzpatrick, *Everyday Stalinism; Ordinary Life in Extraordinary Times: Soviet Russia in the 1930s* (New York: Oxford Univ. Press, 1999). Stephen F. Cohen, *Soviet Fates and Lost Alternatives; From Stalinism to the Cold War* (New York: Columbia Univ. Press, 2011), a most interesting and provocative work. F. Lee Benns and Mary Elisabeth Seldon, *Europe, 1939 to the Present* (New York: Appleton-Century-Crofts, 1965). Max Hastings, *Inferno; The World at War, 1939-1945* (New York: Vintage Books, 2011), vividly describes the conflict between the Soviet Union and Nazi Germany. Tony Wood, "Collapse as Crucible; The Reforming of Russian Society," *New Left Review,* 74, March/April 2012, pp. 5-38. On the wealthier groups playing the market, Ekaterina Shamonina, "Still Living Paycheck to Paycheck," *NYT,* Feb. 21, 2013. Michael A. Lebowitz, *The Contradictions of "Real Socialism," The Conductor and the Conducted* (New York: Monthly Review Press, 2012).

Chapter Sixteen: China

The successful Communist revolution in Russia was a great spur to the founding of a Chinese Communist Party (CCP), founded in 1921 – Mao Zedong, its preeminent leader by the mid-1930s, being among the founding members.

The Communist revolution in Russia not only played a significant role in the founding of the CCP, but also reinvigorated the Guomindang (the Chinese Nationalist Party—GMD) founded by Dr. Sun Zhongshan (Sun Yat-sen) in 1912; Sun was thoroughly versed in Western ideas of progress. The GMD under Sun was a progressive middle-class and democratic party whose 1924 platform skirted socialism; it was this party that played an important role in overthrowing the Manchu Dynasty and establishing a republic in 1912. However, it temporarily lost ground to Western imperialist-backed conservative elements under General Yuan Shikai (Yuan Shih-k'ai), who, true to form, outlawed the GMD and even became emperor of China in 1915-16. With his death in 1916, however, the central government collapsed and a pervasive warlordism followed between 1916 and 1928, in which rival generals and the GMD fought one another in various combinations for political supremacy. In this situation, distrusting the West, the GMD under Sun accepted Comintern support in 1923. Soviet advisors led by Michael Borodin, quickly infused it with new vigor through reorganization and a CCP-GMD alliance, which allowed communists also to be members of the GMD. The goals of the alliance were to end landlordism by establishing a strong central government and to abrogate the humiliating and unequal treaties which the imperialists had imposed on China. The Comintern's objective was to aid the development of a progressive bourgeois national revolution to become a bridgehead for a socialist one.[1]

In 1925, when Sun died, his chief lieutenant, Jiang Jieshi (Chiang Kai-shek), an ambitious and basically conservative general, replaced him as a leader of the GMD. In April 1927, after defeating the northern warlords, Jiang enter Shanghai, the bastion of the Western business community, where he simultaneously made an agreement with it to maintain the status quo—as part of which Western capitalists lent Jiang large sums of money—and murdered thousands of communists. Jiang's victories had freed him from Comintern dependence, which allowed him to crush rising CCP influence in the GMD (in its Second Congress 100 of 250 delegates had been communists). For all practical purposes, thus, the alliance between the two parties ended and a new civil war began. (The CCP unsuccessfully cooperated with a left GMD group until July 1927).[2]

Civil war between the CCP and the GMD followed with periods of truce necessitated by the Japanese invasion of China in 1937. With the defeat of Japan in 1945, renewed civil war between the CCP and the GMD results in the victory of the former over the latter. On October 1, 1949 in Beijing, Mao formally inaugurated the birth of the People's Republic of China (PRC).

The history of the PRC from its inception in 1949 to the death of Mao in 1976 was largely etched by him. During this period Mao served as head of the CCP, as chairman of the central committee—and, until 1958, as state chairman—but above all else he was the charismatic leader who symbolized revolution and communism.[3]

The first period of the PRC's development, 1950-54, followed the contours of Mao's *On People's Democratic Dictatorship* (1949), which restated the proposition of forming a four-class bloc as necessary precondition to socialist banks, large enterprises of industry and commerce (1949-50), and large-scale industrialization by the first five-year plan (1953-7) based on the Soviet model that emphasized heavy industry.[4] In the rural sector the landlords lost their lands to the poor peasantry, while the middle and rich peasantry kept their lands.[5] In these changeovers, some terror was employed, especially in the countryside in 1951, where approximately two million former landlords were killed. Mao justified this on the ground that landlords had been ruthless as leaders of the GMD.[6]

In laying the groundwork for future social change, the CCP did not neglect the women of new China. The traditional male-superior/

female-inferior social roles were made illegal by the 1950 marriage law, which institutionalized legal, social, and economic equality for women; committees were formed throughout China to see the law implemented.[7]

Nineteen fifty-five was a memorable year for China, as collectivization of agriculture began and nationalizations in commerce and industry were completed; since China was and is an overwhelmingly peasant society, the first of the two changes had the greater impact on the lives of its people. Mao's aims specifically in agricultural collectivization (to form three-quarters of a million collectives of 125 million households) were (1) to intensify the class struggle, especially between the poor and rich peasantry; and (2) to increase production through collective endeavors. Certain inequalities continued, since each family had its private plot and individual work on the collective was measured by work points as member of a team (twenty to thirty families working together).[8]

With the completion of the economic and social changes just enumerated, Mao in late 1956 launched a movement with the slogan, "Let a Hundred Flowers Bloom," in which debate was encouraged to examine not only the recently effected changes, but all avenues of Chinese life, including shortcomings within communism. However, when serious criticism of the basic ideals of communism was undertaken by intellectuals and others, Mao backtracked by terminating the experiment.[9]

Partially in response to condemnation of communism and in order to accelerate the drive towards it, Mao boldly opted in 1958-59 for a "Great Leap Forward," which pushed for a more intensive collectivization in the thousands of people's communes. (Their formation caused great controversy in the Communist camp; when Nikita Khrushchev, the secretary to the Soviet Communist Party, derided them, it contributed to the Sino-Soviet split in the early 1960s). The basic aim of the communes was to create a milieu— at once economic, social, political, and psychological—for the development of a new communist person. Mao held that human will and the intensive collectivization of the communes were decisive interrelations in reaching communism.[10]

Through the communes, Mao formed an urban-proletarian social milieu and concomitant culture in the countryside. For example, the intensive collectivization allowed for the concurrent development of agriculture and light industry in which the peasantry could become part-time industrial workers, thus being able to familiarize themselves at least with the rudiments of modern machine technology. This decentralized industrialization, serving agriculture and closely tied to it, was a clear departure from the Soviet model, which emphasized heavy industry or the urban sector at the expense of the rural one. The communes also provided for nurseries, common dining halls, and education. In the initial outburst of enthusiasm in 1959-60, a concerted attempt was made to leap into the communist future of "From each according to his ability, to each according to his need"— work on private plots and work points were abolished for a wageless system that included free distribution of food based on need.

Closely intertwined with the attainment of a society of socioeconomic equality were the communes' embodiment of political (governmental) decentralization and observance of democratic forms under party auspices: all at age sixteen could vote and be eligible as representatives in a commune's congress (its chief governing body). This political organ then elected a management committee headed by a president. A military factor was also included: each commune had its own militia.[11]

There are certain theoretical problems with respect to the communes. In Marxism-Leninism, there is a two-stage development in attaining the Communist goal: Marx, in *Critique of the Gotha Program*, saw the first stage (socialism) as one in which various economic, social, and other contradictions would still remain (manual versus intellectual labor, city versus country, governors versus governed) until their resolution, which then would usher in the second or final phase (communism).[12] During the first stage, both Marx, in *The Civil War in France*, and Lenin, in *State and Revolution*, saw that the contradictions or tension points just mentioned would not negate general social and economic equality and pervasive democratic political forms.[13] The rise of Stalinism in the Soviet Union neglected the preceding features. The Chinese believed that the Soviet model, emphasizing the rapid development of heavy industry and thus exacerbating great socioeconomic, political, and cultural strains— as between manual and intellectual labor and so forth—provided the groundwork for Soviet revisionism in the 1960s. Furthermore, the Chinese criticized the Soviet model for eschewing the ideals of communism by creating a privileged elite. Mao, by developing the communes, consciously tried to forestall this development by creating institutional structures that would keep the various contradictions and antagonisms within reasonable parameters until their ultimate resolution. The problems here were enormous for China achieved revolution in a much lower stage of economic development than Russia in 1917, or as envisaged by classic Marxism. (Yet in many of his works Marx hoped for a socialist revolution in Western Europe which outside of England was still mainly rural.) Obviously, there are certain contradictory elements here: between revolutionary élan for democracy and equality as opposed to necessary historical progression through successive economic phases and concomitant social and political struggles involving rather lengthy time periods; the latter may justify some social, economic, and other inequalities until the productive forces have reached the required advanced levels for communism. Mao definitely stressed the former elements at the expense of the latter in the people's communes experiment and in his next inspired upheaval, the Cultural Revolution.[14]

The intensive drive toward communism in the 1958-60 period was met with great resistance among the more privileged layers of society, which, together with poor crops caused by inclement weather and especially poor planning led to a partly man-made famine in which twenty million perished, necessitating a partial retreat: small private plots and food distribution based on work points in collective work were reintroduced in 1961. Now, the basic work group was the team again, as the former collective pattern resurfaced. The communes' political structure, however, remained, as well as the reliance on small industry and certain other features.[15]

Politically, for Mao, the economic failures associated in the early commune phase led to some power slippage: he chose not to run as chairman of the PRC in 1958, being replaced by Liu Shaoqui (Liu Shao-ch'i), an important CCP functionary and theoretician. However, Mao retained the party chairmanship and the country's respect as preeminent revolutionary. Those in the party who favored greater individual economic incentives by means of wage differentials and more attention devoted to heavy industry were gathered around Liu.[16]

After a five-year pause, the next period of storm and stress in the PRC occurred with the Great Proletarian Cultural Revolution (GPCR), which Mao unleashed for a variety of reasons. A principal one was the erosion of his dominant power position in the Party to Liu, who was supported by well-entrenched elements in the bureaucracies of party, government, army, and industry. (In this connection we may note that most of the party's central committee was against the GPCR.) Also, Mao's many years as a guerilla undoubtedly had a role here, where equality and spontaneity had precedence over inequality and hierarchy.

From a Marxian revolutionary perspective, the GPCR was an extension and deepening of the people's communes' period. All the more was Mao now concerned with the various contradictions, already mentioned, inherent in a socialist society straining for communism—especially in an economically poor one. From a theoretical perspective, he characterized contemporary Chinese society—one under the aegis of the Party—as one still in the throes of an intense class struggle between those wishing for a return to capitalism ("capitalist-roaders") and the average people and officials who wished to continue the drive toward communism. In his fear of an embourgeoisement process within a socialist society and need for a concomitant class struggle to forestall it, Mao breaks into new territory concerning Marxism (although he was anticipated in this regard by Leon Trotsky, among others). To broaden the revolution, that is, to intensify the class struggle, Mao did something unheard of in the Soviet bloc nations: he involved the masses in the power struggle raging within the party.[17]

Mao's decisive advantage in the power struggle, apart from his position of party chairman, was the allegiance of his close colleague Zhou Enlai who was premier and thus had great influence in the state bureaucracy, and the support of Lin Biao (Lin Piao), who was an army chief (rewarded by Mao in 1969 with designation as Mao's successor).

The critical mass-revolutionary element of the GPCR (Mao tapped the revolutionary potential of the first generation of Communist youth) were the army-sponsored Red guards, some thirty million strong, who spearheaded the attack on the more privileged groups. Mao appropriately began the onslaught in his big character poster, "Bombard the Headquarters," of August 5, 1966, by calling on the masses to struggle against the privileged bureaucrats, who, if not checked, would return to capitalist ways, in which economic incentive and hierarchy would win over equality and revolutionary élan.[18] To insure general equality and mass democratic participation, the Maoists urged that the ideas enunciated by the Paris commune of 1871 be followed as a model; Marx's *The Civil War in France* and Lenin's *State and Revolution* were, as before, among the key theoretical works stressed.[19]

The shock on daily life made by the GPCR was profound, for China was involved in a miniature civil war as schools were closed, the Party organization was destroyed (replaced by revolutionary committees), and production in various economic sectors was sharply curtailed.[20] It was in this chaos that the Maoists in 1966 established throughout the nation permanent revolutionary committees—in the communes of the countryside and in factories, schools, and so forth in the cities. These committees were permeated by a pervasive democratic spirit: members (many noncommunist) were elected by the people for only a brief office tenure and could be freely criticized or even recalled; in addition, they neither received pay nor were allowed absence from regular work.[21]

In this period of revolutionary exaltation, Mao emerged as a messianic revolutionary figure; the Red guards and masses assiduously read his works and always carried with them the little red-bound book, *Quotations from Chairman Mao Tse-tung*. From a humanistic socialist perspective, this hero worshipping is obviously deplorable, but may at least be understood as the focal point for continual revolution to achieve communism.[22]

The GPCR did not merely bring about greater socioeconomic equality and mass participation in the various institutions of society, but, as its name implies, it launched a concerted attack on the entire cultural baggage of thousands of years of class society. As Mao told André Malraux in an interview held in Beijing (October, 1965—just before the GPCR): "The thought, culture and customs which brought China to where we found her must disappear; the thought, customs, and culture of proletarian China, which does not yet exist, must appear."[23] Thus, the "Four Olds" (the traditional "ideas, customs, culture and habits") were pitilessly denounced for a systematic and conscious communist alternative that emphasized a new proletarian world view.[24] Mao, in this respect, recognized that for communism to succeed, the elimination of private property alone was not enough; the traditional cultural patterns also had to be quickly destroyed lest they be used as springboards to restore the past.[25]

Education, for example, was one key area in which the GPCR brought about great changes. Even with the advent of the PRC in 1949, bourgeois and landlord groups continued to play a significant role as students and teachers. The schools, as before, stressed memorization and testing, methods which at the same time fostered contempt for manual labor and induced a strong competitive spirit inimical to communism. Now, theoretical and practical work were closely interwoven and testing was downgraded, as a revolutionary political attitude took precedence (those aspiring to university education from rural backgrounds, for example, needed the approval of the commune); all this allowed more students of proletarian and peasant backgrounds to attend schools of higher education. In addition, thousands of May Seven Schools were founded, in which urban youth and bureaucrats went to the countryside to perform manual labor in the fields; thus would they bring the modern urban world to the countryside, but in turn, by working alongside the peasantry, would become more sympathetic to them and be cleansed of an attitude of superiority. For Mao, education was vital in resolving the various contradictions impeding the drive to communism; his solution was to intellectualize the workers as quickly as possible while proletarianizing the intellectuals.[26]

The acrimonious power struggle that tore China apart for three years, one in which the Maoists defeated the Liu group (by the time the CCP was reconstituted in 1969, approximately three quarters of its central committee had been replaced and many party members purged), did not bring an end to intraparty conflict.[27] Soon Mao and Lin were involved in a fight for supremacy; although Lin had the loyalty of much of the army, Mao, with the aid of Zhou, was able through a complicated series of maneuvers to defeat him. (Lin was reportedly killed in an airplane accident over Mongolia while fleeing to the Soviet Union.)[28]

Mao's last significant achievement was the Cultural Revolution. He died in September 9, 1976.

Within a month after Mao's death, a power struggle erupted among the top leadership of the CCP, which soon saw the emergence of Hua Guofeng (Hua Kuo-feng), already premier, as new party chairman. Apparently, with the aid of the party Center and Right, he purged the elements most clearly identified with the Cultural Revolution, the "Gang of Four," who prominently included Mao's widow, Jiang Qing (Chiang Ch'ing), and Vice Premier Zhang Chunqiao (Chang Chunqiao). Although they were arrested in October, 1976, trials and sentencing were completed only in late January, 1981.[29]

With the general purging of the Left in 1977—those most favorable to the Cultural Revolution—and reinstatement of those purged during the Cultural Revolution, the party inexorably drifted rightward. The return to power of the party's vice chairman, Deng Xiaoping (Teng Hsiao-p'ing), signifies this. Purged in the Cultural Revolution, rehabilitated in 1973, stripped of his power position in 1976, but restored in 1977, he was now considered the leading personality of the CCP, his followers in key party and state positions. Deng's real power was in his post as chairperson of the Central Military Committee.[30] The governmental power relations in China are in this descending order: president, prime minister, and unicameral legislature. But real power resides in the twenty-five member Politburo of the CCP and its six member Standing Committee, which includes the president and prime minister. This small ruling group consists of about 100,000 individuals in the higher bureaucratic echelons.

The rise of the Right under Deng, especially since the mid-1980s in the CCP, has continued to the present: by 1957, professionals/intellectuals/experts who came from former bourgeois and landlord families outnumbered the workers in the CCP. They had joined the CCP because of disgust with GMD corruption and weak response to Japanese aggression. Let us add that even with the rise of the Right, urban workers until the 1980s enjoyed the "iron rice bowl"— job security, free medical care and education, subsidized housing, disability insurance, and guaranteed pensions.

The basic economic unit in urban areas was the work unit in factories, schools, hospitals, and so forth. To be sure, surplus-value was extracted from workers, but it was of a reasonable amount because labor was not treated as a mere commodity of production as it is under capitalism. As such, material incentives for workers were limited because Mao did not desire a divided workforce of highly paid workers as opposed to average ones; also, the socialist aim was to increase worker participation in running industry.

In the rural areas, the basic economic unit was the production brigade. Before de-collectivization, the peasantry had free healthcare and education, disability insurance, and childless couples supported by the collective; afterward free healthcare and other social benefits were reduced or eliminated.

To be sure, there was considerable central economic planning necessitating that it be wrung from workers because China as a poor nation had to construct basic industries and an infrastructure to modernize; these realities would ultimately lead to a sharp division in income between manual and mental labor.

The de-collectivization of agriculture by Deng occurred between 1979 and 1984. Although initiated from the top down, the majority of the peasantry supported it. Indeed, a third of the collectives were not performing well, and with higher government prices for farm produce, peasant income rose considerably.

The household-responsibility system which replaced collectivization allowed peasants to work on their own plot of land (1.2 acres was the average). Although technically the village owned the land, in effect this system brought back private property. Let us add that the 1.2 acre farm makes mechanization difficult and not as profitable as large-scale farming. In addition, town and village enterprises (TVEs) were encouraged to stimulate commerce; they were privatized in 1992. The decollectivization of agriculture resulted in the redundancy of more than 150 million farmers by 2010, who went to the cities to work for Chinese and foreign capitalists. One result from the preceding developments was increased class divisions.

To be sure, de-collectivization of agriculture was the first step to destroy the actual socialism of China. Furthermore, it severed the worker-peasant alliance and allowed capitalist relations in the countryside involving the vast majority of Chinese. From 1978 to 1992, China's economy was still largely run by state-owned enterprises (SOEs) and TVEs. The work-unit system continued with job security and other mentioned social benefits, although by the late 1980s workers had multi-year employment contracts and unprofitable small SOEs were allowed to go bankrupt. Overall, however, there were only a few layoffs. This period could be characterized as a socialist market economy, not a capitalist one. Labor as yet was not considered as a mere commodity of production.

The transformative economic change for privatization occurred in 1992, followed by the 1997 CCP Congress that demanded that SOEs operate on market principles. Thus many SOEs and all TVEs (already mentioned) were privatized under the ownership of their managers. The SOEs, traditionally providing many social benefits with their added costs, now found it difficult to compete successfully with the many private companies offering no social benefits, and which had assured markets in the West.

Thus it is that the socioeconomic conditions of workers were adversely affected by marketization and increasing private enterprise, with managers having the right to discharge workers and prevalence of piece-work, a device which Marx noted could not but heighten the exploitation of labor. Between 1992 and 2005, fifty million workers lost their jobs, most with scant or no compensation, including loss of free health insurance. Even many employed workers lost housing subsidies and healthcare, with its recipients being only twenty-five million government bureaucrats (fully insured) and seventy-five million SOE workers, half of whose medical expenses were covered, and some insurance for TVE workers. By and large, most Chinese paid more than 70 percent of health care costs. The "iron rice bowl" was no longer universal.

In the realm of education, examinations were now emphasized, with higher education given great priority in the drive for rapid modernization, favoring the children of mental labor, further exacerbating status and class differences.[30]

The 1990s were a critical time for Chinese socialism; either it would endure, or capitalism would triumph. The basic struggle here occurred within the CCP, which meant that the mass of workers and peasants were not involved. To be sure, the fall of the Soviet Union in 1991 emboldened the capitalist roaders inside the CCP to push for capitalism, and they largely succeeded. The status/class forces of the experts/bureaucrats in the CCP overwhelmed those of the workers whose unions were under the auspices of the CCP. If worker-power in the work units had been paramount in decision-making, the drive to capitalism could have been averted.

There were many workers' protests during this transition period, but they were not coordinated, principally because the layoffs occurred over time and in scattered sites. There was no independent working-class organization outside the CCP which could have stopped the march to capitalism.

All in all, the CCP and economic/state bureaucracies reinforced their normal dominance over the base of farmers and workers who were increasingly economically/socially atomized, pitted against one another. Indeed, the current capitalist or market-orient economic model neglects the economic inefficiency in human terms of mass unemployment and underemployment with their concomitant increased alienation of socioeconomic misery. A socialist society should not necessarily focus on economic growth at the expense of basic human needs. Surely, proper economic planning can at once allow for technological modernization and full employment, including universal health care and other social needs, without victimizing large sections of the working class. Failure to do so indicates a betrayal of basic socialist principles.

The capitalist spirit is so pervasive that the People's Liberation Army is one of the leading capitalist conglomerates running a plethora of enterprises. This condition insures the army's loyalty to capitalism, its leading officers profiting handsomely. Economic consolidation now continues under a ferocious capitalism as small factories are replaced by larger ones, small shops/restaurants by corporate chains, and public markets by supermarkets and shopping malls. Today (2013), SOEs comprise 20 percent of industry, but 30 percent of its value, the remainder in the hands of private Chinese and foreign capitalists. In contrast, in 1978, SOEs comprised 78 percent of production, and TVEs 22 percent.

The CCP under the impress of the capitalist roaders has become utterly nepotistic and corrupt, allowing the extended families of its high and other officials to become most of the Chinese wealthy. This nepotism/corruption is so pervasive that many of the children ("princelings") of top CCP officials are either CEOs of many privately-owned companies, or on the boards of directors as CEOs of SOEs.

A detailed description of how families of prominent CCP members enriched their families: (1) sell SOEs into private stockholding ones; (2) appoint family members as managers; (3) acquire loans from state-owned banks; (4) work with foreign capitalists as partners; (5)

go public by stock in the Hong Kong and New York stock exchanges; (6) receive kickbacks from contracts with foreign companies doing business in China. State wealth plundered by the Communist-capitalists is about $5 trillion. This species of capitalism is of the bureaucratic variety. Also SOEs were sold to capitalists at very low prices, an egregious robbery.

Also, in the last decade, Wall Street and other banks have hired many close relatives of top CCP officials to aid their entering the Chinese market. For example, the grandson of the former President Jian Zemin had a position with Goldman Sachs; the daughter of the former Prime Minister Wen Jiabao was an employee of Credit Swisse. Corruption within the CCP is so widespread and profitable that 18,000 of its leading members in the Party, state, and industry have left China for mainly the U.S. and Canada with a minimum of $120 billion. But a large number of CCP officials have also been arrested and imprisoned.

For Deng and his successors, socialism exists simply to build a strong, rich, and modern China, not one that is modern, rich, and egalitarian—they are not socialists. As Deng once stated: "To get rich is glorious." The CCP should now be called the Chinese Capitalist Party. Under Deng, the present bureaucratic-capitalist elite now running China arose, leading a state-owned/capitalist economic system, a hybrid of sorts.[31]

A serious attempt was made to reverse an increasingly bureaucratic/ nepotistic and pro-capitalist CCP on April 17, 1989, when university students in Beijing, China's capital, assembled in Tiananmen Square (the center of state power) to begin the most popular uprising in China since the GPCR. Student demands included freedom of the press, a public listing of the salaries and outside incoming of leading CCP and state officials and their children, that students be allowed to organize their own autonomous organizations free of CCP control, and that a general strike against the government take place, a most revolutionary proposal.

Student demands would expose high corruption and nepotism among leading CCP/state officials, a nascent authoritarian/

bureaucratic capitalist class, involving the mass of workers and peasants in the process, perhaps starting a revolutionary process similar to the GPCR, and return China to an earlier egalitarian Communism with an opening to democracy, perhaps a participatory one. Student demands, however, were within the CCP umbrella. By May 4, 1989, 300,000 students and workers students and workers were at the Square; by May 17, up to two million; by May 25 there were demonstrations throughout China.

The CCP was divided as to the course of action against the students and workers, but finally Deng's views prevailed: crush the reform movement. On 3-4 June, troops opened fire on the demonstrators at the Square, and there were clashes between the forces of order and demonstrations in Beijing and more than a dozen other cities. All told, 2,000-7,000 students and mostly workers were killed, many more wounded, and approximately 40,000 arrested. Students, except for their leaders, were treated leniently by the authorities, many being children of the CCP elite. This uprising was the last serious popular one to prevent the rise of a capitalist China.[32]

Regarding China's class structure: mainly at the very top are the very wealthy CCP members and their families. Its apex is composed of 115 billionaires worth $230 billion in 2012, comprising 3.9 percent of China's GDP. Two examples of CCP member/extended family wealth include Wen Jiabao's (prime minister, 2000-2013) $2.7-4.3 billion; Xi Jinping (president of China, general secretary of the CCP, and Chairman of the Central Military Commission since 2013), billions of dollars. These fortunes were acquired through the symbiotic relationship of government and private business.

Under them are 3,200 families worth more than $15 million, 90 percent of whom are children of CCP/state officials, as are 90 percent of the richest 20,000 families. From a broad economic perspective, the richest 250,000 households have 70 percent of the entire wealth, not counting the worth of primary residences. Inequality is so great in China that one estimate has it as the most unequal nation of twenty-two East Asian ones. China's 2012 Gini coefficient (zero is absolute equality, 1 is absolute inequality) of 0.46 is higher than that of the U.S., whose income inequality is one of the highest of wealthy nations. Indeed, some economists believe that China's Gini coefficient is even higher because some of the wealthy do not report illicit income. One estimate has the richest tenth of the Chinese population as having 31 percent of the income, but I suspect that it is much higher because the U.S., having a little less economic inequality than China, has its richest tenth with 50-56 percent of the income. Chinese income inequality has the top tenth of the Chinese people earning sixty-five times more than the bottom tenth. In contrast, in 1978, under socialism, China had a Gini coefficient of 0.22, one of the world's lowest rates, comparable to Sweden's, indicating a good deal of socioeconomic equality. As far as income tax policy, China has a somewhat progressive system, approximating Western Europe's, the richest citizens taxed at a 45 percent marginal rate, compared to 39.6 percent for the U.S.

In the late 1990s, the occupational structure of China was as follows: underneath the top 1 percent, there was a middle class of 80 million, or 10 percent of the working population, state officials, engineers, teachers, and other educated professionals, along with lower white-collar workers; then 120 million industrial workers or 15 percent of it; then another 20-25 percent blue-collars in various occupations; finally, 40-45 percent of rural farmers and workers. In 2012, 78 percent of the workforce labored in the private sector, and 22 percent in the SOEs. As China has industrialized, the manual blue-collar and mental labor have increased in number, and the peasantry has decreased.[33]

As a developing nation, China is greatly dependent on a large amount of unskilled labor (47 percent of its economy is in manufacturing/construction/mining, twice the U.S. share). Thus it is that, contrary to developed nations, the unemployment rate for 21-to-25 year olds is lower for the less skilled as opposed to the more skilled, who have more education—4.2 percent for those up to elementary education, 8.2 percent with high-school/vocational training, 11.3 percent for completing junior college, and 16 percent for bachelor degree and beyond graduates.

Circa 2013, Chinese colleges/universities graduated seven million students to the U.S.'s three million (China has four times the population of the U.S.). But as a developing (poor) nation, China has still more need of unskilled workers than well-educated ones. Thus, the oversupply of skilled workers has lessened the income disparity between them and the unskilled. For instance, computer science graduates in Shenzen in 2000 earned $725 monthly, ten times that of a manual worker with less than a high school education, but in 2012 the former earned $550 monthly, the latter approximately half. In the last four years, the wages of unskilled blue-collar workers have increased 70 percent.

To be sure, the Confucian tradition of denigrating manual labor is also partly responsible for the oversupply of mental labor, with its better income and more social prestige. With GDP rising rapidly, so to have living standards in the last decade; 2012 Chinese government statistics have average annual disposable income for urban dwellers at $4,000 and $1,300 for rural ones. The economic impact and consequent social and political ones in China of foreign capital are immense; in 2012, foreigners invested $119.7 billion, over half of it by overseas Chinese, in 120,000 companies employing up to 15 percent of the urban workers, conducting about half of foreign trade. About a third of Chinese manufacturing is by factories working with foreign companies. Overall, foreign investment has contributed about 10 percent to China's GDP.

With the aid of foreign investment, capitalist exploitation of labor, and an export-driven capitalist mercantilism creating a favorable trade balance, China's GDP growth has been phenomenal, averaging almost 10 percent annually from the early 1980s to2012, in 2013, expanding in the high 7 percent range. In 2012, China's GDP was $8.36 trillion, second to that of the U.S. of $15 trillion. In 2011, China's per capita GDP was $7,600 and by 2013 should be near $9,000, a fourth of Western Europe's. In 2012, China's import/export value was $3.87 trillion and $317 billion, first in the world, the U.S. second at $3.82 trillion. In 2010, Chinese foreign investment, mostly by its SOEs and Hong Kong, was $317 billion, a third in Europe, a fifth in North America, a fifth in Asia, and a sixth in South America. China in 2012 is the world's leading export workshop, producing 500 million tons of steel annually (first in the world) and its electricity generates 1,000 gigawatts annually (first in the world; the U.S. is second.) In 2010, Chinese exports to the U.S. domestic market accounted for 20 percent of furniture and household goods, and 36 percent of clothing and shoes. The U.S. trade deficit with China annually is in the hundreds of billions of dollars.

Wasteful government investment in roads leading to nowhere, unused airports, and elaborate public buildings, much capitalist speculative investment, especially in unoccupied apartment buildings, itself the result of excessive income inequality between the rich and the workers, and a high personal savings rate has led to a drop in consumption as a percentage of GDP, from 44 percent in 2002 to 35.7 percent in 2012, investment itself rising from 36.2 percent in 2002 to 46.2 percent in 2010. (U.S. domestic investment circa 2013 is 16 percent of DGP while consumption is 70 percent of it.) On the whole, investment rates in developing nations, like China, as percentage of GDP are much higher than in developed nations like the U.S. Excessive apartment building by capitalists has recently lowered their high purchase prices, leading to the rich losing much of their investment value. If the working class had higher wages to consume or had saved less of their income, the preceding economic waste would not have occurred.

This speculative frenzy in China based on easy credit and its twin of rapid economic expansion has recently burst in a number of cities, one of which is Shenmu in northwestern China, with a half-million people in a coal-industry area. Falling coal prices here have led to failing coal mines, bankruptcies for their rich owners, and for the luxury establishments of conspicuous consumption serving them— clothing stores, restaurants, night clubs, and auto dealerships of Audis and BMWs. To be sure, these developments have resulted in high worker unemployment in the industrial and retail sectors, workers demonstrating in the streets, insisting that helpless city officials provide work for them and compensate them for back wages not paid by capitalists. These are the fruits of capitalist uneven development and speculation, leading to economic boom and bust, as illustrated by the dire consequences just mentioned.

China's modernization now has half of its people living in cities. In a reformist vein, the government is extending its social security system of healthcare pensions, and housing for urban workers (50 percent now have it) and the peasantry, quite an accomplishment for a still poor nation, a remnant of its socialist ideology. Nevertheless, many peasants and rural immigrants to the cities as yet do not have a *hukou*, a household registration card bestowing many social security benefits, like public medical care, forcing them to save much of their earnings for emergency medical and retirement needs. Nevertheless, by 2011 95 percent of Chinese have health insurance. Circa 2013, the Chinese working class is expanding rapidly as China is the workshop of the world; up to two-thirds of China's urban population comprises manual workers, a third of whom are in industry, like manufacturing and construction. This mass, as will soon be observed, is in an ugly mood.

Despite rising living standards of Chinese workers, their working conditions are abysmal, especially outside the SOEs. In the export-driven Pearl River Delta, two-thirds of workers have more than an eight-hour day (some at times up to sixteen hours), with two days off monthly. Furthermore, a fourth of workers (200 million) labor in dangerous conditions; in 2010, for instance, 364,000 were seriously injured, and 80,000 killed.

The socioeconomic misery of the Chinese working class has led to increasing waves of strikes, riots, and demonstrations, annually rising from 87,000 in 2005 to 280,000 in 2010, presaging a revival of an egalitarian socialism. Already, 60 percent of the workforce is outside of agriculture, to be 70 percent by 2020, which, according to Minqi Li, a respected Chinese scholar, is the critical number to effect significant reform, reinforced by the many unemployed college graduates. This social discontent has prompted the CCP in 2013 to call for narrowing the income gap between workers and the wealthier groups.

Of the world's population, land, and fresh water, China has 22 percent, 7 percent, and 6 percent respectively. To remedy this imbalance the Chinese government instituted a two-child per couple policy in the 1990s, and a one-child policy in the 1980s. But in the next half century, population (975 million in 1990; 1.3 billion in 2010) will continue to increase because of life longevity. There are incentives for parents to have one child, including more favorable school and employment admissions for their children, and retirement pensions for parents, and so forth. Later, the policy was relaxed to allow a second child if the first was a girl. On the whole, this program succeeded in significantly lowering the birth rate from 7.5 per woman in 1963 to 1.5 today, one of the world's lowest.

China's rapid industrialization has resulted in a serious pollution problem: two-thirds of its urban dwellers breathe polluted air and 70 percent of its lakes and rivers are polluted. Finally, coal air pollution is especially shortening the lives, by 5.5 years, of the 500 million Chinese who live north of the Huai River, compared with those who live south of it, in the 1981-2000 period. This condition is related to China now using half of the world's coal.[34]

In 2012, the CCP has a membership of 82.6 million, about an eighth of the active population; its presence is ubiquitous in Chinese life, schools, factories, religious groups, and so forth. Party indoctrination begins in early education as all students are enrolled as Young Pioneers; in high school, interested youth join the Communist Youth League. Despite this indoctrination for Communist ideals, corruption is widespread and today capitalism basically reigns.

The experiences of Soviet and Chinese Communism during the last nine decades indicate that a viable Marxist socialism is at least for now rather remote in economically backward/rural societies attempting to industrialize rapidly. The be sure these Communist societies promoted highly egalitarian socioeconomic policies at first, but in not allowing any form of participatory democracy for workers and peasants outside of brief periods, their Communist parties soon sponsored inegalitarian socioeconomic policies, ultimately leading to the return of capitalism. Furthermore, Russia had only a small working class in a peasant sea when it Communist revolution occurred, and China had scarcely any working class at all (overwhelmingly peasant) when its Communists won in 1949. It should also be remembered that the elitist structures of the Communist parties of the Soviet Union and China themselves were of a militaristic nature, organized to win battle (revolution and civil war). As already observed, the Soviet one in the early stages of War Communism had worker control of industry for a brief period of time only, and the Commune period in China was of brief duration. Thus, the nationalizations consummated by both Communist parties were not socialist in nature, although non-capitalistic. For Marx, socialization of production signified that property and production be in the hands of the "associated workers" themselves. Nationalized property is not socialist but state property, and those controlling the state were not the workers and peasants, but a bureaucracy supposedly ruling in their name.

Endnotes

1) On the rise of the Guomindang (GMD) and Soviet assistance, see Stuart Schram, *Mao Tse-tung* (Harmondsworth: Penguin Books, 1996, rev. ed., 1967), pp. 72 ff. On Sun Zhongshan and his basic ideology, see his *Memoirs of a Chinese Revolutionary* (New York: AMS Press, 1970), pp. 227-33, on his "Three Principles of the People: Nationalism, Democracy, and Socialism."

2) On the rupture between CCP and GMD, see Edgar Snow, *Red Start Over China* (1937; reprint ed., New York: Grove Press, 1961), pp. 161-66, for Mao's account; and John E. Rue, *Mao Tse-Tung in Opposition, 1927-1935* (Stanford, Cal.: Stanford Univ. Press, 1966), pp. 40-81.

3) On Mao as a charismatic leader, especially during the Great Proletarian Cultural Revolution, see Schram, *Mao*, pp. 338-40.

4) *On the People's Democratic Dictatorship* (1949), in Mao Te-tung, *Selected Works of Mao Tse-tung*, 4 vols. (Beijing: Foreign Languages Press, 1967), 4:411-24.

5) On various problems discussed, see appropriate sections in Franz Schurmann, *Ideology and Organization in Communist China* (Berkeley: Univ. of California Press, 1966).

6) On the terror unleashed against the former landlords by the CCP, see Schram, *Mao*, pp. 226-67.

7) On women in the PRC and Mao's struggle on their behalf, see Schram, *The Political Thought of Mao Tse-tung* (New York: Praeger, 1969), pp. 334 ff.; and Schram, *Mao*, p. 260.

8) On the 1955 collectivization, see Mao Tse-tung, *Socialist Upsurge in China's Countryside* (Beijing: Foreign Languages Press, 1957), and Schurmann, *Ideology and Organization*, pp. 442 ff.

9) On the One Hundred Flowers period, see Roderick Macfarquhar, *The Hundred Flowers Campaign and the Chinese Intellectuals* (New York: Praeger, 1960).

10) Schram, *Political Thought*, pp. 351-53, presented some of Mao's optimistic statements about change.

11) On the People's Communes, see the extensive coverage in Schurmann, *Ideology and Organization;* Edgar Snow, *The Other Side of the River: Red China Today* (New York: Random House, 1962); and Jan Myrdal, *Reports from a Chinese Village* (New York: Signet Books, 1965)—this work recounts life after the retreat of 1960-62. Arthur A. Cohen, *Communism of Mao Tse-tung* (Chicago, Univ. of Chicago Press, 1964), p. 178, saw Mao's People's Commune as a "unique socioeconomic-political-military unit."

12) Karl Marx, *Critique of the Gotha Programme: with Appendices by Marx, Engels, Lenin*, ed. C. P. Dutt (New York: International Pubs., 1938), pp. 8 ff.

13) Excerpts from *The Civil War in France* by Karl Marx, in Lewis S. Feuer, ed., *Marx and Engels: Basic Writings on Politics and Philosophy* (New York: Anchor Books, 1959), pp. 365-70; and V. I. Lenin, *State and Revolution* (New York: International Pubs., 1932), pp. 36 ff.

14) On the Soviet model for industrial development, which gives priority to heavy industry that results in great socioeconomic

inequality—Soviet revisionism according to Mao—see the excellent article by Paul M. Sweezy, "Theory and Practice in the Mao Period," in *Marxism and the Good Society*, ed. John Burke, Lawrence Crocker, and Lyman Legters (Cambridge: Cambridge University Press, 1981). On the Maoist model for industrial development, see John G. Gurley, *China's Economy and the Maoist Strategy* (New York: Monthly Review Press, 1976), pp. 198-228. For a representative Maoist criticism of Soviet revisionism, see "Leninism or Social Imperialism?" as cited in David Milton, Nancy Milton, and Franz Schurmann, *People's China: Social Experimentation, Politics, Entry onto the World Scene, 1966 through 1972* (New York: Vintage Books, 1974), pp. 450-73.

15) Schram, *Mao*, p. 300

16) On Liu Shaoqui, see Milton, Milton, and Schurmann, *People's China*, pp. 50, 104, 316-31; and Winberg Chai, *The Search for a New China* (New York: Capricorn Books, 1975), pp. 142-45.

17) On the problems presented by social and other contradictions in the PRC, see Cohen, *Communism of Mao*, pp. 139-67. Mao Tse-tung, *On the Correct Handling of Contradictions among the People*, as cited in Schram, *Political Thought*, pp. 304-12, with the 1969 and 1973 constitutions of the CCP in Chai, *Search for a New China*, pp. 170-71, 251, for example. In the first citation of this note, Mao does not see great difficulties in class and class-related tensions, while he does so in the latter two. The Great Proletarian Cultural Revolution had changed Mao's perspective. For an excellent presentation of Mao's contribution to the problem of class struggle within a socialist society, see John Bryan Starr, *Continuing the Revolution: The Political Thought of Mao* (Princeton, N.J.: Princeton Univ. Press, 1979).

18) On Mao's "Bombard the Headquarters," see Joan Robinson, *The Cultural Revolution in China* (Harmondsworth: Pelican Books, 1971), pp. 80-81.

19) On the Paris Commune as a model for the Great Proletarian Cultural Revolution, see Milton, Milton, and Schurmann, *People's China*, pp. 93-100, 288.

20) For a good account of the Great Proletarian Cultural Revolution, see Robinson, *Cultural Revolution*; Milton, Milton, and Schurmann, *People's China*; Edward E. Rice, *Mao's Way* (Berkeley: Univ. of California Press, 1974); and Tai sung An, *Mao Tse-tung's Cultural Revolution* (Indianapolis Ind.: Pegasus, 1972).

21) On the sixteen points of the Great Proletarian Cultural Revolution, see Milton, Milton, and Schurmann, *People's China*, pp. 272-83. Point nine called for the creation of "cultural revolutionary groups, committees, and congresses."

22) For an example of hero worship with respect to Mao, see Schram, *Mao*, pp. 338-40.

23) André Malraux, *Anti-Memoirs*, trans. Terrence Kilmartin (New York: Holt, Rinehart & Winston, 1968), p. 374.

24) Robinson, *Cultural Revolution*, p. 55.

25) See the commentary by Milton, Milton, and Schurmann, *People's China*, pp. 21-34. See "We Are Critics of the Old World," in *ibid.*, pp. 257-61; and excerpts from Mao Tse-tung, "A Talk by Chairman Mao with a Foreign (Albanian) Military Delegation," pp. 261-66.

26) On educational reform during the Cultural Revolution, see Jonathan Mirsky, "China After Nixon," *Annals of the American Academy of Political and Social Science*, 402: 88-90; and Milton, Milton, and Schurmann, *People's China*, pp. 106-48, 245-48.

27) On the differences between Liu and Mao, see Lowell Dittmer, *Liu Shao-ch'i and the Chinese Cultural Revolution: The Politics of Mass Criticism* (Berkeley: Univ. of California Press, 1974), pp. 214-93.

28) On the rivalry between Lin and Mao, see Rice, *Mao's Way*, pp. 499-513; and Chai, *Search for a New China*, pp. 148-53.

29) On Party struggles since 1976, see Charles Bettelheim, "The Great Leap Backward," *Monthly Review*, July-August 1978, pp.

37-130; and Frank Ching, "The Current Political Scene in China," *China Quarterly* (December 1979): 691-715.

30) Ching, "Current Political Scene," pp. 691-715.

31) On the rise of capitalism in China after the mid-1980s and especially since 1992, see Minqi Li, *The Rise of China and the Demise of the World Capitalist Economy* (New York: Monthly Review Press, 2008); Maurice Meisner, *The Deng Xiaoping Era; An Inquiry Into the Fate of Chinese Socialism* (New York: Hill and Wang, 1996); Joel Andreas, "Changing Colours in China," *New Left Review*, no. 54 Nov.-Dec. 2008, pp. 123-42. On corruption, Peter Kwong, "Why China's Corruption Won't Stop," *The Nation*, Ap. 22, 2013, pp. 17-21.

32) On the Democracy movement and student/worker rebellion, see Meisner, pp. 396-467.

33) On wealth/class/polarization, especially since the 1990s, and the rise of socioeconomic inequalities, see Andreas and Minqi Li, "The Rise of the Working Class and the Future of the Chinese Revolution," *Monthly Review*, vol. 63, no. 4, June 2011, pp. 44-46; and John Bellamy Foster and Robert W. McChesney, "The Global Stagnation and China," *Monthly Review*, vol. 63, no. 9, February 2012, pp. 1-28, especially p. 13. Meisner, p. 51, for instance.

34) For 2012 wages in Shenzen, urban unemployment for the 21-to 25 age group and Confucian tradition in disdaining manual labor, see Keither Bradsher, "Young Chinese Say No Thanks To Factory Jobs," *New York Times*, Jan 25, 2012, pp. A1 and A9. Hereafter, *NYT*. On Chinese pensions, see Mark W. Frazier, "No Country for Old Age," *NYT*, Feb. 19, 2013, p. A23; and Samir Amin, "China, 2013," *Monthly Review*, Vol. 64., No.9, March 2013. p.32. On decollectivization of agriculture, see Zhur Xu, "The Political Economy and Decollectivization in China," *Monthly Review*, vol. 65, No. 1, May 2013, pp. 17-36. On foreign investment in China, and size of China's GDP in 2012, see "Wary of Events in China, Foreign Investors Head to Cambodia," *NYT*, Apr 9, 2013, p. 136. That 90 percent of China's economic growth is domestic-driven, see Samir Amin, "China, 2013," *Monthly Review* vol. 64, no. 9,

March 2013, p. 23. On China's import/export value in 2012, see *Time*, Feb. 25, 2013, p. 9. On China's high investment spending, see *NYT*, Nov. 7, 2012, p. B1. On China's foreign investment, see "Nice to see you, EU," *The Economist*, Ap. 20-26, 2013, p. 50; Hung Ho-Fung, "China's Rise Stalled?" *New Left Review*, No. 81, May/June 2013, p. 159. On decreasing share of consumer consumption of GDP in China, see Foster and McChesney, p. 6. On China's rapidly expanding college graduates, unemployment rates with regard to educational level and income gains especially by unskilled workers, see *NYT*, Jan. 11, 2013, p. B12. Keith Bradsher and Sue-Lin Wong, "A Humbled Class of 2013," *NYT*, June 17, 2013, pp. B1 and 2. On the economic devastation of excess credit, see Keither Bradsher, "Easy Credit Drives up Crippling Chinese Cities," *NYT*, Aug. 16, 2013, pp. A1 and A3. On China's rapidly increasing working class and high income inequality, see Göran Therborn, "Class in the 21st Century," *New Left Review*, no. 78, Nov/Dec, 2012, pp. 20-22. On horrid working conditions, injuries, and industrial-related deaths, and consequent increasing protests, see Foster and McChesney, pp. 15 ff. and Li, pp. 41-44. On CCP leaders' proposal for more income equality, see Chris Buckley, "China...Gap," *NYT*, Feb. 6, 2013, p. A13. On economic statistics in regard to China, I mainly relied on *NYT* articles. On the ravages of coal pollution on life expectancy, see Edward Wong, "Pollution Leads to Drop in Life Span in Northern China, Research Finds," *NYT*, July 9, 2013, p. A6. On pollution and limited arable land in China, see various articles in *Monthly Review*, vol. 63, no. 9, March 2013.

Chapter Seventeen: A Proper Socialism/Ecology

Before outlining a proper socialist paradigm, a brief recapitulation of the contemporary US capitalist system is needed.

At its apex are the large stockholders, boards of directors, and higher management led by a chief executive officer, the winners with great economic rewards, workers the inevitable losers with stagnant/ falling wages and high unemployment.

To make matters worse, the corporate elite lower workers' wages and increase workers' unemployment by investing abroad in low-wage nations like China, further increasing their income wealth (see chap. 13), and in the 2009-12 period alone, garnered 95 percent of income gains.

Furthermore, as already observed, blue collar workers laboring in polluted workplaces have higher death rates than wealthier cohorts.

A socialist society would strip capitalists to make ever more money also from these free gifts: a well-educated workforce through public-financed education; government research/development of new technologies like computers and in drugs; the military-industrial complex (very costly) that protects corporate investment abroad; through PACs/lobbyists, low taxes, tax havens' limited corporate liability; bailouts in economic downturns; lax federal regulatory agencies and so forth.

Socialism would raise the wages of most blue-white-collar and service workers by eliminating high salaries/perquisites of the higher managerial elite and their investment income; as already observed the richest 1 percent had 22.5 percent of the income in 2012 U.S. Then, the conspicuous consumption of the wealthy (richest 10 percent to 60 percent of consumer spending in the US circa 2010), would cease, diverting these resources into constructing better housing and so forth to the lower half of the population and improving social services. Also, the bloated military-industrial complex, including the intelligence agencies, would be eliminated, their funds again diverted to social welfare. Then, too, the waste of economic downturns with their high unemployment would be replaced by steady growth. To be sure, the wealth of the rich would be confiscated by taxes democratically.

A halfway house to socialism is in such social-democratic nations like Germany, France, Italy, Norway, Sweden, Denmark and Finland with their extensive social welfare programs, having more socioeconomic equality than the US, and some government ownership of industry, also heavily regulated, labor/socialist movements in these nations often govern. Nevertheless, a capitalist class is the dominant one.

Further left would be deformed socialist nations like the Soviet Union and China, already observed, in which capitalism has now prevailed.

My proper socialism would correct the patterns of the failed socialist experiments by having, at its core, democratically self-managed worker collectives, closely cooperating under self-management.

This socialism is greatly indebted to utopian socialism/anarchism, John Stuart Mill, and Marx himself ("united cooperative societies working on a common plan.") In 19th century US, such stalwart thinkers/reformers, as was Ralph Waldo Emerson, Horace Greeley and Wendell Phillips, also advocated this collective view, as did labor unions like The Knights of Labor.

But in the 20th century, where industrial bigness/complexity prevailed, it was indeed folly to imagine that a workers' cooperative had the economic resources to challenge General Motors. Also, the two large communist experiments of the 20th century among developed nations, the Soviet Union and China, subjected workers to state bureaucrats acting like capitalists to create rapid surplus-value. Thus, the idea of workers' collectives running society is less prevalent today than previously, but the Mondragon collective in Spain and the many workers collectives in Italy and the US are models for a future socialism.

In my proper socialism, social services will be free and expansive: as in education, including college, healthcare, daycare, maternity leave, disability payments, vacations, and so forth; many to a large extent are already in place today in social democracies like France, Germany, and Scandinavian nations, among others.

Alongside the producers' collectives stand consumers' collectives, the two negotiate between themselves transparently to determine price/quality of goods based on material/labor costs, profit expanding the means of production and so forth. This dynamic economic model allows for planning and consumer free choice to be complementary, assuring a balance between production and consumption. Computers and a pricing system are employed to ensure maximum efficiency. (In developed nations, like the US, consumer consumption is the largest part of GDP, 70 percent in the US). This producer-consumer system is akin to an expensive wrist watch with its many complications. To be sure, there are economic safeguards in place in case of unforeseen shortages and so forth, like stockpiling raw materials and other resources.

"Government" exists to levy taxes, allocate resources to the social-welfare sector, plan for national projects, and so forth; it operates locally, regionally and nationally (in the future perhaps internationally). Its work is overseen by committees elected and supervised by the electorate. There are no elected executives or legislatures. In this society, socioeconomic and political power is diffused, the media playing an important informational role. Voting is conducted via computers.

Regarding property arrangements, I would allow private personal dwellings/contents/transportation and small privately owned cooperatives, the remainder being socially-owned locally, regionally, nationally and even internationally to be run by democratic self-managed collectives.

Regarding present wage differentials, they are decided democratically and following the successful Mondragon collective, should be about 6.5 to 1. With technological advances and so forth, the dichotomy between manual and mental labor should be progressively erased, integrated labor becoming the norm, a development reducing wage differentials eventually to zero. Ultimately, I envision a society of technical, educational, socioeconomical, cultural and political co-equals.

An advanced technology and reforms already suggested should lead to a shorter workday/week, increased levels of education, social welfare and so forth.

Savings accounts exist at no interest. Regarding artists and other unusually gifted individuals, they would be granted royalties/ bonuses, but are heavily taxed.

It may be asked if scientific/technological dynamism would be impaired under an egalitarian socialism which supposedly might stifle initiative and genius? I would think not. Even in capitalist United States, for instance, most of the advanced research is conducted through the aegis of public monies in government/ university complexes before being presented, especially government gratis to business for commercial development. Scientific discoveries are now highly cooperative, usually employing a team approach, often interdisciplinary, and unthinkable without the contributions of past generations.

Socialism itself will terminate consumer choice of a restrictive capitalism bounded by class and myth of the free market, actually oligopolistic, whose manipulative advertising employs the conditioning techniques of the psychologists John B. Watson and Edward Bernays and utilizes the socioeconomic insights of Veblen as depicted in <u>The Theory of the Leisure Class</u>, which emphasizes "invidious distinction," of identifying the buyer, consonant with the amount of money spent, with the "better people," who set the standards of "excellence," itself related to planned obsolescence of goods for more profit. It is, thus, a myth that consumers today have free choice. A socialist market transcends these capitalist parameters/ criteria for those of technical excellence and utilitarianism, combined with a proper aestheticism, while ending the accumulation of junk goods for the sake of profit.

International trade is allowed, but not to cheapen labor as does contemporary capitalism. But economically advanced socialist nations will surely aid poorer ones with appropriate economic assistance of a non-exploitative nature.

As for gender relations, socialism decrees social equality. Indeed, in wealthier capitalist nations, women today have achieved great gains: in the US today, they are the majority of college students, many now in high prestige occupations, like law and medicine.

In the realm of sexuality, consensual sex prevails and transgendered, gay and lesbian relations are celebrated as part of the human condition. Twelve states, including California and New York, and the District of Columbia, recognize same-sex marriage, encompassing half the U.S. population by 2013, a great boost to gay liberation; in Western Europe, many nations, like France, Britain and the Scandinavian ones, also have legalized it. As for the nuclear family, its future becomes ever more problematic, but various combinations of it may endure.

Finally, a proper socialism rejects Aldous Huxley's Brave New World, a society genetically-based on intelligence-class – see Chapter 8.

Socialists are now deeply concerned to reduce global pollution/ climate warming, 60 percent of it caused by the richest 10 percent of the world's population, the poorest 60 percent causing 18 percent of it. If the world's present population of about 7 billion (10 billion by 2100), were to live like its richest 10 percent today, it would require "four earths to supply the resources and assimilate pollutants," according to Fred Magdoff (Monthly Review, Jan. 2013, p. 22).

In May 2013, carbon dioxide levels in the earth's atmosphere reached 400 parts per million (ppm) – not long ago it was an acceptable 350 ppm. The last time the 400 ppm was reached the earth's atmosphere was 3 million years ago when polar ice caps were smaller and sea levels 60-80 feet higher than now. At present rates of increase, by the early 2040s, carbon dioxide in the atmosphere will reach 450 ppm, increasing under 2 ppm annually.

In the 1750-2012 period (Industrial Revolution and aftermath), 556 billion of metric tons entered the earth's atmosphere, which, at present rates of increase, will reach a trillion tons in the 2040s, rapidly increasing the earth's climate by at least 2 degrees centigrade

(3.6 degrees Fahrenheit) circa 2100. There is a 40-50 years lag between increases in carbon dioxide and temperature. Estimates vary regarding how to prevent this temperature rise: one suggests that carbon dioxide fall to near zero by 2050; another that it fall 20 percent and clean energy increase 20 percent in the next two decades; yet another, to decrease it by 40-70 percent by 2050.

According to James Hansen, formerly head of NASA's Gedard Institute for Space Studies, and other climatologists, a 2 degree Centigrade eliminate temperature rise would lead to more droughts/head waves, heavy rains, storms, flooding to lower flood production, more physical damage to farms/cities, and higher mortality rates.

Furthermore, a warming climate will release a lot of methane trapped underneath the ocean floor and a melting permafrost in cold areas like Siberia, further exacerbating climate warming.

Global warming at current rates will contribute to a 2-4 feet sea level rise circa 2100 and soon afterward, inundating low-lying areas in Eastern (especially Florida) and Western U.S., Eastern China, Bangladesh, many Pacific islands, Europe, Africa and so forth, engulfing such cities as New York, Miami, New Orleans, Tokyo, Shanghai, Venice, and Washington D.C., among others. This will result in relocating hundreds of millions of people.

Another estimate by Jason Box, an Ohio State University glaciologist, has sea levels rising 70 feet in the rather near future – based on current ice melting and 230 feet in the next 9,000 years: for Box, this oceanic rise will be gradual, presenting humanity with a chronic, not an acute, emergency problem. But Box does not take into account that climate warming has many other ill affects already observed.

The conversion to clean energy, mainly wind and solar, in the US faces stiff opposition, from the capitalist/corporate sector, especially the fossil fuels segment. Politically, up to 2014 Republicans have stymied Democratic Party attempts to ameliorate carbon pollution. President Obama, by executive authority in 2014, empowered by the Clean Air Act, has decreed slashing carbon pollution from automobiles and coal-fired power plants.

Furthermore, developing nations like China and India, mostly rely on cheap coal to industrialization because of high initial clean energy costs. Inexpensive coal allowed China to industrialize rapidly and lift more than half billion of its people from abject poverty.

Presently, about 80 percent of the world's energy is from fossil fuels, with only 7 percent from renewable materials. Today in poor nations, adding to pollution, 3 billion people heat and cook using open fires and inefficient stoves. On balance, the wealthy nations should not only convert to clean energy but also aid poorer ones to also use it.

There are now many proposals to reduce carbon dioxide emissions in the atmosphere, including a carbon tax, reforestation, more clean energy, conservation, storing carbon dioxide underground and more nuclear power, the latter I reject.

These measures should reduce carbon emissions, but time is growing short. Indeed, I concur with socialists like John Bellamy Foster and Fred Magdoff that only a concerted effort under socialist auspices, rapidly employing many of the preceding proposals, can avert human-civilization disasters. Its resources could come from eliminating the world's military spending, now annually at more than a trillion dollars; increasing taxes on the rich and ending the capitalist commodity-profit system producing endless piles of polluting junk. I also recommend a progressive reduction of the world's population to protect and conserve the earth's atmosphere/resources.

The preceding facts do not necessarily indicate lower living standards, which are usually related to lower consumption of commodities. To be sure, socialist communal sharing of commodities and services will increase at the expense of individual ones. Furthermore I believe that it is possible, eventually for human scientific ingenuity, to produce more goods without adversely affecting the physical environment, but that in the near term consumption of goods should be greatly decreased.

One such plan to convert to clean energy quickly within the next 20 to 40 years, according to two academics, Mark Jacobson, a professor of civil and environmental engineering and Senior Fellow,

disputes by back-room maneuverings and purges. To be sure, this took place in poor societies whose educational level at first was very low, and which in modernization favored mental labor (often at first not paid much more than manual labor, but that increasingly placed itself over the manual variety) in the state, military, and industrial bureaucracies, which succumbed to the worldwide bourgeois hegemony, in time favoring the return to capitalism. Mental labor itself – yes Communism developed class societies – in the very nature of economic organization of societies up to now, with limited productive forces, in the higher reaches of the economic and political bureaucracies, is organized to command manual labor, in the process losing many of its socialist aspirations, itself a prisoner of a cultural horizon in which the common good is overwhelmed by a competitive individualism, in the individual's formative years it is observed in the school system, the more able or proficient students becoming mental labor. Acclimated by competition in school, the inequality as between manual and mental labor, the authoritarianism inherent in the denial of civil liberties, poverty/scarcity, including labor discipline (the peasantry is uprooted, ever more becoming industrial workers) needed to industrialize, wrung from a largely exploited working class and peasantry – "primitive socialist accumulation" – and the lack of democracy, is it any wonder that in the attempt to overcome economic backwardness, Communist parties put themselves opened the road to capitalism by forming elite social classes which desired the inequalities inherent in capitalism.

Lenin and Trotsky, for instance, aware of the many problems inherent in bringing about socialism in economically backward societies, were fearful that without the aid of a socialist revolution in the West, an economically backward Russia would exact its revenge on a revolutionary Soviet Communism by becoming capitalist.

The tragedy of modern Communism in economically backward nations is reminiscent of Marx's remarks in *The Eighteenth Brumaire of Louis Napoleon:*

> Men make their own history, but they do not make
> it just as they please; they do not make it under
> circumstances by themselves, but under circumstances
> directly encountered, given, and transmitted from the
> past. The tradition of all the dead generations weighs
> like a nightmare on the brain of the living.

The severely deformed socialist experiments which failed in the Soviet Union and are now atrophying in China do not negate the vision of Marx's socialism, which is inextricably linked to a general human equality through a pervasive democracy and respect for civil liberties. In the main, Marx saw socialism succeeding a mature capitalism, accomplished only with the creation of a large working class waging a class struggle against the bourgeoisie. The working class is still a young class, not too many generations removed from the poor/repressive countryside and still heavily alienated by capitalist oppression, unable to yet forge sufficient links among its members to bring about socialism.

From this analysis, the conclusion is that at least, for now and the foreseeable future, the trait for a proper and viable socialism requires an advanced technological/educational/high living-standards society in which the dichotomy between manual and mental labor is not overly pronounced because of much general education, with full socialist civil liberties and pervasive participatory democracy.

The struggle of the working class for liberation continues: along with the accompanying technological changes daily occurring, the balance of social forces favoring socialism can still change quickly. In fact, if several economically advanced nations can become socialist, they can influence a world socialism that will remain democratic and civil libertarian even in the midst of lower levels of economic development. Thus, we may see the Soviet and Chinese Communist experiments, along with other socialist currents, as a continuation of the First and Second Socialist Internationals. The Fourth Socialist International is now occurring in a global capitalism racked by economic crisis/high unemployment, leading to increased socialist activity.

We should also add that the liberation struggles for equality by women, gays, lesbians, transgenders, and African Americans and Hispanics in the U.S. invariably strengthen the working class, itself now including large sectors of mental labor, like teachers and nurses. These developments should lead to increasing working class socialist activity against the bourgeoisie to liberate humanity.

In summary, I still fully subscribe to Louis Althusser's views that Marx principally describes the general laws of historical drift as now understood [1] and to Henri Lefebvre's assertions that the main contours of 20th-century socialism involving continually massive urbanization and ever larger increase of the working class confirm rather than deny the validity of Marxism whose prophetic elements hold that socialism is the principal wave of the future as the proletariat's struggle against the bourgeoisie intensifies, now more timely than ever to save humanity against the destruction of the ecostructure and nuclear war.

Thus it is that today strong labor, socialist, social-democratic, Communist, left-of-center parties exist throughout the world. They have already enacted extensive social-welfare legislation, partial nationalizations, as in France and Italy, and worker power in the workplace, as in Germany, France, Norway, and Sweden, both preludes to socialization, the end of a capitalist class and the establishment of worker power in co-/self-management.

A brief survey of today's world left follows: In Europe, vigorous socialist currents exist in every one of its principal nations – Britain and its Celtic fringe of Scotland and Wales, France, Germany, Italy, Spain, and Poland – and in the others, as in Norway, Sweden, Denmark, Finland, Ireland, Belgium, Netherlands, Austria, Czech Republic, Hungary, Serbia, Romania, Bulgaria, Albania, Greece, and Portugal. In the East, the Russian Federation is a strong Communist Party opposing the governing conservative United Russia Party. The Ukraine has a socialist movement and Belarus and Serbia are socialist nations.

In Latin America, leftist/labor/socialist parties are in power in Brazil, Argentina, Bolivia, Nicaragua, Uruguay, Ecuador, El Salvador, and Venezuela. In Chile, Dr. Salvador Allende Gossens, its Marxist Socialist President, was overthrown by its military with U.S. involvement, but since 2000 it has had two Socialist presidents. In Mexico, the leftist Andrew Manual Lopez Obrador was cheated out of the presidency in 2006. Cuba is Communist, now becoming increasingly a society of cooperatives.

In North America, the U.S. has a viable social-democratic faction in the Democratic Party, the House Congressional Progressive Caucus of 70 members, advocating universal healthcare, government jobs programs, free college tuition in public schools, extending social security, protecting the physical environment and so forth. In Canada, there is universal healthcare, and the social-democratic new Democratic Party is a key player in its politics, particularly in the provinces.

Australia and New Zealand for many generations have had powerful labor parties often in power.

In Asia: In India, the Congress Party, social democratic, is usually in power; the Indian states of Kerala and West Bengal have had Communist governments. Sri Lanka is socialist China is officially Communist as is Vietnam and North Korea. Japan has a viable socialist party.

In the Arab world, Iraq was basically socialist before the American invasion, as was Libya under al-Qaddafi until he was deposed by mainly the U.S. Egypt has nationalized the banking sector and much of the industry. Algeria also is largely socialist and there is a large nationalized sector in Syria. Iran, Moslem, but not Arab, has a large socialized sector. Israel in the Near East was founded by Labor Party Zionists.

In sub-Sahara Africa, Angola, Mozambique, Zimbabwe, Kenya and the Democratic Republic of the Congo are socialist. In the Republic of South Africa, there is a strong communist party.

Thus it is that Marx's prophecy of a future socialist world – despite the deformities of actual socialist/communist parties and despite setbacks as in the Soviet Union and China – is still on track. History, after all, does not proceed linearly in the short and medium term. Finally, with impending ecological disaster and still the possibility of nuclear war, the necessity for a socialist world based on cooperation/ mutuality becomes ever more imperative.

Endnotes

1) Louis Althusser, *For Marx,* trans. Ben Brewster (New York: Pantheon Books, 1969), pp. 89-128. Henri Lefebvre, *The Sociology of Marx* (New York: Pantheon Books, 1968), pp. 89 ff. On the 20ᵗʰ century/contemporary socialism, for instance, see Donald Sassoon, One Hundred Years of Socialism: The West European Left in the Twentieth Century (New York: The New Press, 1996). David Priestland, The Red Flag: A History of Communism (New York: Grove Press, 2009). Eric Hobsbaum, The Age of Extremes: A History of the World, 1914-1991 (New York: Pantheon Books, 1994). Articles in The New York Times, New Left Review, Monthly Review, Z Magazine, Science and Society.

Index

W

Wages 88 ff., 113, 372-373

Wallace, Henry A. 406

Ward, Lester Frank 182-184

Wealth (U.S.) 373-374

Weathermen/Weatherpeople 408

Weber, Max 150, 248

Weil, Simone 211, 264, 292

Western European Unions/Socialism
406-413

Wilson, Edward O. 186-187

Winstanley, Gerrard 15

Wolfe, Bertram xi

Wollstonecraft, Mary 335-336

Women 335-345

Working class 110 ff., 402

Working day 111, 116-117

Wrangham, Richard 339

Wright, Eric Olin 139-145

Y

Yeltsin, Boris 429 ff.

Printed in the United States
By Bookmasters